RELIGIOUS RIVALRIES AND THE STRUGGLE
FOR SUCCESS IN SARDIS AND SMYRNA

Studies in Christianity and Judaism /
Études sur le christianisme et le judaïsme : 14

Studies in Christianity and Judaism / Études sur le christianisme et le judaïsme publishes monographs on Christianity and Judaism in the last two centuries before the common era and the first six centuries of the common era, with a special interest in studies of their interrelationship or the cultural and social context in which they developed.

Studies in Christianity and Judaism /
Études sur le christianisme et le judaïsme : 14

RELIGIOUS RIVALRIES AND THE STRUGGLE FOR SUCCESS IN SARDIS AND SMYRNA

Richard S. Ascough, editor

Published for the Canadian Corporation for Studies in Religion/
Corporation Canadienne des Sciences Religieuses
by Wilfrid Laurier University Press
2005

This book has been published with the help of a grant from the Canadian Federation for the Humanities and Social Sciences, through the Aid to Scholarly Publications Programme, using funds provided by the Social Sciences and Humanities Research Council of Canada. We acknowledge the financial support of the Government of Canada through the Book Publishing Industry Development Program for our publishing activities. We acknowledge the Government of Ontario through the Ontario Media Development Corporation's Ontario Book Initiative.

Library and Archives Canada Cataloguing in Publication

> Religious rivalries and the struggle for success in Sardis and Smyrna /
> Richard S. Ascough, editor.
>
> (Studies in Christianity and Judaism = Études sur le christianisme et le judaïsme
> ESCJ; 14).
> Includes bibliographical references and indexes.
> ISBN 0-88920-472-1
>
> 1. Sardis (Extinct city)—Religion. 2. Izmir (Turkey)—Religion. 3. Turkey—Religion.
> I. Ascough, Richard S. (Richard Stephen), 1962- . II. Canadian Corporation for Studies
> in Religion. III. Series: Studies in Christianity and Judaism ; 14.

BL1060.R44 2005   200'.939'22   C2005-901388-5

© 2005 Canadian Corporation for Studies in Religion /
Corporation Canadienne des Sciences Religieuses

Cover by Leslie Macredie. Cover photograph by Peter Richardson: looking north across the marble courtyard of the Imperial Cult building in Sardis's Bath Gymnasium.

Text design by Catharine Bonas-Taylor.

Printed in Canada

Order from:
Wilfrid Laurier University Press
Wilfrid Laurier University
Waterloo, Ontario, Canada N2L 3C5
www.wlupress.wlu.ca

CONTENTS

——➤◦◄——

PREFACE

———⊰•◦•⊱———

This project has received innumerable kinds of support. First, the participants in the Canadian Society of Biblical Studies' Religious Rivalries seminar have, over the past nine years, provided deep insight and provocative discussion on the issues raised by the papers presented in the seminar sessions. I am grateful to the members of the seminar's steering committee who have served with me since 1995: Leif Vaage, Steve Wilson, Michele Murray, Phil Harland, Steve Muir, and especially Terry Donaldson, who was chair of the seminar from 1995 to 2000, when he handed me the leadership opportunity.

Noteworthy help in bringing this volume to publication was provided by my research assistants over the past few years. Erin Vearncombe tracked down important publications and did significant work in putting together the Works Cited. Elaine Reid insured conformity in the in-text citations. Helena Medeiros provided a thorough proofreading of an early version of the manuscript. Rachel McRae was invaluable in compiling the indexes. I am grateful to Queen's University and the Social Sciences and Humanities Research Council of Canada for providing funding to employ these talented students.

Peter Richardson has been a great source of help and encouragement on this project, both through his ongoing participation in the seminar itself and in his role as editor of the Wilfrid Laurier University Press ESCJ series. As the volume neared publication, the role of ESCJ editor was taken over by Stephen Wilson, who, as always, provided helpful guidance. Finally, I am grateful for subvention support for this volume, provided in part by Bishop's University. This book has been published with the help of a grant from the Canadian Federation for the Humanities and Social Sciences, through the Aid to Scholarly Publications Programme, using funds provided by the Social Sciences and Humanities Research Council of Canada.

Richard S. Ascough
Kingston, ON, Canada

ACKNOWLEDGMENTS

Figure 1 on page 57 is reproduced, with permission, from Georg Petzl, *Die Inschriften von Smyrna*, Teil II/2, *Grabschriften, postume Ehrungen, Grabepigramme* (Osterreichische Akademie der Wissenschaften; Bonn: Rudolf Habelt, 1990) plate 17.

Figure 2 on page 177 is reproduced, with permission, from Jane C. Waldbaum, *Metal Works from Sardis: The Finds through to 1974.* (Cambridge, MA: Harvard University Press, 1983) 221.

Figures 3 and 4 on pages 178 and 179 are reproduced, with permission, from John S. Crawford, *The Byzantine Shops at Sardis* (Archaeological Exploration of Sardis. Monograph 9. Cambridge, MA, and London: Harvard University Press, 1990), figures 3 and 2.

Portions of chapter 15, "Religious Coexistence, Co-operation, Competition, and Conflict in Sardis and Smyrna," have been previous published in Richard S. Ascough, "The Canadian Society of Biblical Studies' Religious Rivalries Seminar: Retrospection, Reflection, and Retroversion." *Studies in Religion / Sciences religieuses* 32 (2003): 155–73, and are used here with the permission of the editors.

I am grateful to all of the above authors and publishers for allowing the reproduction of their work in this volume.

CONTRIBUTORS

Reidar Aasgaard	University of Oslo, Norway
Richard S. Ascough	Queen's University, Kingston
Lloyd Gaston	Vancouver School of Theology
Keir E. Hammer	Centre for the Study of Religion, University of Toronto
Philip A. Harland	Concordia University, Montreal
Tim Hegedus	Waterloo Lutheran Seminary
James Knight	Wycliffe College, University of Toronto
Jack N. Lightstone	Concordia University, Montreal
John W. Marshall	Department for the Study of Religion, University of Toronto
Wayne O. McCready	University of Calgary
Steven C. Muir	Concordia University College, Edmonton
Michele Murray	Bishop's University, Lennoxville
Dietmar Neufeld	University of British Columbia, Vancouver

ABBREVIATIONS

AASOR	*Annual of the American Schools of Oriental Research*
ABSA	*Annual of the British School at Athens*
ABD	*The Anchor Bible Dictionary*, ed. David Noel Freedman. New York: Doubleday, 1992.
ACM	*Ancient Christian Magic: Coptic Texts of Ritual Power*, ed. Marvin Meyer and Richard Smith. San Francisco: Harper, 1994.
AE	*Archaiologike Ephemeris*
AGJU	Arbeiten zur Geschichte des antiken Judentums und des Urchristentums
AJA	*American Journal of Archaeology*
AJP	*American Journal of Philology*
AJSL	*American Journal of Semitic Languages*
ANF	The Ante-Nicene Fathers
ANRW	*Aufstieg und Niedergang der römischen Weld*, ed. H. Temporini and W. Haase. Berlin: Walter de Gruyter, 1972–.
ApJn	*Apocalypse of John*
Arch	*Archaeology*
ArtB	*Art Bulletin*
ATR	*Anglican Theological Review*
BA	*The Biblical Archeologist*
BARev	*Biblical Archaeology Review*
BASOR	*Bulletin of the American Schools of Oriental Research*
BETL	Bibliotheca Ephemeridum Theologicarum Lovaniensium
BGBE	Beiträge zur Geschichte der Biblischen Exegese
BJRL	*Bulletin of the John Rylands University Library of Manchester*
BJS	Brown Judaic Studies
BSHJ	Baltimore Studies in the History of Judaism
BSR	*Papers of the British School at Rome*
BTB	*Biblical Theology Bulletin*
CCAG	*Catalogus Codicorum Astrologorum Graecorum*. Brussels: Aedibus Academiae, 1898–1953.

CCCA	*Corpus cutus Cybelae Attidisque*, ed. M. J. Vermaseren. 7 vols. EPRO 50. Leiden: Brill, 1977–89.
CCIS	*Corpus cultus Iovis Sabazii*, ed. M. J. Vermaseren. 3 vols. EPRO 106. Leiden: Brill, 1983–89.
CCL	*Corpus Christianorum,* Series Latina.
CERP	*Cities of the Eastern Roman Provinces,* A. H. M. Jones. 2nd ed. Oxford and Amsterdam: Clarendon and Hakkert, 1971–73.
CH	*Church History*
CIG	*Corpus inscriptionum graecarum*
CIJ	*Corpus inscriptionum iudaicarum*
CIL	*Corpus inscriptionum latinarum*
CIMRM	*Corpus Inscriptionum et Monumentorum Religionis Mithriacae*, ed. M. J. Vermaseren. The Hague: Nijhoff, 1956–60.
CRAIBL	*Comptes rendus de l'Académie des inscriptions et belles-lettres*
CSBS	Canadian Society of Biblical Studies
DHA	*Dialogues d'histoire ancien*
EMC	*Echos du Monde Classique = Classical Views*
EPRO	Études preliminaries aux religions orientales dans l'Empire romain
ESCJ	Studies in Christianity and Judaism / Études sur Christianisme et le Judaïsme
ET	English Translation
ExpTim	*Expository Times*
GCS	Griechischen christlichen Schriftsteller
GOTR	*Greek Orthodox Theological Review*
GRBS	*Greek, Roman, and Byzantine Studies*
HDR	Harvard Dissertations in Religion
HE	*Historia ecclesiastica,* Eusebius
HSCP	*Harvard Studies in Classical Philology*
HTR	*Harvard Theological Review*
HTS	Harvard Theological Studies
HUCA	*Hebrew Union College Annual*
IAphrodSpect	*Performers and Partisans at Aphrodisias in the Roman and Late Roman Periods: A Study Based on Inscriptions from the Current Excavations at Aphrodisias in Caria*, ed. C. Roueché. JRS Monographs 6. London: Society for the Promotion of Roman Studies, 1993.
IDeols	*Inscriptions de Délos*, ed. P. Roussel and M. Launey. 7 vols. Paris: Champion, 1926–72.
IDidyma	*Didyma. II. Die Inschriften*, ed. R. Rehm. Berlin: Mann, 1958.
IEph	*Die Inschriften von Ephesos*, ed. H. Engelmann, H. Wankel, and R. Merkelbach. 8 vols. IGSK 11–17. Bonn: Habelt, 1979–84.
IG	*Inscriptiones Graecae*
IGBulg	*Inscriptiones graecae in Bulgaria repertae*, ed. G. Mihailov. 4 vols. Quellen und Abhandlungen zur griechischen Epigraphik 4. 1900. Repr. Hildesheim: Olms, 1976.

IGladiateurs   *Les gladiateurs dans l'orient grec*, ed. Louis Robert. Bibliothèque de l'école des hautes études IVe section, Sciences historiques et philologiques 278. Paris: Champion, 1940. Repr. Amsterdam: Hakkert, 1971.

IGLAM   *Inscriptions grecques et latines recueillies en Asie Mineur*, ed. P. Le Bas and W. H. Waddington. 2 vols. Subsidia Epigraphica 1–2. Hildesheim: Olms, 1972. Repr. of vol. 3, parts 5 and 6 of *Voyage archéologique en Grèce et en Asie Mineure*, P. Le Bas. Paris: Firmin-Didot frères, 1870.

IGR   *Inscriptiones Graecae ad res Romanas*

IHierapJ   "Inschriften," ed. C. Humann. In *Altertümer von Hierapolis*, ed. C. Cichorius, W. Judeich, and F. Winter, 67–202. Jahrbuch des kaiserlich deutschen archäologischen Instituts, Ergänzungsheft 4. Berlin: Reimer, 1898.

IKnidos   *Die Inschriften von Knidos*, ed. W. Blümel. 2 vols. IGSK 41–42. Bonn: Habelt, 1991–92.

IKyzikos   *Die Inschriften von Kyzikos und Umgebung*, ed. E. Schwertheim. 2 vols. IGSK 18, 26. Bonn: Habelt, 1980–83.

ILydiaKP   *Bericht über eine Reise in Lydien*, ed. J. Keil and A. von Premerstein. 3 vols. DAWW.PH 53.2, 54.2, 57.1. Vienna: Hölder, 1908–14.

IManisaMus   *Greek and Latin Inscriptions in the Manisa Museum*, ed. Hasan Malay. Ergänzungsbande zu den Tituli Asiae Minoris 19. Vienna: Verlag der österreichischen Akademie der Wissenschaften, 1994.

IMiletos   *Inschriften von Milet*, ed. Peter Herrmann and Albert Rehm. 2 vols. Milet: Ergebnisse der Ausgrabungen und Untersuchungen seit dem Jahre 1899 6.1. Berlin: Walter de Gruyter, 1997–98.

IPergamon   *Die Inschriften von Pergamon*, ed. M. Fränkel and C. Habicht. 3 vols. Altertümer von Pergamon 8.1–2. Berlin: Spemann, 1890–95.

IPhrygR   *The Cities and Bishoprics of Phrygia*. W. M. Ramsay. 2 vols. Oxford: Clarendon, 1895.

ISardBR   *Sardis*, VII, 1, *Greek and Latin Inscriptions*, ed. W. H. Buckler and D. M. Robinson. Leiden: Brill, 1932.

ISardGauthier   *Nouvelles inscriptions de Sardes II*, ed. P. Gauthier. Hautes études du monde gréco-romain 15. Geneva: Librairie Droz S.A., 1989.

ISardH   "Mystenvereine in Sardeis," Peter Herrmann. *Chiron* 26 (1996): 315–41.

ISardRobert   *Archaeological Exploration of Sardis: Nouvelles inscriptions de Sardes I*. Hautes études du monde gréco-romain 15. Paris: Librairie d'Amérique et d'Orient Adrien Maisonneuve, 1964.

ISGK   Inschriften griechischer Städte aus Kleinasien

ISmyrna   *Die Inschriften von Smyrna*, vol. 1: *Grabschriften, postume Ehrungen, Grabepigramme*, ed. G. Petzl. 2 vols. Österreichische Akademie der Wissenschaften. IGSK 23–24. Bonn: Rudolf Habelt, 1982–90.

JAC   *Jahrbuch für Antike und Christentum*

JBL   *Journal of Biblical Literature*

JECS	*Journal of Early Christian Studies*
JFA	*Journal of Field Archaeology*
JFSR	*Journal of Feminist Studies in Religion*
JHS	*Journal of Hellenic Studies*
JJS	*Journal of Jewish Studies*
JMS	*Journal of Mithraic Studies*
JQR	*Jewish Quarterly Review*
JR	*Journal of Religion*
JRS	*Journal of Roman Studies*
JSJ	*Journal for the Study of Judaism*
JSNT	*Journal for the Study of the New Testament*
JSP	*Journal for the Study of the Pseudepigrapha*
JTS	*Journal of Theological Studies*
LCL	Loeb Classical Library
LSAM	*Lois sacrées de l'Asie Mineure*, ed. F. Sokolowski. EFA, Travaux et mémoires 9. Paris: De Boccard, 1955.
LSCG	*Lois sacrées de cités grecques*, ed. F. Sokolowski. EFA, Travaux et mémoires 18. Paris: De Boccard, 1955.
LTP	*Laval théologique et philosophique*
LTQ	*Lexington Theological Quarterly*
Mart. Pion.	*Martyrdom of Pionius and His Companions*
Mart. Pol.	*Martyrdom of Polycarp*
MAMA	*Monumenta Asiae Minoris Antiqua*, ed. J. Keil, W. H. Buckler, and W. M. Calder. 10 vols. London: Society for the Promotion of Roman Studies, 1928–93.
MDAI(A)	*Mitteilungen des Deutschen Archäologischen Instituts. Athenische Abteilung.*
NewDocs	*New Documents Illustrating Early Christianity*, ed. G. H. R. Horsley, S. R. Llewelyn, and R.A. Kearsley. 9 vols., North Ryde, Australia, and Grand Rapids: Ancient History Documentary Research Centre and Eerdmans, 1981–2002.
NovT	*Novum Testamentum*
NovTSup	Novum Testamentum Supplements
NPNF	Nicene and Post-Nicene Fathers
NTS	*New Testament Studies*
OECT	*Oxford Editions of Cuneiform Texts*
OTP	*Old Testament Pseudepigrapha*, ed. James Charlesworth. 2 vols. Garden City, NY: Doubleday, 1983–87.
P.Cairo.dem.	*Die demotischen Papyrus*, ed. W. Spiegelberg. Strassburg: Schlesier und Schweikhardt, 1908.
PG	*Patrologiae cursus completes.* Series Graeca, ed. J.-P. Migne. Paris: Migne, 1857–87.
PGM	*Papyri graecae magicae*, ed. K. Preisendanz. 3 vols. Leipzig: Teubner, 1928–41.

P.Köln	*Kölner Papyri*, ed. B. Kramer and R. Hübner. 9 vols. Abhandlungen der Rheinisch-Westfälischen Akademie der Wissenschaften. Sonderreihe Papyrologica Coloniensia 7. Opladen: Westdeutscher Verlag, 1976.
P.Mich.Tebt.	*Papyri from Tebtunis*, ed. A. E. R. Boak. University of Michigan Studies Humanistic Series 28. Ann Arbor: University of Michigan Press, 1933.
P.Oxy	*The Oxyrhynchus Papyri*, ed. B. P. Grenfell and A. S. Hunt. 42 vols. London, 1898–1974.
RAC	*Reallexikon für Antike und Christentum*, ed. Th. Klauser. Stuttgart: Hiersemann, 1950–.
RE	*Realencyclopädie der klassischen Altertumswissenschaft*, ed. A. Pauly, G. Wissowa, W. Kroll. Stuttgart: A. Druckenmüller, 1893–.
REA	*Revue des études anciennes*
RevPhil	*Revue de philologie et de literature et d'histoire anciennes*
RR	*Review of Religion*
RSC	*Rivista di Studi Classici*
SBL	Society of Biblical Literature
SBLTT	Society of Biblical Literature: Texts and Translations
SC	*Sources chrétiennes*
SecondCent	*Second Century*
SEG	*Supplementum Epigraphicum Graecum*
SFSHJ	South Florida Studies in the History of Judaism
SHR	Studies in the History of Religions
SJLA	Studies in Judaism in Late Antiquity
SR	*Studies in Religion / Sciences religieuses*
StLit	*Studia Liturgica*
StPatr	*Studia Patristica*
SVTP	Studia in Veteris Testamenti Pseudepigrapha
TAM	*Tituli Asiae Minoris*
TAPA	*Transactions of the American Philological Association*
TMMM	*Textes et monuments figurés relatifs aux mystères de Mithra*, Franz Cumont. Brussels: Lamertin (2 vols., 1896–99).
TynBul	*Tyndale Bulletin*
USQR	*Union Seminary Quarterly Review*
VC	*Vigiliae christianae*
VCSup	*Vigiliae christianae Supplements*
WBC	World Bible Commentary
WUNT	Wissenschaftliche Untersuchungen zum Neuen Testament
ZNW	*Zeitschrift für die neutestamentliche Wissenschaft*
ZPE	*Zeitschrift für Papyrologie und Epigraphik*

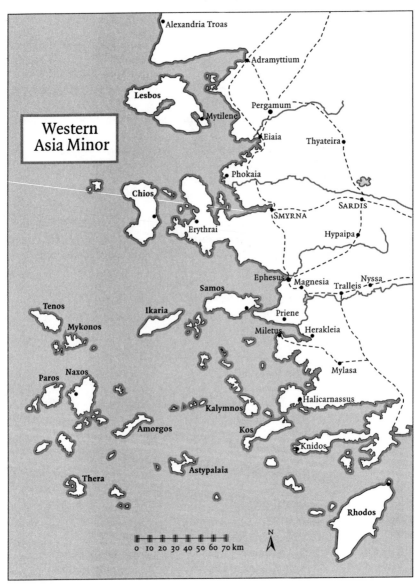

Map by Pam Woodland

INTRODUCTION

1

Interaction among Religious Groups
in Sardis and Smyrna

Richard S. Ascough

Introduction

Building on a long-standing tradition of focused New Testament seminars dating back to 1977, in 1995 the Canadian Society of Biblical Studies inaugurated a new seminar under the title "Religious Rivalries and the Struggle for Success: Jews, Christians, and Other Religious Groups in Local Settings in the First Two Centuries CE." It is a complex and perhaps overly lengthy title, but one chosen carefully and with not a little debate in order to convey the full scope of our project. There are things in the title that many participants would now change as a result of the work done in the seminar—a good sign that the seminar did not remain static vis-à-vis the problematic as first conceived. The seminar's purpose was to explore the relationships and rivalries among Jews, Christians, and Greco-Roman religious groups in the context of local urban settings and *realia*, in the first few centuries of the Common Era. Although the intent was to limit the time frame to the first and second centuries CE, that was an aim difficult to achieve, in part because the available literary and archaeological data were limited, in part because interests of seminar members expanded.

Terry Donaldson laid out the foci, or "interconnected sets of issues," of the seminar in the initial seminar proposal. First, the seminar was identified as undertaking "urban studies." At the foundational level we were interested in the "concrete urban realities of the Roman empire" from the perspective of particular cities. We began with a focus on a single city, Caesarea Maritima (1995–97), followed by a pair of geographically proximate cities, Sardis and Smyrna (1998–2001), and concluded with a region, North Africa (2002–3). For each city or region we sought to inform ourselves about the current state of knowledge (including architectural, social, economic,

---

Notes to chapter 1 start on page 253

3

regional, and political aspects) available through the evidence (e.g., archaeological, literary, numismatic, and inscriptional).

Our second interconnected issue was that of religious groups. Having set the context of a city or region, we aimed to investigate religious groups as one aspect of urban reality. The urban context was important, for, as Jack Lightstone notes, the social structure of the urban setting defines much of how a city's inhabitants understand themselves (2003, 2). Peter Richardson frames it thus: "Careful attention to the architecture and urban design of cities, especially religious structures, will tell modern students important things about past cultures" (2002, 160). The seminar gave attention to this urban context by examining "the roles of religious groups in the life of the city, the way in which religions as social entities are shaped by the realities of their urban settings, and in the relationships...among religious groups" (Donaldson 1995, 1).

Richardson has been a constant and consistent resource in orienting the seminar to the *realia* of the urban sites under investigation. His presentations constantly reinforced the notion that the concrete urban realities of our chosen sites revealed the importance of studying "precise local expressions" far more successfully than would simply leaping to "generalizations" (Richardson 2003, 9). Donaldson makes a similar point in his introduction to the book he edited on Caesarea Maritima: "As urban phenomena, then, religious groups cannot be understood apart from the cities in which they are embedded, nor can the relationships between and among them be understood without an understanding of the social dynamic of their urban mix" (2000, 3).

Finally, the seminar was interested in what was first conceived of as the struggle for "success" among religious groups (see Vaage 1995). We attempted to mine our textual and physical resources for information that revealed the degree to which these religious groups were engaged in competition and/or co-operation. We wanted to know how religious groups competed in their appeal to the same people within the public arena, defining for ourselves the concept of "success" as garnering sympathy, support, respect, status, new members, influence, and power. In doing so, we hoped to learn what factors might be identified in specific contexts that led to the eventual dominance of Christianity over other religious expressions within the late Roman Empire. We wanted to know, as Leif Vaage put it in 1995, "what is at stake in getting the chronicle of Christianity's 'rise,' Judaism's on-going development, and 'paganism's' prolonged displacement cum resistance, 'right' or 'better' or at least endeavouring to make sure that 'all the facts' are laid out on the scholarly tableau" (1995, 23). Our greatest hope and expectation for the seminar lay in the third of the three interconnected issues. Religious groups of interest, we expected, *were* attempting to appeal to the same people and thus would be thrust into direct competition with one another.

Even after looking at a single site, although with considerable methodological reflection on the way, Donaldson was able to conclude that the evidence for a range of possible interrelationships, "from peaceful co-existence, through competition implicit and explicit, to confrontation and conflict," demands that the interpretive model be well thought out and move beyond simplistic dichotomies (Donaldson 2000, 5). It is to this end that the seminar members wrestled with a number of papers that tackled the issue of how one understands the scholarly enterprise of reconstructing relationships among Greco-Roman religious groups (see Vaage, 2005).

Like many of the CSBS seminars before it, the Religious Rivalries seminar has been a highly productive one, with one book of essays published (Donaldson 2000), two others in production (Vaage; Muir), and one "spin-off" book already out (Richardson 2002).[1] As a result of the seminar's three years of work on Sardis and Smyrna, we identified a need for the publication of a number of papers of high scholarly calibre that made a distinctive contribution to the field. The result is this volume of essays. Most of the essays were first presented in draft form during the seminar sessions, and all have since been revised. A couple of essays (Marshall, chap. 7; Aasgaard, chap. 11) were commissioned for this volume as a result of the respective authors' interest in the cities of Sardis and Smyra. It is not the intention of this volume to undertake a comprehensive overview of either city. Rather, the goal is to make some contributions to the refinement of our understanding of both cities. Nevertheless, it is worth a brief overview of salient features of the civic sites themselves.

Overview of Sardis

The city of Sardis is located at the foot of the Tmolos mountain range, where the Pactolus River runs through the Hermus plain. It has a long history, extending well before the eighth century BCE.[2] According to ancient sources, the rise of the Mermnadae dynasty came about in the seventh century through the exploits of Gyges, who, at the urging of the Heraclid king Candaules, spied on the naked body of the king's wife but, when she caught him, he was compelled to kill the king. Gyges' descendant Croesus, famous for his wealth, was later defeated by the Persian king Cyrus (546 BCE) when he wrongly interpreted a Delphic oracle (see Herodotus 1.76–84).[3] Cyrus had Croesus placed on a pyre and set it alight. However, when Croesus prayed to Apollo for help, a downpour from the clear sky extinguished the flames! Although such stories are of doubtful historicity, it is clear that Persia played an important role in the history of Sardis. It was during the Persian occupation that the Royal Road was constructed linking Susa in Persia to Sardis, where the road ended.

Political control of Sardis changed hands a number of times, beginning with the coming of Alexander the Great, who ordered the building of a temple to Zeus Olympios[4] and who allowed the Sardians to use their ancestral laws (Hanfmann 1983, 113). The rule of the Pergamene kings followed, beginning in 213 BCE. The city finally passed into the hands of the Romans in 133 BCE when the Pergamene king Attalus III willed it to them. It was during this time that a temple to Artemis was built, and she became a national goddess for Seleucid Asia Minor (Hanfmann 1983, 129; Pausanias 7.6.6; Xenophon, *An.* 1.6.6–7). The priesthood of Roma became the major priesthood of the city itself, although other religions continued to flourish. During the Hellenistic period, the deities at Sardis, and in Lydia generally, were never completely Hellenized but retained characteristics of their historical development in the local context—their Lydian and Persian forerunners. Nevertheless, most of the material from Sardis is in Greek and reflects Hellenistic practices (Hanfmann 1983, 134).

For the most part, any sort of architectural continuity in religious sites at Sardis will date only from 17 CE, since the city suffered an earthquake in that year.[5] The emperor Tiberius gave generous aid to Sardis in the form of the direct payment of 10 million sesterces and remission of taxes for five years.[6] The Roman authorities had almost the entire city levelled, and thus earlier Hellenistic structures have disappeared (Mierse 1983, 109). Nevertheless, the city was soon revived with new Roman buildings (see Foss 1976, 2; Yegül 1987, 59),[7] and it became part of a strategic network of highways that connected it with all parts of the province (Hanfmann and Waldbaum 1975, 19).

The shift that occurred at Sardis after 17 CE was perhaps more dramatic than elsewhere in Asia Minor because the earthquake was so devastating. Some religious groups still maintained vestiges of their Lydian and Hellenistic forerunners. In fact, by the second century CE there was a renaissance of older Persian and Anatolian cults.[8] Hanfmann attributes this resurgence to an attempt "to rediscover their ancient and mythical past as a source of pride and superiority toward the Romans" (1983, 135). By the second century CE, Sardis was a large, prosperous city, with a population of between sixty thousand and one hundred thousand people (Aune 1997, 218), including a flourishing Jewish community (see Seager and Kraabel 1983, 168–90; Hammer and Murray, chap. 12 of this volume).[9]

There is quite a bit of helpful material available for a study of Greco-Roman religions at Sardis. One source is the collection of ancient literary references to Sardis by John Pedley (1972). Pedley has set out these sources in chronological order in relation to the development of the city (rather than the chronological order of the writers themselves). Each text is given in the original language, followed by a translation into English (although sometimes longer texts are only partially given and then summarized in English). While many are not pertinent to the topic of religions at Sardis, a few do touch on the topic (esp. 73–75, nos. 270–74). However, for the most part, these texts inform us more about the religious structures of the city during the fifth to second century BCE.

Early inscriptional finds from Sardis have been collected in Buckler and Robinson (1932 = *ISardBR*). Robert's volume (1964 = *ISardRobert*) publishes further inscriptional finds but also offers a critique of Buckler and Robinson's collection (cf. Pedley 1972, 62). More inscriptions have been published by Gauthier (1989 = *ISardGauthier*), although he is concerned primarily with royal documents from the time of Antiochus III (III–II BCE). Hermann (1995; 1996) has published some inscriptions not appearing elsewhere.

The secondary material on religions at Sardis is fairly plentiful, much of it arising from the work of the Harvard-Cornell expeditions of 1958–75 and continuing to today.[10] The most comprehensive overview is that edited by George Hanfmann, *Sardis from Prehistoric to Roman Times* (1983). This is really a collection of survey articles jointly written by a number of those involved in the digs at Sardis. It is a good starting point to become acquainted with the religious milieu of Sardis. Other, more specialized studies are also readily available, particularly the reports and monographs in the Archaeological Exploration of Sardis series.[11]

Overview of Smyrna

Smyrna, traditional birthplace of Homer, has a long history. It was founded by the Aeolians in the tenth century BCE and by the ninth had become a thriving commercial centre. The city's name comes from the goddess Myrina, a local variety of Cybele, known as the Sipylene Mother (Cadoux 1938, 215; Ramsay 1994, 192). Ionian Greeks settled in the area at the end of the eighth century and soon occupied the city (Strabo 14.1.4; Pausanias 7.5.1). Herodotus (1.150) tells the story of how, sometime before 688 BCE, the Ionians seized the city while the Aeolians were outside the walls celebrating a festival of Dionysos (see Potter 1992, 73). The Lydians destroyed the city in the sixth century. However, it was refounded again on Mt. Pagos (Strabo 14.1.37) as the result of a dream Alexander the Great had in 334 BCE while resting at the temple of Nemeseis. But work on the new city did not begin until 323 BCE.[12]

During the 190s BCE the city of Smyrna defied the Seleucid king Antiochus III and aligned itself with Rome, building a temple to Roma in

195 BCE (Tacitus, *Ann.* 4.56; Potter 1992, 74). In fact, Smyrna was the first city of Asia Minor to build such a temple (ibid.). Later, this cult was closely aligned with the worship of the emperors (Cadoux 1938, 224). As a provincial centre for the Roman imperial cult, Smyrna vied for the title "first of Asia" with other prominent cities such as Pergamum and Ephesus. In 29 CE the city competed for the right to build a temple to Tiberius and was chosen to be a *neōkoros*, "temple warden" (Tacitus, *Ann.* 4.15; Friesen 1993, 15–21) on the basis of its long years of loyalty (Tacitus, *Ann.* 4.37–38, 55–56).[13] Later, it acquired another Temple under Hadrian (117–38 CE) and another under Caracalla (211–17 CE).

By the first century BCE Smyrna had become a bustling, cosmopolitan port city of about one hundred thousand. Strabo describes the city of the late first century BCE in the following terms: "Their city is now the most beautiful of all....The division into streets is exceptionally good, in straight lines as far as possible; and the streets are paved with stone; and there are large quadrangular porticoes, with both upper and lower stories" (14.1.37, LCL).

Of great pride to the Smyrneans was the "crown of Smyrna," a street lined with public buildings that encircled the top of Mt. Pagos.[14] A frequent image on Smyrnean coins is the patron goddess of the city, Cybele, seated on a throne and wearing a crown of battlements and towers (Ramsay 1994, 188). As such, she is representative of the city itself. The philosopher Apollonius of Tyana plays on this image when advising the Smyrneans that it would be better to take pride in a "crown of persons" (Philostratus, *Vit. Ap.* 4.7; see further Ramsay 1994, 189).

Christianity was introduced at Smyrna early, perhaps by Paul or one of his companions (see Acts 19:10, 26; Pseudo-Pionius, *Life of Polycarp* 1.2.1). By end of the first century CE a small Christian community was solidly in place. The writer of Revelation encourages them through the words of the risen Jesus, "Be faithful until death, and I will give you the crown of life" (Revelation 2:10–11).[15] This image of the "crown" contrasts with the "crown of Smyrna" composed of public buildings. For the Christians of the city, a "crown of life" is to be preferred. Here, we have our first indication of "rivalry" between Christians and their non-Christian neighbours at Smyrna (see further the essays by Hegedus and Marshall in this volume, summarized below).

Early in the second century, Ignatius, bishop of Syrian Antioch, was escorted through Smyrna while en route to his martyrdom in Rome. While there, he encouraged the local Christians, including their bishop, Polycarp. He also met with representatives from churches in nearby cities. After his departure, Ignatius sent two letters back to Smyrna, one to the church and one to Polycarp, thanking them for their hospitality and addressing a number of important issues facing the Asian churches (e.g., the role of a bishop; heterodox teachings, and contact with the Antiochian church).

In 156 CE, Polycarp was arrested by the authorities and brought before the proconsul in the arena during a festival. When ordered to deny his faith. Polycarp responded, "For eighty and six years have I been his servant, and he has done me no wrong, and how can I blaspheme my King who has saved me" (*Mart. Pol.* 9.3, LCL). For his faithfulness Polycarp was placed on a pyre and burned to death (see further McCready, chap. 10 in this volume).

The ancient city of Smyrna was renowned for its beauty among ancient writers (see, for example, Aelius Aristides, *Or.* 17, 18, 19, 20, 21).[16] It was also highly regarded for its fine wines, its beautiful buildings, and its wealth, and it was viewed by the Romans as a centre for science and medicine (Strabo 14.1.15). In the mid–third century CE, a civic honorific inscription for an athlete proclaims Smyrna "first city in Asia for beauty and size, most glorious, mother city of Asia, adornment of Ionia" (*CIG* 3202).[17]

The ancient site of Smyrna is now occupied by the modern Turkish city of Izmir. As the third-largest city in Turkey, and as one of the country's major ports, it has the feel of a fast-paced, prosperous city. Unfortunately, so much of what is of primary interest to the ancient historian remains buried under the modern city or has been destroyed by war, fire, and earthquake. However, Smyrna is slowly revealing its secrets through literary texts and the archaeologist's spade. Today, the most prominent archaeological site in Smyrna is the agora. Built in the fourth century BCE by Alexander, it was destroyed by an earthquake in 178 CE. The emperor Marcus Aurelius rebuilt it, along with much of the town, soon afterwards. Also visible today are traces of the Roman theatre and the Roman aqueducts. The archaeological museum is an excellent place to appreciate the richness of Greco-Roman antiquity, both in Smyrna, and in Asia Minor generally.

In contrast to Sardis, there is less primary and secondary source material for the study of religions at Smyrna. The main source of primary material is the three volumes of inscriptions in the IGSK series (Petzl 1982-90). These make the inscriptional finds up to 1990 readily available, with brief descriptions given in German. In total, just over nine hundred inscriptions of varying lengths, types, and dates are available.

The secondary literature is even more sparse. Despite its publication date at the early part of the last century (1938), the primary starting point for a study of religions at Smyrna is Cecil J. Cadoux's *Ancient Smyrna: A History of the City from the Earliest Times to 324 A.D.* He includes a comprehensive bibliography of earlier works on Smyrna. There is, in addition, the collection of essays and inscriptions in *Mouseion kai Bibliothēk tēs Euangelikēs Sxolēs* (see Cadoux 1938, xxxviii, for a description; see also Broughton 1938, 750-52; Cook 1958/59).

Outline of the Volume

The opening section of this volume contains four essays that together provide an "Overview of Religious Groups in Sardis and Smyrna." Lloyd Gaston surveys Jewish communities (chap. 2), Dietmar Neufeld notes the evidence for Christian groups (chap. 3), and Richard Ascough examines Greco-Roman religions (chap. 4). The order in which these essays appear follows that set out in the subtitle of the Religious Rivalries seminar: "Jews, Christians, and Other Religious Groups in Local Settings in the First Two Centuries CE." All three essays make the case, however, that the time frame for the examination of religious interaction at Sardis and Smyrna needs to be extended into the beginning of the fourth century CE. Indeed, this is what occurs in the subsequent essays that examine particular topics.

These three essays are complemented by Philip Harland's study of rivalries among voluntary associations in Sardis and Smyrna (chap. 5). While noting that there was a high degree of co-operation among associations, Harland gives attention to evidence that reveals associations competing for benefaction and membership. However, Harland also draws attention to the important notion of what he terms the "rhetoric of rivalry," which, in many cases, may not accurately reflect the actual situation. This becomes an important rubric for understanding the Jewish, Christian, and polytheist texts and examined in the subsequent essays, all of which eschew a simplistic understanding of the historical circumstances behind the rhetorical flourishes of the sources.

The second section of the book, "Indirect Contact among Jews and Christians in Sardis and Smyrna," examines in detail some aspects of the New Testament book of Revelation. This book, probably written somewhere between 90 and 135 CE, names among its intended audience seven Christian communities at different locales in Asia Minor, including Sardis and Smyrna. Thus, it provides us with one of the earliest references to Christian communities in these cities. At the same time, the book makes reference to other religious groups, both Jewish and polytheistic. The three essays in this section all explore the nature of the interaction among Christians, Jews, and polytheists reflected in the text. Tim Hegedus (chap. 6) demonstrates how astrological motifs are used in Revelation in a manner that maintains much of its traditional religious significance in polytheism. John Marshall's essay (chap. 7) similarly looks at astrological motifs in Revelation, showing how the Jewish integration of their patriarchal narratives with the zodiac is reflected in Revelation. Together these two essays show that, despite the "rhetoric of rivalry" found in the texts, the book of Revelation reveals a considerable amount of uncritical, if indirect, integration of the practices of Judaism and polytheism.

James Knight balances out this section with a study of the identity of the prostitute portrayed in Revelation 17. His study raises important hermeneutical questions about how one understands the cult of the goddess Roma in antiquity (chap. 8). Knight cogently argues that the common scholarly assumption that the worship of Roma was "just" political are mistaken, since there was no separation of religion and state in antiquity. Thus, the book of Revelation's critique of Roma worship was not only "religious rhetoric" but has embedded in it a critique of the empire itself.

"Interaction among Religious Groups at Sardis and Smyrna" is the third section of the book. The four essays in this section challenge the prevailing scholarly understanding of ancient texts that sees in the "rhetoric of rivalry" actual and direct conflict among Jews, Christians, and polytheists. These four essays are presented according to the chronology of the texts and artifacts that they treat. The first, by Steven Muir, examines how natural and human disasters in the second and third century provided opportunities for religious groups in Sardis and Smyrna to provide charity to others (chap. 9). This becomes a test case for examining Rodney Stark's controversial theory that Christianity grew exponentially because of its charitable work (1996). Muir concludes that while there is no evidence to contradict this claim, the evidence in support of it is not widespread at Sardis or Smyrna. For the most part, Christian charity, like that of the healing cult of Asclepius, focused on its own adherents.

Wayne McCready's close examination of the text of the *Martyrdom of Polycarp*, which is set in Smyrna, reveals that the "rhetoric of rivalry" therein is no more than one would expect from two sibling religious groups (chap. 10). Indeed, the literary production of the *Martyrdom of Polycarp* has much more to do with the formation of a Christian identity distinct from Judaism. Thus, while "the Jews" are vilified in the text, this rhetoric tells us more about the need to assert Christian identity within Christian ranks than it reveals about actual Christian–Jewish conflict in the city of Smyrna. Reidar Aasgaard's treatment of Melito of Sardis (chap. 11) comes to a surprisingly similar conclusion. Looking at the works of the Christian bishop Melito, particularly his *Peri Pascha*, Aasgaard shows that the "rhetoric of rivalry" likely reflects Melito's sense that Christians need to assert for themselves a distinct self-identity—namely, his particular version of it—within their urban environment.

The final paper in this section moves from text to artifact by examining the physical evidence for the interactions among Jews, Christians, and polytheists in Sardis in the third to sixth centuries. Keir Hammer and Michele Murray (chap. 12) show that when one does not *a priori* assume a theory of religious conflict, it is possible to interpret the archaeological evidence from the Sardis synagogue and the Byzantine shops adjacent to it in a way that shows coexistence rather than competition among the adherents of various religions.

The two essays in the final section, "Broadening the Context," set the volume within the larger Greco-Roman context by examining Jewish, Christian, and polytheist interactions in different locales, inside and outside Asia Minor. These essays not only function to fill in the context but also provide important points of comparison for the detailed studies of Sardis and Smyrna while raising important methodological issues.

Michele Murray (chap. 13) provides a description of religious interaction at the ancient city of Priene as a point of comparison for understanding Sardis and Smyrna. Although other comparative sites could have been selected, perhaps one of the five other sites mentioned in the book of Revelation (Ephesus, Pergamum, Thyatira, Philadelphia, and Laodicea), Priene is a fitting choice because "it may be that the second-century Sardian Jewish community resembled...the neighboring one in Priene" (Cohick 1999, 127). Given this similarity, perhaps the evidence from fourth-century Sardis for the location of a Christian domicile surrounded by Jewish shops and residences and backing onto the synagogue (see Hammer and Murray, chap. 12) reflects earlier interactions among the Jewish, Christian, and polytheist inhabitants of Sardis. More significant, from the methodological viewpoint, is Murray's demonstration that when one assumes a "conflict" model for religious interaction, it affects how archaeological and literary evidence is interpreted. Questioning the assumption of conflict when one religious group reuses the religious artifacts of another, Murray sounds a warning bell when we approach the study of religious rivalry.

Jack Lightstone's essay (chap. 14) provides a thick description of the nature of Roman urbanization, particularly in the eastern part of the empire (Palestine and adjacent areas), and its effect on Jewish and Christian communities across the empire. He gives due attention to the relevance of the transformations that took place during the Roman Empire for understanding inter- and intra-religious relations. Of particular importance is the challenge that Jewish and, especially, Christian groups eventually posed to the Romans' sense of a highly structured urban social map. Lightstone concludes with a call for any study of religious rivalries to pay due attention to the reality of Roman urbanization throughout antiquity—the very thing that the volume's studies of Sardis and Smyrna have done. Furthermore, undertaking a study of a specific point of comparison (Murray) and a broader analysis of the urban phenomenon in antiquity (Lightstone) not only sheds further light on Sardis and Smyrna, it also prepares the way for the next volume of essays arising out of the CSBS's religious rivalries seminar, which will focus on methodological issues explored during the nine-year duration of the seminar (Vaage 2005).

This volume's concluding essay, by Richard Ascough (chap. 15), attempts to draw together the conclusions of the essays around the rubric of religious coexistence, co-operation, competition, and conflict at Sardis and Smyrna. Ascough shows that, together, the essays reveal a considerable amount of coexistence and co-operation among Jews, Christians, and polytheists and a surprising lack of competition and conflict. What evidence there is for competition and conflict more often than not reflects inner-group conflict rather than inter-group conflict.

All of the essays in the volume are not only linked thematically but are substantially integrated through the use of cross-references that show how the arguments of individual essays interact with one another to form a cohesive study of religious rivalries at Sardis and Smyrna.

OVERVIEW OF RELIGIOUS GROUPS
IN SARDIS AND SMYRNA

2

Jewish Communities in
Sardis and Smyrna

Lloyd Gaston

Introduction

In approaching the question of Jewish communities in Sardis and Smyrna during the first two centuries CE, my first task was to try to find primary source material—literary, archaeological, or inscriptional. However, I could find very little within the given limits of place and time.[1] It was necessary then to colour outside the temporal lines. There is some secondary material, largely Christian literature, and it was a useful exercise in itself to evaluate what light it could cast on our subject. As a general rule, lack of evidence is usually supplemented by unwarranted assumptions, and I freely admit approaching the task fully warned by Tom Kraabel's "Six Questionable Assumptions" (Kraabel 1982, 445–64).

Jewish Communities in Sardis

I begin with the city of Sardis, where the evidence for "rivalry" is somewhat richer than in the city of Smyrna. Settlement of Jews in Sardis occurred at least as early as ca. 210 BCE when Antiochus III brought 2,000 Jewish families from Babylon to keep order in Phrygia and Lydia, whose capitol was Sardis.[2] Antiochus writes also that "they should...use their own laws. And when you have brought them to the places mentioned, you shall give each of them a place to build a home and land to cultivate and plant with vines" (Josephus, *Ant.* 12.150–51, LCL).

Very important for understanding the situation of Jews in various Asian cities is a series of decrees and letters supposedly collected and cited by Josephus. Unfortunately, their authenticity is questionable, and there is some corruption in the texts, whether deliberate or not.[3] I cite in full those concerning Sardis specifically:

Notes to chapter 2 start on page 254

17

1. Lucius Antonius, son of Marcus, proquaestor and propraetor, to the magistrates, council and people of Sardis, greeting. Jewish citizens (*politai*) of ours have come to me and pointed out that from the earliest times they have had an association (*synodos*) in accordance with their native laws and a place of their own (*topon idion*), in which they decide their affairs and controversies with one another; and upon their request that it be permitted to do these things, I decided that they might be maintained, and permitted them to do so. (*Ant.* 14.235, LCL)

2. Decree of the people of Sardis. "The following decree was passed by the council and people on the motion of the magistrates. Whereas the Jewish citizens (*politai*) living in our city have continually received many great privileges from the people and have now come before the council and the people and have pleaded that as their laws and freedom have been restored to them by the Roman Senate and people, they may, in accordance with their accepted customs, come together (*synagōntai*) and have a communal life (*politeuōntai*) and adjudicate suits among themselves, and that a place (*topos*) be given them in which they may gather together with their wives and children and offer their ancestral prayers and sacrifices to God,[4] it has therefore been decreed by the council and people that permission shall be given them to come together on stated days to do those things which are in accordance with their laws, and also that a place (*topos*) shall be set apart by the magistrates for them to build and inhabit, such as they may consider suitable for this purpose, and that the market-officials of the city shall be charged with the duty of having suitable food for them brought in." (*Ant.* 14.259–61, LCL)

3. Gaius Norbanus Flaccus, proconsul, to the magistrates and council of Sardis, greeting. Caesar has written to me, ordering that the Jews shall not be prevented from collecting sums of money, however great they may be, in accordance with their ancestral custom, and sending them up to Jerusalem. I have therefore written to you in order that you may know that Caesar and I wish this to be done. (*Ant.* 16.171)

If it is permitted to take these three texts at (almost) face value, we learn much about Jews living in Sardis.[5] First, some Jews who were Roman citizens, perhaps not from Sardis, reported that Jews living in Sardis had from earliest times (at least 210 BCE, and probably earlier) an "association" of their own, a voluntary association (Richardson 1996a). In addition, they also had their own "place" to meet, whether a separate building or a designated area in a public structure. They had their native laws and decided their own affairs. In other words, they formed an independent *politeuma* within the Greek city of Sardis.[6]

Second, the response of the people of Sardis was to confirm the situation of the Sardian Jews. They will continue to come together in their association or synagogue, to exercise their functions as a *politeuma* and to offer prayers and worship to God. They come together on Sabbaths and holidays ("stated days") and live according to their own laws.[7] Again, they have a "place," but here it is a place "set apart for them to build and inhabit," surely a building of some kind. Provision is made for them to have their own licensed market, presumably so that kosher food will be available. Finally, the collection of the temple tax is protected.

Jews in the cities of Asia, if I may generalize, seemed to be very much at home in those cities, having lived there for centuries (in the case of Sardis, at least). At the same time, they appeared to be faithful to the traditions of their ancestors. They lived and governed themselves according to their own laws and customs, including keeping the Sabbath and abstaining from prohibited food. They tried to keep all the biblical commandments that applied in their situation. What specifically these were we do not know, for we do not have a Diaspora Mishnah.[8] But they still remained loyal to the temple and Judea and contributed the temple tax.

While there were definitely Jews who were Roman citizens, it is doubtful that any were citizens of the Greek cities in which they lived before the end of the second century (Applebaum 1974, 440–44). When we hear that the decree of Sardis called the Jews there both citizens (*politoi*) and inhabitants (*katoikontes*) of the city, there seems to be a basic contradiction in terms. Either "citizens" is an interpolation, by Josephus or his sources, or the word is used imprecisely for members of a *politeuma*. One debated issue, which need not be resolved here, is the question raised by decrees other than those found in Sardis whether all Jews in Asia were exempt from military service or only those who were Roman citizens (Applebaum 1974, 458–60).

The curtain now closes for two-and-a-half centuries on the Jews of Sardis. We do not know how they survived the major earthquake of 17 CE, or whether or not their synagogue was rebuilt afterward. We do not know what they thought about the three great revolts, 66–70 and 132–35 in Judea and 115–17 in Egypt, Cyrenaica, and Cyprus, although we can assume that they did not participate, since there is no sign of Roman hostility to Asian Jews (Smallwood 1976, 356–57; Trebilco 1991, 32–33). Presumably, they paid the *fiscus Judaicus* like all other Jews in the empire. We can, however, extrapolate forwards and backwards into the middle, since the evidence of the decrees of the last century BCE is corroborated by the extraordinary evidence of the excavated synagogue from the third and fourth centuries CE.

The synagogue was converted from part of a large civic complex in the heart of the city, probably in the second half of the third century.[9] It was a large

building, with a capacity of over a thousand people, and it was richly decorated. A large marble table, probably used for the reading of the Torah, was
supported by two (formerly Roman) eagles and flanked by two (formerly
Lydian) lions. There are over eighty inscriptions on tablets, which had been
attached to the walls, dealing with donations or vows (Kraabel 1992f, 229).
Many donors call themselves "Sardinians," and at least eight are members of
the city council (*bouleutēs*). There is also one former procurator, one count,
and one official of the city archives. One refers to Samoe, "priest and teacher,"
probably more like Philo than a rabbi. The synagogue was never converted
into a church but continued as the centre of Sardian Jewish life until the
whole city was destroyed by the Sassanian armies in 616 CE.

It is doubtful whether Melito of Sardis can tell us very much at all
about Jews in Sardis. Kraabel once thought he was able to present a vivid
contrast between Melito's bitter attack and the powerful and prosperous Jewish community in their new synagogue (see Kraabel 1992c, 197–207).[10] But
it now appears quite impossible to make Melito's sermon and the refurbish-
ing of the civic building contemporary events.

There is no evidence that the Sardis Jews knew of Melito's wrath;
indeed, later evidence indicates that Jews and Gentiles here were generally
on better terms than Christian leaders like Melito might wish. The *Peri
Pascha* does not mean a Jewish–Christian conflict in late second-century
Sardis; there is no evidence from the Jewish side for that, and in addition,
Jewish wealth and influence at Sardis in this period suggest Christian envy
of the Jews from afar rather than an actual confrontation with them. There
is no firm evidence that Sardis Jews were even aware of Melito, or that a
direct hostility on their part provoked his attacks (Kraabel 1992e, 264).[11]
Important as Melito is in the self-definition of the early church and his
place in the development of Christian anti-Judaism,[12] he cannot be used as
a source for Jews and Judaism in Sardis.

Jewish Communities in Smyrna

There is much less evidence of "rivalry" at Smyrna than there is for Sardis,
although it is possible to uncover some traces. There certainly was rivalry
between Christians and Jews in ancient Smyrna, if we can believe a classic work on the history of the city. In 1938 Cadoux published a lengthy
and loving work on the city of his birth, in which he claims to know about
"the bitter hatred of the Jews. There was a considerable Jewish community
at Smyrna; and we have seen in the 'Apocalypse' of John evidence of their
feelings toward the Christians" (Cadoux 1938, 348; cf. also 318, 378).

He also knows how their hatred contributed to the death of Polycarp:
"Uncontrolled by the police and assisted by the degenerate Jews (who

showed their usual bitter hostility to the Christians), the crowd collected timber and faggots from the neighbouring workshops and baths" (Cadoux 1938, 361). Part of the reason for this hostility must lie in the (undocumented!) fact that the church at Smyrna "consisted largely of converted Jews" (Cadoux 1938, 319).

Such myths about ancient Diaspora Jews continue in later writers. A respected work published in 1986 claims that Revelation 2:9 refers to Jews who were actively persecuting Christians in Smyrna and suggests that indeed they were the cause of Christian poverty there (Hemer 1986, 66–68). That same author seems to find no contradiction when he says that ancient Diaspora Jews were "particularly unpopular in a Greek city, and the Jews in turn hated their pagan environment" and later that ancient Diaspora Jews had a "long-standing accommodation to surrounding pagan culture" (Hemer 1986, 151). We need to sort out the evidence and our assumptions more carefully than that.

I argued some years ago that those who say that they are Jews but are not (Revelation 2:9; 3:9) and those uncircumcised people who preach Judaism (Ignatius, *Phil*. 6.1) are Gentile Judaizers and not Jews at all. I will not repeat those arguments here (Gaston 1986a, 33–44). With respect to Jewish Christians in Smyrna, the only argument (as opposed to assertion) I have seen is based on Ignatius, *Smyrneans* 1.2: "his saints and believers, whether among the Jews or among the Gentiles in the one body of his church" (Thompson 1990, 126, 143).[13] But the phrase is part of a creedal formula and says nothing about the church in Smyrna specifically (Schoedel 1985, 220–24). Some of the Christian apocryphal Acts probably come from Asia Minor but, differing from the canonical Acts, contain no reference to Jews at all.

It is remarkable how widespread the idea has become among church historians that Jews were the instigators of the persecution of Christians in the ancient world,[14] when there is so little evidence to support the claim.[15] Since the only martyr Acts that mention Jews come from Smyrna, we need to look at them carefully to see what they can tell us about the Jews of Smyrna.[16] The *Martyrdom of Polycarp* begins by speaking of "blessed Polycarp who put a stop to the persecution by his own martyrdom as though he were putting a seal upon it. For practically everything that had gone before took place that the Lord might show us from heaven a witness in accordance with the Gospel. Just as the Lord did, he too waited that he might be delivered up" (1.1–2). It ends by saying, "He was not only a great teacher but also a conspicuous martyr, whose testimony, following the Gospel of Christ, everyone desires to imitate" (19.1). His martyrdom is then told in such a way as to show conformity to the pattern of Christ's passion in the Gospels (see Simon 1986, 122).

Many of the details confirm this parallel. Polycarp had his Gethsemane also outside the city but refused to escape, praying that God's will be done (7.1). He was arrested by a police captain named "Herod"(!),[17] having been betrayed by those of his own household, and destiny decreed that "those who betrayed him might receive the punishment of Judas" (6.2). The arresting party set out "as though against a brigand" (7.1; cf. Matthew 26:55). Polycarp was led back into the city riding on a donkey (8.1). The mob shouted for his death (12:2), and he was pierced in his side (16.1). Clearly, the martyr Polycarp died as a faithful follower of the martyr Jesus.

On the other hand, what is said of the Jews is most improbable. When the "mob of pagans and Jews" shout for his death, calling him "the destroyer of our gods," it seems the Jews are not so much part of history but added from the Gospels (12.2). When Polycarp was to be burned, "the mob swiftly collected logs and brushwood from workshops and baths, and the Jews (as is their custom) zealously helped them with this" (13.1); and yet this happened on the "great Sabbath" (8.1, 21). Much effort has gone into the identification of which Sabbath the Jews of Smyrna would call "great,"[18] but the designation simply comes from John 19:31 (it is found also in Pionius 2.1; 3.6). It "was at the suggestion and insistence of the Jewish people" that the governor was petitioned not to give up the body of Polycarp, but their reason is given as: "Otherwise...they may abandon the Crucified and begin to worship this man" (17:2). In my opinion, one cannot learn anything about Jews in Smyrna from the *Martyrdom of Polycarp*.[19]

Some ninety-five years later came the *Martyrdom of Pionius*, also on the Great Sabbath, an event worth mentioning here because of the vivid retelling of the story and the vigorous defence of its authenticity by Fox (1986, 450–92). But the (mostly biblical) Jews appear only in Pionius's two impressive speeches (4–6; 12.4–14.16) and are not part of the story of the martyrdom at all. These martyrdom Acts then are a good example of Christian anti-Jewish rhetoric but do not inform us very much about Smyrnian Jews. Fox makes the interesting and somewhat romantic claim that the "Great Sabbath" refers to the coincidence of the city's Dionysia and Purim when the large crowd of "Greeks, Jews, and women" all were on holiday together and were free to attend Pionius's hearing. But it is not certain that the Jews of Asia Minor celebrated Purim at all in this period.[20] Although it has become traditional to speak of the Jews as instigating polytheists to persecute Christians, it seems that we shall have to add this "questionable assumption" to Kraabel's list. It did not happen and cannot be cited as evidence of rivalry.

We turn now to inscriptional evidence. One such piece, probably from the second century, includes among the donors *hoi pote Ioudaioi*, who gave 10,000 *drachmai* for the public good (*ISmyrna* 697; 124 CE). According to

Frend, this indicates "outright apostasy" (1965, 148), while according to Cadoux this refers to "erstwhile Jews, presumably polytheists who, after conversion to Judaism, had reverted to their former beliefs and wished to advertise the fact" (1938, 348). But it is much more natural to translate the phrase as "former Judeans," who had perhaps emigrated to Smyrna after the Bar Kochba troubles.[21] *Ioudaioi* is a political or ethnic category and only occasionally (in the case of converts) purely a religious one (see further Harland, chap. 5).

There are four Jewish inscriptions, to be sure from the third or fourth century, that give evidence for a synagogue (Goodenough 1953, 79–81). One refers to two presbyters, father and son, who donated seven gold coins for the pavement. One refers to "L. Lollius Justus, a scribe of the people in Smyrna." The most interesting provides the starting point for Bernadette Brooten's important *Women Leaders* (1982): "Rufina, a Jewess, head of the synagogue (*archisynagōgos*) built this tomb for her freed slaves and the slaves raised in her house. No one else has the right to bury anyone (here). If someone should dare to do, he or she will pay 1500 denars to the sacred treasury and 1000 denars to the Jewish people. A copy of this inscription has been placed in the (public) archives (*CIL* 741, translation in Brooten 1982, 5).

Here is a woman head of a synagogue, rich enough to own slaves and integrated enough into the community to have part of the fine paid to the Jewish people and part to the Smyrna treasury. Although we have no evidence for it, I assume that there was a synagogue in Smyrna also in the second century. I also assume that the Jewish community there was similar to that of other Asian cities.

There is one further matter that needs to be discussed about religious rivalry for Smyrna, that of competing missionary activity. The only possible evidence comes from the *Martyrdom of Pionius*, when he says, "I understand also that the Jews have been inviting some of you to their synagogues" (13.1). This shows that some Smyrnian Christians were interested in Judaism and that Smyrnian Jews were hospitable, but it does not necessarily refer to missionary activity at all. That Judaism was characterized by missionary zeal is one of Kraabel's "questionable assumptions," and recently McKnight (1991) and Goodman (1994) have argued persuasively that it was not (but see Feldman 1992, 1993a; cf. Carleton-Paget 1996).

Conclusion

In this brief overview of Jewish communities in Sardis and Smyrna in the first two centuries CE, I find nothing that could be called a "rivalry." Barclay has argued that Josephus' decrees show evidence of tension between Jews and Greek cities in Asia in the first century BCE (Barclay 1996, 276).

While he may be correct, and while there were major conflicts in Alexandria in the first century CE, one cannot say anything similar about the Jews in Asia in the first two centuries CE.[22] Particularly, the Sardis excavations show a large Jewish community living in peace with their polytheist neighbours and as far as we know also later with Christian neighbours.[23] They were at home there and continued to be at home as long as the city stood. At the same time, there is no evidence of syncretism or lack of loyalty to Torah or Temple or Judaism as they understood it. They felt no need to persecute Christians or to make proselytes of polytheists. In short, I do not believe that the Jews of Smyrna and Sardis were in competition with any of their neighbours. The best way to understand relations among Jews, Christians, and polytheists in antiquity is probably not through the perspective of "conflict theory" at all.[24]

3

Christian Communities in
Sardis and Smyrna

Dietmar Neufeld

Introduction

While obtaining information about religious practices of Christians in the first two centuries of the Common Era in Smyrna and Sardis is difficult, enough exists to reconstruct how polytheists, Jews, and Christians there coexisted and co-operated during the first three centuries CE. The "conflict model" of defining relationships between these groups has buried within it assumptions of group antagonism and a struggle for survival vis-à-vis the other. The question, however, of religious rivalries and relationships must first be set into the much larger context of the realities of urban life and the characteristics of Sardis and Smyrna that made them "receptive" or conducive to Christianization. This will lead to more accurate descriptions of the nature of the relationships and rivalries among polytheists, Jews, and Christians in the cities of Sardis and Smyrna.

This essay will highlight some of the distinctive features of Christianity in Sardis and Smyrna and will raise questions of method related to the interests in this volume: "religious rivalries and the struggle for success." I have included (1) a description of some of the primary source material that is available for both Sardis and Smyrna, noting that most of what we do have that is of interest to us is from a later period, (2) a brief overview of the history and development of the Christian communities in Sardis and Smyrna, although once again, the task is difficult because of the paucity of material evidence from the first 200 years CE, and (3) a description of several cases, texts, and issues that might be investigated in greater detail.

The relationships and rivalries of Jews, Christians, and polytheists is complex and difficult to determine, complicated because of the self-imposed time constraints of the current book and because sources are

Notes to chapter 3 start on page 255

relatively scarce from the early period (Kraemer 1992, 311–329). For the most part, the question of *Adversus Judaeus* traditions has dominated the discussions. It is generally assumed that the polemic in Christian texts (Matthew, Mark, John, Apocalypse, *Martyrdom of Polycarp*, Melito's *Peri Pascha*, etc.) reflects an external environment of mutual hostility and hatred. Recent scholarship, however, has questioned the idea of a direct line of development of anti-Judaism from the first century CE through to the fourth century CE. Instead, the sources are examined in their own contexts and on their own merits, with the result that a different picture emerges (Millar 1992; Olster 1994; Setzer 1994; Rutgers 1995; Lieu 1996, 4–19; Limor and Stroumsa 1996; Robbins 1996a; Lieu 1998; Cohn-Sherbok and Court 2001). Very different social conditions in the third century CE, provoked by invasions, economic crisis, and changes in organization of cities in various parts of the empire, shaped factors internal to Christianity and Judaism: thoughts, attitudes, literature, responses, composition, and structure. All of these factors must be considered as components within the larger Greco-Roman world.

Christian literature or discourse played a significant role in the second century in giving shape to the inner structures of Christianity. It was not a straight line of progression and perpetuation from the first through to the third century, but rather a mosaic of opinion and attitude, determined by the local context (Wilson 1995; Lieu 1996, 4–19). Cameron has demonstrated that many features of Christian discourse fitted the circumstances of society at large very well (1991, 14–46). Religious literature became the vehicle of competition and choice, set within a context of religious vitality and choice (Cohen 1996). Nowhere was this function of religious literature more visible than in the cities of Smyrna and Sardis. Situated in Asia Minor, they benefited from both a literary and cultural vibrancy while also being home to a variety of Christian groups and literature.

One of the great puzzles of the *Adversus Judaeus* tradition is that there is no solid evidence that any of this literature was answered or even provoked by Jews who had come into contact with early Christians. Evidence for Jewish polemic against Christianity is vaporous, apart from, perhaps, the occasional banning of books (prohibited *sifre minim*), occasional expulsion, and liturgical malediction (*Birkat ha-minim*; Kimmelman in Sanders 1980, 226–44; Wilson 1995, 169–95). The same appears to be true of polytheist attitudes that run from benign neglect to indifference, at least in the early period (MacMullen 1973; Fox 1986; Foss 1976, 27–34). The view of Judaism or polytheism meeting Christianity blow for blow well into the fourth century is difficult to maintain. Scholarship has sought to paint Judaism as well as polytheism, for that matter, as real and vital contenders with Christianity.

Part of the problem lies in trying to define Greco-Roman Judaism and polytheism with Christian criteria. For example, when it comes to Judaism, the question of mission and proselytizing is often considered. If Jews proselytized aggressively, their action might help to explain the hostility in some of the Christian texts. While there may be some evidence for a Jewish mission in the late fourth century, there is no firm evidence in the Jewish sources to indicate a Jewish mission to non-Jews in the early period (Feldman 1993b, Feldman and Reinhold 1996, 123–335; Goodman 1994; Stark 1996, 49–71). Why some Christians were preoccupied with Judaism and things Jewish and the hostility it appeared to generate might not necessarily find its answer in the traditional assumption of mutual animosity and antagonism. Instead, what emerges from our texts is a varied picture of Christianity. It is not until the end of the third century CE that we see the foreshadowing of what would in later centuries become a focused stance against Judaism (Lieu et al. 1992, 1996).

While there are numerous literary sources pertinent to Sardis and Smyrna, they do not give us the direct information needed to establish the nature of the relationships between Jews, Christians, and various Greco-Roman religious groups. These sources, however, do reveal many fascinating aspects of the life of a city and its people. Nevertheless, the textual sources usually used to reconstruct the rivalries and relationships of Jews, Christians, and polytheists must be set within a historical context that is chronological, geographical, and social, taking into account the commerce and economic development of the cities, the patronage system, wealth, upward mobility of polytheists, Jews, and Christians, industry, architecture (White 1990 and 1997), guilds, and politics. Important texts include Revelation (ca. 100 CE),[1] Ignatius' letter to the Smyrneans and to Polycarp (ca. 115),[2] Polycarp's letter to Philippi (ca. 115), the *Martyrdom of Polycarp* (ca. 160),[3] Melito's *Peri Pascha* (ca. 150), and the *Martyrdom of Pionius and His Companions* (ca. 250).

Traditional questions of place, date, and authorship of these works, although important, are often driven by historiographical and theological interests that are idealized and harmonized. While such questions are important, we also require an awareness of both the archaeological and sociographic data available. Such information is crucial in our efforts to understand and describe the relationships among the inhabitants of Sardis and Smyrna. For example, it is important to note that rivalries and internal wrangling in Sardis and Smyrna appear to be normal features of urban life; Apollonius of Tyana wrote to Sardis, drawing attention to its internal struggles (Apollonius of Tyana, *Epistles* 75; 76). Setting the question of *rivalries* into a larger context of internal strife, city disturbances, and public disorder that erupted around issues of rights, privileges, and influence will help to nuance and clarify the nature of the conflict among polytheists, Jews, and Christians.

Christianity in Sardis

Of the authors who contribute to our knowledge of Sardis at the turn of the era, two are of paramount importance: Strabo and Nicolas of Damascus. Strabo gives us a detailed description of Sardis's geography, landmarks, and political history. During the first and second centuries CE, a number of other authors contribute important knowledge of Sardis (Pedley 1972, 3–5). The works pertinent to an understanding of the origins and development of the Christian community in Sardis and Smyrna include Revelation 2:8–11 and 3:1–6, Ignatius' *Letter to the Smyrneans*, Melito's *Peri Pascha*, and Eusebius' *Historiae ecclesiasticae*. On the basis of these sources it is possible to reconstruct a profile of Sardis.

The history and origins of the Christian community are difficult to determine, and the suggestions of an origin in a synagogue, in a Pauline mission, or in the unrecorded activity of the other evangelists are conjectural (Hansen 1968; Kraabel 1992f, 233). The name of the founder of the Christian community at Sardis may be preserved in a tradition of the Greek church. One of the Greek calendars names a certain Clement as the first Gentile to believe in Christ, later to become bishop of Sardis. This Clement is sometimes identified as one of Paul's fellow workers, mentioned in the Epistle to the Philippians (Phil 4:3; *Synaxarium* 621). His identity, however, has never been clearly established.

Whatever the origins of the church in Sardis, the writer of Revelation considers the church in Sardis important enough to mention it. In the last decade of the first century CE the writer of Revelation addresses the Christian community there as once having a reputation that it no longer deserves:

> And to the angel of the church in Sardis write: These are the words of him who has the seven spirits of God and the seven stars: "I know your works; you have a name of being alive, but you are dead. Wake up, and strengthen what remains and is on the point of death, for I have not found your works perfect in the sight of my God. Remember then what you received and heard; obey it, and repent. If you do not wake up, I will come like a thief, and you will not know at what hour I will come to you. Yet you have still a few persons in Sardis who have not soiled their clothes; they will walk with me, dressed in white, for they are worthy. If you conquer, you will be clothed like them in white robes, and I will not blot your name out of the book of life; I will confess your name before my Father and before his angels. (Revelation 3:1–5, NRSV)

The language seems to imply that certain members of the community had lapsed from an earlier stronger state, while others had not defiled their garments, i.e., they had not lapsed into polytheism or heterodoxy (Revelation 1:11, 3:1–6; Johnson 1961, 81–90).

By the middle of the second century CE the Christian community in Sardis appears to be flourishing, for it produced an apologist and writer, the bishop Melito, who presided during the time of Antonius Pius and Marcus Aurelius (Rescript of Antonius Pius, ca. 139 CE [Petzl 1990], Eusebius, *HE* 4.13.8, III–IV CE). While Melito was a prolific writer, only one of his works survives almost complete, the *Peri Pascha* (Foss 1976; Hall 1979; Wilson 1995). The following has been established about Melito and his community:

1. He is numbered with the disciples of Philip and John and the mar-tyr bishop Polycarp of Smyrna as one of the "great luminaries" of the church in Asia Minor: "Melito the eunuch who lived entirely in the Holy Spirit and who lies in Sardis"—according to Polycrates of Ephesus (ca. 195 CE) as quoted by Eusebius (*HE* 5.24.8 [trans. by Williamson 1965]).

2. As bishop, Melito addressed an apology to the Emperor Marcus Aurelius (fragments in *HE* 4.26.5–11) in which for the first time it is argued that the empire should support the church because they began together in the time of Augustus, prospered when together, and thus belong together: "Our philosophy first grew among the barbarians, but its full flower came among our nations during the glorious reign of your ancestor Augustus; and became a good omen for your empire, since from that time the power of the Romans has grown mightily and magnificent" (*HE* 4.26.7). This apology may have been presented to Lucius Verus, who passed through Asia in 166 CE; a statue was erected in the Sardis gymnasium, and a Hebrew inscription may have been put up in his honour in the synagogue as well.

3. Melito was an accomplished orator, a man of fine oratorical genius (*elegans et declamatorium ingenium*—according to Tertullian (as quoted by Jerome in *Lives of Illustrious Men*, 24 [trans. NPNF]). His rhetoric resembles the Asian style of the second Sophistic (Wil-son 1995, 241–57).

4. Melito is the first Christian known to have made a pilgrimage to the Holy Land (*HE* 4.26.13). The purpose of the trip was to secure an accurate canon of the books of Jewish scriptures (Wilson 1995, 253).

5. Melito was a Quartodeciman: like many other Anatolian Christians of his time, he celebrated Easter on the day the Jewish people cel-ebrated Passover (14 Nisan), no matter what day of the week it might be (other Christians, those in the west, celebrated Easter on the Sunday following Passover). He was probably a celibate and was noted for his prophetic powers (Wilson 1995, 241–57).

Melito's *Peri Pascha* is often regarded as the result of conflict between a large, well-established, and prosperous Jewish community and a small, somewhat lesser Christian community. Some would argue, however, that this projected image of a small and struggling Christian community is erroneous. Melito's rhetorical flair may in fact betray an established educational and social background not inferior to that of the Jewish contemporaries (Norris 1986; Taylor 1995; Lieu 1996, 207). Lieu writes, "The strength of Melito's rhetoric need not imply the strength of the Jewish community at the time. It is only scholarly imagination that makes Melito's major motivation the Jewish community of Sardis, vibrant, self-confident and influential, while the Christians struggled with poverty of members, poor self-image and insecurity" (1996, 228).[4] Melito's rhetoric is more about the desire to create reality than a response to reality.

To some extent the idea of the *Peri Pascha* as rhetoric is found in Wilson's excellent discussions of Melito. But privilege is nevertheless given to the historical reality of the piece as representing the tensions and animosities between the communities. While it is likely that the text reflects a certain historical reality of interaction between communities, it is Melito's own concerns, the logic of his arguments, and the traditions from which he draws, especially the Hebrew Bible, that helped to create and cast the terms within which he spoke. His rhetorical flourish helped to create a stereotyped image of the other. This representation or image then became reality for later generations. Such literature has a clear rhetorical function, a world-creating rhetoric, and the details serve to produce a stereotyped image of the other (Lieu et al. 1996, 5–13).[5]

Melito's *Peri Pascha* was written in relative isolation, from within a particular community, attempting both to encourage members of the community to stay and to discourage others from defecting. It was not intended directly to criticize the Jewish community of Sardis (Seager and Kraabel 1983, 179; Kraabel 1991, 237–55). A number of complex issues and forces collectively motivated him to shape the vehemence of his attack: Marcion, the Quartodeciman controversy, his Christological heritage, and scriptural tradition (Wilson 1995, 285–301). Kraabel suggests that "Melito's vituperation may be a backfire set to defend himself from the charge by fellow Christians that, as a Quartodeciman who followed the Jewish calendar annually in setting the date of Easter, he was *Judaizing*" (Kraabel 1992a, 348).

An indication of the size and vitality of the Christian community in Sardis is that it is said to have produced two martyrs in the persecutions of the third century: a priest from Sardis, executed at Satala at Lydia under Valerian (*Synaxarium ecclesiae Constantinopolitanae*, May 26, ca. 257) and Apollonius, about whom virtually nothing is known (*Synaxarium ecclesiae Constantinopolitanae*, ca. III CE [?]).

While the names of the bishops of Sardis are recorded for the early period, few of them achieve distinction. The following is a list of the metropolitan bishops of Sardis from the first century CE through to fifth century CE (Germanos 1928; Laurent 1928; Foss 1976, 135–36):

Clement	I CE
The "Angel" of the Apocalypse	I CE
Melito	160–180 CE
Artemidorus	325 CE
Leontius	359 CE
Heortasius	360 CE
Candidus (Arian)	363 CE
Maeonius	431 CE
Florentius	448–451 CE
Aetherius	457 CE
Julianus	553 CE

The bishops of the fourth century CE were preoccupied with the controversies on the nature of Christ and the Trinity and, hence, are not helpful for understanding the early period.

Byzantine Sardis (early Byzantine, ca. 395–616 CE) with its shops and large synagogue provide good evidence that its inhabitants enjoyed a high standard of living. Restaurants, probably owned by Christians, have been excavated by the Harvard-Cornell Sardis Expedition. A plate decorated with a cross was discovered along with the presence of pig bones and shellfish, as well as a graffito on a shard showing a Latin cross and the name *Kyriak...(os)*. He may have been the restaurant owner. An ampulla with a Latin cross has been found. The residence/restaurant had a Latin cross with a *rho* top carved on a door jamb. A residence/wine shop with mussel shells in it has also been discovered and may have been owned by either Christians or polytheists (Crawford 1996, 17–18). The Byzantine shops on the main highway adjacent to the gymnasium signal an active commercial life. Archaeological evidence points to Jews, Christians, and polytheists living, moving, and working in close proximity and cooperatively, manufacturing and selling a large variety of goods, including metal tools, utensils, glass vessels, and jewellery (Foss 1974, 18; Crawford 1996, 38–70). Many individuals could also afford to set up dedicatory monuments and memorials in marble and engage in generous acts of benefaction.

One of the significant discoveries in Sardis is the synagogue, a very large building built in several phases from the third to the seventh centuries CE. The synagogue revealed approximately eighty inscriptions mainly having to do with donations of wealthy citizens and office-holders of some status—city council members, a count, a procurator, an assistant in the state archives (Kraabel 1992f, 229). The first Jewish settlers in Sardis may have arrived shortly after the fall of Jerusalem in 586 BCE. The book of Obadiah mentions exiles from Jerusalem who lived in *Sepharad*—the Semitic name for Sardis. By the first century CE they had become wealthy and influential with a place of worship (Josephus, *Ant.*14.235; 259–612; 16.171), with the right to send the temple tax to Jerusalem (Josephus, *Ant.* 16.171), and were assured the provision of ritually pure food (Josephus, *Ant.* 14.261).

A letter from the proconsul of Asia, Gaius Norbanus Flaccus, conveying the decision of the Caesar that the Jewish practice of collecting money and sending it to Jerusalem should not be hindered, seems to indicate the influence of the community (Pedley 1968, 212). On the basis of the decrees and the synagogue, Kraabel concludes (not uncontested) that the decrees are a sign "not of the community's need for protection, but of its prestige," and that the "Sardis synagogue reflects a self-confident Judaism, bold enough to appropriate polytheist shapes and symbols for itself," (Kraabel 1978b, 242–44). At Sardis, proximity of Jews to polytheist culture, rather than producing syncretism and capitulation to polytheism, produced clarity and the enjoyment of a Gentile culture (Kraabel 1978, 255).[6]

It also appears that Sardis was an intellectual centre of some importance in the fourth to fifth centuries CE. Rhetoric and philosophy flourished and are perhaps best exemplified by the *Lives of the Sophists* written around 400 by Eunapius. Chrysanthius appears to have been the founder of one such school in Sardis. He came from a family of senatorial rank. He studied Plato and Aristotle, the gods, Pythagoras, and Apollonius of Tyana, and eventually practised theurgy. In due time, he attracted the attention of the young Julian, who came to the throne in 361 CE. Chrysanthius was appointed by Julian to restore polytheism in Sardis, and he did that, not by persecuting Christians or building new temples, but by restoring existing temples (Eunapius, *Vitae Sophistarum* 503, ca. 375).

Tangible marks of early Christianity are difficult to trace because little or no archaeological remains survive. White (1997) points out that the followers of Jesus met in homes of members. He argues that recent studies show that the house church setting conditioned the nature of worship, assembly, and communal organization, as did its urban context: "The social location of the Pauline communities reflected the character and conditions of urban households and other private domestic activities" (White 1990, 4). The place in which the community met remained long unchanged from its basic domestic function, but within three centuries this was to change. These private houses were eventually renovated, in what White calls architectural adaptation, to become Christian house churches in the early period, approximately 240 CE. With time, in stark contrast to the loosely organized house church, the monumental church building arose. The one was random and informal, the other hieratic and formal. From the fourth century CE onward, the basilica epitomized Christian architecture, and under the patronage of Constantine and his mother Helena Augusta, monumental church structures proliferated in the Roman Empire.

Christianity in Smyrna

The book of Revelation indicates the presence of a Christian community in Smyrna sometime before the end of the first century CE, but nothing is known of the origin of the Christian community there. In Revelation 2:8–10 we find these words:

> And to the angel of the church in Smyrna write: These are the words of the first and the last, who was dead and came to life: "I know your affliction and your poverty, even though you are rich. I know the slander on the part of those who say that they are Jews and are not, but are a synagogue of Satan. Do not fear what you are about to suffer. Beware, the devil is about to throw some of you into prison so that you may be tested, and for ten days you will have affliction. Be faithful until death, and I will give you the crown of life."

The mention of Jews and of the "synagogue of Satan" also indicates the presence of Jews in Smyrna at this time.

This Jewish presence in Smyrna is confirmed by a number of inscriptions. A famous inscription 123–24 CE, during the reign of Hadrian, refers to a contribution of 10,000 drachmae for some unknown public works project by *hoi pote Ioudaioi* (*CIJ* 2.742.29; *CIG* 3148). The phrase is sometimes translated as "former Jews," but Kraabel has argued that the phrase should be translated "people formerly of Judaea," and thus probably immigrants from Palestine (1982, 455). Many of the Christian inscriptions are dated to the fifth and sixth centuries CE and, hence, beyond the scope of this overview (Petzl 1982, 263–71).

During Ignatius's stay in Smyrna in the early second century CE he wrote four of his seven letters. From Troas, he wrote two letters to Smyrna, one to the church itself, and the other to its bishop, Polycarp. In these letters, Ignatius comments briefly on Jews and Judaism. In his letter to the Smyrneans he makes one brief mention of the Jews occurs in a formulaic expression of praise: "...for all ages, through his resurrection, for his saints and the believers, whether among the Jews, or among the heathen, in one body of his church" (*en Ioudaiois eite en ethnesin*; 7.1.2).[7] In his letters to the Philadelphians and Magnesians several passages are frequently taken to indicate the social relationships between Jews and Christians. He wrote to the church at Magnesia while staying at Smyrna, where he was visited by their bishop, two elders, and a deacon.

Magnesians 10.1.3 reads, "For this cause let us be his disciples, and let us learn to lead Christian lives [*christianismos*]. For whoever is called by any name other than this is not of God....It is monstrous to talk of Jesus Christ and to practice Judaism. For Christianity did not base its faith on Judaism [*ioudaismos*], but Judaism on Christianity."

Philadelphians 6.1 reads, "But if anyone interpret Judaism to you do not listen to him; for it is better to hear Christianity from the circumcised than Judaism from the uncircumcised. But both of them, unless they speak of Jesus Christ, are to me tombstones and sepulchers."

Magnesians 8.1–2 reads, "Be not led astray by strange doctrines [*heterodoxia*] or by old fables which are profitless [*mutheuma*]. For if we are living until now according to Judaism, we confess that we have not received grace. For the divine prophets lived according to Jesus Christ. Therefore they were also persecuted, being inspired by his grace, to convince the disobedient that there is one God, who manifested himself through Jesus Christ his son, who is his Word proceeding from silence, who in all respects was well-pleasing to him that sent him."

And *Magnesians* 9.1 reads, "If then those who walked in ancient customs came to a new hope, no longer living for the Sabbath [*sabbatizontes*], but for the Lord's Day, on which also our life sprang up through him and his death—though some deny him—and by this mystery we received faith, and for this reason also we suffer, that we may be found disciples of Jesus Christ our only teacher; if these things be so, how then shall we be able to live without him of whom even the prophets were disciples in the Spirit and to whom they looked forward as their teacher?"

These passages have caused a great deal of speculation about the identity of these uncircumcised interpreters of Judaism. A number of options have been examined without a consensus of opinion (Lieu 1996, 35). Some suggest that they are Gentile converts who have been attracted to Judaism. Others suggest they are God-worshippers who are imposing their Jewish practices on other Christians. Still others think that they are docetic teachers who have adopted Jewish themes. Ultimately, there is probably more rhetoric than reality in these passages. Nevertheless, the rhetoric not only clearly denigrates a system but also excludes it, because anyone who lives according to Judaism puts himself outside the compass of salvation that the Gospel offers. In the world of the text, it would appear that Ignatius pays little attention to the Jews as a group outside the Christian community. For him, the relationship between the two is necessary but is one that permits movement in one direction only—from Judaism to Christianity. For Ignatius, this one-way relationship hinges on the question of the place and interpretation of the Hebrew Bible—to whom do the scriptures belong?

For Ignatius, there is no need to understand the scriptures outside of a Christocentric perspective.

Thus, as Lieu points out, nothing can be concluded with any certainty about Christian–Jewish relations at that time from Ignatius's letters (1996, 70–79). Indeed, argues Lieu, Ignatius's letters are clearly driven by several concerns that shape the attitudes, manner of presentation, and content, against which the role of the Jews should be understood. Ignatius's intense preoccupation with his journey to Rome and impending death colours the letter and renders it opaque when it comes to answering questions of relationships and rivalries.

By the end of the second century CE the Christian community at Smyrna could boast of having a bishop who was eventually martyred. Polycarp's martyrdom and the appearance of Jews at dramatic points in the story are taken to illustrate the growing tension between the Christian community and the powerful local Jewish community. The text is often simplistically seen as an early example of anti-Semitism or as an example of the pervasive presence in second-century Asia Minor of Jews who were bent on persecuting early Christians (Lieu 1996, 94). In *Martyrdom of Polycarp* 12.2 a whole crowd of Gentiles and Jews (*hapan to plēthos ethnōn te kai Ioudaiōn*) with uncontrollable rage shout that Polycarp should be done away with. Traditionally this outbreak has been taken to demonstrate that the Jews played some historical role in early Christian persecution.

In *Martyrdom of Polycarp* 13.1, a mass of Smyrneans, Gentiles, and Jews are pictured boiling over with anger and shouting for Polycarp's life ("the crowds [*ochloi*] immediately gathering from the workshops and baths wood and firewood, with the Jews assisting at this particularly enthusiastically [*malista Ioudaiōn prothumōn*] as is their custom"). The crowds rush about seeking fuel for the pyre, with the author commenting that the "Jews as usual joining in with more enthusiasm than anyone" (Eusebius, *HE* 4.15.23).

In *Martyrdom of Polycarp* 17.1–18.1 the Jews are once more pictured as eager and hostile. "And this with the Jews inciting and urging, who also kept watch, as we were about to take him from the fire. For they did not know that we would never be able to abandon the Christ....When the centurion saw the contentiousness of the Jews that took place, he placed him in the midst and burnt him." This text in particular, along with Revelation 2:9 ("synagogue of Satan"), is understood by many scholars to demonstrate tensions between Jews and Christians in Smyrna.

A number of issues, however, have thrown into doubt this traditional assumption that these texts reflect an actual conflict and rivalry between Christians and Jews in Smyrna. Though Polycarp is thought to have been martyred in 155 (Eusebius, *HE* 4.14.8–4.16.3), the date of the literary text concerning the event is problematic. In two different contexts of the Polycarp narrative the text mentions the "great Sabbath" (*sabbatos megalos*) and the feast of the Passover (*Mart. Pol.* 8.1; 21.1; Lieu 1996, 70–79). Rather than see these two references simply as part of the theological thought world of the narrative, as does Conzelmann (1978, 41–58), or as indicative of Christian–Jewish conflict, one should understand them as reflecting a conflict about dates and calendars that takes place *within* the Christian community at the time of writing of the *Martyrdom of Polycarp*.[8]

An additional important early and celebrated martyr, according to Eusebius, was Pionius (died in 250 CE; Eusebius, *HE* 4.16.3). Historians and scholars doubt the text's authenticity and reliability, not least because it presents a textual challenge. The earliest Greek text dates ca. XII CE. Earlier versions appear in a variety of languages: Latin, Armenian, and Slavonic, each confirming the tone and detail of the Greek manuscript (Cadoux 1938, 374ff.; Fox 1986, 460). Fox argues, however, that the various texts, for the most part, match in detail and, if carefully analyzed, illustrate Pionius's views of polytheist culture, the great city of Smyrna, and its sophists and Jews (Fox 1986, 460–92).

The conflicts and rivalries during Pionius's time are contrived and artificially accentuated because of the Decian persecution and, thus, do not give us an accurate picture of what everyday relationships were like among Pionius, polytheists, and Jews. Pionius showed disdain for the learned polytheists, chastised the city for its vanity, warned the Jews not to gloat over the Christians who had apostacized. He pointed to the scriptures to show that many Jews had sinned of their own free will, that they had killed their prophets, that they had also murdered Christ. In a prison diary, he lamented the state of disarray of the church because of the quarrels and disputes within it and then once again turned his attention to the Jews. Quite significantly he pointed out that he had heard that the Jews were inviting some Christians into their synagogues. He attacked them for this practice, suggesting that they were using "crisis" and fear of death as a pretext to recruit. Apparently, the Jews believed that Christians would rather belong to the synagogue than eat "demonic" polytheist meat. Pionius was of the opinion that once in the Jewish community, Christians would be exposed to slander about Jesus and the Resurrection. In a counterattack, he argued that Christians must remember the history of the Jews; they killed Jesus and the prophets. He labelled them as "rulers of Sodom and the host of Gomorrah" (Fox 1986, 479). Fox concludes that here we are being treated to a rare glimpse of ongoing Jewish missionary interest, one that the Christians were no longer willing to tolerate.

Fox is of the opinion that Pionius's words fit the context at Smyrna only too well. While no synagogue has been found in Smyrna, inscriptional remains suggest a Jewish community of some size and influence. According to Fox, even as early as the 150s Jewish mobs and individuals had had a direct involvement in the death of Polycarp (Fox 1986, 481–82). One wonders whether Pionius's diary captures an actual state of affairs or whether his rhetoric gets away from him in much the same way as it does from Melito in his homily. It seems to me that the influence and social rank of a religion, Jewish or polytheist, in society need not necessarily imply the existence of animosity and conflict but may imply rather an attitude of benign indifference.

Indeed, the greater the rank, influence, and power of a community, the less the need to recognize the other. Hence, it is possible that the Christian community was not openly or maliciously harassed by its Jewish neighbours (MacLennan 1990, 107; Wilson 1995, 298).

To protect themselves, and to dissuade members of the Christian community from defecting to the dynamic and more attractive Jewish community, leaders of the Christian community erected elaborate, artificial rhetorical edifices (Melito is often regarded as the first poet of deicide). These rhetorical edifices of slander and opprobrium tell us more about the internal dynamics of establishing identity than they do about the establishment and existence of conflict (Gaston 1986a; Satran 1996; Limor and Stroumsa 1996). These writings, though arising within the shadow of a respectable Judaism, were not addressed to the Jews but to both polytheists and Christians.

Conclusion

In very few of the descriptions of Sardis and Smyrna offered to date in commentaries, monographs, books, and journal articles is much made of the economical, political, archaeological, architectural, and commercial enterprises, and numerous other factors that define daily life in large, prosperous urban centres. Generally, it is acknowledged that these cities were prosperous, powerful, and influential and that the decadence associated with power and wealth probably corrupted the churches in Sardis and Smyrna in some way (Caird 1984, 47–50). But there has been little investigation into how such urban realities specifically shaped the inhabitants, religious groups, and other social institutions. Studies are, however, beginning to appear that take seriously how a city's urban realities, its commerce, economy, and trade, determine how its inhabitants, communities, groups, and associations relate to each other, to the governing powers, and to institutions, religious or otherwise (Kraybill 1996).

A contextual study ("thick" description; Geertz 1973, 3–30) of both Smyrna and Sardis in terms of conflicts, economics, the military, political and religious conditions, and special relationships nuances the nature of the rivalries and relationships between Christians, polytheists, and Jews. The urban realities of Sardis and Smyrna are read as kinds of texts for clues to these issues (MacLennan 1990, 17; Satran 1996, 57–58). The available archaeological evidence, literature from the cities, ancient writings about the cities, and descriptions of special places such as libraries, graves, buildings, and synagogues in the cities of Sardis and Smyrna, reveal that the reasons for rivalries or cooperation were complex and invariably related to difficult urban problems (Foss 1976; Pedley 1972).

The category of *Adversus Judaeus* is problematic because there are many assumptions about rivalries and relationships implicit within it. The interaction of Jews and Christians should not be seen in isolation but as part of a vital religious life and activity in Asia Minor. Epigraphic conventions and formulae indicate that there was far more interaction of an amicable kind between Jews, Christians, and polytheists than the literary sources would lead us to expect. Lieu argues that as late as the sermons of Chrysostom, *Against the Jews*, ordinary church members thought it quite acceptable to attend a synagogue service, to join in the celebration of Jewish festivities, and to regard the synagogue as a sacred place in which to take oaths (Lieu 1996, 24; Mitchell 1993, 40–51). Moreover, it would be beneficial to use the categories of *image* and *reality* in the way Lieu has done when analyzing Melito, Polycarp, and other writers.

The conflict often posited between Jews and Christians is implicitly based on the assumption that Jews from the early period were preoccupied with polytheists and Christians, actively seeking to convert them for fear of being converted themselves. Moreover, a "conflict model" has encouraged the perception that Christian documents reveal a climate of hostility, competition, and conflict between Christianity and a Judaism that had not lost its combativeness and dynamism (Taylor 1995; Seager and Kraabel 1983, 178). As pointed out, some regard Melito's *Peri Pascha* as indicative of the social relations between Christians and Jews in the city of Sardis during the second century (Johnson 1961; Frend 1984; Kraabel 1992f). While the documents are polemical, their tone and content need not necessarily imply the existence of external conflict. The hostile tone was also the result of the dynamics of internal debate relative to the group and not only the result of open, mutual hostility between the Christians and Jews. In the words of Gaston, the rivalries and debates between Christians and Jews "arise out of an inner-Christian theological debate rather than out of rivalry with a living Judaism" (Gaston 1986b, 163; see also Gaston's essay in this volume).

To view this literature, however, as belonging mainly to the Christian discourse of self-definition would be misleading. Such a model is too static, for it does not take into consideration the dynamic character of religious identity in the Greco-Roman world. In order for Christianity to construct an identity, it constructed the identity of "the other," of Judaism and of polytheism (Lieu 1996, 1). This literature, at its heart, is not about Judaism per se but about those who articulated those views. In giving expression to them, an image was created that was drawn from a particular social, cultural, and religious milieu. Jews and polytheists were presented in particular ways by particular authors in particular contexts. Literary presentations of "the other," therefore, cannot be taken to accurately reflect or mirror the external reality from which they arose. Needs that were both internal and external to the literature itself shaped the presentation of the image of the other, which, though arising out of the reality of Jews and polytheists in Sardis and Smyrna, did not directly address the situation implied.

4

Greco-Roman Religions in Sardis and Smyrna

Richard S. Ascough

Introduction

In this essay I will undertake a brief survey of the many polytheistic religious groups[1] of Greco-Roman antiquity that are manifest distinctly, and perhaps distinctively, at Sardis and Smyrna. In its original form, delivered to the CSBS Religious Rivalries seminar in 1998, the essay had two primary goals. First, it aimed to provide an orientation to the important deities attested at Sardis and Smyrna. Second, it attempted to highlight issues of "religious rivalry" that might warrant further research. In its present revised form I have retained the survey nature of the essay but have indicated where some of the issues raised have been taken up by others who have contributed to this volume. Other issues are raised that continue to await further exploration.

Greco-Roman Religions in Sardis

At Sardis, Artemis was an important figure during the Hellenistic and early imperial age (Hanfmann, Robert, and Mierse 1983, 129), as she was seen as the protectress of the city. Her temple at Sardis is the fourth-largest Ionic temple known from the ancient world (Hanfmann 1983, 129).[2] The first phase of building began shortly after 281 BCE and ended in 222 BCE. The temple incorporated a limestone altar dedicated to Artemis that probably dates from the sixth century BCE. It was unfinished, and work on it resumed around 175 BCE, although again it was left unfinished. During this time Zeus Polieus joined Artemis as the object of worship in the temple. Although earlier studies tended to see a conflation of Artemis with Cybele at Sardis, Hanfmann (1983, 129) points out that "no inscription found in the Artemis Precinct ever refers to Cybele, Meter, or Kore. It is no longer permissible after

Notes to chapter 4 start on page 256

our archaeological, linguistic, and sculptural findings...to conflate Artemis with Cybele."[3]

At Sardis the only deity to be associated with Artemis was Zeus Polieus ("Zeus [protector] of the city"), who joined her in the temple from 220 BCE.[4] A colossal statue of Zeus was set up in the temple of Artemis, probably balancing a similar colossal statue of Artemis (Ramage 1987, 31).[5] After the earthquake of 17 CE, the temple of Artemis lay in ruins for over fifty years, presumably because these gods were viewed as having failed to protect the city. "Not unnaturally, from gods that had failed them, they turned to the *praesens divus*, the 'present god,' the Emperor who was the first to help them in their dire plight" (Hanfmann 1983, 135). The third building phase was completed around 150 CE, at which time it became the locus of the worship of the emperor Antoninus Pius (138–51). The double cella in the temple came to house statues of Antoninus and the Empress Faustina.[6]

The other major female deity at Sardis was Cybele, known there as the "mother of the gods," or in Roman times, *Meter Oreia* ("mother of the mountain"). A seventh- to mid-sixth century BCE altar to Cybele has been uncovered near the Pactolus River, where she watched over the finding and refining of gold.[7] Iconographically, she is often depicted as enthroned between two lions.[8]

After the earthquake of 17 CE, Artemis rarely appears on coins from Sardis. Instead, there is the depiction of a figure that looks like Kore but is in actuality an ancient deity (Hanfmann 1983, 129).[9] Hanfmann (1983, 131) suggests that before the earthquake of 17 CE there existed at Sardis an archaic cult of a Lydian "corn maiden." After 17 CE her archaic image became the official representative of the city, thus displacing Artemis from the role. This change of status may have resulted from the failure of Artemis to protect the city in 17 CE, along with the shift from grapes to wheat as the primary agricultural product (Hanfmann 1983, 136, 144, 147). Eventually, the mother goddess (Cybele) and the corn maiden were seen as a pair and were assimilated into the Greek legend of Demeter and Kore.

Most relevant for this investigation is the rivalry between the various Greco-Roman religions as they vied for the allegiance of the people of the cities. In Sardis we find a late first- or early second-century CE inscription warning the temple warden *therapeutai* of Zeus the Legislator not to participate in the mysteries of Sabazios, Agdistis, and Ma:[10]

> In the thirty-nine years
> of Artaxerxes' reign,
> Droaphernes, son of Barakis,
> governor of Lydia, dedicated a statue
> to Zeus the Legislator. He (Droaphernes)

instructs his (Zeus') temple-warden
devotees who enter the innermost sanctum
and who serve and crown the god,
not to participate in the mysteries of
Sabazios with those who bring the burnt
offerings and (the mysteries) of Agdistis and Ma.
They instruct Dorates the temple-warden
to keep away from these mysteries. (*ISardH* 4 = *CCCA* 1.456,
trans. by Horsley 1981, 21–22)

This inscription is a Greek rewriting of an earlier Aramaic edict from ca. 365 BCE.[11] The primary deity in the latter case was Zeus Baradates ("the Legislator"), the epithet being a Greek translation of the name of a Persian deity (Ahura Mazda).[12] Both Sabazios and Agdistis are also of Persian origin, while Ma is a Cappadocian goddess (Horsley 1981, 22). That the text legislates against participation in the mysteries of these deities suggests that their cults existed at Sardis in the fourth century BCE.[13]

On the issue of "religious rivalries," it is interesting that only a select group, the "inner" circle, of Zeus worshippers is prevented from participating in other cults (Horsley 1981, 22). That an earlier text is later translated and re-inscribed shows the force of the prohibition over a five hundred-year period.[14] According to Horsley (1981, 23), "What we are looking at here is one voluntary religious association in one particular locality which has retained alive and apparently in not too contaminated a form Iranian religious traditions long after the Persian empire had disappeared." In the first or second century CE, a certain Dorates had transgressed the exclusivity requirement, which resulted in the recutting of the stone (Horsley 1981, 23). This entire scenario is interesting because it shows that religious exclusivity is not confined to Jewish and Christian groups (Horsley 1981, 23).[15]

Herrmann (1996, 29–35) draws four general conclusions from the archaeological evidence: (1) there existed a private religious association at Sardis from the first century BCE to the second century CE, since we have four inscriptions from this group; (2) there is some continuity with the fourth century BCE evident in the act of re-inscribing a text from that time during the second century CE, but this continuity itself raises a number of problems; (3) all four inscriptions were found in the neighbourhood of the temple of Artemis (and Zeus), but a direct connection has not been determined; (4) there existed for this group some sort of inner sanctum (*ton adyton*) in which rituals took place (see Horsely 1981, 22).

A further spinoff of this inscription is the conservatism reflected in it. Kraabel points out that, for at least this one cult at Sardis, the second century CE was "not a period of syncretism of 'religious creativity' but of conservatism, reinforcing the piety of the past" (1992d, 254). This conservatism is also true in the case of a column that recreates the image of a goddess with her essential features coming from the seventh century BCE, an image that is also represented on Sardian coins from the time of Hadrian and beyond (see Kraabel 1992d, 254).[16]

Another important cult in Asia Minor is that of Sabazios, a Thracian-Phrygian deity whose mysteries existed at Sardis as early as 367 BCE (Hanfmann 1983, 132).[17] In the inscription mentioned above we saw that the Zeus officials are prevented from participating in the cult of Sabazios. This regulation was first in place in the fourth century BCE and reaffirmed in the first or second century CE, indicating the existence of the Sabazios cult at Sardis, like that of Zeus, for a period of over five hundred years. A second-century BCE altar dedication set up by a priest of Zeus Sauazios [sic] has also been found (see Johnson 1961, 82; 1968).[18]

Johnson (1968, 545) is of the opinion that "the cult of Sabazios shows continual syncretism and variation." The similarity of names and titles between this cult and Judaism—for example, "Lord Sabazios" is similar to "Lord of the Sabbath" or "Lord of Hosts"—caused some in antiquity to equate the two. This confusion has, in turn, led to the modern suggestion that the Sabazios cult influenced Jews in Asia Minor (e.g., Johnson 1961, 83; 1968, 547–49; see Kraabel 1992d, 250–52). Kraabel attempts to dismantle this view by pointing out that no evidence of Sabazios (or Dionysos) has been found in the Sardis synagogue building (1992b, 282–83; 1992d, 252–54). He argues that, as was the case in the Zeus inscription, the members of the Jewish community at Sardis were restricted from participation in the Sabazios cult. He highlights the fact that the cult of Sabazios invited "syncretism" and did so for a very long time at Sardis, so much so that other religious groups considered it imperative to resist it.[19]

There are a number of inscriptions dedicated to the moon god Men, including localized designations such as Men Axiottenos and Men Tymoleites (*ISardBR* 17, 159; *ISardRobert* 31, 32, 34, 35). The earliest depiction of Men, which shows him as a horseman riding towards an altar, comes from the late Hellenistic period (*ISardBR* 96a). He appears on coins from the time of Vespasian, and the fountains list of about 200 CE indicates that he had a sanctuary at Sardis. Hanfmann (1983, 133) notes that the cult of Men "came to cooperate with and rival Artemis."

Hanfmann notes that "Dionysus must have had a temple and image at Sardis, but apart from the vaguely Praxitelean head on autonomous coins...we have no evidence for either" (1983, 133). However, it is clear that the annual festival of Dionysos was established before 150 BCE. Two inscriptions testify to an active association of Dionysiac artists during the time of Hadrian (*ISardBR* 13, 14). Both inscriptions were set up to celebrate Hadrian as the "new Dionysos."

Other deities mentioned in the inscriptional record from Sardis include Athena, Asklepios, Herakles, Attis, Hermes, Eros, and Iaso (the goddess of healing). We find more generic designations of "god" used of deity. Apollo is one of the male deities most often depicted on coins from Sardis (Hanfmann 1983, 132). Voluntary associations at Sardis include an association of *mystai* of Apollo Pleurenos (Herrmann 1996, 319), which Hanfmann wonders "may not after all be related to Plans (Qldans), probably a Lydian god" (1983, 132).

The cult of Roma was present at Sardis possibly as early as 125 to 100 BCE, although neither her shrine nor her image has been found.[20] She does not appear on coins until the time of Hadrian (Hanfmann 1983, 134). Veneration of the emperor occurred in the city before the earthquake, as there was a temple to Augustus on the acropolis from at least 5 BCE (*ISardBR* 8). However, no reference to this temple has been found from after 17 CE.[21]

From the time of Tiberius, if not earlier, the city referred to itself as Caesareia *Sardianeon*, a designation that continued through the reign of Claudius (Hanfmann 1983, 144; Ramsay 1994, 268).[22] Tiberius himself was called "Founder of the City" (*tēs poleōs ktistē<n>*), as a result of his generosity following the earthquake.[23] His mother, Livia, is depicted on coins as a seated goddess offering grain to the people.[24] Nevertheless, in 29 CE Sardis failed in its bid to be the first city of Asia to be granted the right to build a temple to the emperor and become *neōkoros* (see further below).

A fairly recent discovery at Sardis is a pseudodipteral temple of the first century CE, probably dedicated to the emperor Vespasian (see Ratté, Howe, and Foss 1986, esp. 66–68).[25] This temple seems to have fallen into disuse by the mid-second century CE, although Ratté, Howe, and Foss (1986, 67) postulate that Sardis could still claim the honour of *neōkoros* that it brought. They suggest that it became too costly to maintain two sites of imperial worship at this time. The second site is attested in a dedicatory inscription on a marble pedestal dating to 161–69 CE, which states that Sardis was at this time twice *neōkoros*.[26] The city probably received a second neokorate during the reign of Antoninus Pius (138–51 CE; Johnson 1961, 86–87; Yegül 1987, 50; cf. *ISardBR* 64, 72). Rather than build a new temple, it was decided to move images of Antoninus and his wife Faustina Maio into the temple of Artemis.[27] As a result, second- and early third-century CE Sardis could claim the distinction of being "autochthonous and sacred to the gods, first city of Hellas and metropolis of Asia and of all Lydia, twice neokoros of the Augustan gods by decree of the most sacred Senate" (*ISardBR* 64, lines 2–9; III CE).[28] By the time of Elagabalus (218–22) coins with four temples, three for the imperial cult and one for Kore, indicate that Sardis had become thrice *neōkoros* (Hanfmann 1983, 145).[29]

The bath-gymnasium complex of Sardis and its relationship to the synagogue provides an interesting case study in relationships among diverse religious groups.[30] From its very inception, the bath-gymnasium complex would have been associated with deified emperors and the gods—it was "the central location in the city for the promulgation of 'pagan' culture and piety" (Kraabel 1992d, 243, citing *ISardBR* 21). By the mid-first century CE, the construction of the elaborate substructure of the bath-gymnasium complex was underway at Sardis (Yegül 1987, 47), and the bath block completed by the middle of the second century CE (Yegül 1987, 53). Within the complex is the open-air marble court that was built in the early third century and was lavishly decorated (and is now partially restored). This area was intended to honour one of the Roman emperors and his family (Ramage 1987, 32), probably Septimus Severus or Caracalla.[31] It may even have been associated with the imperial cult, with the main apse holding a statue of the emperor or an altar of the imperial cult (although no traces of either were found *in situ*; Yegül 1987, 53).

That the synagogue was later found within the larger bath-gymnasium complex indicates a high degree of contact between Jews and polytheists. However, there is no evidence of syncretism or dilution of Judaism at Sardis (Kraabel 1992d, 244). An obvious point for investigation is the elaboration of the connections between the bath-complex and the imperial cult and an exploration of the presence of a Jewish synagogue within this complex—two tasks taken up by Hammer and Murray in chap. 12 of this volume.

A related issue is the reuse in the synagogue decoration of items taken from polytheistic religion. For example, in the synagogue two Lydian lions (VI–V BCE), like those at the altar of Cybele, were found beside a table, each leg of which is decorated with a Roman eagle clutching thunderbolts. It is interesting that the eagles have been defaced (literally) by having their heads knocked off (see further, Kraabel 1992d, 244–46).[32] It is instructive to explore both the political issues and issues of religious sensitivity implied in such reuse of sacred objects, as done by Hammer and Murray (chap. 12).

Similar reuse of polytheist material occurred in Christian architecture of the fourth century CE (Kraabel 1992d, 247). In fact, a Christian chapel was constructed against the southeast corner of the Temple of Artemis, thus transforming the temple into a Christian religious edifice.[33]

Crawford (1996, 42–44) notes a number of other examples from Sardis in which Christians and Jews deliberately defaced polytheist images. For example, "an archaic monument of Cybele was reused in a pier in the synagogue's main hall in a way that completely obscured her image" (Crawford 1996, 42);[34] a brass lion-shaped lamp found in a Christian residence (E5) has had the image of Cybele removed from it; in one of the Christian restaurants (W1) a depiction of Attis has had its face removed; a marble table leg in the form of Dionysos has his face and genitalia smashed. This defacing suggests to Crawford that an anti-polytheist sentiment was widespread between these two groups, at least during the fourth and early fifth centuries CE, although this idea is now challenged by Hammer and Murray (chap. 12).

A number of third-century BCE inscriptions that have come to light in Anatolia, including Sardis, are referred to as "penitential inscriptions." These public confessions take the form "I did…and the goddess punished me with…I erect this stele in commemoration of the manifestation of her power."[35] Such appeals to placate the deity reflect a concern to remain in a good relationship with him or her. Since these attempts reflect the "religious frame of mind" of those in Lydia-Phyrgia (Kraabel 1969, 82–83), perhaps it is in this arena that the Christian message of "forgiveness of sins" had some impact among the polytheists. However, I also suspect that the ultimate concern of these "penitentials" was not with the experience of forgiveness per se but with establishing a pattern of prosperity and good health in one's life, for which one was dependent upon the deity. Nevertheless, it might have played a part in converting polytheists to Christianity.

One of the more controversial, and to my mind one of the more interesting, issues of religious rivalries vis-à-vis Sardis is the existence of God-fearers. In numerous works Kraabel has made clear that he does not find any evidence that Jews actively sought to convert Gentiles in the city of Sardis (or elsewhere, for that matter; see 1994, 79–81).[36] Yet even his conclusion warrants our attention: "The God-fearers, once thought of as persons on the verge of converting to Judaism, in many cases have proved to be 'friends of the local Jews' for economic and/or political reasons, or they were motivated by pure neighborliness" (Kraabel 1994, 82).

One cannot leave Sardis without mention of its numerous voluntary associations.[37] Herrmann (1996) has collected and commented on many of the inscriptions of mystery associations at Sardis, and a judicious examination of the associations at both Sardis and Smyrna is provided by Harland in chap. 5 of this volume.[38] With respect to voluntary associations, it is worth briefly mentioning the article of Marianne Bonz on the acquisition of the Sardis synagogue. Although the "Jewish" side of this question is beyond my immediate focus, I do want to dispute one of Bonz's central points. Bonz argues that in around 225 CE the Jews of Sardis were able to take over the polytheist south hall of the bath-gymnasium complex and turn it into the foundational stage of what becomes the large synagogue of the fourth century. She suggests that the Jews of Sardis had the money to acquire it because Jewish benefactors contributed modest amounts to a common community fund (1993, 150–53), in contrast to the polytheistic associations, which relied on large gifts from wealthy benefactors and did not keep a common fund (1993, 148–49, 151). While the evidence Bonz cites for both synagogues and associations is correct, it is incomplete. In fact, examples of associations that received a number of smaller donations exist,[39] as do examples of associations with a common fund.[40] Thus, as intriguing as is Bonz's argument for the means of acquisition of the synagogue, it cannot be sustained.

Greco-Roman Religions in Smyrna

A number of deities are attested at Smyrna.[41] From the very beginning of Smyrna in the tenth century BCE, the mother of the gods (Cybele) was worshipped: "She was in a real sense the patroness or tutelary deity of the city" (Cadoux 1938, 215–16). An inscription from the second century CE probably refers to her as "our foundress" (*tē [archēgeti]di hēmon*; *CIG* 3387, note the restoration by the editor). As such, she became merged with the mythical foundress Amazon Smyrna. During the third century BCE, there existed a temple (Metroon) for her. From the second century CE, inscriptions testify to a voluntary association called "the synod of the initiates of the goddess," who are joined by the rest of the Smyrneans in honouring certain women (*tan theologous*) who have "strenuously done everything connected with the pious worship of the Goddess and the feast of the initiates" (*ISmyrna* 653, 654).

According to Cadoux (1938, 217–19), Cybele is probably to be identified with variations of the Great Mother (although this claim may need to be re-evaluated in light of the earlier note that at Sardis recent evidence has argued against seeing Cybele merged with other deities). The worship of this latter deity, Atargatis (also known as Astarte), involved the keeping of sacred fish. A Smyrnean inscription stipulates that anyone who harms the fish or damages the property of the goddess will be consumed by the fish in the sacred ponds (*ISmyrna* 735, I BCE; Cadoux 1938, 219).

Closely related to the mother goddess was the goddess Nemesis, whose worship at Smyrna goes back to the time of the Aeolians. A distinctive feature of her cult at Smyrna was the worship of two Nemeseis (Ramsay 1994, 192). Cadoux (1938, 220) gives a number of possible explanations for this duplication: "the twin peaks called 'the Two Brothers,' the good and evil types of retribution, the combination of the old and new cities by Alexand[er the Great], the combination of the European Nemesis with the local Asiatic deity."

It is the last that he thinks to be the correct explanation.[42] The cult of the Nemeseis flourished and was most influential in the third and second centuries BCE (Cadoux 1938, 222), although during the first century CE the Nemeseis, either alone or as a pair, appear on coins from Smyrna (Cadoux 1938, 211; Ramsay 1994, 192). "In 250 A.D. the Nemeseion was the scene of a struggle between the magistrates and a group of Christians over sacrificing to the emperor Decius: the renegade Christian Bishop swore an oath by the emperor's Fortune and the Nemeseis" (Cadoux 1938, 222; *Mart. Pion.* 6.3, 7.2, 15.2, 16.1, 18.13–14).

During the first century CE the temple of Aphrodite Stratonikis at Smyrna was a place of refuge for debtors, runaway slaves, and criminals.[43] When ordered by the Roman senate to defend this status for the temple, the Smyrneans successfully argued that an oracle of Apollo had long ago conferred upon the city the privilege of building the temple to Aphrodite Stratonikis as a place of refuge (Cadoux 1938, 238). Other female deities attested at Smyrna include Tyche, Boubrostis,[44] Athena, Here, Hestia, Isis, Persephone, Semele, the Graces, Nymphs, and Muses, and the Fates (Cadoux 1938, 223–26).

Of all the male deities, Zeus seems to have been the most widely acknowledged at Smyrna, probably as a result of his status as leader of the gods (Cadoux 1938, 202). Zeus is known by a number of names in the city, including Zeus Polieus (Zeus [protector] of the City), Zeus Akraios (Zeus dwelling on the height), Zeus Soter, and Zeus Asklepios. The ruin of what was once a magnificent temple to Zeus was noted at the site in 1824 but by 1938 had long since disappeared (Cadoux 1938, 202). The temple had twenty-three marble Corinthian-style pillars along each long side and ten along the short side. It was serviced by a Roman aqueduct. There was also an altar to Zeus in the agora (McDonagh 1989, 237), and somewhere in the city, a colossal statue of Zeus (Cadoux 1938, 203).

The worship of Asklepios was brought to Smyrna from Pergamum during the early to mid second century CE (Pausanias 2.26.9) and began to flourish immediately (Cadoux 1938, 205). An Asklepieion was built at the site somewhere near the water, although the exact location is not known. Asklepios was noted not just as a physician but also as "saviour" (*CIG* 5974; *IG* XIV 967; *Mouseion* 1.69).

Dionysos was worshipped at Smyrna from early in the city's history. He is known by a number of names including Breseus, the name used for the depiction of Dionysos as an older, bearded adult, in contrast to the clean-shaven youthful depiction found more usually elsewhere. Coins from the first and the third centuries CE depict Dionysos as a beardless youth but place a bearded figure in the background, showing "that both types were recognized" (Cadoux 1938, 209). Dionysos's temple probably stood outside the city gates, as indicated by reference to him as "Dionysos before the City" (Cadoux 1938, 209). It was during a Dionysiac festival outside the city walls that the Ionians were able to overrun the Aeolians and take the city in the seventh century BCE. During the Roman imperial period, the worship of Dionysos took place under the auspices of a voluntary association that called itself "the sacred synod of experts and initiates associated with Breiseus Dionysos" (*ISmyrna* 600; Cadoux 1938, 208).[45]

The worship of the Smyrnean native epic poet Homer continued right through the pre-Constantine period. During the first century there existed a "Homereion, a quadrangular portico, containing a shrine and wooden statue[46] of Homer" along with a bronze coin called a "Homereium" (Strabo 14.1.37, LCL).[47] Numerous coins also bear the image of Homer.

Apollo was a popular deity at Smyrna, as is indicated by his appearance on coins from 400 BCE through to the imperial period and the popularity of personal names derived from "Apollo" (Cadoux 1938, 206). In the imperial period there were at least two temples to Apollo at Smyrna (Cadoux 1938, 206). Other male deities at Smyrna include the personified and deified rivers Meles[48] and Hermos, as well as Ares, Hermes, Hades, Eros, Herakles, Poseidon, the Dioskoroi, and the Egyptian gods Sarapis, Harpokrates, and Anubis (Cadoux 1938, 212-14).

"With the accession of Augustus to supreme power, there began for Smyrna a new epoch of peace, prosperity, and brilliance," although Smyrna was not one of the few free cities at that time (Cadoux 1938, 228). During the first century CE Smyrna gained a reputation as a centre of learning (especially its library) and medicine (Cadoux 1938, 232). In Augustus's early years, the *koinon* (League) of Asia came into prominence. Each spring a festival that focused on the public worship of the deified emperor was held. It was first celebrated in Smyrna, but rotated each year among that city and three other participant cities, Sardis, Pergamum, and Ephesus (although later it was expanded and took place in other cities). This festival involved great displays of athletics, music, and literature, with the accompanying social activities that surrounded any public festival in antiquity (especially eating and drinking).

During the reign of Tiberius, the city of Smyrna gained permission to build a temple to the emperor Livia (Tiberius's mother), and the Senate (Tacitus, *Ann.* 4.37-56)[49] and gained the title *neōkoros*.[50] Eleven Asian cities vied for the status of possessing this honour: "The construction of such temples was always preceded by a fiercely competitive atmosphere as cities bid against each other for the honour" (Kearsley 1992, 203). In 29 CE the Senate at Rome finally resolved the issue.[51] The choice from among eleven was narrowed down to two: Sardis and Smyrna. By appealing to their ancient ties to the Etruscans, their ancient wealth, their colonization of Greece, letters of commendation from Roman generals, their treaty with Rome during the Macedonian war, and the natural advantages of their region, the Smyrneans were able to garner 400 votes in contrast to the nine votes cast for Sardis (details in Cadoux 1938, 239-40, Ramsay 1994, 277; Tacitus, *Ann.* 4.55). In this competition over the title *neōkoros*, a direct religious rivalry is apparent.[52]

During the second century. Smyrna became "twice neokoros" when Hadrian allowed it to build a second temple to the emperor (himself). The Smyrneans worshipped Hadrian as "Olympian Zeus" and gave him titles such as "saviour" and "founder" (see *ISmyrna* 622–25; Cadoux 1938, 257). On coins from the time, Smyrna is designated "Hadriana Smyrna," and new games were instituted, the "Olympia Hadriana." In return, Smyrna not only received a large sum of money but was exempted from tribute (Broughton 1938, 740). The building of the temple to Hadrian entailed the appointment of a number of religious officials, including a priest of the god Hadrian (*IG* II² 3623),[53] a prophet of the mysteries of the god (*ISmyrna* 597), *theologoi*, and singers (*hymnōdoi*). Perhaps one might predict competing claims for the title "soter" among Zeus,[54] the emperor Hadrian,[55] and Jesus, although there is little evidence for direct rivalry.[56]

Such rivalry might be seen in light of the martyrdom of Polycarp and others at Smyrna for their refusal to acknowledge the emperor. According to the account of the martyrdom of Polycarp (which occurred in the mid-150s CE), Christians were considered "atheists" (*Mart. Pol.* 3.2) and denounced for refusing to "take the oath and offer sacrifice" (*Mart. Pol.* 4.1; cf. 8.2). That is, they refused to acknowledge the divinity of the emperor (*Kyrios Kaisar*). This story indicates that, despite the early arrival and growth of Christianity at Smyrna, there was considerable resistance to it among those who held affinity for the emperor. One might even see this as early as the book of Revelation, where the author writes to encourage the Christians who are supposedly suffering at the hands of both Jewish and polytheist opponents in the city (Revelation 2:8–11).

A third temple to the emperor was added under Caracalla (211–17 CE). The city was recognized as the centre for the cult in Asia Minor, and it served as warden for the province (Potter 1992, 74). The priests were Smyrnean citizens and others from elsewhere in the province who "were expected to expend a good deal of their own money in the performance of their duties" (Potter 1992, 74). Thus, by well into the third century CE Smyrna is officially entitled "leading city of Asia in beauty and size, most splendid metropolis, thrice neokoros of the Augustan gods according to the decree of the most sacred Senate, glory of Ionia, city of Smyrna" (*ISmyrna* 640, 3–12).[57]

In considering such claims to civic greatness, one question that remains is how much "religion" plays a factor in the worship of the emperor and how much is driven by civic politics.[58] Obviously both are present, and in many ways the distinction is artificial, but how is each aspect played out? One might ask what roles are taken on by the acquisition of other temples or the claim of patron deities in the rivalry over civic claims of greatness by these cities.[59] One obvious entry point is the coins and inscriptions from each of our chosen sites. Another avenue for investigation is the rhetoric surrounding the inter-city rivalry at the annual festival of the *koinon* of Asia, found in the inscriptional record. These, and other, issues are taken up by Harland (chap. 5) and Knight (chap. 8) in this volume.

One famous resident of Smyrna in the second century was the orator Aelius Aristides, who first arrived there in 143 CE.[60] He suffered greatly from an illness and underwent a number of cures in several parts of western Asia, beginning at Smyrna. While there, he had visions of Asklepios, Isis, and Sarapis, all of whom helped him greatly and continued to speak to him. It was not until late 146 that he underwent his greatest healing. Asklepios instructed Aristides to bathe "in the river which flowed in front of the city" of Smyrna. When he did so, to the cries of the crowd's "Great is Asklepios," he experienced great relief. After that, Aristides became a fairly regular resident at Smyrna and spent his time there relaying instructions from Asklepios to the Smyrneans. Often the god would direct him to speak to the people or to the council chamber, much like the Spirit is said to have directed Paul and the other missionaries in the biblical book of Acts. It was at this same time that the temple to Asklepios was being constructed at Smyrna (Tacitus, *Ann.* 3.63; Pausanias 2.36.9; 7.5.9). There are obviously interesting connections between the healing and revelatory powers of the Christian God as manifest in Jesus and the healing and revelatory powers of Asklepios evidenced in the life of Aristides, as explored by Muir in chap. 9 of this volume.

Nearing the end of the second century, Smyrna suffered a number of earthquakes (177–78 and 180 CE) in which much of the city was destroyed, although Marcus Aurelius rebuilt it. Aristides (*Or.* 21) celebrated this rebuilding by comparing Smyrna with the rise of the phoenix (Aune 1997, 161). According to Cadoux (1938, 235), the ancient Asiatic calendar "is in all probability that of Smyrna." In this calendar a number of the month names were taken from the names of the emperor (e.g., Kaisarios, Tiberios). With regard to the name of the eighth month, Euangelios (April/May), Cadoux writes,

> For the reflective fancy it is perhaps not without interest that history seems as it were to pause in silence at this stage in the onward march of time, and that the very word "Good News," which the Smyrnaians probably in celebration of the advent of Augustus had taken as the name for one of their months, was destined on the contrary to connect itself exclusively with the birth and career of one of the lowliest subjects of one of the great Emperor's vassal-princes. (1938, 235)

Cadoux points out that the month name Euangelios was introduced at a point earlier than the advent of Christianity in Asia. In Smyrna it derived possibly either from the name of an obscure deity or hero ("Euangelos"),[61] from its use as a title for Hermes and Zeus, or as a commemoration of some particular event such as the triumph of Augustus over Antony in 31 BCE.

Conclusion

It is clear from the preceding survey that the Greco-Roman religions at Sardis and Smyrna, like those of most other cities in antiquity, reflected a broad range of religious groups. Our examination suggests that, for the most part, the religious groups in these cities co-inhabited the urban centres with little antagonism among them. Nevertheless, the archaeological, epigraphic, and literary sources do give some indications that there were some, if occasional, points in which conflict possibly occurred, or was perceived to occur. The task befalls other scholars in this volume to examine in detail the amount and the degree of these areas of interaction.

5

Spheres of Contention, Claims of Pre-eminence
Rivalries among Associations in Sardis and Smyrna

Philip A. Harland

Introduction

The monuments and inscriptions of Roman Asia Minor give us important glimpses into the lives of unofficial groups and guilds that regularly
met for a range of activities. In several respects, these "associations" in cities
like Sardis and Smyrna provide an entry into the complicated world of
social and religious interactions and rivalries in antiquity. Moreover, the
evidence from these cities demonstrates quite clearly that rivalries could
encompass various practices, realms of activity (social, religious, economic, and otherwise), and levels of engagement. Associations were contenders for economic support and benefactions and for the honour and
prestige that such connections with the elites entailed. In fact, participation in monumentalizing was one important means by which associations made claims about their place within society in relation to, or over
against, other groups and institutions. Furthermore, associations were
competitors for potential adherents and for the allegiances of members.
While some groups could be more self-consciously competitive than others in specific ways, competition (alongside co-operation) was inherent
within civic life in Asia Minor, and virtually all associations took part in
this context in some way.

Overview of Associations at Sardis and Smyrna

A brief overview of the evidence for associations in Sardis and Smyrna (in
the first to third centuries CE) will set the stage for a discussion of rivalries.
In many respects, the range of groups attested in these two cities is quite typical of cities in Asia Minor generally.[1] I further explore the activities and connections of such groups elsewhere (Harland 2003).

Notes to chapter 5 start on page 259

There were a variety of associations at Sardis. The surviving evidence for occupationally based associations here is somewhat limited. We do catch glimpses of guilds of Italian businessmen in the Republican era, slave-merchants in the late first century CE, and performers devoted to Dionysos in the second century (*SEG* 46 1521 [ca. 88 BCE], 1524 [90s CE]; *ISardBR* 13-14 [time of Hadrian]).

More prevalent in the record are other groups that explicitly identify themselves with particular patron deities. There were associations in connection with Attis, Zeus, Apollo, and the emperors (*ISardBR* 17 [Attis]; *ISardBR* 22; *ISardH* 3, 4 [Zeus; I-II CE]; *SEG* 46 1520 [Apollo Pleurenos; I BCE]; *ISardH* 2 [Apollo; I CE]; *ISardBR* 62 [emperors; II CE]). Some inscriptions refer to "initiates" (*mystai* or *archenbatai*) without designating the deity in question, one of which is also a group of athletes (*ISardH* 1, 5 [athletic group]). Other monuments from the vicinity of Sardis vaguely refer to other associations using common terminology, one making reference to the *koinon* and another mentioning the meeting hall of the *symbiōsis* (*ILydiaKP* III 14-15).

Turning to Smyrna, the surviving evidence for associations that epigraphers have managed to document is even more varied. Regarding occupationally based groups, here there is more than one "family" (*phamilia*) of gladiators, a synod of athletes, a group of porters (devoted to Asklepios at one point), and guilds (*synergasiai*) of basket-fishermen, tanners, and silversmiths/goldsmiths (*IGladiateurs* 225, 240-41; *ISmyrna* 217, 709 [athletes, I CE]; *ISmyrna* 204, 205, 713 [porters, ca. 150-80 CE and 225 CE]; *ISmyrna* 715 [fishermen, III CE]; Petzl 1977, 87, no. 18 [tanners]; *ISmyrna* 721 [goldsmiths/silversmiths, ca. 14-37 CE]; cf. *ISmyrna* 718). As in many cities in the region, there was a group of merchants with Italian connections, this one emphasizing its province-wide character in calling itself the "Romans and Hellenes engaged in business in Asia" (*ISmyrna* 642 [mid to late II CE]).

Several associations at Smyrna make reference to a favourite god or goddess. Among our earliest evidence is the membership list of a group devoted to the worship of Anubis, an Egyptian deity (*ISmyrna* 765 [early III BCE]). Particularly prominent in the Roman period was a group of "initiates" (*mystai*) devoted to Dionysos Breseus (*ISmyrna* 598-99, 600-1, 622, 639, 652, 729-30, 731-32). Other Dionysiac inscriptions, which may or may not be related to the "Breiseans," refer to a sanctuary of Dionysos (with Orphic-influenced purity rules for entrance) and to a "Baccheion," a common term for a meeting place among Dionysiac associations (*ISmyrna* 728, 733 [II-III CE]; cf. Nilsson 1957, 133-43).[2]

Demeter and Kore find their place here, too. One inscription refers to those who had "stepped into" Kore's mysteries (hence *enbatai*; cf. *ISardH* 5), and several others refer to a synod of initiates of the "great goddess" Demeter (*ISmyrna* 726 [Kore], 653–55 [I–II CE]). It is likely that the group that calls itself "the former Judeans" on a list of donors to the city was dedicated to the deity of its homeland (*ISmyrna* 697 [ca. 124 CE], discussed further below). Rulers and emperors once again find their place here, as at Sardis: one group called itself the "Friends-of-Agrippa companions" (*synbiotai*), and another in the nearby village of Mostenae was an association (*koinon*) of "Caesarists," regularly engaging in sacrifices for their patron deities, the emperors (*ISmyrna* 331; *IGR* IV 1348 [Caesarists]).[3] Less certain are the specific identities of other associations that simply call themselves *synbiotai, synmystai, mystai, thiasōtai, synodos, synedrion,* or *philoi,* "friends" (*ISmyrna* 330, 534, 706, 716, 718, 720, 734).

Rivalries among Associations

As the above survey suggests, we have considerable evidence for associations at Sardis and Smyrna with which to work. At times, however, it will be beneficial to draw on sources from other cities in the same region of Roman Asia to shed more light on issues of rivalry. Here I would like to discuss issues that suggest the range of possibilities in contentious encounters among associations. I begin by discussing competition that was inherent within systems of benefaction and honours, before going on to discuss competition for membership and for the allegiance of members. This will lead us into an exploration of what I call "the rhetoric of rivalry," encompassing associations' claims of pre-eminence for their deity or group. As this paper concentrates on rivalries, I would like to preface the following discussion with a very important qualification: *co-operation* was also inherent within social relations in the cities of Roman Asia and within association life generally.

Rivalries Related to Benefaction

The conventions of benefaction and honours evince several important dimensions of rivalries within the civic context. First, associations were competitors for the benefaction or support of the elites (civic, provincial, and imperial; see van Nijf 1997, 73–128; Harland 2003, 137–60). Prominent women and men of the city were potentially the benefactors of several groups and institutions (including the city itself); yet presumably their resources were not limitless, and groups of various kinds were contestants as potential beneficiaries. Rivalries for connections with a particular patron are illustrated by the case of T. Julius Lepidus at Sardis and his family elsewhere in Asia. Both the official, gymnastic group of young men (*ephēboi*; ISardBR 46 with revisions in *SEG* 46 [1996] 1523) and an association of merchants honoured him, probably with expectations of continued support.

The latter group joined with the civic assembly in honouring this prominent benefactor: "According to the decree passed by the assembly, the people of the Sardians honoured T. Julius Lepidus, the Emperor-loving high-priest of both Asia and the city and foremost man of the city, because of his love of glory [*philodox(ian)*] and unmatched goodwill towards the homeland. Those engaged in business in the slave-market [*(tōn en tō) statariō pra(gmateuo)menōn*] set up this honour from their own resources."[4] The guild of merchants was, evidently, quick to join in honouring such a prominent benefactor.

Lepidus's kin at Thyatira, C. Julius Lepidus, was also the benefactor of a gymnastic group (*TAM* V 968). The Thyatiran Lepidus's cousin (or second cousin), Claudia Ammion, included among her beneficiaries the guild of dyers: "The dyers honoured and set up this monument from their own resources for Claudia Ammion—daughter of Metrodoros Lepidas and wife of Tiberius Claudius Antyllos who was thrice gymnasium director—who was priestess of the *Sebastoi* and high priestess of the city for life, having been contest-director in a brilliant and extravagant manner with purity and modesty, excelling others."[5] Claudia's husband was also a benefactor of a gymnastic organization there.[6] Associations, groups, and institutions of various kinds were in competition for contacts with and financial support from elite families like the Lepidi.

Making initial connections with a benefactor helped to ensure continued cross-generational support (financial and otherwise) from the same family and hence continued success in competing with potential rivals. This is what is hinted at in the following inscription from Sardis: "The *therapeutai* of Zeus—from among those who enter the shrine [*adyton*]—crowned Sokrates Pardalas, son of Polemaios, foremost man of the city, *for following in his ancestors' footsteps* in his piety towards the deity (*ISardBR* 221, cf. Herrmann 1996, 323).

It is more explicit in the case of the guild of dyers at Thyatira who honoured T. Claudius Sokrates, civic benefactor and imperial cult high-priest, just before 113 CE, as well as his son, Sakerdotianos, about twenty years later, praising him for his "love of honour since he was a boy" (*TAM* V 97, 980 = Buckler 1913c, 300–306, nos. 4–5 [with family tree]).

It is important to remember that inscriptions give us only momentary glimpses of a larger picture, and it is hard to measure the level of competition or the number of groups involved. We never, for example, have monuments telling us that an association failed to gain support from a particular benefactor. Not surprisingly, we hear of only the "winners" not the "losers." I would suggest, however, that the associations in question were not assured of such support, but rather had to struggle with others, including more official groups or institutions, to be recognized in this way.

Before moving on to the more varied nature of benefaction and its significance, it is worth noting that associations were not always competing *for* benefactors but could become competitors *as benefactors*. The guild of silversmiths and goldsmiths at Smyrna, for instance, became a benefactor when it repaired a statue of the goddess Athena "for the homeland" (*ISmyrna* 721). Such actions could improve or maintain an association's standing within the civic community. A list of donors to civic institutions at Smyrna included several groups who, because of their willing contributions to the homeland, could expect honour and prestige in return. Among them were "theologians," a group of "hymn-singers," and an association of "former Judeans," immigrants from Judea (*hoi pote Ioudaioi*; *ISmyrna* 697 [ca. 124 CE]).[7] Associations were competitors not only as recipients but also as donors seeking the appropriate honours and prestige in return.

ISmyrna 697, lines 29–35 (from Petzl 1990, plate 17, used by permission). ©J. Biegart.

There was far more to benefaction than simple material support; connections with the elites could be a source of *prestige and honour* for an association. Here, too, associations were potential rivals as they sought to establish or maintain a place for themselves within society. The case of the initiates (*mystai*) of Dionysos Breseus at Smyrna will serve us well in illustrating the feelings of importance that arose from such connections.

This synod of initiates is first attested in the late first century and evidently had a long life, existing well into the third century (*ISmyrna* 731, 729). At a certain point in the second century, the membership apparently encompassed a significant number of performers (*technitai*), who were likely responsible for performing the Bacchic theatrical dances (*ISmyrna* 639; cf. Lucian, *de Saltatione* 79; Artemidoros, *Oneirokritika* 4.39; *IPergamon* 486 [association of "dancing cowherds"]). The synod maintained connections with important figures within civic, provincial, and imperial networks; these connections were a source of prestige for this group, presumably over against other associations within the same context. The group honoured a member of the local elite who had displayed love of honour in his role as contest-director on one occasion (*ISmryna* 652 [I CE]). About a century later, they erected a monument in honour of a functionary in the imperial cult and in the worship of Dionysos:

> The sacred synod of performers and initiates which are gathered around Dionysos Breseus honoured Marcus Aurelius Julianus, son of Charidemos, twice-asiarch, crown-bearer, temple-warden of the *Sebastoi* and "bacchos" of the god, because of his piety towards the god and his goodwill towards the homeland in everything; because of the greatness of the works which he has done for it; and because of his endowments for them. This was done when Menophilos Amerimnos, son of Metrophanes, was treasurer and Aphrodisios Paulus, son of Phoibion, was superintendent of works. (*ISmyrna* 639 [II CE])

Perhaps more important in illustrating how connections could enhance reputation is this group's activities in relation to emperors (or emperors-to-be). The group set up a monument in honour of Hadrian, "Olympios, saviour, and founder" (*ISmyrna* 622 [ca. 129–31]), and even maintained correspondence with both Marcus Aurelius and Antoninus Pius (*ISmyrna* 600; cf. Krier 1980; Petzl 1983). The most well-preserved part of the latter inscription involves the future emperor Marcus Aurelius, then consul for the second time (ca. 158 CE), responding to the initiates who had sent a copy of their honorary decree by way of the proconsul, T. Statilius Maximus. Aurelius's response to the decree, which pertained to the association's celebration at the birth of his son, acknowledges the goodwill of the initiates, even though his son had since died. That these diplomatic contacts continued with Lucius Verus when Aurelius was emperor is shown in a fragmentary letter from these emperors to the same group around 161–63 CE, perhaps in response to further honours (*ISmyrna* 601). While this correspondence with emperors on the part of a local association is somewhat special (though certainly not unique),[8] this synod of initiates was by no means alone among associations in its engagement in monumental honours.

The significance of such connections for understanding rivalries is better comprehended once one realizes that groups (publicly) advertised their connections by *monumentalizing* these instances of contacts with important persons in civic, provincial, and imperial networks. In the Roman Empire, monumentalizing was a means by which individuals and groups advertised connections, enhanced their standing, and claimed their place within society. Inherent in the action of making a monumental statement, I would suggest, was a mentality of competing against others in the same context.

A few more words of explanation are in order about the symbolic significance of erecting monuments, or monumentalizing. Since MacMullen's article on the "epigraphic habit" of the Roman Empire (1982), some scholars have been turning their attention to explaining the significance of the epigraphic phenomenon and the visual messages of statues and other monuments. Of particular interest is what they can tell us about society and the behaviour of actors within it, whether communities, groups, or individuals (see MacMullen 1982, 1986; Millar 1983; Meyer 1990; Woolf 1996; Smith 1998).

Woolf's recent work (1996) on "epigraphic culture" provides a useful starting point on the significance of monumentalizing, though his theory about the social settings that led to the predominance of the epigraphic habit is problematic. Woolf looks at the uses and significance of monumental inscriptions, arguing that they can be viewed as statements about the place of individuals and groups within society. But then, depending on common scholarly assumptions that I have challenged elsewhere (Harland 2003, 89–97), he attempts to link the popularity of monumentalizing with supposed widespread feelings of social dislocation and anxiety, which coincided with the "rise of individualism." Nevertheless, his observations on the meaning of acts of monumentalizing, seeing them as "claims about the world" (1996, 27), are very insightful and applicable to situations involving associations.

According to Woolf, "the primary function of monuments in the early Empire was as devices with which to assert the place of individuals [or collectivities] within society" (1996, 29). Those who set up a monument were, in a very concrete manner, literally carved in stone, attempting to symbolically preserve a particular set of relations and connections within society and the cosmos for passersby to observe: the visual and textual components of epigraphy "provided a device by which individuals could write their public identities into history, by fixing in permanent form their achievements and their relations with gods, with men [*sic*], with the Empire, and with the city" (1996, 39). Monumentalizing, then, was one way in which groups, such as associations, could express where they fit within society, simultaneously attempting to enhance their standing in relation to other competitors in the same context.

Rivalries over Membership and Allegiances

Associations could also be competitors for members and for the allegiances of those who were already members. The evidence for dual or multiple affiliations suggests that many associations were, to some degree, competitors in this regard. Yet there are clear signs that some groups, more than others, were self-consciously competitive for allegiances, sometimes tending towards "exclusivity" of some sort.

The most general, yet instructive, evidence we have about the potential for multiple affiliations, or plural memberships in several associations, comes from imperial legislation. In the late second century, Marcus Aurelius and Lucius Verus re-enacted a law to the effect that it was not lawful to belong to more than one guild (*non licet autem amplius quam unum collegium legitimum habere*; Digest 47.22.1.2). Regardless of the rationale behind, or (in)effectiveness of, such imperial legislation,[9] what is clear from such actions is the commonality of one person belonging to more than one association. In other words, membership in a guild or association was often non-exclusive; belonging to one group did not hinder the possibility of belonging to or affiliating with another (see also Ascough 2003b, 87–88). In this regard, associations were competitors both for new members and for the allegiances of the members they had.

Turning to Roman Asia, there are clear hints of multiple affiliations or memberships in associations (despite the vagaries of epigraphy). There is at least one confirmable case in which the same man (L. Aninius Flaccus) is named as a member of both the Dionysiac "dancing cowherds" and the association of "hymn-singers of god Augustus and goddess Roma" at Pergamum (Conze and Schuchhardt 1899, 179–80, no. 31 [ca. 106 CE]; *IPergamon* 374). The inclusion of Jews on the membership list of a young men's (*ephēboi*) organization at Iasos, and Jews (or Christians) named as members of the local elders' (*gerontes / gerousia*) association at Eumeneia, are also suggestive of additional memberships alongside participation in the synagogue (*CIJ* 755; Robert 1946, 100–101; 1960, 436–39 [II–III CE]; cf. Lüderitz 1983, 11–21, nos. 6–7 [Jewish names among the *ephebes* at Cyrene in Cyrenaica, late I BCE—early I CE]). The occupational status of Jews represents an array of occupations comparable to the known guilds, and there are cases in which, it seems, Jews maintained memberships in local guilds without necessarily giving up their connections to the synagogue. The guilds of purple-dyers and carpet-weavers at Hierapolis (ca. 190–220 CE) most likely included Jews in their membership (see *CIJ* 777; Harland 2000, 109–21; 2003, 206–10).

There is also evidence of multiple affiliations from Sardis and Smyrna. Quite telling are cases in which an association attempted to curb such tendencies towards multiple affiliations, making apparently "exclusive" claims to the allegiances of members. Such was the case with the *therapeutai* of Zeus in Sardis, who in the mid–second century re-engraved a Greek translation of an apparently ancient Aramaic edict by the Lydian governor (ca. 404–359 BCE; *ISardH* 4 = Robert 1975 = CCCA I 456 = *NewDocs* I 3; also see Ascough, chap. 4 of this volume).[10] As the edict reads, the temple-keeping *therapeutai* of Zeus "who enter the shrine [*adyton*] and who crown the god [are] not to participate in the mysteries of Sabazios—with those who bring the burnt offerings—and the mysteries of Agdistis and Ma." Moreover, "they instruct Dorates, the temple-warden, to abstain from these mysteries." What is most significant for us here is that the leaders or certain members of this group in the Roman era felt a need to reinforce the allegiances of members to the association, tending towards an exclusive view that would limit participation in other groups or mysteries. The "confession inscriptions" characteristic of Phrygia and Lydia suggest similar claims to the allegiances of those devoted to a deity. One of these involves a man from Blaundos who set up a monument after he was punished by the god "frequently" and "for a long time" "because he did not wish to come and take part in the mystery when he was called" (*MAMA* IV 281 = Petzl 1994, 126, no. 108 [I–II CE]).

Even without such explicit demands for allegiances, many associations could count on members' allegiances and pride in belonging to the group (whether they felt a sense of belonging in other groups simultaneously or not). A grave epigram (probably from the area around Magnesia Sipylos) expresses a deceased member's renowned allegiance to the association: "I, who at one point set up a monument of the leader of the association-members, lie here, I who first observed zeal and faith towards the association [*thiasos*]. My name was Menophilos. For honour's sake these men have set up this grave-inscription; my mother also honoured me, as well as my brother, children and wife" (*IManisaMus* 354; trans. by Malay 1994: with adaptations; 180 or 234 CE).

Continuing family traditions of allegiance to the Dionysiac initiates at Smyrna, for instance, shows through when members proudly state that their father was also an initiate in the group, claiming the title *patromystai* (*ISmyrna* 731–32; ca. 80–90 CE; cf. *IEph* 972, 1573 [*patrogerōn*, son of a *gerousia*-member]). Discussion of proud assertions on monuments leads us to a final, more general, observation pertaining to the expression of rivalries.

The Rhetoric of Rivalry

Competitive mentalities among associations (often though not always along "religious" lines) are further indicated in language and expressions of identity, or in what I would like to call "the rhetoric of rivalry." Thanks to the work of Broadhurst (1999), among others, we have become much more cautious in making the step from rhetoric to reality. Yet I would suggest that the rhetoric of rivalry among associations would, at least on occasion, find social expression in realities of life, as when members of different groups came face to face. Let me illustrate what I mean by the rhetoric of rivalry.

Sometimes associations and guilds express pride in identity by attaching appropriate appellations to their name on monuments. Many, like the Dionysiac initiates at Smyrna, felt that their group was "sacred" (*hieron/hiera*), others claimed to be particularly "emperor-loving," and still others called themselves "great" or "worldwide/ecumenical."[11] Associations of performers and athletes illustrate the conscious rivalry involved in titles. Two particular groups, which were quite active throughout Asia Minor, piled on the self-designations: "the sacred, worldwide synod of performers, sacred victors and associate-competitors gathered around Dionysos and emperor Trajan...new Dionysos" versus "the sacred, athletic, travelling, pious, reverent synod...gathered around Herakles and emperor... Hadrian..." (*IAphrodSpect* 88 [127 CE], 90; cf. *IAphrodSpect* 91–92; *ISardBR* 13–14; *IEph* 22).

Rarely do we have evidence of explicit claims to superiority by a particular association. But a monumental statement by the Iobacchoi at Athens is suggestive (*IG* II² 1368 = *LSCG* 51 [ca. 178 CE]; cf. Tod 1932, 71–96). When this group gathered in assembly they did so "for the honour and glory of the Bacchic association [*Baccheion*]," acclaiming their new high-priest, the wealthy C. Herodes Atticus, and calling for the engraving of the associations' statutes. The minutes for the meeting record the enthusiastic shout of the members: "Bravo for the priest! Revive the statutes!...Health and good order to the Bacchic association!" The meeting culminated with the members' acclamation: "*Now we are the best of all Bacchic associations!*" Presumably Dionysiac associations were superior to those devoted to other deities, but this group was the best of all! We find other such rhetorical claims to pre-eminence among associations, sometimes with reference to the superiority of the patron deity or deities.

Occasionally we encounter rhetoric about whose god is the best, most protective, or most worthy of honour. Aelius Aristides of Smyrna reflects this sort of rhetoric among participants in associations in his discussion of those devoted to Sarapis:

> And *people exceptionally makes this god alone a full partner in their sacrifices*, summoning him to the feast and making him both their chief guest and host, so that *while different gods contribute to different banquets*, he is the universal contributor to all banquets and has the rank of mess president for those who assemble at times for his sake...he is a participant in the libations and is the one who receives the libations, and he goes as a guest to the revel and issues the invitations to the revellers, who under his guidance perform a dance.[12] (*Orations* 45.27–28, trans. by Behr, 1981, with adaptations and my italics)

Evidently, it was in associations devoted to Sarapis, more so than any others, that participants truly experienced communion with their god, according to the sentiment expressed here.

There is further evidence from Smyrna specifically. Seldom does the rhetoric of rivalry in inscriptions clearly identify the "competitors." This is why the case of associations devoted to Demeter and to Dionysos at Smyrna is so interesting, serving as a fitting conclusion to a paper on religious rivalries. For each of these associations, which existed simultaneously (I–II CE), we have the typical claims about the "greatness" of its patron deity. But what is even more telling is the terminology used by each group, such that it seems that we are witnessing conscious attempts to rival the other with claims of pre-eminence. On the one hand is "the synod of initiates of the great goddess *before the city* [*pro poleōs*], Demeter Thesmophoros"; on the other is "the initiates of the great Dionysos Breseus *before the city*" (*ISmyrna* 622 [ca. 129–31 CE], 655 [note the lack of an article in the Greek]).[13] In reference to the Dionysiac group, Cadoux (1938, 175) interpreted "before the city" as a simple reference to locality: "his temple stood just outside the walls." However, as Robert and Robert point out, there likely is a double meaning here, which directly pertains to our focus on rivalry: *"Il semble que pro poleōs unisse là les deux sens: devant la ville, protégeant la ville"* (1983, 172). Members of each association felt that their deity was foremost in protecting the civic community, and *their group, not the other*, was pre-eminent in the homeland of Smyrna.

Conclusion

The preceding analysis has revealed the complexity of social and religious interactions among associations at Sardis and Smyrna. The evidence demonstrates that associations could engage one another at several levels and through a variety of practices and activities. Associations contended with one another for economic support and benefactions from the elite and for the honour and prestige that such connections entailed. Through monumentalizing these connections and proclaiming their superiority, associations not only made claims about their place in society and their relationships with other groups and associations, but sought to attract new members while solidifying the adherence of those who already belonged.

INDIRECT CONTACT AMONG JEWS AND
CHRISTIANS IN SARDIS AND SMYRNA

---⇒►◦◄═---

6

Some Astrological Motifs in
the Book of Revelation

Tim Hegedus

Introduction

Astrological beliefs and practices are found in many religious traditions, ancient and modern. In classical Greco-Roman religion and culture, astrology was arguably the most popular form of divination; one recent scholar has described astrology as "the most important and widespread Hellenistic system of piety" (Martin 1991, 59). Many astrological texts have come down to us from the Greco-Roman period from writers such as Manilius, Ptolemy, Vettius Valens, and Firmicus Maternus, writings that display great diversity, complexity, and sophistication.

Of course, the modern distinction between astrology and astronomy did not hold in antiquity. While some scholars understand Greco-Roman astrology within the context of the history of science, in this paper I approach it as a religious phenomenon, following the lead of the great nineteenth-century historian of religions Franz Cumont.[1] The first part of the paper presents a summary of some basic elements of Greco-Roman astrology: the doctrine of cosmic sympathy, the view of the planets and the stars as divine, and the practice of delineating relationships between the planets and the signs of the zodiac, which allowed astrology to function as a form of divination. The second section of the paper underscores these religious attributes of Greco-Roman astrology by focusing on one of the most significant astrological treatises from the ancient world, Firmicus Maternus's *Mathesis*. In the third section, I point out the religious rivalry that leaders and writers in the early church saw between astrology and emerging Christianity. The fourth section then looks at a remarkably nuanced expression of this religious rivalry between astrology and early Christianity found in sections of a late first-century text from western Asia Minor, the Revelation to John.

Notes to chapter 6 start on page 262

Basic Elements of Greco-Roman Astrology

"L'astrologie hellénistique est l'amalgame d'une doctrine philosophique séduisante, d'une mythologie absurde et de méthodes savantes employées à contre-temps." His value judgments aside, in these words A. J. Festugière summarized the basic components of Greco-Roman astrology (Festugière 1950, 89). The philosophical aspect of astrology to which Festugière refers is the doctrine of cosmic sympathy, according to which everything in the cosmos is interconnected and interdependent (Beck 1991; Boyce and Grenet 1991, 497; Barton 1994, 103–104). The second, mythological component of astrology is the identification of the planets and the stars as animate, divine beings. In this way, astrology construed the relationship between the heavens and the earth as personal. As well, the identification of the planets with Olympian gods entailed their association with the characteristic mythological traits of the gods (Cumont 1929, 161).[2] Thus, for example, in keeping with the traditional view of Jupiter as the "father of the gods," the planet that bore his name was regarded as benevolent and beneficial in astrology.

Other considerations also affected the traits that astrologers attributed to the planets. For example, the association of Kronos/Saturn with old age was influenced by the planet's pale colour and slow movement, as well as by the mythological account of Kronos (the father of the Olympian gods) and word play of *Kronos* with *Chronos*, "time"; such notions, as well as Saturn's location as the farthest planet from the earth, led astrologers to ascribe to it primacy among the planets (Bouché-Leclercq 1899, 94–95; Festugière 1950, 96–97).[3] The signs of the zodiac—the twelve figures applied to twelve constellations that were allotted twelve equal portions (each thirty degrees) of the ecliptic circle—were similarly regarded as animate beings endowed with particular characteristics that were derived from mythology as well as other sources.[4] For example, the following influences were rather ingenuously ascribed to Aries the Ram: since it is the first in the usual order of the signs, Aries corresponds to the head in the system of zodiacal melothesia; since the ram produces wool, those born under the sign of the Ram are destined to work with wool; since the ram is shorn of its wool and then grows it back, those born under Aries will experience sudden losses and recoveries of fortune (see the perilous adventures recounted in the myth of the Golden Fleece) and live in hope (note that the sign of Aries ascends rapidly; Bouché-Leclercq 1899, 131–32).

The third component of Festugière's description—astrology's *méthodes savantes*—refers to the relationships that could be calculated between astrological signs and planets,[5] which allowed astrology to function as a type of divination in ancient society. The bringing about of a "completed event" (*apotelesma*) was precisely the object of astrological divination (*apotelesmatikē technē*; Festugière 1950, 101). Ptolemy divides predictive astrology into two main divisions: general (or "catholic" astrology) and genethlialogy (or horoscopic astrology), of which the former is more universal, and hence, prior to and more significant than, the latter (*Tetrabiblos* 2.1, 3.1; Boll 1894, 121). Alongside catholic astrology and genethlialogy, the third type of divination by astrology in the ancient world was katarchic astrology, which was concerned with forecasting the favourable moment for a specific undertaking.

Religious Attributes of Astrology in Firmicus Maternus's *Mathesis*

The specifically religious aspects of Greco-Roman astrology (theology, worship, and cultic ritual, mysticism, ethics, and eschatology) were emphasized by Franz Cumont (1912, xii–xxl, 10–21, 58–110, passim; 1929, 158ff.). Astrology retained much of the older Greek and Roman religious tradition in many of the attributes, and the very nomenclature, of the planets and the constellations. In astrological texts, astrology was often portrayed as being of divine origin: Manilius describes it as a body of knowledge revealed to ancient kings and priests, while Vettius Valens affirms astrology to be a holy and divine gift to humanity (Cumont 1929, 158). Astrology also had its own authoritative, sacred writings, and treatises attributed to legendary figures such as Nechepso, Petosiris, and Hermes Trismegistus.[6] Moreover, astrologers were regarded as religious professionals in their own right (Cumont 1912, 82). One of the traditional terms for astrologers—magi—originally referred to a priestly caste of ancient Persia, and the term still carried (exotic) sacerdotal connotations in the Greco-Roman world.[7] An association between astrologers ("hour watchers," *hōroskopoi* and *hōrologoi*) and the Egyptian priesthood is suggested by references in the hermetic literature (Cumont 1937, 124–25), Porphyry,[8] and Clement of Alexandria.[9] As well, the discovery of ostraka and papyri containing astrological texts at Egyptian temples, and depictions of the zodiac on temple ceilings, indicate that Egyptian temples were a primary location for astrological activity during the Hellenistic as well as the Roman periods (Barnes 1994, 39–41, 44–45, 47–48).

However, the pre-eminent portrayal of ancient astrology in religious terms is Firmicus Maternus's astrological treatise *Mathesis*. For example, he describes the astrological doctrines that he is imparting in his book as akin to initiation into the mystery religions: "Do not entrust the secrets of this religion to people's erring desires; for it is not right to initiate the degenerate minds of human beings into the divine rites" (*Mathesis* 2.30.14).[10] In

Mathesis 2.30.1, the astrologer is portrayed as one who is in daily contact with the gods: "Form yourself according to the image and likeness of divinity, so that you may always be adorned with the proclamation of goodness. It is necessary for him who daily speaks about the gods or with the gods to shape and furnish his mind so that he always approaches the imitation of divinity."

Mathesis 2.30.1–15 details Firmicus's view of the life and training of the professional astrologer, with emphasis on expected moral virtues (modesty, uprightness, sobriety, temperance, abstaining from love of money; 2.30.2), as well as domestic virtues such as keeping a wife at home, having many sincere friends, abstaining from quarrels, being constantly available to the public, dealing with others in peace, loyalty, honesty, etc. (2.30.8–11). These virtues are reminiscent of the expectations of Christian clergy detailed in numerous early Christian texts. For Firmicus, astrologers are comparable to priests: "Try your hardest with your training and intent to outdo the training and intent of worthy priests; for it is necessary for the priest of Sol and Luna and the other gods, through whom everything on earth is ruled, to always instruct his mind in such a way that he might be acknowledged worthy of such great rites by the testimonies of all humankind" (*Mathesis* 2.30.2).

Then, after warning that an astrologer is not to respond to those who would enquire about the life of the emperor (2.30.4–7), he adds that "this is alien from the purpose of a priest."[11] If astrologers are priests, they must be descended from a long line of priesthood; thus in 8.5.1 Firmicus refers to the legendary Egyptian founders of astrology, Petosiris and Nechepso, as "those divine men and priests of the most holy religion" of astrology. Of course, one of the stock arguments against astrology in the ancient world was that subsuming everything dissuades people from religious worship. However, Firmicus affirms, instead, that astrology promotes piety and worship of the gods, since it teaches that our actions are ruled by the divine motion of the stars:

> For we make the gods to be feared and worshipped; we show their godhead and majesty when we say that all our acts are ruled by their divine setting in motion. Let us therefore worship the gods, whose origin has joined itself to us through the perennial setting in motion of the stars; and let the human race look up at their majesty with the constant veneration of a suppliant. Let us in supplication call upon the gods and devoutly fulfill our vows to their godhead, so that when the divinity of our mind has been strengthened we may resist in some measure the violent decrees of the stars and their powers. (18.2–13)

Religious Rivalry between Astrology and Early Christianity

Especially in light of its religious aspects, it is understandable that astrology was seen as a rival for the allegiance of their constituents by early church leaders. The complaint that church members were in the habit of consulting astrologers is found repeatedly in early Christian literature (Boll, Bezold, and Gundel 1966, 184–85). The exhortations of early church leaders against consulting astrologers reflects a sense of competition between church leaders and the practitioners of astrology: it seems that many early Christian leaders regarded astrology as a rival to Christianity.

Indeed, the most common estimation of astrology expressed in early Christian literature overall is resoundingly negative. Early Christian writers usually viewed astrology with fervent hostility and vehemently denounced it: such polemic attacking astrology recurs frequently in early Christian texts. Aside from polemical digressions in texts devoted to other topics, numerous Christian writers also composed whole treatises "against fate" (Gundel 1958, 2625–26; 1966, 828). For these writers, there was an intimate connection between astrology and belief in fate: for example, in *City of God* 5.1 Augustine writes, "When people hear the word destiny [*fatum*], the established usage of the language inevitably leads them to understand by the word the influence of the position of the stars at the time of birth or conception" (in *CCL* 47, 128.11–14). Christian writers often used the technical term for a person's horoscope, *genesis*, as a synonym for fate (Festugière 1950, 111n7; Prestige 1952, 53–54). Indeed, it is not surprising that fatalism was a primary focus of Christian argumentation, since it was this aspect of astrology that seemed most opposed to early Christian affirmations of divine authority and human free will.

The tradition of Christian anti-astrological polemic has been examined by scholars such as David Amand and Utto Riedinger. Amand (1945) surveyed common arguments against astrology and fate that were marshalled by Greek writers, including several Christian authors, tracing the source of those arguments back to Carneades, head of the New Academy in Athens in the second century BCE. Riedinger (1956), too, focused on anti-astrological polemic, looking at Christian writers from Origen to John of Damascus. Both scholars demonstrated that early Christian writers were frequently motivated by the conviction that astrology posed a significant threat to adherents of Christianity.

Of course, the extent and vehemence of anti-astrological polemic from church leaders provides indirect evidence of ongoing interest in astrology among church members. Their interest is confirmed by the frequent complaints of early Christian writers that believers were in the habit of consulting astrologers. Moreover, as early as the *Didache* (3.4), we find warnings that Christians were not to engage in astrology as a profession, and similar prohibitions are found later in Tertullian (*De Idololatria* 9), Jerome (*Commentary on Isaiah* 13.47.12–15), Augustine (*Sermon* 61), and the so-called *Apostolic Constitutions* (8.32.11). Some writers describe members of Christian congregations who were "hedging their bets": these were Christians who admitted that they believed in Christ for the sake of eternity but that they believed in the power of astrology over life in the here and now.[12] Thus, it is clear that people in the early church continued to be attracted to astrology, and that Christian writers and church leaders perceived astrology to be a serious rival for the allegiance of the faithful.

However, in addition to outright polemic, there is evidence of other expressions of religious rivalry between astrology and early Christianity. It would be incorrect to say that early Christian attitudes to astrology were solely or exclusively polemical. The early Christians did not live in isolation from their environment, for they had been raised and nurtured and shaped within traditional Greco-Roman culture, and they interacted daily with that culture. Since astrology was part of it, we should expect a range of attitudes toward astrology among the early Christians—and upon examination, that indeed proves to be the case.[13]

Some Astrological Motifs in the Revelation to John

Further evidence for the rivalry between astrology and Christianity is available from early Christian texts that incorporated astrological themes and imagery. A text in which such usage is evident is the book of Revelation. In contrast to the standard Christian anti-astrological polemic noted above, the author of Revelation seems to have been surprisingly open to astrology. This receptivity provides some insight into the social and religious context of the cities of the west coast of Asia Minor in the late first century,[14] including Sardis and Smyrna, which are mentioned in Revelation 1:11, 2:9–11 (Smyrna) and 3:1–6 (Sardis).[15] For his readers in these locations, the author of Revelation felt that it would be meaningful to appropriate elements of astrology and to exploit them in order to express specifically Christian ideas.

Of course, many of the themes of Revelation can be related loosely to astrology. Indeed, one recent commentary on Revelation seeks to interpret the book of Revelation entirely in celestial terms as a "sky vision," resulting in a reading of the text that is all too often forced (Malina 1995).[16] Astrology is no doubt the general background for elements in the text of Revelation such as the references to the numbers nine, seven, and twelve (Boll 1914, 20–23). Yet one cannot be sure that behind Revelation's repeated fours, sevens, and twelves (and their multiples) the writer had in mind definite elements of astrology such as the planets or the signs of the zodiac.

Therefore, my present focus is on passages in which astrological features seem especially prominent: Revelation 4:6b–7 (the four living creatures) and 12:1–17 (the woman clothed with the sun).

Revelation 4:6b–7: The Four Living Creatures

> And in the midst of the throne and the circle of the throne are four living creatures full of eyes in front and behind: the first living creature like a lion, the second living creature like an ox, the third living creature with a face like a human being and the fourth living creature like a flying eagle. (Revelation 4:6b–7)

The literary background to this passage is the vision of the divine throne chariot in the first chapter of Ezekiel, with its description of the cherubim as "four living creatures" (Ezekiel 1:5–14) having the faces of a human being, lion, ox, and eagle (Ezekiel 1:10; cf. 10:14). In both Ezekiel and Revelation, the four living creatures clearly correspond to four heavenly constellations. It is of course well known that the author of Revelation borrowed extensively from the Hebrew scriptures. Nevertheless, it is unlikely that the astrological content of Revelation 4:6b–7 can be accounted for by the author's proclivity for literary borrowing alone.

According to the interpretation of Franz Boll, the lion in this passage corresponds to the constellation Leo, the ox to Taurus, the human being to Scorpio, and the eagle to Pegasus. Boll based his view on the bright stars that are located in these constellations: Leo's brightest star is Regulus, the "little king";[17] Taurus contains Aldebaran; and Scorpio Antares. The last two were often referred to together as lying diametrically opposite to (*antikeimenoi*) each other (Boll 1914, 37). Citing a statement from Firmicus Maternus (*Mathesis* 6.2) that "royal stars" are found in the four signs Leo, Scorpio, Aquarius, and Taurus, Boll claimed that Regulus, Aldebaran, and Antares were the royal stars of Leo, Taurus, and Scorpio respectively. He further asserted that the royal star in Aquarius to which Firmicus refers must be the star Alpha Pegasi, and so the fourth living creature of Revelation 4:6b–7 (the eagle) is Pegasus (Boll 1914, 37n3).[18] That, however, entails a departure from Firmicus's statement. In fact, a better candidate for the royal star in Aquarius is Formalhaut (Alpha Piscis Austrini), which is located at the end of the stream of water poured out by Aquarius and which allows us to remain with the constellation actually referred to by Firmicus, Aquarius (Beck 1977, 14n16).[19] Formalhaut is also brighter than Alpha Pegasi.

For Boll, the presence of these royal stars in Leo, Taurus, Scorpio, and Pegasus explains why these constellations were chosen by the author of Revelation: such astrological imagery was useful to the author in portraying a heavenly throne and its surroundings. Moreover, the fact that these four signs are located more or less along the celestial equator sheds light on the bewildering phrase "in the midst of and in the cycle of the throne" (*en mesō tou thronou kai kuklō tou thronou*) in Revelation 4:6b, since the equator divides heaven in half and at the same time surrounds it completely (Boll 1914, 38).

Boll's interpretation has been followed by other scholars.[20] Charles agreed with Boll on the first three beings in Revelation 4:6b–7 (lion = Leo, ox = Taurus, human being = Scorpio) but identified the eagle with the constellation Aquila (Charles 1920, 122–23). And indeed Aquila is *prima facie* a more obvious candidate for the eagle; it is worth noting that Aquila too contains a bright star, Altair.[21] However, Charles's identification of the human being with Scorpio is problematic: since Scorpio's associations with evil were well known, it would have hardly been seen as one of the attendants of the divine throne (Bouché-Leclercq 1899, 143).[22]

Preferable to the readings of the four living creatures proposed by Boll and Charles is that offered by Austin Farrer. Farrer sees the lion as Leo and the ox as Taurus (like Boll) and the eagle as Aquila (like Charles), but he claims that the human being refers to Aquarius, a more plausible interpretation (Farrer 1964, 91–92).[23] As we have seen, the best candidate for Firmicus Maternus's "royal star" in Aquarius is Formalhaut (Alpha Piscis Austrini).

Farrer's interpretation is zodiacal: Leo, Taurus, and Aquarius are all zodiacal signs, and along with Scorpio, they are the middle signs in the four quarters of the zodiac.

Aries	Libra	Cancer	Caprigrain
Taurus	**Scorpio**	**Leo**	**Aquarius**
Gemini	Sagittarius	Virgo	Pisces

Farrer acknowledges that Scorpio's evil reputation would have made it unsuitable for use by the biblical writers in describing the environs of the heavenly throne. He claims that Aquila was chosen as Scorpio's replacement because the heliacal risings of the two signs were equivalent (Farrer 1964, 91–92).

Farrer's purpose in linking the four living creatures of Revelation with the signs of the zodiac is to connect the symbolism of the creatures with the annual festivals of the Jewish calendar (Farrer 1964, 117).[24] In this he is ultimately unsuccessful, however, because the order of the signs that derive from his astrological identification of the four living creatures is problematic: in neither Ezekiel nor Revelation do the four living creatures correspond to the signs in the usual zodiacal order, and indeed, the order in Revelation (according to Farrer: Leo, Taurus, Aquarius, Aquila [i.e., Scorpio]) follows the circle of the zodiac backwards. Farrer states that the writer of Revelation "makes the minimum change in Ezekiel's order which will allow the four signs to be read straight around the Zodiacal ring, Lion (summer), Bull (spring), Man, the Waterer (winter) and Eagle, for Scorpion (autumn)" (Farrer 1964, 92).

However, this does not account for the signs being given in reverse order in Revelation 4:6b–7.[25] Similarly, in Farrer's reading of Revelation 6:1–8 (where the four living creatures give utterance at the opening of the first four seals), the usual order of the zodiacal circle is, again, not found.[26] Moreover, Farrer's claim that the book of Revelation overall can be apportioned to the symbols of the four living creatures in the proper zodiacal order (and that thus the book corresponds to the major Jewish festivals) cannot be substantiated: even if "St. John proceeds in the direct order of the seasons, advancing from summer to autumn, when he goes on from the Lion [of Judah in Revelation 5:5] to the Eagle [in Revelation 8:13]" (Farrer 1964, 92).

There is no basis in the text itself for assigning part of Revelation to the bull,[27] nor for identifying the "one of the four living creatures" of Revelation 15:7 with Aquarius.[28] Farrer's calendrical reading of the book of Revelation is not readily apparent within the text of Revelation itself. Moreover, despite his claim to have found astrological support from Revelation for his calendrical reading of the text, Farrer makes zodiacal identifications of the four living creatures that do not support his conclusions: the creatures and their signs cannot refer the Jewish festivals unless they actually follow the annual circle of the zodiac.

This reading does not invalidate Farrer's identification of the four living creatures per se, which is really more plausible than those suggested by Boll or Charles. It is significant that in all of these interpretations, the astrological signs that are referred to as the four living creatures lie far apart from each other; thus, they may be seen as surrounding the heavens, just as the living creatures are said to surround the throne in Revelation 4:6b. An astrological identification of the living creatures would be entirely in keeping with the cosmic significance of the throne and its surroundings that is being portrayed at this point in the text (Revelation 4:1ff.).[29] The use of astrology in locating the four living creatures around the divine throne in Revelation is remarkably similar to the way that the torchbearers, Cautes and Cautopates, can be identified in the Mithraic mysteries with the bright stars Aldebaran (in Taurus) and Antares (in Scorpio) so as to relate to the figure of Mithras in the tauroctony scene as companions of the god (Beck 1977, 6–7).

Revelation 12: The Woman and the Dragon

At the outset of Revelation 12 the writer portrays a great heavenly portent: a woman clothed with the sun, with the moon under her feet, bearing on her head a crown of twelve stars (12:1). The image of the heavenly crown was not uncommon in antiquity; it is found already in the description of Achilles's shield in *Iliad* 18.485.[30] The crown of the woman in Revelation 12:1, as well as her splendid garments and her footstool, are the trappings of royalty: she is a heavenly ruler, *regina caeli*, like Isis who rules over the stars and fate.[31]

Of course, the crown of twelve stars immediately recalls the zodiac. A literary parallel is Martianus Capella's description of a crown whose twelve flaming jewels are associated with the zodiacal signs and the annual seasons, worn by another heavenly female, Juno.[32] Ancient Greco-Roman iconography also featured the depiction of a figure (e.g., Jupiter, Heracles, Helios/Sol,[33] Pan[34]) or figures (e.g., Dionysus and Ariadne, Helios and Selene[35]) encircled by the zodiac. Such depictions appear frequently in the iconography of the Mithraic mysteries: here the central figure is usually Mithras himself, for example, in the portrayal of his birth from an egg on the Housesteads relief (*CIMRM* 860), his birth from a rock on a relief from Trier (*CIMRM* 985), or in the tauroctony scene (*CIMRM* 75, 810, 1472). A zodiac may have surrounded the representation of the banquet of Mithras and Sol in *CIMRM* 1161 (from Stockstadt), and the serpent-wrapped figure Aion on a relief from Modena (*CIMRM* 695) is also encircled by the twelve signs. Examples of zodiacs encircling a central figure are evident in Judaism as well: for example, a mosaic from the Beth Alpha synagogue includes a figure in a chariot encircled by the twelve zodiacal signs with their names in Hebrew (Gundel 1972, 649, no. 131; Godwin 1981, 83, plate 50).[36]

Female deities were similarly depicted. Examples include Ephesian Artemis with the zodiac as a necklace or encircling her bodice (Gundel 1972, 625, no. 41, 642–44, nos. 92–113),[37] Artemis in her temple surrounded by the zodiac (Gundel 1972, 670, no. 195.1 [a coin from Ptolemais]), a second-century relief with Victory holding a zodiac that encircles another goddess,[38] a stele from Argos depicting Selene with seven stars surrounding her head and shoulders (as well as the zodiac surrounding the whole figure, Patterson 1985, 439–43),[39] and grave paintings from El Salamuni, Egypt, featuring Isis-Sothis encircled by the zodiac (Gundel 1972, 662, nos. 166.4, 166.8).[40]

The presence of the zodiac on these representations had the effect of emphasizing the cosmic, universal aspect of the deity, highlighting the god's role as *kosmocrator*, "lord of the heavens, who controls the progression of time and events" (Patterson 1985, 440). The seven planets similarly were used to express the deity's cosmic power, as in the imagery of the Son of Man holding seven stars in his right hand (Revelation 1:16, 20; 2:1; 3:1).[41] Imagery of the planets and the zodiac were featured together in the temple of Bel at Palmyra: in the northern thalamos of the temple, the ceiling of the cult-niche portrays the god (Bel-Jupiter) surrounded by the six other planets, around which in turn appear the twelve zodiacal signs in a second ring (Drijvers 1976, 9 and plate II).[42]

More specifically, the circle of stars encircling the woman's head would have been readily understood in cosmological and astrological terms to signify that the woman is standing in the midst of the zodiac. She is "clothed with the sun": the sun's annual journey through the signs of the zodiac confers upon her, as it were, a garment. The moon beneath the woman's feet may be merely a mundane astrological reference, i.e., that Virgo rules over a month (Farrer 1964, 141). The imagery is similar to the Egyptian view of the moon (and sun) as a barque on which the gods traverse the sky and the underworld,[43] and in the Mithraic mysteries, the scene in the side panels to the tauroctonies in which the bull (likely to be identified with the moon) rides in a boat or lunar crescent.

In terms of astrology, the woman portrayed in Revelation 12 corresponds to the constellation Virgo. It does not matter that she who wears the zodiac as a crown is one of the twelve zodiacal signs herself: the writer is drawing special attention to her among the zodiacal signs in this way.[44] Boll emphasizes that such an astrological interpretation of the text would have been natural for both the writer of Revelation and his contemporaries. It should not be regarded as an esoteric reading restricted to a learned few but rather as readily accessible to a general audience (Boll 1914, 103).

Isis, too, was interpreted as Virgo in the Greco-Roman world, which offers a clear parallel to this identification of the woman of Revelation 12 with Virgo. The earliest astral association of Isis was with Sothis (i.e., Sirius the Dog Star), whose heliacal rising marked the Egyptian new year (Griffiths 1970, 371–73). That the Egyptian goddess also eventually came to be equated with Virgo is evident from descriptions of Isis with the ear of grain (*spica*), which was a basic feature of the constellation Virgo (Spica is the name of the brightest star in Virgo). While naturally the ear of grain also led to identifications of Virgo with Demeter, the same motif of the ear of grain was also used in portrayals of Isis.[45] For example, Boll refers to a gem that features Isis holding her son Horus in her arms; over her head there is a star, and Horus has an ear of grain; another ear of grain stands in a modius beside the goddess (Boll 1903, 211).[46]

A first-century astrological text by Teucros the Babylonian also refers to Isis under the heading of Virgo: "At the first decan a certain goddess arises, sitting on a throne and nursing a child; some say this is the goddess Isis nursing Horus in the temple" (Boll 1903, 210; 1914, 9–10).[47] Griffiths argues that the term *caelestis Venus* used for Isis in *Metamorphoses* 11.2 refers to the goddess Dea Caelestis, who was worshipped in Apuleius's native Carthage (Griffiths 1975, 116) and who combined the functions of virgin and mother (Ferguson 1970, 215). The identification of Isis as Virgo was, of course, possible only after the latter was incorporated into Greco-Roman (and Egyptian) cosmography (Boll 1903, 216).[48]

Understanding the woman in Revelation 12 astrologically as Virgo is also supported by the next image described in the text of Revelation, a dragon, which corresponds to the constellation Hydra. The introduction of the dragon closely parallels the heavenly woman presented in 12:1: "And I saw another portent in heaven: a great red dragon, with seven heads and ten horns, and seven diadems on its heads. Its tail swept down a third of the stars of heaven and threw them to the earth. Then the dragon stood before the woman." (Revelation 12:3–4a).

The verb *histēmi* (and its compounds) was the technical term used in astronomical texts to position a constellation in relation to other constellations (e.g., in Aratus's *Phaenomena*), or to describe placing a catasterism in the heavens (e.g., in Ps-Eratosthenes' *Katasterismoi*; Boll 1914, 101).[49] Nevertheless, the word *hestēken* in Revelation 12:4a need not indicate any particular astrological position of Hydra in relation to Virgo. However, Boll writes that in some situations (such as Revelation 12) the specific position of constellations cannot be calculated: "das hängt vollkommen in der Luft" (Boll 1914, 101, no. 4). It is more likely that the verb *hestēken* in Revelation 12:4a should be understood in terms of early Christian theology rather than astrology; i.e., it is meant to portray the dragon as the antagonist of the woman and her offspring, in keeping with the curse upon the serpent in Genesis 3:15; indeed, the writer of Revelation explicitly equates the great dragon with "that ancient serpent who is called the devil and Satan, the deceiver of the whole world" (Revelation 12:9, cf. 20:2) and describes the dragon's making war upon the woman's children in 12:17.[50]

The primary confrontation in Revelation 12:1–6 takes place between the woman and the dragon,[51] paralleled in the ancient astrological location of Isis and Seth/Typhon in the northern hemisphere.[52] For example, a royal grave from Thebes refers to the "fore thigh of Seth located in the northern heaven," which is "the seat of Isis" who guards Seth in chains (Boll 1903, 163; 1914, 110–11). In ancient Egyptian cosmology, Seth was identified with the seven stars of Ursa Major (Boll 1903, 162).[53] Like Isis guarding the seven-starred Seth, the Son of Man is portrayed in Revelation as holding seven stars in his right hand (Revelation 1:16). The image of the "third of the stars" being swept down by the dragon's tail (Revelation 12:4) can be understood not only as an example of the frequent use of the number three in the text (cf. Revelation 8:12) but also as a reference to the sheer extent of the constellation Hydra across the heavens. Ancient astrological texts refer to Hydra stretching across four of the signs of the zodiac, from Cancer to Libra (Boll 1914, 102).[54]

Again, the seven heads, seven diadems, and ten horns of the dragon are likely more than just examples of apocalyptic number symbolism:[55] it is significant that Corvus (the Raven) and Crater (the Cup)—the two constellations lying immediately adjacent to Hydra and frequently associated with it (e.g., in the Mithraic tauroctony scene; *TMMM* 1.202)—have seven and ten stars respectively, according to Ps-Eratosthenes's *Katasterismoi* 41 (Boll 1914, 102).[56] Of course, falling stars, like comets, were widely regarded in the ancient world as omens that signified momentous historical events. According to Boll, the use of falling stars as an eschatological symbol belongs specifically to the apocalyptic tradition (Boll 1914, 103–104).[57] The same imagery is also evoked with regard to the *ekpyrōsis*, the Stoic doctrine of the periodic dissolution of the universe into fire, in Seneca's *Consolatio ad Marciam* 26.6.[58]

Aside from the individual correspondences of the woman with Virgo and the dragon with Hydra, the narrative of Revelation 12 also parallels ancient astrological myths. The drama of Revelation 12 begins with the woman giving birth. Once she is introduced in 12:1, the author then relates that "she was pregnant and was crying out in birthpangs, in the agony of giving birth" (12:2). This birth is envisioned as taking place in the sky, not on earth (Boll 1914, 104–105).[59] After the dragon has been brought on the scene in 12:3–4a, a battle ensues:

> Then the dragon stood before the woman who was about to bear a child, so that he might devour her child as soon as it was born. And she gave birth to a son, a male child [cf. Luke 2:7], who is to rule all the nations with a rod of iron [cf. Psalms 2:9]. But her child was snatched away and taken to God and to his throne; and the woman fled into the wilderness, where she has a place prepared by God, so that there she can be nourished for one thousand two hundred sixty days. And war broke out in heaven; Michael and his angels fought against the dragon. The dragon and his angels fought back, but they were defeated, and there was no longer any place for them in heaven. The great dragon...was thrown down to the earth, and his angels were thrown down with him. (Revelation 12:4b–9)

Of course, the motif of birth followed by flight in this text parallels the nativity story in Matthew 2. In the latter, while of course the child is not snatched away to heaven, nevertheless, Herod's pursuit of Jesus and his family mirrors the dragon's attack on the woman and her child. The text also contains an astral battle, a traditional theme that was present in ancient Jewish sources (Judges 5:20) and became more common in apocalyptic texts (e.g., Daniel 8:10; Sibylline Oracles 3.796–808, 5.206–13). A particularly vivid example is the end of Sibylline Oracles 5 (512–31) with its bleak vision of the future:

I saw the threat of the burning sun among the stars
and the terrible wrath of the moon among the lightning flashes.
The stars travailed in battle; God bade them fight.
For over against the sun long flames were in strife,
and the two-horned rush of the moon was changed.
Lucifer fought, mounted on the back of Leo.
Caprigrain smote the ankle of the young Taurus,
and Taurus deprived Caprigrain of his day of return.
Orion removed Libra so that it remained no more.
Virgo changed the destiny of Gemini in Aries.
The Pleiad no longer appeared and Draco rejected its belt.
The Pisces submerged themselves in the girdle of Leo.
Cancer did not stand its ground, for it feared Orion.
Scorpio got under the tail because of terrible Leo,
and the dog star perished by the flame of the sun.
The strength of the mighty day star burned up Aquarius.
Heaven itself was roused until it shook the fighters.
In anger it cast them headlong to earth.
Accordingly, stricken into the baths of ocean,
they quickly kindled the whole earth. But the sky remained starless.[60]

In contrast with a third of the stars being cast down in Revelation 12:4, according to the writer of this portion of the Sibylline Oracles, the eschatological battle will cause all the stars to fall. The theme of astral battle was also present in Greco-Roman literature, as in the celestial attack waged by Typhon against the constellations described at length in Nonnos's *Dionysiaca* (1.163ff.). A later astrological text portrays the planets falling in all directions as they flee before the constellation Draco (*CCAG* 5/2: 134.11–17).

The identification of the woman of Revelation 12 with Virgo is not contradicted by her giving birth to a son. Despite Manilius's description of Virgo as *"sterilis,"*[61] mother goddesses were not incompatible with Virgo in ancient Greco-Roman religion.[62] According to Frances Yates, "The…virgin is…a complex character, fertile and barren at the same time" (Yates 1975, 33). For example, as we have seen, the figure of Isis holding her son Horus was identified with Virgo. Virgo was also associated with various other mother goddesses in antiquity, such as Juno,[63] Dea Caelestis,[64] Ceres, Magna Mater, Atargatis,[65] and even Ilithyia, the Greek goddess of childbirth (Boll 1914, 105).[66] As Boll concludes, *"das alles ist eins"* (Boll 1914, 111). Commonly, the paradox of the goddess being both virgin and mother prompted mockery from early Christian writers: in *De Errore Profanarum Religionum* 4.1, Firmicus Maternus ridicules the mother goddess (Dea Caelestis) worshipped by the Africans as "Venus Virgo—if virginity ever was pleasing to Venus!"[67] Augustine, too, laughs at the identification of the virgin goddess Vesta with Venus:

If Vesta is Venus, how do virgins serve her duly by abstaining from the works of Venus? Or are there two Venuses, one a virgin, the other a wife? Or even three, one for virgins who is Vesta, another for married women, another for harlots? The Phoenicians used to give the latter a gift of their daughters for prostitution before they married them to husbands. Which of these is the noble wife of Vulcan? Certainly not the virgin, since she has a husband. Let it not be the harlot, lest we seem to insult the son of Juno and the fellow-worker of Minerva! Therefore it is understood that she [Venus] was concerned with married women: but let us wish that they do not imitate what she did with Mars! (*De Civitate Dei* 4.10; in *CCL* 47, 107.60–70, my translation)

Augustine prefaces this passage with a sneer: "It was right that all this vanity should be abolished and extinguished by him who was born of a virgin" (*CCL* 56–57).[68] Despite such Christian responses, it is clear that the paradoxical image of the goddess who was both virgin and mother was exploited by the author of Revelation 12, who must have felt it was also understandable to his Christian audience. It is interesting that such a paradox came to be affirmed of Mary in early Christian tradition: the notion of Mary's virginity not only *ante partum* but also *post partum* and *in partu* came to be developed by the fourth century (Brown 1993, 518 and n2).

In Revelation 12:5–6, the woman's flight to the wilderness in her plight recalls Isis's tragic pathos in the face of her loss of Osiris. Meanwhile, the threat posed by the dragon continues until the final defeat of the beast, which derives its power from the dragon (Revelation 13:2), by Christ in Revelation 19:19–20. Similarly, in the myth of Isis, the goddess's son Horus is the one who ultimately defeats their enemy Typhon. Moreover, Plutarch's account of Horus's victory over Typhon in *De Iside et Osiride* 19 refers, in passing, to Horus's killing of a snake. Again, we have a parallel with the defeat of the dragon of Revelation. The snake that Horus killed had been pursuing Thoueris, Typhon's former concubine, who then came over to the side of Horus. Here again, we have the child defending a female divinity. Indeed, in Egyptian tradition, Thoueris had been the protrectress of pregnancy (cf. the connection between Isis and maternity), while in Greco-Roman times, she was identified with Athene.

The woman's flight into the wilderness (Revelation 12:6), of course, implies her descent to earth. This descent is the exact opposite of the astrological myth of the catasterism of the goddess Dike related in Aratus's *Phaenomena* (96–136),[69] according to which at the beginning of the Age of Bronze, Dike (i.e., Justice) had withdrawn herself from the earth to become the constellation Virgo in the heavens. Instead, since the woman's arrival on earth precedes the defeat of the dragon (Revelation 12:7–9), and ultimately anticipates the triumphant coming of Christ (19:11–21), the writer of Revelation is reversing the myth of the catasterism of Dike in a similar way to Virgil's announcement of the return of the Golden Age:

> The majestic roll of circling centuries begins anew:
> Justice returns, returns old Saturn's reign,
> With a new breed of men sent down from heaven.
> Only do thou, at the boy's birth in whom the iron shall cease,
> The golden race arise, befriend him,
> Chaste Lucina; 'tis thine own Apollo reigns. (*Ecologues* 4.5–10,
> trans. J. B. Greenough)[70]

Similarly, according to Hephaestion of Thebes, the appearance of the comet named for Ilithyia (the goddess of childbirth) "signifies humanity's weariness and a change of things for the better" (*Apotelesmatica* 1.24).[71] It seems that the first Christian to claim that Virgil's reference to Virgo's return in the fourth Eclogue was a prophecy of Christ was Constantine, who in his *Speech to the Assembly of the Saints* (19–20) identified Virgil's Virgo with Mary, the mother of Christ.[72] Constantine's contemporary, Lactantius, read the fourth Eclogue more generally as looking forward to the coming of Christ without particular emphasis on Mary.[73] Indeed, Lactantius does not follow the reversal of the myth of the ascent of Dike, but rather dismisses that myth altogether: "Why do you portray a hollow justice and wish for it to fall from the sky, as if it were formed as some kind of statue?" (*Divine Institutes* 5.8.2).[74] For Lactantius, since the reign of justice has come with Christianity, there is no need to look for the return of Dike (Yates 1975, 35).

According to Revelation 12:14 (reprising 12:6), "The woman was given the two wings of the great eagle, so that she could fly from the serpent into the wilderness, to her place where she is nourished for a time, and times, and half a time." As Boll notes, wings were a standard part of Virgo's image in ancient cosmography (1914, 113).[75] An Egyptian inscription from a stele of the eighteenth dynasty describes the goddess Hathor (Isis) as producing wind with her wings while in flight (Brugsch 1891, 398, see also 91–92). The "great eagle," with its definite article, must have a specific reference. While there is precedent for such imagery in Jewish tradition,[76] Boll sees the reference here to the constellation of the Eagle, Aquila (Boll 1914, 113).[77]

The eagle, i.e., the constellation Aquila, also appeared earlier in Revelation. As we have seen, it is one of the four living creatures in 4:6b–7, and in 8:13 its position at mid-heaven is described using technical astrological terminology (*en mesouranēmati*). The narrative of the dragon's opposition to the woman ends in Revelation 12:17 when, having failed to kill the woman herself, the dragon turns to attack her children. The children are the Christians, among whom the author of Revelation is numbered. They are "the rest of her children, those who keep the commandments of God and hold the testimony of Jesus."[78] Thus, in addition to her astrological and mythical correspondences, in Revelation 12:17 the woman receives yet a further identification as the church. Of course, just as Israel was portrayed as the bride of God (Jeremiah 31:32; Hosea 1–2), the church was portrayed as Christ's bride in early Christian texts (e.g., Ephesians 5:22–32). Such imagery is different from, but not contradictory to, the image of the church as mother derived from Revelation 12:17. Indeed, the latter represents a further level of meaning achieved by the incorporation of feminine imagery.[79] The dragon then tries to kill the woman, utilizing water: "Then from his mouth the serpent poured water like a river after the woman, to sweep her away with the flood. But the earth came to the help of the woman; it opened its mouth and swallowed the river that the dragon had poured from his mouth" (Revelation 12:15–16, NRSV).

In the Isis myth, water also features in Typhon's attack on Isis. The killing of Osiris takes place when, after trapping Osiris in a chest, Typhon and his fellow conspirators take it out to the river and let it go to the sea, which carries it to Byblos (Plutarch, *De Iside* 13.15). The symbolism of the latter story is also comparable to the myth of Revelation 12: just as the land "swallows" the flooding of the Nile, so the earth rescues the woman from the dragon's attempt to destroy her (Boll 1914, 109). Water also appears in the catasterism myth of the snake (Hydra/Anguis), raven (Corvus), and cup (Crater) reported by Ovid (*Fasti* 2.243–66) and Ps-Eratosthenes (*Katasterismoi* 41): the raven takes too long fetching water with Apollo's cup and returns carrying a snake on which it blames the delay, with the result that Apollo sets all three together in the heavens. Boll (1914, 109n3) notes the similarity between the words of the raven in Ps-Eratosthenes' version (auton ekpinein kat' ēmeran to gignomenon en tē krēnē hydōr) and Revelation 12:15 (kai ebalen ho ophis ek tou stomatos autou…hydōr).

From Revelation 12:5 we know that the first born son (cf. Luke 2:7) of the woman is Christ; the allusion there to Psalms 2:9 ("he will rule all nations with a rod of iron"), which will be repeated in Revelation 19:15, makes this clear (Boll 1914, 116). This birth took place in the past; the future coming of Christ is still ahead, at Revelation 19:11ff. However, there is a tremendous difference—indeed, according to Boll (1914, 119 and n1), a contradiction—between a "historical" focus on Jesus's life (such as is evident in the Synoptic Gospels, for example) and the heavenly portrayal of Christ in the book of Revelation. Boll argues that early Christian writers were faced with two possible avenues according to which Christ's birth could be described. The point of departure for both of these was the Septuagint of Isaiah 7:14: "Therefore the Lord himself will give you a sign: behold the virgin shall conceive in her womb and give birth to a son and you shall call his name Emmanuel."[80] This text provided the essential connection between the virgin who becomes a mother and gives birth to the Messiah. The one avenue was that taken by Matthew 1:18–25 (cf. Luke 1:27), i.e., to portray the woman as an earthly virgin. Such an approach was developed along the lines of the traditional Jewish view that the Messiah would be a descendant of David. The other avenue saw the Messiah primarily as a heavenly being. From this perspective, the author of Revelation was able to make the virgin of Isaiah 7:14 correspond with the celestial Virgo, which, as we have seen, was long identified with numerous other virgin and mother goddesses of Greco-Roman religion.

There are other examples of the association of Mary with Virgo. For example, among certain spurious works attributed to John Chrysostom is a homily "On the Birth of Christ" in which the angel Gabriel greets Mary with a slightly altered form of the "Ave Maria" of Luke 1:28: "Greetings, favoured one, O unharvested land of the heavenly ear of wheat."[81] The "ear of wheat" (*stachus*) also refers to the image of the sheaf that is a regular characteristic of Virgo, and *stachus* is the Greek name of Virgo's brightest star (Spica). It was by identifying Virgo with Mary that the author of Revelation was able to adapt elements of the myths of Virgo to a Christian perspective. Other early Christian writers who betray almost no interest in the "historical" details of Jesus's life include Paul and the author of the *Gospel of Thomas*.

The Christian perspective of the author of Revelation is also evident in that the woman of Revelation 12 is subordinated to Christ within the work overall. Outside of chapter 12, she makes no further appearance. Moreover, while polytheists could ascribe the aretalogical statement "I am all that has been and is and will be" to the goddess herself (it was an inscription on a statue of Athene/Isis at Saïs, according to Plutarch, *De Iside* 9),[82] for the author of Revelation such a claim could be uttered only by Christ (Revelation 1:4, 8) and not by the woman who is his mother in Revelation 12. In the process of taking her over from polytheist religion, the author of Revelation has subsumed the woman's divine power to that of her son, with the result that she has become a lesser figure than she was before.

The approach taken by the author of Revelation also represents quite a departure from the historical emphasis of traditional Jewish messianic expectation. Rather, the myth of the woman and the dragon in Revelation 12 is an example of the widespread tendency (emphasized, for example, by Franz Cumont) in Greco-Roman religion to situate the gods in the sky (see Cumont 1912, 92–110; Boll 1914, 114, 122). In Revelation 12:6, the woman's descent to the wilderness (on earth) allows for a minimum connection with the earth;[83] therefore, she can be the earthly mother for her other children, the Christians (12:17). Since she does not remain in the sky, the woman is both heavenly and earthly (Boll 1914, 123). A similar balance does not, however, exist in the portrayal of Christ in Revelation 12. Perhaps this was a necessary price for the author's use of astrological myths in this passage. Aside from the reference to "the blood of the lamb" in 12:11, Christ is a predominantly heavenly being in this chapter, though elsewhere the author does affirm Christ's humanity and earthly suffering (Revelation 1:5, 7; 5:9; 11:8).

Conclusion

What is remarkable about these passages from Revelation is that they demonstrate the use of astrological imagery to express Christian meaning. Revelation shows little or none of the suspicion of astrology that would become so fixed in later Christian polemic against astrology. The astrological imagery that is found in Revelation is fairly unsophisticated; the author shows no awareness of learned astrology such as is evident in Ptolemy's *Tetrabiblos*, for example. Instead, the author exploited the symbolism of the heavens (what Festugière described as the "mythological" component of astrology) for the purpose of proclaiming a Christian message. By subsuming the old meanings of astrological imagery (e.g., those associated with the constellation Virgo) to the new religious doctrine, the author of Revelation attempted to enlist traditional veneration of the heavens in the service of Christianity. This had the potential to augment the appeal, as well as the authority, of the new religion.

Nevertheless, the Christian interpretation of astrological imagery failed to displace the traditional polytheist associations of the heavens entirely. Despite the author's attempt to assign Christian meanings to astrological motifs in Revelation, those motifs were still laden with traditional religious significance. This suggests that for ancient readers—and potentially for modern readers as well—the rivalry between Christianity and astrology could still be discerned within the text of Revelation.

7

The Patriarchs and the Zodiac
Revelation 12

John W. Marshall

A great portent appeared in heaven: a woman clothed with the sun,
with the moon under her feet, and on her head a crown of twelve
stars.   —Revelation 12:1

Introduction[1]

Who is the woman in Revelation 12:1, and who or what are the stars?
These questions lead into a fascinating mélange of possibilities that may illuminate the complex interactions between Judaism and astrology in the
ancient world, as well as patterns of interaction and rivalry among religious options.[2] Are the stars the patriarchs, the signs of the zodiac, or the
apostles? These possibilities are only the beginning. How do they overlap,
and if, as I suspect and will argue, John has both the zodiac and the patriarchs (as well as, perhaps, the apostles) in mind, does he stand in any continuity with Jewish thinking about the patriarchs and the zodiac?

Relations between religious groups are rarely played out along a simple line of greater or lesser opposition, much less through a multiple-choice
form: "(a) bitter rivalry, or (b) benign toleration." The seeming opposition
of rivalry and co-operation, enmity and *amiticia*, diminishes what is actually a broad field of possibilities—including the possibility of combinations
ranging from optimistic synthesis to hostile co-optation. Combination can
be sincere or sinister.

For Revelation 12:1, a binary formulation of the question that asks
whether the twelve stars indicate the zodiac or the patriarchs is insuffi-
cient. Two reasons make this clear: (1) the symbolism of the apocalypse is
not so impoverished as to yield to such weak paraphrase, and (2) the forms
of Second Temple Judaism are not hermetically walled off from Greco-

Notes to chapter 7 start on page 268

Roman and Near Eastern religious culture. Here again, the binary formulation "Jews and Gentiles" not only masks the variety of the Gentiles, but makes absolute a distinction that, though undoubtedly proper and valuable, is nevertheless somewhat porous. In Sardis and in Smyrna, two of the cities designated as recipients of John's Revelation, the conflict John addressed consisted substantially in shoring up a boundary across which there should be no commerce and finding passage across the boundaries that would be dissolved in the age to come.

In this essay I will demonstrate that John's reference in Revelation 12:1 is dual, embracing both the patriarchs and the zodiac, and, moreover, that it is actually an instance of a complex of thinking about the patriarchs and the zodiac that is broadly distributed in ancient Judaism. This wider pattern ranges among alternatives that I would call triumphant equivalence, imitative superiority, and habitual correlation. In the tradition preceding Revelation, the evidence for such patterns lies in the Hebrew Bible itself as well as the book of *Jubilees*, Philo of Alexandria, and the *Testaments of the Twelve Patriarchs*. In the aftermath of John's Apocalypse, these patterns continue in the magical papyri, rabbinic considerations of the zodiac, the material remains of synagogue decorations, and the Syriac horoscope of Asaph.

The plan of this essay is like a diamond standing on its point: beginning from a consideration of a single verse in a Jewish visionary text devoted to Jesus,[3] my investigation expands to trace a topic and the patterns of its treatment throughout Second Temple Judaism and beyond, and then narrows again to draw conclusions about Revelation 12:1, supplemented by ways that this single verse—as well as the broader investigations it called forth—can illuminate the configurations of religious rivalry in the ancient world.

Adela Yarbro Collins, whose interpretations of Revelation have been widely and rightly influential in the last twenty-five years,[4] leans decisively in her "Numerical Symbolism in Apocalyptic Literature" (1984) towards the zodiac as the dominant reference and sufficient description of the twelve stars of Revelation 12:1. Her most extensive reference to the text is worth quoting at length:

> In Rev 12 a woman is depicted, clothed with the sun, with the moon under her feet, and wearing a crown of twelve stars. These stars allude to the twelve constellations of the zodiac. On one level of meaning, the woman is a heavenly being, the heavenly Israel. So here too heavenly bodies are subordinated to a heavenly being. The number twelve appears again in the final vision of salvation in connection with the tree of life (22:2). It bears twelve kinds of fruit, one each month. The number twelve here is associated with the rhythm of the year. (1984b: 1269–70)

Collins's direct efforts to interpret the stars point only in one direction: the zodiac. She makes only one subsequent mention of the stars of Revelation 12:1 in her 1984 article: "The image of the twelve stars (12:1) is based on the Zodiac [*sic*]."[5] Her interpretation of the woman—heavenly Israel—is well supported in the scholarly literature, but it seems not to affect her interpretation of the stars. Letting the woman influence the interpretation of the stars that are clearly subordinate to her is the task I undertake here.

Collins's *ANRW* article represents fairly well a consensus of scholarship. For example, in his recent excellent commentary on Revelation, Aune devotes his comment on the meaning of the twelve stars exclusively to the zodiac possibility. There is no doubt that the parallels and referents to which he points are there, but the exclusivity that they hold in his interpretation is another matter altogether. While Collins and Aune may represent a current consensus of leading scholars of the apocalypse, note must also be taken of the longer history of astrological interpretation of Revelation from Gunkel through Chevalier, including the contribution of Hegedus to this volume (chap. 6).[6]

Depicting a situation as comprising only two exclusive alternatives—whether religious formations in antiquity or communities of scholarly opinion in the modern world—is an abetting condition for intense rivalry. And yet, we know that alternatives are often overdrawn, whether they are Judaism and Hellenism, orthodoxy and heresy, Judaism and Christianity, or Greek and barbarian. This insight is not lost on the best commentators on Revelation 12:1, and Collins in particular makes this clear.[7] My task is threefold: (1) to take the insight of the inadequacy of binary oppositions seriously and then work out the neglected element of symbolism in Revelation 12:1, (2) to gather together a larger than heretofore assembled catena of ancient Jewish evidence for the correlation of the patriarchs and the zodiac, and (3) to reflect on the forms of rivalry evidenced in such material.

The Patriarchs and the Zodiac in Early Judaism

Genesis: Seeds

Understandings of the patriarchs of Israel in concert with the signs of the zodiac are dependent first on the coincidence of the number twelve. This sets up the initial possibility of a compelling correlation that I argue ancient Jews forged in a variety of places; such a venture taken in the ancient world is precisely the phenomenon under examination. The basic coincidence of twelve is abetted by two narratives in Genesis that invite a more richly drawn correlation of the sons of Jacob and the signs of the zodiac: Joseph's astral dream in Genesis 37:9 and Jacob's blessing of his sons in Genesis 49:1–28.

In Genesis 37:9, Joseph recounts the second of two dreams to his brothers: "Behold, I have dreamed another dream; and behold, the sun, the moon, and eleven stars were bowing down to me." Jacob, understanding the symbolism in light of the more explicitly subordinating dream of the wheat sheaves (Genesis 37:6–8), objects, saying, "What is this dream that you have dreamed? Shall I and your mother and your brothers indeed come to bow ourselves to the ground before you?" (Genesis 37:10). While Jacob reacts to his young son's dream, later interpreters react to the vision of a virtuous and venerable patriarch. In this latter context, both the dream and Jacob's interpretation have wielded authority: the stars are symbols of the patriarchs. And the twelve stars implied by the dream—Joseph being by implication of the same nature as his brothers, even if he exceeds them in status—refer, as would any group of twelve stars in an ancient description of the heavens, to the constellations of the zodiac.[8]

Later in the Genesis narrative, Jacob issues his dying blessing to his sons. In more or less detail, Jacob characterizes his sons in ways that are often suitable for correlation to the qualities or figures associated with signs of the zodiac: Judah is a Lion (Leo); Dan a serpent (Scorpio); Reuben, proud and licentious (Taurus); Simeon and Levi, a brotherly pair (Gemini). Other instances are not nearly so neat: Joseph as a fruitful bough or Benjamin as a ravenous wolf. The twelveness is also awkward. If Simeon and Levi are correlated with Gemini, then what is to be done about the twelfth position? Obviously the text as it stands is not an ironclad mapping of the patriarchs and the zodiac, but its tantalizing features inspire several ancient interpreters to overcome the deficiencies in Genesis 49:1–28 and make the bond much firmer. Ephraim and Manasseh stand ready, so to speak, to jump in as the twins, and even Dinah may be pressed into service as Virgo—naturally, by her gender, or ironically, by her defilement at the hands of Shechem.

The argument here is emphatically not that Genesis actively correlates the patriarchs and the zodiac, but merely that it proved fertile for later interpreters who wished to do so and posed conundrums for those who would refuse such a correlation. I have in mind *Jubilees*, Philo of Alexandria, and *The Testaments of the Twelve Patriarchs*.

Jubilees: *Symmetrical Opposition*

The treatment of the Genesis narratives that takes place in the book of *Jubilees* is one of the most extensive in the literature of ancient Judaism. Moreover, one of the dominant and animating concerns of *Jubilees*—calendrics—has the potential to bring the zodiac to the fore for the reader. The incidents discussed above—Joseph's astral dream and Jacob's testamentary blessing—receive no treatment in *Jubilees*. The dream sequence, which would fit in at approximately *Jubilees* 39.1, is omitted (within the larger omission of the brotherly betrayal), and the blessing is abbreviated to a blessing and eschatological prediction with no substantial or specific content (*Jubilees* 45.14–15).[9] In tendering the most obvious foundations for understanding the patriarchs in concert with the zodiac, *Jubilees* spurns (as unclean?) the offerings of canonical Genesis.

It seems at first glance that *Jubilees* strives simply to avoid association of the sons of Jacob with the zodiac. Elsewhere in *Jubilees*, astrology is viewed quite negatively.[10] One of the clearest and most colourful examples of *Jubilees*' opposition to astrology is in the secret sin of Arpachshad, the grandson of Noah through Shem. In *Jubilees* 8.3–4, Arpachshad comes upon a rock carving that "some men of old time had carved upon a rock, and he read what was on it and transcribed it; and he sinned because of it, for it contained the teachings of the Watchers, in accordance with which they [men of old] used to observe the omens[11] of the sun and moon and stars in all the signs of heaven." After "sinning" because of this inscription,[12] Arpachshad, copies it out, apparently in secret. Here *Jubilees* makes use of what Nicklesburg (2001, 190) calls the "instruction motif" of the Enochic tradition—the transmission of forbidden knowledge—as a means to engage and oppose the practice of astrology. And just as Arpachshad not only sins by reading the inscription, presumably with positive interest, he also copies it out secretly in an action that provides plot space for the secret transmission of illegitimate esoteric knowledge among the sons of Shem. The corollary to this secret revelation and transmission occurs in the third week of the second jubilee when the "unclean demons began to lead the children of Noah's sons astray and to mislead them and destroy them" (*Jubilees* 10.1). Noah prays for help against the Watchers *redux* and receives it from the righteous angels in the form of remedies and herbal therapies, which, like Arpachshad, he writes down for future transmission (*Jubilees* 8.4). Even clear opposition is fraught with symmetry and imitation.

Upon closer examination, however, the relationship between the patriarchs and the zodiac drawn by *Jubilees* is more than a simple denial of relationship by disregard for the resources in Genesis, or a symmetric opposition to astrology worked out in recasting the tale of the Watchers. The birth distribution of the patriarchs themselves stands as a parallel to the signs of the zodiac, in much the same way that Noah's book of herbal remedies is positioned as the antidote to Arpachshad's astrological tome. The first inkling is in a discussion of marriage possibilities between Rebecca and Jacob in *Jubilees* 25. Though the discussion itself has no direct source in Genesis, the concern—that Jacob not marry a Canaanite woman—does. Rebecca's dissuasion of Jacob from marrying a Canaanite includes a noteworthy promise: "And may he [God] multiply your sons while you are alive, and may they equal in number the months of the year" (*Jubilees* 25.16). The promise goes on to take up the more common pledge of innumerable descendents like the sand of the seashore.

In the narratives of the births of the patriarchs that follow, the author of *Jubilees* offers more information that cannot be derived from the canonical narrative of the sons of Jacob. For each patriarch, the text provides an exact date of birth. The distribution of birthdates approaches (but does not quite attain) a distribution of one patriarch per month.[13] As the text stands, Zebulon and Naphtali overlap in the seventh month, and Benjamin and Gad in the eighth. Correspondingly, the second and twelfth are empty.

This expansion and specification of Genesis is not idle filler in *Jubilees*, especially given the significance of calendrics in the text. Moreover, in the course of transmission and translation (from Hebrew to Greek to both Ethiopic and Latin), such culturally specific elements as calendar are particularly vulnerable to textual corruption. There is no doubt that *Jubilees* does not work to make some theological equivalence, but even its urge to rivalry seems to inspire an imitation designed to supersede rather than to flatter.

Philo of Alexandria: Triumphant Equivalence

Where *Jubilees* shrinks back from the paths sketched out by Genesis, the other major interpreter of Genesis in early Judaism, Philo of Alexandria, is confident in his synthesis of the patriarchs and the zodiac, and is convinced that Joseph's dream in Genesis 37:9 was "about [*peri*]" the zodiac (*On Dreams* 2.6) and that the zodiac is a sign in God's creation of the values and sacralization that show up both in the history of Israel and in the structure of creation.

Book 2 of Philo's treatise *On Dreams* uses the dream of Joseph in Genesis 37 as its pre-eminent example. In addition to the comment in *On Dreams* 2.6 that the dream "has to do with" the zodiac, the more detailed treatment later in the treatise describes the dream specifically as heaven-sent: "He then who saw that heaven-sent vision dreamt that the eleven stars made him obeisance, thus classing himself as the twelfth to complete the circle of the zodiac" (*On Dreams* 2.113, LCL). This association of the patriarchs with the zodiac seems obvious enough to Philo that it requires neither argument to establish it, nor qualification to safeguard the purity of Judaism. The other instance in which Philo treats Joseph's astrological dream, *On Joseph* 9, does not make the zodiac connection explicit but simply transmits the equation of stars and patriarchs that Jacob's reaction in Genesis 37:10 implies.

Philo also takes up the opportunity to identify the patriarchs and the zodiac in his discussion of the vestments of the high priest in *On the Life of Moses* 2.123–24. Here, Philo discusses the vestments of the high priest described in Exodus 28 and 39. The association of the two stones on the shoulders of the ephod with the names of the patriarchs and also the twelve stones with the twelve patriarchs is explicit in Exodus (28:11–12, 21; 39:6–7, 14) as well as in Philo. Without any discussion in Genesis of the stars to prompt him, Philo adds the correlation of the patriarchs and the zodiac:

> A similar testimony is given by their [the two stones on the shoulder of the ephod] colour, for the appearance of the whole heaven as presented to our sight is like the emerald. Six names, too, had to be engraved on each of the stones, since each of the hemispheres also divides the zodiac into two, and appropriates six of the signs. Secondly, the stones at the breast, which are dissimilar in colour, are distributed into four rows of threes, what else should they signify but the zodiac circle? (*Moses* 2.123–24, LCL)

According to Exodus 28:21 and 39:14, the stones are engraved with the names of the patriarchs, and there is no reason to doubt that Philo writes with that understanding. Strikingly, even as Exodus 28:29 provides a rationale for the whole system by noting that with the properly constructed ephod, Aaron (and his descendents) "shall bear the names of the sons of Israel in the breast piece of judgment upon his heart, when he goes into the holy place, to bring them to continual remembrance before the Lord," Philo does not confirm this as the ultimate reference of the symbolism of the decoration of the ephod. Instead, he asserts that the ultimate reference is the zodiacal circuit and its differentiation and individuation of the seasons and elements of the annual cycle (*Moses* 2.124–26). The principle at work here, expressed again in Philo's explicit reiteration of the zodiacal character of the priestly ephod, is that God's commands for the cult of Israel are in harmony with the principles by which he has created and structured the world, and consistent with the reason with which the elite human is endowed.

These striking interpretations force a consideration of the larger place of the zodiac in Philo's thought; when he makes an equivalence with the zodiac, what is he saying? First, the zodiac is an attribute of the heavens, a feature Philo exploits in his discussion of the ephod in *On the Life of Moses*. The heavenly role of the zodiac becomes most explicit when Philo summarily discusses the entirety of high priestly raiment as corresponding to the entirety of the universe:

Thus is the high priest arrayed when he sets forth to his holy duties that when he enters to offer the ancestral prayers and sacrifices there may enter with him the whole universe, as signified by the types of it which he brings upon his person, the long robe a copy of the air, the pomegranate of water, the flower trimming of earth, the scarlet of fire, the ephod of heaven, the circular emeralds on the shoulder-tops with the six engravings [of the names of the patriarchs] in each of the two hemispheres which they resemble in form, the twelve stones on the breast in four rows of threes of the zodiac, the reason-seat of that Reason which holds together and administers all things. (*Moses* 2.133, LCL)

The zodiac stands as one of the constitutive elements of the universe to which a key element in the history of Israel, the patriarchs themselves, stands as a pointer. This indexical function of the patriarchs, as pointers to the more fundamental truth of the zodiac, shows up also in *On Flight and Finding*, during Philo's description of the twelve springs of Elim (Exodus 15.27) and his digression on the number twelve:

And twelve is the perfect number. The zodiac circle in the sky is a witness to this, being adorned with that number of luminous constellations: a further instance is the sun's circuit, for it completes its rounds in twelve months, and men [*sic*] keep the hours of the day and night equal in number to the months of the year. And Moses celebrates this number in several places, telling us of the twelve tribes in the nation, directing twelve loaves to be set forth on the Table, bidding them to wave twelve inscribed stones [with the names of the patriarchs] on the "oracle" in the holy vestment of the high priest's full-length robe. (*Flight* 184, LCL)

Heavenly bodies are not merely concentrations of gas or lumps of drifting ice and rock, but are understood by Philo as uncorrupted elements of God's rational creation. He describes them as "living creatures endowed with mind" and having no partnership with vice, being "excellent through and through and unsusceptible to any evil" (*On Creation* 73, LCL). Moreover, humanity and the heavenlies stand as pairs on a continuum, "one the most perfect of imperishable objects of sense, the other the noblest of things earthborn and perishable, being, in very truth, a miniature heaven" (*On Creation* 82). Obviously, the patriarchs have a little more traffic with evil than do the heavenly bodies, being perishable creatures and an abbreviation of their heavenly counterparts. Philo's strategy of mapping the astrology and patriarchal history triumphs not by simply subordinating the zodiac to the patriarchs of Israel, but by positioning the patriarchs as divinely privileged pointers to the rationality with which the God of Israel has infused his creation.

The Testaments of the Twelve Patriarchs: *Habitual Correlation*

The relation of the *Testaments of the Twelve Patriarchs* to the dream of Joseph in Genesis 37:9 is quite peculiar. On the one hand, the dream itself is absent from the *Testaments*.[14] On the other hand, the betrayal of Joseph is a common theme in the *Testaments* attributed to many of his brothers.[15] Moreover, two factors bring the patriarchs of the *Testaments* into the orbit, so to speak, of the zodiac: the correlations of virtue with the patriarchs and the astrological dreams of Naphtali. The *Testaments of the Twelve Patriarchs* are structured around the correlation of individual patriarchs with specific moral values: Zebulon with compassion and mercy, Simeon with envy, Joseph, predictably, with chastity, etc. Naphtali's testament concerns "natural goodness" (*peri physikēs agathotētos*). This correlation of the celestial figures and specific dispositions of moral significance is known in Judaism as Philo's discussion of the heavenly bodies, treated above (Philo, *On Creation* 73, 82). The basic structuring device of the *Testaments* positions the sons of Jacob in the same function as the ascription of signs and qualities to heavenly bodies.

One of the most common elements of the *Testaments* is the prediction of future transgressions by the descendents of an individual patriarch. Often this projection takes the form of a claim that such transgressions are prophesied in the books of Enoch and are commonly cast in terms of going astray (*planaō*).[16] This contrast between the ideal course of behaviour—straight[17]—and the error of going astray corresponds to the wider ancient contrast between planets that wander around the heavens and the perfect fixity of the constellations. The use of this contrast is not in itself remarkable, even if its association with the patriarchs is noteworthy. Within the *Testaments*, the patriarchs' citations of Enochic literature, with its detailed astrological speculations in the astronomical apocalypse and its description of the Watchers as stars that have wandered from their appropriate station, does intensify the specifically astronomical import of the *planaō* terms.

The buildup of this mode of discussion before the astral vision of Naphtali in *Test. Nap.* 5 is particularly intense. Naphtali's astral vision has thematic parallels to the vision of Joseph's second dream in Genesis 37: most important, the correlation of the sons of Jacob with individual stars or constellations. Prior to Naphtali's vision, the theme of improper change, of acting in conflict with divinely established patterns of order, comes to the fore.

> Sun, moon, and stars do not change their order [*alloiousi taxin autōn*]: so you too must not change the laws of God by the disorderliness of what you do. The Gentiles went astray [*planēthenta*] and changed their order, and they went after stones and stocks, led away by the spirits of error [*pneumasin planēs*]. But you will not be so, my children:

you have recognized in the vault of heaven, in the earth, and in the sea, and in all created things, the Lord who made them all, so that you should not become like Sodom which changed the order of its nature. Similarly the Watchers also changed. (*Test. Nap.* 3.2–5, trans. in Sparks 1984)

In addition to deployment of the astral metaphor, the heavy emphasis on change recalls the most concise formulations of the results of the Watchers' sins: "And the world was changed" (*1 Enoch* 8.2 [Sparks 1984, 191]).[18]

Naphtali's astral vision follows the formulaic citation of the Enochic literature in *Test. Nap.* 4. The dream itself is somewhat similar to that dreamt by Joseph in Genesis 37:9. In *Test. Nap.* 5, Isaac commands his grandson to grasp the sun and moon that are standing still overhead. Levi and Judah seize the sun and moon, respectively. When Levi receives twelve palm branches, from beneath Judah twelve rays spread out and a great winged bull appears and Joseph ascends upon it. Thus, the three pre-eminent patriarchs each gain a special status, but within an explicitly astral symbolism. Lest there be any doubt that the twelves of the astral visions correlate with the patriarchs, writing appears to Naphtali describing the future captivities of the twelve tribes of Israel.

For most endeavours that attempt to illuminate Second Temple Judaism on the basis of the *Testaments of the Twelve Patriarchs*, the interference of the Christian provenance of the manuscripts usually makes any particular conclusion very insecure.[19] In the case of the vision of Naphtali, however, the meagre evidence we have of Jewish predecessors unaffected by Christianity happens to coincide in a way that intensifies the astral qualities of the patriarchs. While the Naphtali fragments of the Dead Sea Scrolls (4Q215 [4QTNaph]) are too fragmentary to illuminate the dream sequence of *Test. Nap.* 5, the Hebrew *Testament of Naphtali* from the Cairo Geniza (Charles 1913a, 361–631913a, 361–63) provides a valuable witness against any possibility that the visions in *Test. Nap.* 5 are Christian compositional or redactional material. In fact, the visionary portions of *Test. Nap.* are what is most closely paralleled in Hebrew Naphtali. In both the case of the astral vision in *Test. Nap.* 5 and the shipwreck vision of *Test. Nap.* 6, the visionary account is more elaborate in Hebrew Naphtali.[20] In the case of the astral vision, Hebrew Naphtali is not only more extensive, but also more specific. Before Joseph rides the celestial bull, and after Levi and Judah grasp the sun and moon, Hebrew Naphtali describes actions of the patriarchs that correspond to the prominent actions of Levi and Joseph: "So did all the tribes; each rode upon his star and his planet in the heavens" (Heb. Nap. 2.6).

The *Testaments of the Twelve Patriarchs* are an integration of the figures of the patriarchs with the astrally inflected treatment of morality that characterizes the Enochic literature. The fortunate remains from Cairo Geniza confirm that the astral allegory of the patriarchs is not a product of their eventual Christian provenance. They also show how extensively the patriarchs and the zodiac may be integrated in ancient Judaism.

Revelation 12:1

Here we are at the fattest point of the diamond-shaped structure of this essay. Leading up to the deployment of the twelve stars in John's Revelation, we have seen several modes of setting together the patriarchs of Judaism's foundational mythic-historical narrative: competition between the patriarchs and the zodiac, which leads to imitation (*Jubilees*); confident and clear-headed theology of equivalence that has the zodiac as a pointer to the patriarchs, which are in turn pointers to the will of God (Philo); and what appears to be a habitual manner of "thinking with patriarchs" that parallels broader patterns of ancient Mediterranean "thinking with constellations" (*The Testaments of the Twelve Patriarchs*). All of this sits on top of the clear provocations to rub the patriarchs and the zodiac against each other. These parallels are in addition to those implicit in Joseph's astral dream in Genesis 37:9 and Jacob's peculiar testamentary blessing in Genesis 49:1–28. In a Second Temple Judaism that provides the context for all these ways of thinking about the patriarchs and the zodiac, it makes sense that a visionary account of a figure representing Israel surrounded by twelve stars should refer both to the patriarchs and to the zodiac.

This juxtaposition is more than a scholarly eagerness to dodge a tough decision or to have it both ways. Instead, this "both/and" interpretation of the twelve stars—rather than an "either/or" interpretation—represents the way that many Jews in the Second Temple period thought. We can be more specific and see elements of this sort of "both/and" thinking in an unrelated and unambiguous phenomenon in John's apocalypse: his predilection for Greek/Hebrew doublets[21] and Greek/Hebrew gematrias.[22] In spite of broad claims that "dualism" lies at the heart of apocalyptic literature, one cannot say that John is simply habituated to thinking in dualistic terms. On the contrary, what is important to John is demarcating the "right" dualisms: Jew and Gentile is not adequate, for there will be Gentiles among those who dwell in heaven.[23] Similarly with the patriarchs and the zodiac, John does not seek the simple, though incomplete, rejection attempted by *Jubilees*. Nor does John articulate a relationship in the discursive manner that Philo of Alexandria does when he tames the zodiac. Instead—and a kinship with another apocalyptic work ought not to come as a surprise—John simply and without obvious anxiety gestures simultaneously to both the patriarchs of Israel and the zodiac circle of the wider Greco-Roman and Near Eastern world.

After Heaven's Queen

From this fattest point of the diamond, perhaps we can proceed more quickly to show that the correlation between the patriarchs and the zodiac continues in Judaism, at least as long after Revelation as it existed before John's vision. As in the previous section, four instances illustrate the motif: the magical materials in Greek and Coptic, the art of early synagogue buildings, comments by the rabbis, and a peculiar Syriac text that brings the patriarch-zodiac synthesis to a fine point.

The Magical Materials

The materials collected in the Greek magical papyri (*PGM*; Preisendanz 1973; Betz 1986) form an environment within which an association of the patriarchs and the signs of the zodiac would find a congenial home. Obviously, this is a weaker formulation than an unambiguous mapping of the patriarchs and the zodiac would justify, and there is, to my knowledge, no such obvious mapping in the magical papyri.

The presence in the Greek magical papyri of figures and expressions from Jewish sacred texts is a well-known phenomenon, suggestive of a certain appeal exercised among polytheists by Jews, and of an impulse among Jews to undertake the sort of private and sometimes spiritually inflected operations that the magical papyri represent in a mode that drew upon familiar figures and resources. Such is the invocation of the power of "the god of Abraham, Isaac, and Jacob" in *PGM* XXXV.15. Likewise, *PGM* XXIIb. 1–26, described as the "Prayer of Jacob," invokes the "Father of the patriarchs" who causes "the fixed and movable stars to pursue all things" and calls on this God to fill the summoner's heart with good.

Much more extensive, however, is the set of materials assembled under the patronage of Moses in *PGM* XIII. In three variorum editions, "the eighth book of Moses" offers instruction for, techniques of, and applications for invoking the great names of God under the power of the paradigmatic magician Moses.[24] Tantalizingly, the materials of *PGM* XIII also refer to a much more extensive corpus of Mosaic magical material: "The Key of Moses," "The Archangelic Teaching of Moses," Moses's "Secret Moon Prayer," "The Tenth Hidden Book of Moses," and "The Hidden Book of Moses concerning the Great Name." While *PGM* XIII does not explicitly mention the twelve patriarchs, several of its characteristic analogies and concerns would make a congruous environment for a correlation of the sons of Jacob with the twelve houses of the zodiac. Witness the description of the seven-lettered name of God as the sound that the seven planets utter (*PGM* XIII.775), the direct invocation of Abraham, Isaac, and Jacob (*PGM* XIII.815), and the reference to the "rulers of the twelve months" (*PGM*

XIII.735). The largely lost corpus of Mosaic magical material is a likely setting for the impulse to correlate the patriarchs and the zodiac.

Given the loss of most of the Mosaic material, the magical papyri from Christian Egypt (*ACM* = Meyer and Smith 1994) can illustrate some of the ways the Mosaic materials might have continued and demonstrate ways of thinking about the patriarchs that intensify the potential for connections between the patriarchs and the zodiac in general and in the deployment of astral references within the Greek magical papyri. *ACM* 113 hails various heavenly powers, invokes the seals and organs of the body of Adam, and proceeds through recognition and invocation of Jesus and David. What follows is apposite to the topic of the patriarchs and the zodiac:

> The tribes in the twelve worlds hear them, rejoice and echo him:
> Hail Ab[...]ais [in] heaven and earth! You praise!
>> Spell
> Hail, O Sun!
> Hail, twelve little children who shelter the body of the sun
> Hail, twelve bowls filled with water!
>> They filled their hands (with it)
>> They cast (it) towards the rays of the sun
>> so they shall not burn the fruits of the country (*ACM* 113.26–33)

Here Israel's twelvefold patrimony and the twelveness of the zodiac system are brought together in ways that should be familiar to us by now. This Egyptian text, in which the twelve pursue the son, is also reminiscent of the chasing of the sun in the astral dream of Naphtali (*Test. Nap.* 5) and its more extensive version in the Hebrew Naphtali document from the Cairo Geniza (Charles 1913a, 361–63).

The Christian papyri also extend the association between the patriarchs and individual angels in certain instances and the much more widely attested understanding of angels in astral terms in the apocalyptic speculations of Second Temple Judaism. *ACM* 73 is a spell of erotic compulsion that—perhaps oddly—invokes Gabriel as the matchmaker, and adjures the archangel by various *topoi* of holiness (tears of the father, final judgment, etc.) in order that Gabriel may not delay "until you come forthwith to your sign of the zodiac which I shall set afire." Understood in combination with the speculations of that most prominent Egyptian Jew, Philo, this text offers a certain triangulation by means of which we can see the astral interpretation of the patriarchs. Admittedly, the magical materials are not the richest repository of the correlation of the patriarchs and the zodiac, but two observations might temper this disappointment as well as supplement the significance of the cited instances: (1) the evident under-representation of the Mosaic magical materials that existed in antiquity among those preserved in the contemporary world; and (2) the insight that proceeds from the dearth of discussion of the patriarchs and the zodiac in the magical materials, namely that such a correlation was not a specifically marginal phenomenon.

Synagogue Materials

Many discussions of the zodiac in ancient Judaism concentrate, often exclusively, on the mosaic depictions,[25] and the literature devoted to the zodiac mosaics of Beth Alpha, Hammat Tiberias, Sepphoris, Yafa, Naaran, and Isfiya, as well as the inscription at En Gedi, is vast.[26] The art of the synagogue at Dura Europos has also been interpreted in astrological terms.[27] The examples of Dura and Sepphoris are most suggestive for our purposes.

In the Dura synagogue, the scene at issue is the one in which a robed figure touches a spring with a rod, while twelve streams shoot out to twelve figures in twelve tents arranged on either side of a schematic sanctuary of temple, menorah, censers, and table.[28] This is a deliberately non-identifying description of the picture; Kraeling and Goodenough disagreed sharply in their initial identifications of the scene. Kraeling suggested the well at Beer, and Goodenough the spring at Elim.[29] Later, Goodenough admitted that no single biblical scene stood as the antecedent of the painting but suggested that it was a composite of the various wilderness well scenes from the Penteteuchal accounts of Israel (1953–1968, 10:33). Still, the Elim scene plays a large part in his interpretation, not only as it occurs in Exodus with its encampment and twelve springs, but also, and crucially, in Philo of Alexandria's interpretation of the scene at Elim in both *Flight* 183–84 and *Moses* 1.188, which identifies the springs with the patriarchs, and in the case of *Moses* 1.188 with the zodiac. This is perhaps the clearest comparative instance that Goodenough uses to ground his interpretation of the painting at Dura, but he also relies on other Targumic and rabbinic interpretations of the Elim scene and the patriarchs as well as hypotheses concerning similarities to a reconstruction of a Sassanian temple.[30] Without accompanying Goodenough in all his hypotheses about a coherent and widespread "mystical Judaism," it can be seen that the depiction of the well in the wilderness—in which the patriarchs in their "houses" receive the springs of Elim in a pattern reminiscent of the rays of Helios extending to the houses of the zodiac—is distinctly plausible.

This interpretation of the art of Dura Europos opens a possibility for one of the enigmatic elements of the Sepphoris synagogue mosaic: the youthful male figures that accompany the symbolic representations of the signs. The scorpion is sufficient to represent Scorpio, and the star represents the astral element of this symbol, but what does the robed male add to the astrological symbolism? In both the Beth Alpha and Hammath Tiberias mosaics, a single scorpion is sufficient to represent Scorpio, but at Sepphoris a young man stands beside it. While the Sepphoris synagogue consistently depicts the symbols of the zodiac that are known from other synagogue zodiac mosaics, the addition of human figures within the sectors for each sign is the peculiar constant of the Sepphoris mosaic. Potential and actual exceptions need to be noted: two panels are too fragmentary for a figure to appear, though there is certainly room for one. In addition, there is, of course, the possibility that one or more of the fragmentary figures is female. Nine of the remaining ten panels have complete or incomplete human figures accompanied by traditional symbolic representations of the zodiacal signs. The one panel without a human figure is Sagittarius, which combines the human with the bull in a centaur, so the human is by no means absent. With these qualifications in mind, as well as the extensive reservations that Levine outlines (2000, 561–69), I suggest that the male figures represent the grafting of the patriarchs onto a more traditional depiction of the zodiac wheel.

Here, I look for support not only to Goodenough's interpretation of the Dura Europos depiction of the springs of Elim, but also to Schwartz's programmatic interpretation of the Sepphoris synagogue (substantially a polemic against that of Weiss and Netzer 1996). He introduces an element into his interpretation of two features particular to the Sepphoris mosaic that may make the identification of the human figures with the patriarchs (and thus the patriarchs with the zodiac). Most interpreters note the absence of an anthropomorphic Helios figure from the chariot in the centre of the Sepphoris mosaic; instead, rays of light extend through the central medallion. Schwartz suggests that those responsible for the Sepphoris mosaic refrained from this particular figural representation out of "anxiety," presumably about having a polytheist symbol in such a central place (2001, 255). Likewise, Schwartz attributes the identification of the zodiac figures with the months of the calendar[31] to "anxiety" and an effort to "tame" the zodiac symbols (2001, 256). I am persuaded by Schwartz on this matter, and I see the figures, which I suggest are the patriarchs, accompanying the zodiac symbols as another expression of the anxiety that Schwartz identifies. The makers and sponsors of the mosaic at Sepphoris have refrained from the depiction of an anthropomorphic Helios at the centre of the cosmos and tame the beasts of the zodiac through an overlay of the patrons of the twelve tribes of Israel.

The Rabbis

The nature of rabbinic materials makes it probable that multiple perspectives on any issue will be witnessed in the literature.[32] The most oft-repeated claim is that "Israel is immune from planetary influence [*mzl*]" (*BShab*. 156a),[33] but the context is not as one-sided as the claim itself. The immediate predecessor to this declaration, which appears first on the authority of R. Johanan and is subsequently repeated by several other rabbis, is correlation of birth days of the week with specific character traits, and then a discussion of the constellations of specific hours of birth as determining influences on character. After the elaborate speculations about birth timing and after the declaration by R. Hanina that "the planetary influence gives wisdom, the planetary influence gives wealth, and Israel stands under planetary influence," R. Johanan declares that "Israel is immune from planetary influence." The grounding text for this assertion is Jeremiah 10:2.[34]

Among the other justifications for the repeated declaration that "Israel is immune from planetary influence" is that attributed to Rab, based on an elaboration of Genesis 15:5 in which Abraham blames his infertility on his constellation but is ordered by God to abandon his star-gazing, because God has reoriented the position of Jupiter. God can arrange the stars for his purpose, and the superiority of Israel and Israel's God over the power of the planets is exercised in symmetry to that which it opposes. *Genesis Rabbah* 44.12 elaborates Genesis 15:5 and accomplishes the same end by suggesting that "He brought him out" implies a heavenly ascent in which Abraham is lifted above the stars and can look down on the stars and thus be superior to the zones that they influence. Again the rivalry with the zodiac is won on astrological terms, by ascending higher than the stars and looking down upon them.

Other rabbinic and proto-kabbalistic texts are less concerned with superiority to or immunity from "planetary influence." The discussion of Genesis 49:28 in *Midrash Tanhuma* has affinities to Philo's discussion of the number twelve in *Flight* 184, treated above. As *Midrash Tanhuma* concludes its interpretation of Jacob's testamentary blessing, which had such fertile associations for astrological correlation of the patriarchs, it focuses on the number twelve in Genesis 49:28: "All these are the twelve tribes of Israel."

> As for the tribes, they have a basis in the structure of the world. The day has twelve hours, the night has twelve hours, the year has twelve months, there are twelve planets (*Midrash Tanhuma* 12:16).

Similarly, the early kabbalistic text *Sefir Yezirah* correlates the signs of the zodiac and the patriarchs in a process of Judaizing basic structures of the cosmos and making cosmic the basic value of Judaism. This is another example of the triumphalist equivalence we saw in Philo.

The Horoscope of Asaph

An infrequently cited text of quite uncertain provenance correlates the patriarchs and the zodiac elaborately and unambiguously. The astrological text attributed to an unidentifiable "Andronicus" containing an extract from an otherwise unknown "Asaph" was first published in 1918 by Alphonse Mingana on the basis of a single manuscript from the John Rylands Library.[35] Mingana dated the manuscript, which contained several independent works, to the fifteenth century CE (1917–18, 79–80), but suggested the text of Andronicus was composed in the third or fourth century CE and incorporated a fragment attributed to a Jewish astronomer "in the centuries immediately preceding or following the Christian era" (1917–18, 87). Within the large scope that Mingana's judgment offers, I have cautiously opted to treat the fragment attributed to Asaph as subsequent rather than prior to Revelation.

The fragment attributed to Asaph within Andronicus's "discourse on the twelve *stoicheia* of the sun" is brief enough and worthwhile enough to quote in its entirety:

> Asaph the writer and historian of the Hebrews explains and teaches clearly the history of all these [the signs of the zodiac], but does not write and show them with Greek names, but according to the names of the sons of Jacob. As to the effects and influence of these *stoicheia* he, too, enumerates them fully without adding or diminishing anything, but in simply changing in a clear language their names into those of the Patriarchs. He begins them in the Aramaic language and puts at the head Taurus, which he calls "Reuben." After it comes "Aries," which they call "Simeon." After it comes Pisces, which they call "Levi." After it comes Aquarius, which they call "Issachar." After that comes Capricornus, which they call "Naphtali." After it he sketches a rider while shooting and calls him "Gad," and he is analogous with Kirek of the Greeks. After it comes Scorpio, which he calls "Dan." After it he mentions Libra which he calls "Asher." After it he mentions Virgo, whom he calls Dinah. After it comes Leo, which he calls "Judah." Then he sketches Cancer, which he calls Zebulun. After it he mentions Gemini, whom he calls Ephraim and Manasseh. (Mingana 1917–18, 89)

In the fragment attributed to Asaph, the potential correlation of the patriarchs and the zodiac is deployed without reservation or apology. The particular mapping that the Asaph fragment draws has several close connections to the qualities attributed to individual patriarchs in Jacob's testamentary blessing in Genesis 49. The most obvious connections from Genesis seem to inform the Asaph fragment—Judah the lion is Leo; Reuben the powerful, proud, and incorrigibly virile is Taurus, etc.—as well as several that require more interpretive agency.[36] Especially in comparison to later rabbinic correlations, the scheme attributed to Asaph seems to stand in a tradition that looks positively to Genesis 49 for whatever guidance it may offer in mapping the patriarchs onto the zodiac.

Syntheses

The literary and religious environment in which John wrote Revelation included ample resources for understanding the patriarchs and the zodiac as related phenomena and a broadly distributed pattern of doing so. Moreover, this essay as a whole has assembled the dispersed instances of the idea of mapping the patriarchs onto the zodiac and vice versa with new proposals for understanding this in *Jubilees* and the Sepphoris synagogue. In the case of John's Revelation, the integration of the patriarchs and the zodiac in Revelation 12:1 occurs not by accident—as a result of poorly integrated polytheist narrative and mythological materials—but by John's own design, playing with the correlation while clearly subordinating the stars (zodiac) to the woman (Israel).

Not surprisingly, Jewish texts exhibited manifold strategies for dealing with the potential relationship of the patriarchs and the zodiac, and the way that they dealt with this relationship of mythological elements highlights the variety of ways in which different religious formations can relate to one another. The pattern that I have labelled "triumphant equivalence" is a high gain / high loss strategy. One group may accept the other's euhemeristic claim but acknowledge no triumph. Or, more aggressively, its discourse may reverse the triumphant claim. The conflict between Jews and Christians over the interpretation of the Hebrew Bible is afflicted with the "high loss" that characterizes this strategy at least as often as "high gain" does. "Habitual correlation" is also a two-edged sword. On the one hand, it can help inter-religious relations, yet on the other hand, it sets up an intra-religious conflict—one that can be at least as bitter as any inter-religious conflict—between those who want to maintain high boundaries and those who want more flexible relations. In the Christian heresiological literature in one mode, and substantial strands of Jewish rabbinic literature in another, this intra-religious conflict rages. Imitative superiority often involves something that might uncharitably be called a safety based on self-deception, where difference itself is a matter of principle that trumps any observation that might suggest similarity. These suggestions do not exhaust the patterns of rivalry over the patriarchs and the zodiac, but they ought to serve as a well-grounded caution against monolithic interpretations of very plural symbols and simple characterizations of very complex relations.

8

Was Roma the Scarlet Harlot?
The Worship of the Goddess
Roma in Sardis and Smyrna

James Knight

Introduction

The great harlot continues to be one of the more striking and enigmatic images of the empire in the book of Revelation. The vision itself begins with the invitation of one of God's avenging angels to the seer to come and see the judgment of the great harlot (Revelation 17:1). After embarking on a spiritual journey, the seer arrives in the wilderness, where he receives the vision (17:3b–6a) and is offered an angelic interpretation of the vision (17:7–18). At the close of the angel's interpretation, the harlot's demise is predicted (17:16), leading to the depiction of the various reactions to her destruction in the subsequent section (18:1–19:8).

In an effort to unravel the symbolism of the harlot vision, some scholars have attempted to situate the image within the book's historical context by proposing a connection between the goddess Roma and the whore of Babylon (Beauvery 1983, 257–60; Collins 1984a, 121; Bauckham 1993, 17; Aune 1998, 920–28). Bauckham, for example, argues that the author's portrayal of the goddess Roma as "a stunning personification of the civilization of Rome," in the guise of "a Roman prostitute," functions as an arresting critique of the empire (1993, 17–18).

Emphasizing the uniquely static or tableau-like character of Revelation 17:1b–6, Aune contends that this vision-report is an *ekphrasis*, an accepted Greco-Roman literary device, which he defines as a "detailed description [of a work of art]," employed for rhetorical purposes (1998, 923). He further posits that this particular *ekphrasis* describes a marble or bronze relief of Roma, which is no longer extant, but may be represented by the image of Roma found on a sestertius minted in Asia Minor during the reign of Vespasian (1998, 923–25, 928; see also Beauvery 1983, 243–60). The obverse of the coin has a portrait of the emperor with the inscription "IMP CAESAR VESPASIANVS AVG PM TP PP COS III" ("Greatest Priest, Tribunal Power, Father of the Fatherland, Counsul for the Third Time"; Aune 1998, 920). The reverse depicts a female figure identified as ROMA seated on seven hills. She wears a crested helmet and a short tunic, and she holds a small sword (*parazonium*). Flanking Roma are the letters *S* and *C*, which stand for *senatus consultum* (a resolution of the senate). Roma is joined by old man Tiber on her right and a she-wolf nursing Romulus and Remus on her lower left (Cohen 1880–92, 398; Carson and Mattingly 1923–62, 187; Vermule 1974, 41; Beauvery 1983, 260). Citing Vermeule's classic study on the goddess Roma in Roman art, Aune maintains "it is reasonable to suppose" that this coin is a copy of a marble or bronze frieze that was prominent in Asia Minor (1998, 921, 928).

Although Aune's focus is on the influence of Roma on the harlot vision, he does recognize its composite nature by acknowledging possible allusions to the Hebrew Bible (e.g., Jeremiah 51:13; 1998, 925–26). The crux of his argument, however, rests on the striking similarities between the Vespasian sestertius and the harlot vision. The image of the woman seated on seven hills (Revelation 17:9) represents the most conspicuous feature linking the goddess Roma and the harlot vision (Aune 1998, 926). However, Aune mentions a possible problem with this connection, since the image of the harlot seated on the seven hills is not part of the initial description in 17:3b–6 but is found in the angel's interpretation in 17:9 (1998, 926). Rounding off his argument, Aune notes other, less obvious affinities (1998, 925–27). The presence of the she-wolf on the coin may have contributed to a "subversive joke" that Roma was a harlot, since the Latin word for wolf, *lupa*, also had the connotation of "prostitute" (Aune 1998, 925; see also Beauvery 1983, 257–58). As well, the description of the harlot "seated *by* the many waters" (17:1) may refer to the image of Roma's foot touching the Tiber River, yet in making this assertion, Aune argues that the preposition *epi* should be translated "by" rather than "on" (1998, 907). In addition, the mysterious name on the harlot's forehead (17:5) may reflect the popular legend that Roma had a concealed, unutterable name (Aune 1998, 926–27). Finally, Roma's *parazonium* or sword, signifying the military prowess of the empire, may represent the harlot's intoxication from the blood of the saints in 17:6 (Aune 1998, 927).

So was Roma the "scarlet harlot"? According to Aune, the seer was acquainted with this image of the goddess and employed elements from it in the composition of the harlot vision. However, I am not as convinced as Aune for a number of reasons. First, given the polyvalent nature of Revelation's symbolism, it is difficult to establish a one-to-one correspondence between an image in the text and an element from the historical context.

The notion of polyvalence acknowledges that symbolic texts, such as vision-reports, operate on different levels of meaning, affecting the reader with a synergy of historical, literary, mythical, and archetypal allusions. Yet polyvalence is a misunderstood notion. Some contend that acknowledging the polyvalence of a symbolic text severs the text from its historical context (Collins 1984a, 19–20). An example of this severance is found in Pippin's analysis of Revelation, where she desires to "play with the polyvalence of the symbols, unanchoring them from any specific historical context" (1992, 16). Humphrey, on the other hand, presents a more preferable view of polyvalence, stating that "to call a text 'open' is to suggest that it has a range of meanings, but not that it can mean anything and everything" (1995, 69). Illustrating this point, she compares the task of reading the biblical text with the art of interpreting and performing a musical score, arguing that there can be differing approaches to the performance of Bach, yet "some renderings will not work" (1995, 69–70).

The second reason for my uncertainty, a corollary of the first, reflects some personal observations on the current state of biblical scholarship. Although the discipline today comprises a diversity of approaches, the continuing emphasis upon *realia* or "objective evidence" may stifle other avenues of inquiry. In other words, the tendency to relate a biblical text to a coin, a statue, or an inscription in such a way that one cries, "Eureka, I've unlocked its meaning," places a particular set of parameters around the text. While Collins is correct in asserting that "the symbolic universe of every text is shaped by its historical context and cultural milieu" (1984, 19), the "historical context" is not the sole arbiter of a text's meaning, since its literary character opens up a range of meanings that go beyond historical realities. This is not to nullify the importance of historical study; rather, it is to acknowledge the value of other approaches. After all, no methodology is completely objective. Even history is something pieced together from a wide array of evidence, which has been categorized, weighed, and interpreted.

Finally, there are a few difficulties with Aune's proposed similarities between the Roma coin and the harlot image. The most obvious parallel, the harlot and the goddess seated on seven hills, is not as compelling when one considers details within the passage itself. In the specific section that Aune describes as an *ekphrasis* (17:1b–6), the harlot is depicted as being seated on "many waters" (17:1b) and on "a scarlet beast" (17:3b). It is only later, in the angel's interpretation of the vision, that reference is made to the beast's seven heads as seven hills on which the harlot sits (17:9). To further complicate matters, the angel adds that the beast's seven heads are also seven kings. It becomes apparent then that the actual vision of the harlot does not portray her as being seated on seven hills; rather, she sits upon a seven-headed, ten-horned scarlet beast.

Whereas Aune's study of Roma and the harlot concentrated on a particular image of the goddess in relation to Revelation17:1b–6, one that we do not find convincing, this essay will examine the larger issue of the nature of Roma worship in Asia Minor and consider how it pertains to Revelation's critique of the empire. By examining the impact of the Roma cult in the lives of the citizens of cities such as Sardis and Smyrna, we can gain some insight into the harlot vision as a subversive image of empire.

The Roma Cult in Sardis and Smyrna

Mellor's work on the Roma cult represents the classic study of the cult's place in the Greco-Roman world (1975, 1981). The explicit aim of his earlier monograph is to examine "the origins of this goddess, where, when and why she was 'invented,' and what meaning she had for those who worshipped her" (Mellor 1975, 14). The book's structure facilitates this goal. Part 1 analyzes the evidence for Roma in the Greek world within the context of historical and political currents of the time, attempting to explain the origins and development of the cult. Part 2 examines "the various manifestations of Roma and her cult" (epithets, poems, temples, altars, statues, festivals, games, and cult officials) in order to discover how the cult was perceived by the Greeks.

Mellor's study succeeds in assembling, organizing, and analyzing a mountain of material into a coherent picture of Roma worship in the Greco-Roman world. His project, however, is flawed as a result of a clear bias toward a political interpretation of the Roma cult. His notion that "for the Greeks such cults were political and diplomatic acts…based on political, rather than religious experience" represents the principal argument of the study, influencing his presentation of the evidence and leading to an inevitable set of conclusions (Mellor 1975, 16).

Mellor describes the cult of Roma as "a political tool" that was devoid of any religious affections (1975, 16). To bolster this assertion, he draws similarities between the cult of Roma and the cults of the Hellenistic rulers and the Roman emperors, arguing that they constituted successive phases of political allegiance to various rulers (1975, 20–26; 1981, 957–58). Within his scenario, the Roma cult was a transitional phase between the worship of the Hellenistic kings and the deification of the Roman emperors. These political cults, Mellor notes, enabled the citizens of Asia Minor to adapt to the changing political landscape of their world (1975, 26, 111). When power shifted from the Hellenistic kings to the Roman republic, the Greek cities did not have a new monarch to attribute divine honours to, so they deified the Roman state, and the Roma cult was born (1975, 26). Subsequent modifications in Roman rule, primarily when the republic evolved into the empire, signalled the cessation of the Roma cult, since "there was no longer any political rationale for the inclusion of Roma in the imperial cult," for "if she remained, it was usually out of inertia and religious conservatism" (1975, 26). By depicting the worship of rulers and of Roma as lacking "any religious dimension," Mellor is able to conclude that "the significance of the cults was political; the motivation was political; the desired consequences were political" (1975, 20–21).

Mellor's view that the Roma cult was more about political diplomacy than "true religion" corresponds to similar notions concerning the imperial cult argued elsewhere (Nock 1935, 481–503; Nilsson 1948, 177–78; Bowersock 1965, 112–21). For instance, Mattingly characterizes the imperial cult as lacking "warmth and personal appeal," never passing "from official to heartfelt acceptance" (1954, 28). Along similar lines, Mellor characterizes the "formal religious practice" of the Greeks as having "nothing to do with what we would call 'religious experience.' For that experience they turned increasingly to the new popular philosophies and the mystery cults" (1975, 22).

His notion of "religious experience," however, reflects modern ideas of religion, as he states in a footnote: "Use 'Religious' here in its modern sense, in antiquity a far broader spectrum of social and political activity might be termed 'Religion'" (1975, 21). This is the essential problem with Mellor's assessment of the Roma cult. A religion of antiquity, in this case the cult of Roma, is viewed through a modern lens, which defines religion as a transcendent, individualistic, and affective phenomenon that is untainted by worldly, political matters.

This particular critique of Mellor's definition of religion is not new, as Price and Fox have offered similar assessments, focusing largely upon the imperial cult (Price 1984, 7–22; Fox 1986, 39–41). Fox, for instance, asks why the imperial cult took on religious characteristics, if it was merely an expression of political loyalty (1986, 40). Price offers a more extensive critique, questioning many of the preconceived notions about ritual, religion, and politics in the study of the imperial cult (1984, 7–22).

Price's insights provide a helpful evaluation of Mellor's study, especially of the relationship between emotion and religion. Mellor's description of the Roma cult as lacking "any religious dimension" or "experience" (1975, 16, 22) is criticized by Price for a "Christianizing" approach to ancient religion that questions the religious aspects of the imperial cult, a criticism based solely on the criterion of affect (1984, 9–10). According to Price, such an approach is misguided since it defines religion from the angle of "interiorized beliefs and feelings of individuals" (1984, 10). He points out that such an assessment of the religions of antiquity wrongly applies modern concepts of spirituality to another society "without consideration of their relevance to indigenous standards" (1984, 10). Biased evaluations of other faith groups are present within modern Christianity as well. A Christian from a non-liturgical tradition might characterize an Anglican worship service as meaningless ritual, since the prayers are read from a book instead of being offered spontaneously "in the Spirit." A fair and accurate examination of religion, ancient or modern, is not possible if one clings to a set of preconceived notions of what constitutes true religion.

Another questionable notion within Mellor's works is the division between religion and politics. Throughout his book Mellor gives the impression that the worship of Roma was a mundane, political affair that never approached the status of true religion (1975, 16, 18, 21, 22, 84, 111, 133, 161, 195). Price refutes similar opinions about the imperial cult, that it was merely "imperial propaganda" and "provincial diplomacy," with the following analysis: "Both arguments assume that an examination of overt initiatives and of the interests served by the cult exhausts the significance of the phenomenon" (1984, 16). Price is not denying the political aspects of the imperial cult; instead, he is reacting against the analysis of the cult, a response based *solely* on the political motives of the empire and its citizens. Again, the problem lies with modern presuppositions that hinder a fair assessment of ancient religions. Price has made the comment that "the preoccupation with a distinction between religion and politics in the study of the imperial cult is a perpetuation of the perspective engendered by the struggles and eventual triumph of the Christian Church" (1984, 19). The modern dogma of the separation of church and state may keep us from imagining a world where religion, economics, and politics were closely linked.

The cult of Roma emerged in a world where religion, economics, and politics were entangled, yet Mellor's review of the evidence for the cult focuses solely on its political character. For instance, he presents the establishment of the first temple to Roma in Smyrna as an act of political expediency (Mellor 1975, 15–16). The primary reference to the temple in Smyrna is found in Tacitus's account of an incident in 29 CE in which eleven cities in Asia Minor were vying for the privilege of constructing the temple to Tiberius, Livia, and the Senate (*Ann.* 4.55–56). According to Tacitus, Tiberius and the Senate listened to the arguments of the key cities and narrowed it down to Sardis and Smyrna. As both cites argued their case, the emissaries from Smyrna noted, among other things, that "they had been the first to erect a temple to the City of Rome [*seque primos templum urbis Romae statuisse*], at a period when the Roman fortunes stood high indeed, but had not yet mounted to their zenith, as the Punic capital was yet standing and the kings were still powerful in Asia" (*Ann.* 4.56, LCL, referring to the consulate of Marcus Porcius [ca. 195 BCE]). Tiberius and the Senate were swayed by the apparent devotion of the Smyrneans, and they awarded them the temple to Tiberius, Livia, and the Senate.

Mellor concentrates on Tacitus's allusion to the first temple to Roma in Smyrna, examining the historical circumstances surrounding this incident. The resulting historical reconstruction portrays the origins of the cult as an example of political manoeuvring during the superpower showdown between Rome and the Selucid dynasty (Mellor 1975, 15–16; 1981, 958–59; see also Gruen 1984, 178–79). According to Mellor, thirty years prior to the construction of the Roma temple, Smyrna and Lampsacus had given their allegiance to King Attalus of Pergamum. At that time, Selucid power was weakening in the east, and Antiochus could not gain control over the Greek cities. In 197 BCE, however, Antiochus III had some important victories in Egypt and he sailed to Ephesus, demanding allegiance from the key cities of Asia Minor. The majority of the cities submitted, but Smyrna and Lampsacus refused, appealing to Rome for help. To gain favour with Rome, the Smyrneans created the cult of Roma as a sign of their loyalty. According to Mellor's scenario, the building of the first temple to Roma was more the result of political diplomacy than of religious devotion.

Indeed, all appearances suggest that the birth of the cult of Roma was a political strategy on the part of the Smyrneans to solicit the support of the Romans against Antiochus III. If the emergence of the Roma cult in Smyrna was an example of power-playing political diplomacy, why, as Fox has asked, "was it a cult, taking religious forms?" (1986, 40). Surely there were means of diplomacy in the ancient world other than the formation of a cult around new or emerging powers. In addition, a focus on the political events surrounding the formation of the Roma cult ignores the religious features of the cult. Price makes a similar point, commenting that an explanation of the origins of the cult only in terms of "overt initiatives" or "interests served by the cult," specifically Smyrna's political overtures to Rome, does not thoroughly explain its inception or continued existence (Price 1984, 16). In other words, a limited "political" interpretation of the cult's origins fails to account for the complex set of factors behind its formation.

An accurate assessment of the cult of Roma should account for the interplay of these various components, that is, the political, social, economic, and religious features of the cult. Although Price is critical of Mellor's political explanation of the cult of Roma, he does recognize the political function of the ruler cults, describing them as "reactions to power" (1984, 52). However, he counters the narrow interpretation of the ruler cults as expressions of political loyalty by pointing out that the issue of power was as much a religious problem as a political one in the ancient world (1984, 52). Price emphasizes that the citizens of Asia Minor relied on religion to help them with the problem of "making sense of an otherwise incomprehensible intrusion of authority in their world," specifically the emergence of Roman power in their region (1984, 247–48). In his words, the "imperial rituals...were a way of conceptualizing the world" (1984, 7; see also Will 1969, 79–85). In this society, religion was the means of defining the place of the powerful, enabling the people to comprehend their status within the great rabble of humanity. From this perspective, the cult of Roma emerged out of an essential need to categorize Roman power within the particular symbolic universe of the inhabitants of Asia Minor.

Mellor's analysis of the Roma cult is guided by the idea that "the worship of Roma can only be properly understood in the context of the political history of these cities and regions and of their relations with Rome" (Mellor 1975, 27). In this way, he seems to accept the notion that the correct perspective of history is "from above" or that "history is the memory of states," in the words of Henry Kissinger (Zinn 1995, 9). This raises the important issue of the kinds of presuppositions adopted by historians. In his book on American history, Zinn points out that historians select, simplify, and emphasize certain facts over others in their presentation of history and that this process is guided by an ideological bias (1995, 8–10). History is not simply an objective study of the facts; it is influenced by the perspective of the one telling the story. Mellor's choice to examine the Roma cult in light of the "political history" of the cities of Asia Minor and "their relations with Rome" reveals a belief that history is primarily about the rising and falling of the superpowers and the impact upon the peripheral regions.

The process of selecting, simplifying, and emphasizing is apparent in Mellor's study of the Roma cult as its political function is stressed and its religious aspects are minimized. To his credit, the study is a fine compendium of a massive amount of material on Roma, yet he consistently maintains that the honours paid to the goddess, whether epithets, poems, temples, altars, coins, or festivals, were of a political and not of a religious nature (Mellor 1975, 112–63). An example of this bias is found in Mellor's treatment of temples to Roma. Emphasizing the small number of temples dedicated exclusively to Roma, he remarks that "the most visible manifestation of devotion to a divinity is the temple built in his or her honour," implying, of course, that Roma failed to receive full divine honours (Mellor 1975, 134). The temple to Roma in Smyrna is an obvious exception to Mellor's argument, yet he plays down its significance by stressing that there were too few temples to Roma as compared to other gods to make her a bona fide divinity worthy of religious devotion (Mellor 1975, 135). Thus, the number of temples reveals the depth of religious enthusiasm. But mere numbers cannot be the true measure of religiosity. The existence of a temple to Roma in Smyrna does in fact constitute, in the words of Mellor, "the most visible manifestation of devotion to a divinity" (1975, 51). In addition, the temple to Roma in Smyrna continued to be prominent long after the emergence of the imperial cult, as shown by coins issued at Smyrna in the second and third centuries CE that depict the goddess and her temple (Mellor 1975, 135).

Temples that granted joint honours to Roma and the emperor may also represent exceptions to Mellor's "too few" temples argument. Mellor acknowledges that there were "more than a dozen temples" dedicated to Roma and the emperors (1975, 135), but his prevailing focus is on the "few temples built to Roma before she was associated with Julius Caesar and Augustus" (1975, 134). Implicit within Mellor's argument is the idea that only the temples specific to Roma can be used to gauge the level of her religious appeal. The temples to Roma and the emperors merely reflect a transitional stage in the evolution of the ruler cults as the imperial cult emerged and the cult of Roma began to wane (Mellor 1975, 26, 82, 111, 195–96). Such an assessment diminishes the significance of these joint temples, the most prominent being the temple to Roma and Augustus at Pergamum (awarded in 29 BCE). The temple of Roma and Augustus was the centre of the imperial cult in the province of Asia Minor as well as the focal point for the religious and political activities of the Koinon of Asia (Mellor 1975, 141). For example, the Koinon assembled annually at Pergamum for *Romaia Sebasta,* a series of meetings and games held in honour of Roma and Augustus (Mellor 1975, 81).

In addition, a series of coins issued in Asia Minor during the reigns of Augustus, Claudius, Nero, Vespasian, Domitian, Nerva, and Trajan attest to the enduring importance of the temple to Roma and Augustus at Pergamum. The reverse of these coins depicts the temple with the inscription "ROM ET AVG" (Roma and Augustus) on its apex and having the words *COM ASI* (Commune Asia) on either side of it. Roma and the emperor stand inside the temple. Roma is fully draped in flowing cloth, wears a crown, holds a *cornucopia* in her left hand, and places a crown upon the emperor with her right hand (Vermeule 1974, 135). These coins reveal an intimate connection between the Roma cult and imperial worship, demonstrating the importance of the goddess within the "theology" of the inhabitants of Asia Minor.

The presence of temples dedicated to Roma, whether specific to her or combined with emperor worship, reveals that Roma was worshipped as a goddess, regardless of the political aspects of the cult. Nevertheless, Mellor diminishes the religious features of the cult with the following analysis: "Roma had few temples but numerous festivals and games, akin to the honours offered to the Hellenistic kings" (1975, 134). In one swift stroke Mellor manages to eliminate the religious significance of the "few" temples to Roma by emphasizing the "numerous" festivals and games held in her honour, which, he alleges, served a political function, similar to those honouring the Hellenistic kings. Taking his argument further, he contends that the religious festivals devoted to Roma, called *Romaiae*, do not indicate that she was worshipped as a goddess (Mellor 1975, 165). In his words, "every *panegyris* [a religious assembly celebrating the festival of a god or goddess] was a religious festival and therefore included certain religious ceremonies, however devoid of true religious content the cult of Roma might be" (Mellor 1975, 161). Mellor's attempt to minimize the religious aspects of the Roma cult becomes even more conspicuous as he acknowledges that the festivals held in her honour were "religious" and included "religious ceremonies," while maintaining that the cult was "devoid of true religious content." Clearly, this argument is difficult to maintain unless one accepts the apparent contradiction that the cult had the marks of a religion, yet fell short of some modern definition of a "true" religion.

Another way of diminishing the significance of the festivals honouring Roma is to portray them as non-religious, mundane affairs. Nilsson offers the typical argument for this view: "Religion runs a serious risk of being profaned and materialized by all such festivity and merry-making" (1925, 260). Nilsson's critique of religious festivals stems from a narrow view of religion that sees these public ceremonies as a corruption of true religion. Implied is the idea that genuine religion is characterized by individual observance and private, emotional experiences. In response to this notion, Price, citing noted anthropologist Clifford Geertz, makes the point that the study of ancient religion and ritual should not be limited to the inaccessible world of private sensation, but should be seen as part of the collective mentality or "the intersubjective world of common understandings" that shapes the individual's world by establishing a particular outlook on the world and the person's place in it (1984, 8). The religiosity of the cult of Roma, then, should not be defined in terms of individuals and "their interior mental states," but as a "public cognitive system" that was manifested in the public sphere (Price 1984, 9).

Understanding ancient religion as a "public cognitive system" enables one to view the religious dimensions of the Roma festivals in a completely different light. In a thorough discussion, Price describes the imperial festivals as public expressions of religious devotion involving the entire population of a city (1984, 107–21). Mellor notes that the festivals in honour of Roma included a procession through the city, the presentation of gifts and the singing of hymns to her as a goddess, and the staging of various athletic, musical, and dramatic competitions (1975, 165–67). From the standpoint of the residents of Asia Minor, *Romaia* was a religious festival where Roma was worshipped as a goddess.

Furthermore, festivals and games honouring Roma were a substantial part of the religious and social life of the inhabitants of Asia Minor. For instance, the Koinon of Asia celebrated *Romaia* in Pergamum, as well as in other principal cities of Asia Minor such as Sardis and Smyrna (Mellor 1975, 81–82, 167–68). By the reign of Tiberius, the joint festival honouring Roma and the emperor, *Sebasta Romaia*, was celebrated in a number of cities in Asia Minor (Mellor 1975, 168). Inscriptions confirm the celebration of *Romaia* in Pergamum (*IPergamon* 269; *IGR* IV 498; *IPriene* 105) and in Smyrna (*I Delphes* 550, ca. III CE), as well as the presence of the *agnothete* (the director of the contests honouring Roma and the emperors) in Smyrna (*ISmyrna* 591, ca. 54–68 CE; *IGR* IV 1410) and in Sardis (*ISardBR* 8 = *IGR* 1756).

There are further indications that the worship of Roma did have religious elements and was not merely a sign of political loyalty. Significant cultic acts, such as sacrifices, were part of the worship of Roma. Mellor offers an example of a treaty document from 130 BCE (*IGR* IV 1692) in which the citizens of Pergamum agreed to make sacrifices to Roma and other deities (1975, 157). Another inscription from Pergamum requires each new candidate to the association of *hymnodes* to pay an entrance fee of 100 *denarii* to cover the cost of the sacrifices made to Roma and Augustus (*IPergamon* 374, II CE). Clearly, Roma was worshipped as a goddess.

Epithets used to describe Roma may also reflect her divine qualities, demonstrating the religious dimensions of her cult. Mellor identifies *thea*, *sōtēr, euergetēs, epiphanēs, nikēphoros, egemon, archēgetēs, aenaos, polis*, and *basileius* as the primary epithets applied to Roma (1975, 112–19). Yet he diminishes the religious significance of these terms, describing them as "rather weak epithets" that do not imply the divinity of Roma (1975, 112, 115). In making his case, Mellor argues that *sōtēr* (saviour) and *euergetēs* (benefactor) could be applied to mortals as well as deities and that *epiphanēs* (manifest), a term typically denoting divinity, had lost this particular connotation, speaking more of the sudden appearance of Roman power in the east (1975, 112–115). Certainly Mellor is correct in claiming that some of the epithets, such as *euergetēs* (benefactor), were applied to humans as well as to gods. However, Roma is clearly presented as *thea* (goddess) alongside the divine emperors in inscriptions from Sardis and Smyrna (*ISmyrna* 591, ca. 54–68 CE; *ISardBR* 8), so the other epithets must be viewed from this divine perspective. At the same time, these epithets demonstrate the fusion of the religious, social, and political aspects of life in Asia Minor. Realities in the material world had religious implications, so the terminology of power, rule, benefaction, and salvation enabled the inhabitants of Asia Minor to construct a myth of empire that fit their symbolic universe.

The cohesion of the religion, politics, and social activities in Asia Minor can also be seen in the descriptions of the priests of Roma. Their responsibilities were not limited to the political sphere but embraced various facets of life in this ancient society. The majority of inscriptions from Smyrna and Sardis referring to the cult of Roma list only the name of the particular priests of Roma, giving little information about the goddess or the specific practices of the cult (*ISmyrna* 591; *ISardBR* 8, 27, 93, 112, 113, 114, 115; *SEG* 46 1520) as a way of dating official documents, municipal decrees, and cinerary chests. For example, a sepulchral inscription from Sardis reads, "In the year when Kotobes was priest of Roma on the fifteenth of the month of Artemisios, Artemidoros (died) at the age of seventeen" (*ISardBR* 113, ca. I BCE).

At first glance, inscriptions naming the priests seem to tell us little about the cult itself, but on closer inspection, they indicate the prominent administrative role that the priest of Roma had in the cities. An inscription found in Sardis on a marble cinerary chest names Dionysios as the *stephanephoros* and the priest of Roma (*SEG* 45 1651, 9 BCE; see also *ISardBR* 93 [date in dispute]). This is significant because during the Attalid dynasty, the *stephanephoros* was the eponymous magistrate of the city, by whose name the year was identified and decrees and city documents were marked (Mellor 1975, 182). Sometime after the end of the Attalid dynasty (133 BCE), the priest of Roma took on the role of *stephanephoros*. One inscription from Sardis, dated in the late first century BCE, drops the designation of *stephanephoros* and names only the priest of Roma, indicating that at a certain point "the priest of Roma" became the accepted term for the eponymous magistrate of the city (*ISardBR* 8; see also *ISardBR* 112, 113, 114).

The priests of Roma played an important role within the administration of the city, but their responsibilities went beyond. An inscription from Smyrna from the time of Nero reveals the religious, political, and social duties of the priest of Roma (*ISmyrna* 591). This particular inscription reads, "It was resolved by the Hellenes of Asia, on motion of Tiberius Claudius Hero [high priest] and revealer of the divine images [*sebastophant*] and director of the contests [*agonothete*] for life of the goddess Roma and the god Sebaste Caesar." Tiberius Claudius, the high priest described here, had a multifaceted role within the Asian league. His administrative or civic responsibilities are evident from the prominent place of his name upon the decree itself. Furthermore, he performed specific duties within the religious practices of the cult of Roma. He is described as the *sebastophant* or the revealer of the divine images. The *sebastophant* had the task of uncovering the images of the *Sebastoi* within the religious ceremonies of the cult (Pleket 1965, 338–41). Finally, he was named the *agonothete* or the director of the contests honouring Roma and the emperor. As mentioned earlier, the contests and the festivals were prominent features of the cult of Roma within the cities of Asia Minor.

The evidence from Asia Minor, specifically from Sardis and Smyrna, reveals that the cult of Roma was not simply a political affair. The cult had a pervasive role within Asia Minor that touched the various facets of city life. Unfortunately, the classic study of the cult of Roma by Mellor limits its role to the political sphere, overlooking the religious and social impact of the cult on the people of Asia Minor. The problem lies in the major pillar of Mellor's argument that the Roma cult was "the bastard offspring of the Hellenistic ruler cult" and the "model for the worship of the Roman emperors" (1975, 195). He has drawn these lines of development in order to prove that the cult of Roma was merely a political tool, an act of loyalty by a subjugated people. He further contends that when the "power of Rome could be more appropriately embodied in the emperor and his family," the Roma cult ceased to be necessary politically and faded from view (1975, 195–96). This assertion is contradicted by evidence from Mellor himself that several cities in Asia Minor, including Smyrna, maintained the Roma cult into the third century CE (Mellor 1975, 196–97). In light of this fact, Mellor admits that something other than simple political manoeuvring was behind the cult, noting that "the innate conservatism of religion gave the cult an existence independent of its origin and political significance" (1975, 198). Ultimately, Mellor is unable to explain the phenomenon of Roma's enduring appeal and admits that "a certain part of the impact of Roma on the citizens of the eastern empire remains beyond our understanding" (1975, 198).

The impact of Roma upon the citizens of Asia Minor may be "beyond our understanding" because of our modern views of religion as a transcendent phenomenon, separate from worldly, political affairs. A world where politics, economics, religion, and social interaction are enmeshed is somewhat foreign to us. Yet this is the type of world where the cult of Roma emerged and flourished. Price notes that the characterization of religion as mystical and politics as mundane ignores the fact that both "are ways of systematically constructing power" (1984, 247). The cults of Roma and the emperors were "reactions to power" (Price 1984, 52), that is, they represented the response of the inhabitants of Asia Minor to a new political power. Using the paradigm of their particular symbolic universe, they were able to conceptualize the role of the emperor (and of Rome) "in the familiar terms of divine power" (Price 1984, 248).

Revelation as Subversion

In the preceding section I have illustrated that our preconceived notions about the cults of Roma and the emperors can influence our understanding of religion in antiquity. In addition, these notions, especially the distinction between religion and politics, can distort our reading of Revelation.

Price notes that the political reading of imperial religion has led some scholars of Revelation to conclude that when confronted with the cults of Roma and the emperors, followers of Christ faced "a stark choice between Christ and Caesar, between religion and politics" (1984, 15). A more nuanced approach to Revelation and religion needs to acknowledge the multifaceted nature of the cults of Roma and the emperors in the cities of Asia Minor. Fortunately, contemporary interpreters of Revelation, such as Bauckham (1993, 35–39) and Kraybill (1996), have recognized the close association of religion, politics, social life, and economics in Asia Minor.

The harlot vision of Revelation 17 reveals that the seer did not separate the various political, social, economic, and religious factors in imperial rule, but placed them side by side in one figure. On one level, the harlot vision can serve as a cautionary tale of the dangers of imperial religion. The primary description of the woman as a harlot (*pornē*) committing harlotry (Revelation 14:8; 17:1, 2, 4, 5, 15, 16; 18:3, 9; 19:2) triggers allusions from the Hebrew scriptures where harlotry is associated with idolatry. Further indications of the religious antagonism of the harlot are evident in the "abominations" (*bdelygmatōn*) that fill her cup (17:4), her portrayal as the "mother of harlots and of earth's abominations" (17:5), her impurity (17:4b; 18:2), and her sorcery (18:23d). Finally, the harlot is seated upon a scarlet beast, which is covered with blasphemous names (17:3) and is identical to the arrogant, blaspheming beast of Revelation 13:1–8 that receives the worship of the peoples of the earth (13:4, 8, 12, 14, 15).

At the same time, the vision criticizes the overwhelming political power of the empire. The harlot is nicknamed "Babylon" (17:5), indicating her status as an empire in opposition to Zion, the city of God. Furthermore, the harlot is portrayed as being "seated," implying that she is *enthroned* and has political authority over the earth (17:1c, 3b, 9b, 15; 18:7b). Being seated "upon the many waters" (17:1b), interpreted as "peoples and multitudes and nations and tongues" (17:15), the harlot is shown to reign over the peoples of the earth. As well, the beast's seven heads are interpreted as "seven hills" upon which the harlot is seated (17:9). This reference to "seven hills" would have been clearly recognizable as an allusion to the ruling city of Rome (Aune 1998, 944–45). Finally, the use of ruling and reigning language confirms the political aspects of the harlot figure. This is most explicit in the angel's remarks that the harlot "is the great city which has rule (*basileian*) over the kings of the earth" (17:18). This is reiterated in 18:7 as the harlot states, "I sit as a queen" (*basilissa*).

The seer condemns the harlot's political rule as arrogant and bloodthirsty. The extreme arrogance of the empire is seen in the harlot's inner thoughts that boast of her perpetual enthronement: "I rule as a queen; I am no widow, and I will never see grief," (18:7b). In addition, the harlot's reign has resulted in the slaughter of God's people. Using a military metaphor, the seer characterizes the harlot as being "drunk with the blood of the saints and the blood of the witnesses to Jesus" (17:6). A similar charge is made in 18:24 where "a mighty angel" declares, "In you was found the blood of prophets and of saints, and of all who have been slaughtered on earth." The harlot's hubris results in the swift judgment of God (18:7–8). As the harlot episode concludes, the chorus of heaven breaks out in celebration, proclaiming that God "has avenged on her [the harlot) the blood of his servants" (19:2b). Through these statements, the seer highlights the culpability of the harlot in the slaughter of God's people.

Finally, the seer reproaches the "harlot city" for her excessive wealth. The seer's description of the harlot contains significant remarks on her clothing and adornment (17:4). Although there are various options for interpreting the harlot's attire, the seer appears to be using her apparel as an expression of her great wealth. For instance, when the merchants lament the demise of the city (18:16), they describe it with language strikingly similar to 17:4, adding that "in one hour all this *wealth* has been laid waste." In addition, the harlot's clothing and jewellery are listed in the catalogue of luxury cargo (18:12), signalling their role as indicators of wealth. Finally, references to the harlot's opulence are made elsewhere, stressing that her wealth is a factor in God's judgment of her, and its removal manifests the outcome of God's judgment (18:3c, 7a, 9a, 11, 14, 15, 19, 23c).

Conclusion

In Revelation, the seer's critique of the empire was not merely about the dangers of religious syncretism, political allegiance to the empire, or the excesses of wealth; rather, the image of the harlot exposed the extensive web of imperial power that infiltrated the lives of his readers. Bauckham places the harlot image within the context of the propaganda of the Roman Empire, the ideology of *Pax Romana,* which promoted the idea that Roman rule brought peace, prosperity, and civilization to the world (1993, 35–36). Arguing that "Revelation portrays this ideology as a deceitful illusion," Bauckham points to the harlot vision and the beast vision as the unmasking of "the pretensions of Rome" (1993, 35–39). The harlot vision exposes the dark underside of the glitter of the empire. For readers familiar with the standard propaganda of the empire, the process of deciphering the image would open their eyes to an alternative view, one that sees Rome as the antithesis of God's rule. In light of the harlot vision, the crimes of the empire become manifest: abomination, idolatry, impurity, deception, opulence, murder, and hubris. With this new perspective, the seer's audience are urged to cease their collaboration with the corrupt empire (18:4).

If, as Price suggests, imperial religion, including the cult of Roma, was a means by which the citizens of Sardis and Smyrna "systematically constructed power," specifically, the power of the empire, then John's Apocalypse represents a contradictory perspective on power. Through his visions, the seer enabled his readers to challenge the conventional notions of their world in order to imagine a different set of power relationships with God Almighty and the Lamb, rather than the empire, ruling over the cosmos.

INTERACTION AMONG RELIGIOUS
GROUPS IN SARDIS AND SMYRNA

9

"Caring for All the Weak"
Polytheist and Christian Charity
in Sardis and Smyrna

Steven C. Muir

Introduction

This essay[1] is a continuation of work done in analysis of Rodney Stark's 1996 book *The Rise of Christianity*. In an earlier essay, soon to be published, I critiqued the material covered in chapters 4 ("Epidemics, Networks, and Conversion") and 7 ("Urban Chaos and Crisis: The Case of Antioch") of Stark's book (Muir 2005). Stark assumed there was a sharp contrast between Christianity and the polytheist world, in particular concerning charity to the sick and poor. He asserted that one factor in the rapid rise of Christianity was its developed ideology of charity and its organized program of social ministry. He found nothing comparable in the polytheist world; hence, in his opinion, Christianity in its pre-Constantinian phase had a "market" opportunity. This opportunity was advanced by two crisis periods identified by Stark: widescale epidemics in 165 and 250 CE, and more general conditions of urban poverty. The sick and poor benefited from the charity extended by Christians, and converted to the movement.

My earlier essay argued that Stark had an inadequate appreciation of the roles that Greco-Roman philanthropy and medicine could have played in ameliorating sickness and poverty, and thus overstated the contrast between Christianity and polytheism in this regard.[2] Stark also failed to consider charismatic or supernatural healings. Healing cults and magicians were common in the ancient world, and they could have been competitors not only to the palliative care but also to the charismatic healings enacted within Christian circles. Christianity did not have a corner on the ancient world's market for health care.

In this essay I examine Stark's arguments in light of a detailed study of Smyrna and Sardis. It is both fascinating and frustrating to move from

Notes to chapter 9 start on page 272

the broad and intuitively appealing theses of Stark, albeit unsupported by primary sources, to the variety of historical evidence from specific locations. Here, Stark's large and bold black-and-white portrait is necessarily replaced by small-scale, impressionistic sketches done in local colours. Nevertheless, there is some tantalizing evidence that supports Stark's theses.

It is clear at the outset that the primary sources, particularly the Christian ones, are often obscure on the mundane but important social factors at work. Theissen notes, "It is a characteristic trait of religious tradition that it masks its mooring in human activity, preferring to speak of the god's activity or to testify to an experienced reality lying beyond the world of human sense perception" (1982, 175–76). No matter how closely we interrogate our primary sources, or even how many sources we bring in, they may refuse to yield the kind of information we seek. Hence, my essay is longer and less conclusive than I would like it to be. In many cases, I discuss evidence that is merely suggestive or even inconclusive, precisely to show that although Stark's assertions make sense, they are difficult to prove in a rigorous way when we look at Smyrna and Sardis.

Furthermore, Stark posits that Christians, by offering charity to outsiders, drew them into the circle, creating obligations, and that these factors then facilitated affiliation with the group and eventually led to conversion to the movement. My essay makes clear that indeed Christians did "care for all the weak."[3] The issue is who precisely these "weak ones" were. The evidence from the Christian sources suggests that the majority of Christian charity was extended to those "in the household" of believers. What remains unclear is precisely what Stark assumes—how non-believers accessed the charity offered by Christians.

Living Conditions in Sardis and Smyrna

Stark's estimation (1996, 131–32) of various city sizes, with Sardis at one hundred thousand and Smyrna at seventy-five thousand, is consistent with other scholarship.[4] These sites were among the top twenty most populous cities of the empire. We can also assume that Sardis and Smyrna had numerous groups of subsistence-level artisans and day labourers, and poverty-stricken people who would live in crowded and unsanitary living quarters (Carney 1975, 87–88; Scobie 1986, 399–433). For example, according to Strabo, Smyrna is praised for its beauty but "there is one error, not a small one, in the work of the engineers, that when they paved the streets they did not give them underground drainage; instead, filth covers the surface, and particularly during rains, when the cast-off filth is discharged upon the streets."[5] Many health problems would result from such conditions, as well as the inevitable factionalism and class conflict, for which we have evidence in both Sardis and Smyrna.[6]

Along with these social problems came numerous natural disasters. Among the most devastating were the two plagues that swept through Asia Minor in 165 and 250 CE, including Sardis and Smyrna.[7]

Both plagues were to the result of infections picked up by troops at the eastern fringes of the empire (Boak 1955, 26).[8] As the legions returned west, the plagues came with them. Thus, the eastern provinces of the empire would have had the first exposure to the disease and perhaps were hit harder than the western ones (Boak 1955, 26). We may reasonably suppose that cities were more afflicted than the countryside, because of the greater potential for contagion to spread in crowded living conditions (Littman and Littman 1973, 252-53).

Two inscriptions from around 165 CE, one from Pergamum and one from Caesarea Trocettis, mention the plague (*IGR* 360 and 1498). A temple to Apollo in Hierapolis, constructed on the advice of the oracle at Claros (see below), was consulted during the plague (Yamauchi 1980, 150-51). Aelius Aristides gives us firsthand information about the 165 CE plague in Smyrna (discussed below). The river Meles, which passed through Smyrna, is praised in a second century inscription for preservation from plague: "I sing the praises of the river (-god) Meles, my saviour, now that every plague and evil has ceased" (*CIG* 3165). The plague is often identified as that of 165 CE (Cadoux 1938, 11; Magie 1950, 663).

Many other natural and human disasters occurred during the first to fourth centuries in Asia Minor, albeit mostly on a smaller scale than the two plagues noted above,[9] including bouts of famine, widespread disease, and localized plagues[10] (Magie 1950, 1543; Gilliam 1961, 235-36; Robinson 1991, 71-72; Hill 1999, 39).

Asia Minor was a region prone to food shortages, and this situation was perhaps particularly acute because of its dense population.[11] A well-known legend recorded by Herodotus 1.94 (also recorded by Plutarch) was that the Lydians under King Atys had a great famine (Pedley 1972, 11-12 nos. 23, 24; 14 no. 31). Some scholars see an allusion to famine in Revelation 6:6 (Robinson 1924, 8-18; Rostovtzeff 1957, 201, 599-600; Hanfmann 1983, 144; further discussion below). MacMullen notes evidence for famine or food shortage around 93 throughout the eastern provinces,[12] in Prusa (northern Asia) and Aspendus (Pamphylia) during the reign of Vespasian, in Pisidian Antioch sometime in the late first century,[13] in Termessus (Pamphylia) in the late second century, and in Ephesus and Phrygia under Marcus Aurelius (1966, 252). Galen records that starving country folk of Asia Minor in the second century had to eat weeds for lack of food (cited in Garnsey 1988, 26, 29, 48, 55, 61).

Fires were always a hazard in crowded conditions that are typical of the poor quarters of cities, and we know of at least one major conflagration in Smyrna (Cadoux 1938, 280). The region around Sardis was unstable geologically (as was Asia Minor generally), and we know of several earthquakes in the area.[14] We have evidence of earthquakes in Smyrna in 177–78 and at other times (Hill 1999, 41–43).

Such harsh living conditions and regular natural and human disasters would provide many opportunities for charity from polytheists and Christians. We turn our attention first to the polytheists.[15]

Polytheist Responses to Human Need

Cults of Asclepius and Other Healing Gods

The cult of Asclepius had reached new heights by the second century CE. It was popular and widespread in the empire. The Asclepieion at Pergamum was an extensive complex, exceeded in size and influence only by the mother-site at Epidaurus in Greece (Hoffmann 1998, Yamauchi 1980). Pergamum was well connected to other locations in Asia[16] and was an influential city.[17] We should not be surprised, therefore, that there was religious activity related to Asclepius in Sardis and Smyrna and throughout Asia Minor; it would be more unusual if there had been none. That being said, it is worth noting specific evidence.

First we can consider the Asclepius cult in Smyrna. Pausanias, in *Descriptions of Greece* V.9 (cf. XXVI.8), describes a sanctuary to Asclepius in Smyrna, built in his own time (mid-II CE) and originating from the main sanctuary at Pergamum.[18] An early third-century CE inscription in a theatre lists the assignment of four rows of seats to porters attached to that Asclepieion.[19] About the end of the second century CE the rhetor Herakleides took part with others in providing a golden-roofed oil fountain in the gymnasium of Asclepius.[20] There is a Smyrnaen inscription to Asclepius *Paieon* (the Healer).[21] A citizen of Smyrna dedicates a statue of Zeus *Soter* (Saviour) to Asclepius *Ieter* (Healer).[22] From Galen, the well-known physician of Pergamum, we have the following laconic statement: "The whole body of Nichomachus of Smyrna swelled excessively and it was impossible for him to move himself. But this man Asclepius healed" (Edelstein and Edelstein 1945, 459). There is some Smyrnaen coinage of Asclepius (Walton 1894, 204nn2–3). At Rome, the Smyrnaen physician Nikomedes dedicates a statue of Asclepius.[23]

Next we turn to the Asclepius cult in Sardis. In an inscription of the Hellenistic period, a shrine (or image) of Asclepius is dedicated to the Nymphs of the local hot springs and the donor gives thanks for his health

(Buckler 1932, 96–97 no. 94). There is a votive stele to Iaso, the goddess of healing and daughter of Asclepius, dated 173 CE (Buckler 1932, 99 no. 97). There is a statue of Asclepius from the Hadrianic period and two fragmentary bases of other votive statues to Asclepius (Hanfmann and Ramage 1978, 83, 111–12 no. 125). A votive relief of a patera and two snakes may also relate to the Asclepius cult (Hanfmann and Ramage 1978, 127 no. 158). Other relevant artifacts at Sardis are mentioned by Hanfmann (1983, 133, 271–81), including Asclepius and Hygeia portrayed in relief and pottery.[24]

Healing cults other than that of Asclepius also play a part in the religious life of Asia Minor and the cities of Sardis and Smyrna. Apollo, in his aspect as healer, received a dedicatory inscription in fulfillment of a vow (Cadoux 1938, 207). The hybrid healing and oracular cult of Glycon—the new Asclepius, manifested as a snake—set up by Alexander of Abonduteichus in the Paphlagonia region received a satirical report by Lucian. Several Hellenistic period gravestones from Smyrna have the picture of a bearded snake (Ridgeway 1993, 235). The patron deity of Sardis was Artemis-Cybele, and healing powers, even the ability to raise the dead, were attributed to the goddess there.[25] A river in Sardis was also believed to have healing powers (Pedley 1972, 7 no. 5). Hot springs about four km from Sardis are still in use and famed for their curative powers. The river-god Meles of Smyrna was also believed to have healing powers, as is shown in a second-century CE inscription, and by Aristides, who bathed in the river and thought the healing was due to Asclepius.[26]

Very interesting and well attested throughout Asia Minor are first- and second-century CE petitionary or confessional inscriptions on stelae.[27] They usually mention some person's affliction (such as an illness), which was seen as divine punishment for some transgression against the god. These are evident in the rural areas, and the addressee often is an indigenous (Lydian, Phrygian), pre-Hellenic deity, sometimes with a Greek epithet. In return for relief, the person vows to set up a monument. A few such stelae have been found in Sardis, including one by someone seeking—or celebrating—a cure from blindness.[28]

The Evidence of Aelius Aristides

Aristides was born in northern Mysia, a district north of Smyrna and Pergamum, in 118 CE. Both he and his father, a wealthy landowner, were citizens of Smyrna.[29] As a citizen, Aristides owned houses both in the city (*Or.* 48.43) and in the suburbs (*Or.* 48.38–39, 51.2). He suffered from one or more chronic ailments. Aristides spent an extended convalescent period at the Asclepieion in Pergamum.[30] He saw Asclepius as not only healer but also as the patron of Aristides's career as a sophist and travelling rhetorician. To pursue this career, Aristides assiduously dodged appointments to various civic offices (the usual reward for elites), including high priest of Asia, priest of the temple of Asclepius in Smyrna, tax collector in Smyrna, and *eirenarch* or chief police officer in Mysia (see Behr 1968, 61–63).

Nevertheless, Aristides was not lacking in civic pride. He lectured in Smyrna and addressed the city council on a few occasions,[31] he wrote an oration praising the beauty of the city, in particular the splendid amenities and living conditions (*Or.* 17), and he was influential in persuading Emperor Marcus Aurelius to rebuild Smyrna after the disastrous earthquake of 177 CE (Behr 1968, 112–13).[32] In his letter urging the rebuilding of Smyrna, Aristides mentions an earlier time when "there were frequent earthquakes and famines about the coast of Asia in this region and some places had even been destroyed by the fissures and various misfortunes afflicted the cities."[33]

Aristides gives us a valuable, unique first-hand description of the 165 CE plague in Smyrna:

> I happened to be in the suburbs at the height of summer. A plague infected nearly all my neighbors. First two or three of my servants grew sick, then one after another. Then all were in bed, both the younger and the older. I was last to be attacked. Doctors came from the city and we used their attendants as servants. Even certain of the doctors who cared for me acted as servants. The livestock too became sick. And if anyone tried to move, he immediately lay dead before the door. Everything was filled with despair, and wailing, and groans, and every kind of difficulty. There was also terrible sickness in the city. (*Or.* 48.38, in Behr 1981)[34]

As a devotee of Asclepius, Aristides thought that the god had not only saved him from that particular plague, but sustained him through many other lesser illnesses:

> And years later that plague occurred, from which the Saviour and Lady Athena manifestly saved me. And for some six months after this, my condition was wonderful. Then I became very constipated, and other things troubled me, all of which the god settled, and if I may say so by his grace, he still settles them with daily regimens and predictions. (*Or.* 50.9, in Behr 1981)

In addition to comments on the plague, Aristides gives us other important testimony about Smyrna, particularly in religious healing. He confirms the popularity in Smyrna of the healing and mystery cult of Isis and Sarapis: he mentions that there was a temple to Isis in Smyrna (*Or.* 49.45) and that he once had an oracular vision of Sarapis and Asclepius there.[35]

Another time in Smyrna, Aristides reports having an oracular vision of Asclepius and Apollo (*Or.* 48.18; Walsh 1931, 195–96; Cadoux 1938, 150–51, 204, 210, 232, 266). The "Warm Springs" was a resort and healing site about five km from Smyrna. Aristides records that it was at that site that he had his first vision of Asclepius and healing by him.[36] Aristides records (*Or.* 47.61–68) that while in the city of Smyrna he had an immense tumour in his stomach, which he believes was healed through the miraculous efforts of Asclepius (Behr 1968, 62). Another time (*Or.* 48.19–23), an afflicted Aristides bathed (in mid-winter!) in the healing river Meles just outside Smyrna and was cured by Asclepius. Aristides gives us glimpses of the Asclepius cult in Smyrna: he notes that there was at least one temple in the city to that god.[37] In summary, Aristides gives us first-hand, personal information about how a person (admittedly a member of the elite) could find satisfactory relief from illness in the Asclepius cult in Asia Minor. It is probable that such healing cults were the first resort of the lower classes, who could seldom afford to pay the fee of a physician.

Local Medicine and Philanthropy

Not surprisingly for a Hellenistic city of its size, Smyrna had an established and well-known medical centre. Smyrna had a medical school and eminent physicians, and Galen went there to study for two years (Walsh 1931, 195–96; Cadoux 1938, 150–51, 204, 210, 232, 266). Pliny the Elder mentions two Smyrnaen writers on medical and scientific matters whom he cites as authorities (Cadoux 1938, 233). We have the epitaph of a physician (*hiatros*) in Sardis (Buckler 1932, 123–24, no. 142). Physicians were associated with Sardis as well, though our evidence for them is from the fourth century (Foss 1976, 22–28). Occasionally, a physician would donate his services, so it is possible that more than the elites could benefit from such services (Muir 2005).[38]

Evidence of the usual Greco-Roman social system of donations and philanthropy can be seen in Smyrna and Sardis, and in Asia Minor generally (Thompson 1990, 151–52). According to inscriptions, wealthy citizens took seriously their responsibility to underwrite doles and public banquets (especially during food shortages) and undertake public works.[39] For example, a monument to a prominent citizen of Sardis records that "when want came among the people, he nobly contributed toward its alleviation out of his private means a modius for each citizen" (Buckler 1932, 63, no. 47). We also see that entire cities would assist each other in times of calamity. Aristides (*Or.* 19.12) speaks of Smyrna having helped cities of Asia Minor with gifts of food and money, when those cities were visited by a severe earthquake. The favour was returned when Smyrna was devastated by the earthquake of 177 CE: cities from Asia sent assistance (Cadoux 1938, 245, 280). The gymnasium in Smyrna was built with funds donated by the emperor Hadrian (Yamauchi 1980, 58). Philanthropy in this context was not targeted specifically at the poor: while all citizens except the disenfranchised urban poor could benefit, in practice allocations were distributed according to status (see MacMullen 1966, 180).

Christian Responses to Human Need

Christianity took several competing forms in western Asia Minor; it was inchoate and still very young when it reached this area, and its often independent missionaries addressed different audiences in a variety of ways (Kraabel 1992b, 284).

Asia Minor was an important centre of early Christian activity.[40] In the first century, Paul and the authors of the Johannine tradition are associated with this area. Letters of Paul or of the Pauline corpus (Galatians, Philemon, Colossians, Ephesians) are addressed to churches or persons in Asia Minor. The Pastoral letters (Timothy and Titus) have been linked with Ephesus. Revelation contains epistolary messages to the "Seven Churches of Asia," including Smyrna and Sardis. Ignatius and Polycarp are well-known local figures of the second century. From the same period, we have Pliny's letter to Trajan, giving an outsider's view of Christianity in Bithynia. Yet it is in the area of early Christian evidence that testing Stark's theses is the most difficult. Our assessment of the degree of Christian charity, and Christian response to plagues and other calamities, is constrained by the very limited explicit references to these subjects. In many cases, we are left to our own inferences, and in at least some cases it is noteworthy that the texts do not address our issues.

Pauline Communities

Paul does not write to communities in Sardis or Smyrna, although the apocryphal *Acts of Paul* places him in Smyrna (see below). Yet we know that one of his primary theatres of operation was Asia Minor.[41] Our only Pauline evidence is from other locations in Asia Minor, and I discuss them assuming that these situations can shed some tangential light or that there is continuity or connection between the centres. In Paul's letters we can infer that the churches he addresses practised charity, or were at least familiar with the concept. Entailed in this supposition is the view that the "love" (*agapē*) of which he speaks was not left as an abstract concept but was enacted in practical deeds.

Paul's tantalizingly brief comments in Galatians about his affliction are made in the context of his reminder of the community's initial friendship towards him. We might suppose Paul received palliative care during his physical ailment (4:13–15).[42] Paul concludes this commendation of their friendship and support by praising the community's self-sacrificing nature. We wish Paul would have revealed more about the circumstances of this event. One wonders—and this is pure speculation—if the Galatians sympathized with Paul in part because many among them had been or were still experiencing their own illnesses.[43] In other words, were they what we might call a therapeutic community?

In typically Pauline parenesis, he then urges the community "through love [*agapēs*] be slaves [*douleuete*] of one another,[44] and to love the neighbour as the self" (Galatians 5:13–14). Paul reminds the Galatians of the fruit of the Spirit (community attitudes): love, kindness, generosity (5:22). He urges them to bear one another's burdens[45] and so fulfill the law of Christ (6:2). The picture we have is of mutual service within the community, a practice Paul advocates as a community-building tactic (see Betz 1979, 273–74). In 6:9–10 he tells the Galatians to "sow [presumably good works] to the Spirit so as to reap eternal life," and then continues, "So let us not grow weary in doing what is right [*kalon poiountes*],[46] for we will reap at harvest time, if we do not give up. So then, whenever we have an opportunity, let us work for the good of all [*ergazōmetha to agathon pros pantas*], and especially for those of the household of faith."[47] Given Paul's concern about community factions, his qualification is thus understandable.[48] Yet although Paul wishes his flock to direct the majority of their efforts to fellow believers, he apparently does not exclude work among others.

In addition to charitable ministry, perhaps we can see healings and exorcisms among the Galatians, in the charismatic miracles or powerful deeds (*dynameis*) that Paul asserts continue to happen (3:5, cf. Betz 1979, 135n78). Lending credence to this supposition are accounts in Acts of Paul's miracles in southern Galatia: the healing of the cripple at Lystra (Acts 14:8–18), and the unspecified "signs and wonders" (*sēmeia kai terata*) done by Paul and Barnabas at Iconium (Acts 14:3). We know that healing was performed and considered to be one of the gifts of the Spirit in at least one Pauline community (1 Corinthians 12:28, *charismata iamatōn*).[49] The Pauline-related healing located closest to Sardis and Smyrna is recounted in Acts 16:8: the resuscitation or resurrection of Eutychus at Alexandria Troas (on the northwestern coast of Asia).

We next consider deutero-Pauline material. The city of Ephesus was a hub for western Asia Minor,[50] and thus the letter to the Ephesians may be an encyclical letter, one generally applicable to churches throughout western Asia Minor (Arnold 1989, 6, 13–14). Ephesus was a centre of magic in western Asia Minor.[51] Since a common use of magic is for its supposed apotropaic powers (the ability to ward off or relieve demonic influence), and since illness in the ancient world was commonly attributed to demons, one might suppose that Christian healers would be in competition, in the popular imagination, with magicians.[52] This is certainly the picture presented in Acts 19:11–20, as Paul engages in contests of power with the sons of Sceva (who exorcise) and the magicians of Ephesus (Arnold 1989, 30–31). This picture is not developed in the epistle to the Ephesians.[53] The general theme of this letter is the cosmic plan of God, enacted by the *ekklēsia* in group unity and practical adherence to household codes. The impression we get is of an inward-looking community, and there is no sense of open networks to the outside world.[54] This does not seem to be of much relevance to the points we examine in this letter. For example, in Ephesians 4:11, the list of gifts of the Spirit (cf. 1 Corinthians 12:4–11), there is no mention of healers.

Colossians likewise has few matters for us to consider. Some teachers were urging the Colossian church to engage in esoteric worship of celestial beings and strict observance of holy times (Lohse 1971, 3). To counter this, the Pauline writer urges the community to bear fruit in God-pleasing practical social matters. He mentions that they should do every good work (1:10, *en panti ergō agathō*), and clothe themselves with good action-oriented attributes, including merciful compassion, kindness, and love (3:12, 14, *oiktirmou, chrestotēta, agapēn*; see Lohse 1971, 146–47).

In the Pastorals, we see early second-century church documents concerned to establish features of institutionalization (MacDonald 1988, 159–20). The location of these texts is often identified as Ephesus. Church order, the regular performance of good works, and job descriptions for group leadership are typical concerns in these texts. The Pastoral writer mentions an office of deacons, and possibly female deacons as well (1 Timothy 3:8–13),[55] and an order of widows (5:3–16). Among the tasks of these groups were charitable acts of ministry to the sick and poor.[56]

In particular, widows' tasks are to be charitable and to perform the typically domestic duties of the ideal woman in Greco-Roman society (1 Timothy 5:10). She must be well attested for her good works (*ergois kalois*), as one who has brought up children, shown hospitality, washed the saint's feet, helped the afflicted (*thlibomenois epērkesen*), and devoted herself to doing good in every way (*panti ergō agathō epēkolouthēsen*).[57] This list of activities seems primarily to be in-house (especially hospitality and ministry to the "saints"); however, some activities could also be directed to outsiders or potential converts.[58] The same could be said for the next section, where the writer urges the wealthy to do good (*agathoergein*), to be rich in good works (*ploutein en ergois kalois*), to be generous (*koinōnikous*), and to be ready to share (1 Timothy 6:18). In Titus 2:7 and 14 we see a similar concern with the performance of good works.

Johannine Community

From the perspective of this paper, the Apocalypse of John truly presents a two-edged sword (1:16; 2:12, 16; 19:15, 21)! On the one hand, we have references to the churches of Sardis (3:1–6) and Smyrna (2:8–11) and their local situations. Other churches in western Asia are also named (1:4, 11) and discussed: Ephesus (2:1–7), Pergamum (2:12–17), Thyatira (2:18–28), Philadelphia (3:7–13), and Laodicea (3:14–22). These passages should give us some of the evidence we need.[59] Yet these references are narrowly focused, and the prophetic material that follows the epistolary greetings is (to put it mildly) symbolic and cryptic. Prosaic matters such as charity are low on the seer's agenda. He seeks to strengthen his audience in the face of anticipated persecution, by means of exhortation and disclosure of his visions of the near future. His message is that the present conditions in Asia Minor (most likely 95, during the Domitian persecutions)[60] are a time of testing. Local churches must cultivate patient endurance, wait watchfully, and reject false teachers.

Antagonism towards the "world" (the Roman Empire) suggests that Stark's theory of open network interactions does not apply here at this time, at least not in the seer's opinion. The network is, in fact, quite closed, as is further indicated by the concern with avoiding heterodox teachers. We might also expect that heightened parousial expectations (e.g., 1:7; 3:11; 22:20) would make mundane activities such as charity or a social ministry seem irrelevant.[61] That being noted, it is still possible to glean some potentially relevant information from this text.

First, we examine the sections on Sardis and Smyrna. There seems to be little of use for this paper in the greeting to Sardis (Revelation 3:1–6). References to being alive and then dead may relate to apostasy, indifference, or accommodation to the Greco-Roman society. There is some information relevant to our case in the greeting to Smyrna (Revelation 2:8–11). There are references in 2:9 to affliction (*thlipsis*) and poverty (*ptōchos*).[62] Revelation 2:10 warns of impending persecution and the prospect of martyrdom (see also Revelation 6:9–11). Mounce (1977, 92) speculates that believers in Smyrna faced pressures from the imperial cult and a large, possibly antagonistic Jewish population (Revelation 2:9): "In an antagonistic environment it would be difficult for a Christian to make a living, and thus many were economically destitute. They may also have been the victims of mob violence and looting" (cf. Hebrews 10:34). Hemer speculates that a contributing cause to the suffering and poverty was "devoted Christians [who] on occasion reduced themselves to penury by the liberality of their own giving" (1986, 68).[63]

We should also consider whether the vision portion of the text provides background information. Here the images are of interest. Of course they are symbolic, and that means two things: that their meaning derives primarily from tradition (apocalyptic stock images), and that they may not be referring literally to local events. However, I would suggest that if conditions matched the images, the images would be a powerful rhetorical tool and would resonate more with the audience—the goal of the seer, surely.[64] We know that the chief causes of famine are drought and war: the influx of troops places stress on limited food supplies. Famine leads to disease and death, compounding the deaths that result from war (Garnsey 1988, 25-26, 32-33; Hamel 1990, 44-56). These factors come into play strikingly in the depictions of the various horsemen. The rider on the red horse represents war (6:4), the rider on the white horse represents military conquest (6:2),[65] the rider on the black horse represents famine (6:5-6),[66] and the rider on the pale horse is someone who will kill with sword, famine, pestilence, and ravaging wild animals (6:8). The visions also contain references to plagues and diseases[67] and earthquakes.[68]

We can also consider the Johannine letters. Second-century traditions locate them in Ephesus (Brown 1979, 98-99). The only issue relevant to our case in these short letters is that of hospitality. We have seen reference to hospitality in other texts, and in all cases what we see are in-house efforts. Itinerant Christian teachers are being provided with food and lodging for a brief period by settled Christian householders. So there is no open network here, contra Stark. In fact, the matter is even more definite, and closed. In 3 John 5-8, giving service to brethren, especially visiting strangers, is described. To encourage his audience, the letter-writer notes that these travelling teachers "accept no support from the non-believers" (*apo tōn ethnikōn*).[69]

Apocryphal Acts

When we consider this segment of early Christian literature we move into interesting and controversial areas.[70] On the one hand there is a strong endorsement of asceticism and celibacy in the texts. On the other, there are often many fantastic accounts of the apostles engaging in contests of miraculous power with opponents or before skeptical crowds. Disdain for the physical body is balanced by healing of the body.

In this section, I focus on an area of conversion ignored by Stark, that of charismatic healing and the propaganda value of miracle accounts. The second- to fourth-century world was one in which miracles and magic were part of the basic world view. MacMullen pointedly summarizes this perspective: "The people of the Roman Empire...took miracles quite for granted. That was the general starting point. Not to believe in them would have made you seem more than odd, simply irrational, as it would have seemed irrational seriously to suppose that babies are brought by storks"

(1984b, 22).[71] We must, therefore, take seriously the appeal of a religion that could point to miraculous activities happening through its leaders. Quite apart from the prosaic palliative care, which Stark identifies as instrumental in the growth of Christianity, more sensational inducements were offered to potential converts. MacMullen stresses the role of miracle accounts (and the underlying charismatic activities) in producing converts to Christianity: "If the subject of religion arose, it would be the aspects most commonly talked about; and, given the concentration of ancient religion on the relief of sickness or deformity, an exchange of views might most likely begin with the wonderful cures wrought by this or that power. Of all worships, the Christian best and most particularly advertised its miracles by driving out of spirits and laying on of hands" (MacMullen 1984b, 40–41; see also 22, 25–29, 36).

The connection between miracle and conversion is a striking and recurring theme in the apocryphal Acts.[72] Time and again, an apostle heals, exorcises, or resurrects, and in most cases, conversion results. Perkins finds that in the apocryphal Acts, Christianity distinctively promotes itself as a "superior healing cult" (1995, 126, 129). Davies proposes the following highly credible scenario: in many cases, Christianity was spread by itinerant wonder-workers, and the people who preserved the apocryphal traditions about the apostles knew them and perhaps had been healed by them (1980, 30–31). These traditions themselves become an evangelistic tool when the charismatic activity diminishes in the community: stories about miracles become an effective substitute for the miracle itself in attracting adherents.[73] Christian preaching is validated first by charismatic actions (according to many apocryphal Acts accounts), then subsequently by an appeal to traditions about such actions (as the accounts function for their audience).

As noted above, there is a strong connection between charismatic healing and conversion, according to the apocryphal Acts.[74] The Asia Minor provenance of these Greek texts alone makes them worthy of note here. But the *Acts of John* also places many of the accounts in Asia Minor,[75] including Ephesus[76] and Smyrna. So we can examine this text in a little more detail. In *Acts of John* 55, the apostle receives a request from the Smyrnaens to visit the city. In *Acts of John* 56–57, the entire city is assembled to watch John exorcise the twin sons of Antipatros, a prominent citizen. Antipatros offers to pay John, but the apostle demands his conversion instead. The exorcism is effective, and in gratitude the father falls down at John's feet. John instructs the family about trinitarian doctrine, baptizes them, and exhorts the father to give money to the poor.

The *Acts of Paul* is another text worth mentioning. According to Tertullian (*De Bapt.* 17), the text was composed by a presbyter in Asia Minor. *Acts of Paul* 4 places Paul in Myra (a city on the southern coast of the Roman province of Lycia in Asia Minor), where he heals Hermocrates, who converts. Other manuscripts of *Acts of Paul* note that he visited Smyrna, but we lack further information on his activities there (Schneelmelcher 1992, 263). There are folk traditions in southern Asia Minor about Thecla, Paul's associate in *Acts Paul*. These accounts credit her with miraculous healing abilities (discussed in MacDonald 1983, 92).

There is another feature associated with the apocryphal Acts: Aside from charismatic healing, the social factor most often associated with conversion is hospitality. Maier (1991, 151) notes,

> The household is the primary setting of these Acts. There are numerous passages which describe the hospitality offered by a wealthy householder to the wandering apostle, worship services conducted by the apostle in a wealthy person's home, and even leadership arising from patronage. All of the passages which describe hospitality offered to an apostle present wealthy people who either become Christians or are attracted to the apostle in such a way that they invite him to lodge with them. This inevitably results in the establishment of the wealthy person's home as a place of teaching and worship.

In the case of the healing of Lycomedes and his wife (*Acts of John* 19–25, above), the apostle is rewarded for his efforts by hospitality at the cured person's home. On the basis of patterns of benefaction, we might assume that in the hospitality and leadership we have wealthy people seeking to advance their status in society by becoming patrons of a group, in this case Christianity.[77]

Ignatius and Polycarp

The writings of two bishops inform us about Christianity in early second-century Asia Minor. Ignatius, bishop of Antioch (ca. 35–107 CE), writes several letters to churches he visits (including Smyrna and Ephesus) on his farewell tour prior to martyrdom in Rome.[78] Ignatius's young associate, Polycarp (ca. 65–156 CE), is bishop of Smyrna. Polycarp collects the correspondence of Ignatius and also writes a letter from Smyrna to the church at Philippi. From this correspondence, we have brief but valuable evidence that Christian charity—perhaps including ministry to the sick—was practised in Asia Minor.

In his letter to the Smyrnaen group (*Smyrn.* 6.2), Ignatius commends them and contrasts their behaviour with that of others whom he views as schismatic dissenters:

> Now observe those who hold erroneous opinions about the grace [*tēn charin*][79] of Jesus Christ which came to us, how they are opposed to God's purpose: for love [*agapēs*] they have no care, none for the widow,

none for the orphan, none for the distressed,[80] none for the afflicted [*thlibomenou*], none for the prisoner [*dedemenou*], or for him released from prison [*lelumenou*],[81] none for the hungry or thirsty; they remain aloof from eucharist and prayers because they do not confess that the eucharist is the flesh of our savior Jesus Christ.[82]

Assessing the social reality behind Ignatius's rhetoric is no simple task. He probably has polarized the situation. First, we must note the context of this discussion. Ignatius is concerned with a faction in the Smyrnaen Christian community that has heterodox theology and, perhaps reflecting this theology, has withdrawn from common eucharistic celebrations. We know from *Smyrn.* 8.2 that this group had their own eucharistic meal, one not supervised by Polycarp the bishop. In Ignatius's mind, the practice of the group is linked to their theology,[83] and it threatens group unity.

Second, we should adopt a cautious assessment of the extent of the love or charity that the "heterodox" Smyrnaens are extending. Most likely, it is primarily the collection gathered at the eucharist celebration and distributed later to the poor and sick of the church.[84] If the Eucharist is also an *agapē* meal (suggested by Ignatius's choice of words; see also *Smyrn.* 8.2), then the meal itself could have been a form of charity. Ignatius's critique here is that since the schismatics are not partaking of the common Eucharist, they are not engaging in the "love" (formal charitable elements) that the love-meal entails (Shepherd 1940, 148; Lampe 1966, 55; Schoedel 1985, 242). The faction may well have been sympathetic to the poor and sick of the church,[85] but since the group is docetic[86] and possibly "incipient Gnostic,"[87] their primary concern would have been with individual spiritual advancement rather than social ministry, and there may have been a tendency to elitism (Schoedel 1985, 240). So we have evidence that charitable ministry was the norm for Smyrnaen Christians, though it was probably in-house.[88]

A few other passages from Ignatius add to the picture. In his letter to Polycarp, Ignatius advises him that a bishop must act as a strong leader in several ways, in particular to "bear the illnesses of all [*pantōn tas nosous bastaze*] as a perfect athlete" (*Pol.* 1.3). Unfortunately (for our purposes) this seems to be a stock rhetorical flourish[89] rather than practical advice on ministry to the sick. More significant is Ignatius's attitude towards the polytheist world. He advises the Ephesian church,

> But pray on behalf of other people unceasingly, for there is hope of repentance in them that they may attain God. Let them learn at least from your deeds to become disciples. Before their anger be gentle, before their boastfulness be humble, before their slandering [offer] prayers, before their deceit be fixed in faith, before their fierceness be mild, not being eager to imitate them in return. Let us be found [to be] their brothers in gentleness. (*Eph.* 10.1, in Schoedel 1985, 69)

This is a remarkable passage in its irenic tone and accommodation towards outsiders.[90] However, it is not quite as positive as it seems at first glance—most notably in the characteristics of the non-believers, who are portrayed as angry, boastful, slanderous, deceitful, and fierce! However, Ignatius still calls them brothers. Unfortunately, for our purposes, nowhere does he mention extending charity or healing to them. The "deeds" enjoined upon the Ephesians that may result in conversion are those done by role models of patient suffering. We do see here an open network, at least in theory.

Polycarp instructs the church at Phillipi to ensure that charitable works continue: "Let the presbyters also be compassionate, merciful to all, bringing back those that have wandered, caring for all the weak [*pantas astheneis*], neglecting neither widow, nor orphan nor poor [*hē penētos*]" (Polycarp, *Phil*. 6.1).[91] Since Ignatius also mentions "the widows" in his letter to Polycarp (*Pol*. 4.3), we can assume that this group existed in Smyrna, receiving charity and perhaps giving it to other women.[92]

Other Evidence

Other evidence from Christian sources is sketchy. Early Christian inscriptions in Asia Minor attest to the presence of deacons and bishops overseeing their efforts (Buckler 1932, 185). In the middle of the second century in Bithynia, Pliny interrogates two female *ministrae*, likely deaconesses (10.96). We also have late evidence of deacons in Sardis (V–VI CE stele in Buckler 1932, 148, no. 189).[93]

Montanism arose in Asia and Phrygia in the mid-second century and flourished there for a few hundred years. According to ancient sources, Christianity at the time of Montanus, Priscilla, and Maximilla faced persecutions, inner conflicts, and social turbulence (including warfare and plague).[94] One wonders about the connection between conditions of plague and warfare and the appeal of the new prophecy of the Montanists. Charismatic prophecy had a long lineage in the region: aside from the Johannine seer, we know of Philip and his four daughters, active in Phrygian Hierapolis.[95] Part of the answer to this question may lie in the appeal of prophecy and apocalypse during periods of economic hardship and social upheaval. Dickey provides an interesting discussion of this issue. In outlining the various causes of social unrest (famine and food shortages, inflated food prices, class conflict, economic exploitation of the urban poor), he notes, "Therefore when Christianity entered with its promise of a 'new age' of righteousness inaugurated by divine power, which involved 'feeding the hungry with good things' and 'exalting those of low degree,' it could not help but get a hearing" (1928, 411).

In addition to the *Apocalypse of John* and the earlier messianic age perspective of Paul, Dickey points out that another apocalyptic tradition can be associated with Asia Minor: "Irenaeus of Lyons, himself a native of Asia Minor, attributes to the Elders, who saw John the disciple of the Lord in Asia, the story found in the Syriac *Apocalypse of Baruch*, of the fabulous vine-stocks of the Messianic age, each of which bore a thousand branches, etc." (1928, 412).[96] Furthermore, according to Irenaeus, this vision of an overflowing abundance of vines, grain, fruit, and meat for the faithful is attested in the writings of Papias, the disciple of John, friend of Polycarp of Smyrna, and bishop of Hierapolis in the second century. Dickey continues, "If this was the sort of gospel Papias preached up and down the Lycus valley, we can picture without much difficulty wherein lay the point of its appeal. Nor was Papias alone. The whole Chiliastic movement, of which he was a distinguished representative, was a literalistic emphasis on Christian apocalypticism. Montanism, again, was a recrudescence of the apocalyptic elements in Christianity, and Montanism was primarily a phenomenon of Asia Minor" (1928, 412). The connection between the utopian visions in some apocalypses and social conditions may also be linked to Christian charitable work, although how remains unclear.

Post-Constantinian evidence reflects either the institutionalized setting in which Christianity found itself, or the growing trend of hagiography and legendary stories about saints. In Sardis, we have a sixth-century Christian inscription concerning at least one polytheist who was interned in a *xenon*, a hospice for the sick poor (Duff 1926, 85, 89; Buckler 1932, 43, no. 19; Foss 1976, 22, 29, 116). Popular legends about Gregory Thaumaturgus, the hero figure of Christian evangelism in the Pontic countryside, portray him as a miraculous protector against plague, earthquake, and demons.[97] Therapon, a third-century saint associated with Sardis, had a healing site associated with the spot where he was arrested and tortured: "The earth, enriched by his blood, brought forth a great oak tree which is shown, always blooming, up to the present day; it cures every disease and weakness."[98]

Significant are the actions of Basil of Cappadocia during a prolonged famine in the region in the late 360s (Holman 1999). In his panegyric on Basil, Gregory Nazianzus describes how Basil, in his capacity as bishop, alleviated the suffering:

> For by his word and advice he opened the stores of those who possessed them, and, so, according to the Scripture dealt food to the hungry, and satisfied the poor with bread, and fed them in the time of dearth, and filled the hungry souls with good things. And in what way? For this is no slight addition to his praise. He gathered together the victims of the famine with some who were but slightly recovering from it, men and women, infants, old men, every age which was in distress, and obtaining contributions of all sorts of food which can relieve famine, set before them basins of soup and such meat as was pre-

served among us, on which the poor live. Then, imitating the ministry of Christ, Who, girded with a towel, did not disdain to wash the disciples' feet, using for this purpose the aid of his own servants [deacons], he attended to the bodies and souls of those who needed it, combining personal respect with the supply of their necessity, and so giving them a double relief. (*Or.* 43.35, in NPNF 7.406)

Here we see an example of a development in the post-Constantinian church: bishops become "protectors of the poor." Drawing on the patronage exchange system prevalent in the Greco-Roman world, bishops increased their power and influence by tapping into a previously unaffiliated group, the urban poor. Charity towards these poor resulted in their loyalty and support.[99]

Conclusion

The evidence for Stark's theses in Smyrna and Sardis is suggestive but sparse. It appears that the churches of Smyrna and Sardis, like many other Christian communities, practised charity, including care of the sick and poor, at least within their own communities. The plagues identified by Stark, along with other social problems, created opportunities for Christian groups to practise charity towards outsiders. However, it also appears that there would have been competition from the Asclepius cult, other healing cults, magicians, and sometimes even physicians.

Christian engagement in charismatic healing, and the development of traditions around such events, may have exerted an appeal to join the group. However, the actual evidence for Christian charity beyond their own groups is difficult to find, particularly in the first few centuries. Our investigation of the evidence for Smyrna and Sardis, and the surrounding region of Asia Minor, suggests that while Stark's argument is at least plausible, the lack of firm evidence means that it is somewhat exaggerated.

10

Martyrdom
In Accordance with the Gospel

Wayne O. McCready

Introduction

Robert L. Wilken, in *The Land Called Holy: Palestine in Christian History and Thought*, observes that Christians, from their earliest origins, were inclined to express their religiosity at places where fellow-Christians were buried. "Like Greeks and Romans who built shrines to mark the place where they buried their famous dead or celebrated the exploits of mythical heroes, Christians constructed memorials to their dead. Called *martyria* (places that bear witness), these rooms were erected over the site where the martyr had been buried" (Wilken 1992, 91).

This study investigates how martyrdom, as a feature of ancient religion, assists investigation of relations between Jews and Christians in the second century CE—and demonstrates the coming-to-be of a particular religious self-definition when two sibling religious movements interact. Specifically, the study will consider the account of Polycarp's martyrdom, in a letter addressed by the church of Smyrna to the church of Philomelium that was written shortly after Polycarp's death in 155 CE. The letter, written for a wide readership, eventually gained significant profile for Christians when Irenaeus and Polycrates affirmed Polycarp's death as a martyrdom in the emerging apostolic tradition. At the beginning of the fourth century CE, Eusebius cites the letter extensively in *Historia ecclesiastica* 4.15, either by direct quotation or by paraphrase, with the consequence that the martyrdom of Polycarp functioned as a core reference for Eusebius's depiction of early Christian history.

Smyrna dates from the tenth century BCE, when Aeolians migrated to this portion of Asia Minor to be displaced later by Ionian exiles from Clazomenai in the eighth century (Cook 1958/59). Excavations indicate that

---

Smyrna had a centralized civic organization early in its history, but the city gained prominence in the second century BCE when it aligned with Rome against Antiochus III by building a temple to the goddess Roma (Cadoux 1938, 94–141). By the beginning of the Common Era, Rome viewed it as one of four important centres in Asia Minor (along with Ephesus, Sardis, and Pergamum), and eventually it served as the provincial *neokoros* (ward) of temples (Price 1984, 258). Primary source materials, and scholarly critique of those sources, suggest that Smyrna was frequently a city of conflict between wealthy and poor, as well as between local and imperial authorities (see, for example, Philostratus, Polemo, and Aelius Aristides; cf. Cadoux 1938, 254–281; Bowersock 1968, 22–49; see further, Ascough, chap. 1).

The depiction of the larger societal context frames most assessments of the early Christian community at Smyrna, which is understood to be in conflict with a powerful local Jewish community (see Cadoux 1938, 343–400; Fox 1986, 462–92). This study will consider alternative assessments of Jewish and Christian relations at Smyrna, and review the predominant working hypothesis of conflict theory. Miriam Taylor's book *Anti-Judaism and Early Christian Identity: A Critique of the Scholarly Consensus* (1995) provides a helpful directive in this regard—especially with reference to using rhetorical analysis rather than conflict theory for understanding relations between religious rivalries at Smyrna. The essential questions to be addressed are (1) what is the role of Jews depicted in the *Martyrdom of Polycarp*, and (2) what does that role tell us about religious rivalry between Jews and Christians in Smyrna?

Parameters for the Question and Related Issues

Taylor examines a range of views on Jewish–Christian interaction in the patristic period, and she estimates that Marcel Simon's *Versus Israel: A Study of Relations between Christians and Jews in the Roman Empire* (ET 1986, 135–425) sets the tone for widespread consensus about Christian anti-Judaism that can be characterized as "conflict theory" (Taylor 1995, 2). The essential feature of the theory is that Christian anti-Judaism in antiquity was a consequence of spirited competition between Jews and Christians, when Jewish mission came into conflict with Christian mission. Baumgarten has noted that Simon's analysis has the benefit of locating Christian anti-Judaism in a certain time and place, and hence countered the tendency to see anti-Judaism as necessarily endemic to Christianity (Baumgarten 1999, 472). Although Simon attempts to correct long-standing theological biases against Judaism in Christian scholarship, as a consequence of his analysis conflict theory became the normative starting point in assessing the social settings for Christian anti-Judaism in antiquity. Will and Orrieux argue that much of the evidence used by Simon in his assessment of Judaism was internal to Jewish communities and was not directed toward early Christians (Will and Orrieux 1992). Goodman proposes that relations between Christians and Jews in the first two centuries of the Common Era cannot be reduced to a single theory, and that much of the evidence used by Simon should be understood with reference to God-fearers (Goodman 1994, 130; also Reynolds and Tannenbaum 1987; for an alternative position to Goodman's, see Feldman 1993b; cf. Carleton-Paget 1996). Taylor finds the theory wanting as a hermeneutical principle and as a helpful directive for assessing historical and social relationships between Judaism and Christianity in antiquity. She argues that it fails to adequately account for the anti-Judaism expressed in early Christian literature.

As an alternative working thesis, Taylor applies the theoretical analysis of Clifford Geertz (1966, 1973, 1983) to the importance of religious symbolism for communicating and developing a distinctive culture—in this case, a Christian culture promoting a divine destiny for the new people of God. The anti-Jewish viewpoints expressed in early Christian literature were theological motifs that emerged from the internal theoretical process of identity-formation in Christianity. Taylor observes that minimal attention is paid to the genre and theological language of patristic texts that express anti-Jewish viewpoints; undue weight is frequently placed on an "empathetic reconstruction" intent on discovering a social reality behind the text that can even be expressed unconsciously and unintentionally (Taylor 1995, 156). She recommends cultural analysis as a helpful hermeneutical tool for investigating Christian anti-Judaism, as it has the capacity to allow such anti-Jewish statements to remain in their theological context. There is no need to push unduly for a more "objective" social and psychological reality if the source material does not warrant it. Indeed, anti-Jewish sentiments can be viewed as motifs created to provide a distinctive understanding of the world; they are parts of a larger holistic theological vision that sought to interpret salvation history, define early Christianity within that salvation context, and articulate how it fit within a divine destiny (Taylor 1995, 159; cf. Geertz 1966, 3). A similar strategy is helpful when investigating the synagogue expulsion episode in John 9 (see McCready 1990).

The emerging tension between the early Jesus movement and its larger Jewish heritage was the essence of, and challenge for, a new religious identity. The narrative in John 9 is a demonstration of discontinuity with the Jewish component of the early Jesus movement, and it gives insight into the dialectic of Christian definition. The point to be underscored is that the episode represents something about Christian self-definition, and attention must be paid to the primacy of the gospel message that gives form and substance to the narrative. John 9 is not a source for the origins of a rift between Judaism and Christianity—it is a distinctive statement about being a first-century CE Christian. The *Martyrdom of Polycarp* will be treated in a similar manner in this study. We will begin by determining how it represents ancient Christian religiosity before moving to matters of Jewish and Christian relations in Smyrna.

The *Martyrdom of Polycarp* and Rhetorical Analysis

The *Martyrdom of Polycarp* belongs to the genre of *martyria* (see Dehandschutter 1979, 157–89). However, the narrative in the *Martyrdom* has a specific focus and warrants rhetorical analysis, as it fits the profile of a deliberative discourse in persuading its readership of a particular viewpoint: the martyrdom of Polycarp is in accordance with the gospel (*Mart. Pol.* 1.1), his martyrdom is worthy of imitation since it follows the gospel of Christ (*Mart. Pol.* 19.1), and, most important, Christians will not abandon Christ or worship another god (*Mart. Pol.* 17.2). These primary features of the deliberative discourse are illustrative of an observation of Barth on ethnic identity and attitudinal boundaries (1969; 1981, 9–10). Emerging ethnic identity frequently develops strong convictions about a select and limited number of values or behaviours that define them in comparison with other groups with whom they may have close contact. The select and distinctive factors of difference create boundaries that have a positive impact on a developing identity.

On a related point about deliberative discourse as addressing essential principles for self-definition, Classen observes that almost all Greek and Roman rhetoric is closely related to educational purposes and intention—with the aim of defining oneself by means of contrast (1995, 522).[1] Such self-definition has an "agonistic" dimension (based on *agon*—"contest, combative, having to do with competition") that promoted a competitive spirit, as well as mutual criticism and self-criticism (Classen 1995, 533).

This aggressive dimension of rhetoric is also noted by Eden in *Hermeneutics and the Rhetorical Tradition* (1997): a great deal of rhetoric had to do with the adversative and antagonistic environment of law courts. Eden also calls attention to the importance of determining the whole over against the parts when dealing with Greco-Roman rhetoric. An advocate was trained to consider both the whole text and the whole set of circumstances when arguing a legal case before the courts. What a person meant to say or do was best understood in its broadest context (Eden 1997, 18–19).

Martyrdom as Discourse

Daniel Boyarin's research (1999) serves as an essential directive for this study. Boyarin argues that Judaism and Christianity interacted in complex ways in the first centuries of the Common Era, with martyrology (perhaps better understood as proto-martyrology until the third and fourth centuries CE) functioning as a multi-faceted discourse that was shared between the two religions in their formative stages. His examination of proto-martyrological discourse suggests there was close contact and dialogue between the religions; martyrology was an important factor for self-definition in the coming-to-be of each religion. His recommended metaphor for this circumstance is "the entwining of the ways" (Boyarin 1998, 578). Boyarin's analysis seeks to find a middle ground between Frend's view (1967) that martyrdom was a Jewish practice taken over by Christians, and Bowerstock (1995) who views martyrdom as inherent in Roman society, which became Christianized and was subsequently adopted by Judaism (cf. Laurence and Berry 1998; Rutgers 1995; Rajak 2001). Boyarin cautions that both Frend and Bowersock work from a faulty first principle: that Judaism and Christianity were two separate entities, and hence there are distinct sources of origin for martyrdom.

Boyarin proposes that the relationship between the two emerging religions had less to do with argument and exchange between religious authorities and more to do with "complex dialectical processes of negotiations of difference and sameness, samenesses masked as differences, and sometimes differences that appear as sameness" (1998, 581). He notes the similarities between accounts of Akiba and Polycarp (e.g., the proconsul speaks to the respective sages with concern for their well-being, and both sages are unwavering in their resolve, even with death immediately before them). Working from a third-century CE Tosefta passage (cf. *Ḥullin* 2.24) about Rabbi Elie'zer being arrested as a Christian and avoiding difficulties through a clever play on words ("I trust the judge") rather than cursing Jesus, Boyarin makes a spirited case for understanding the complex relationship that existed between Judaism and Christianity in antiquity. Rabbi Elie'zer may have been attracted intellectually and spiritually to early Christianity—without giving up his Judaism in an either/or circumstance. Rather than curse Jesus, he took his chances with wordplay in a critical life situation; for Boyarin (following Lieberman 1944), Rabbi Elie'zer thematizes the complexities of relations between Jews and Christians. He suggests that there is circulation and reworking of common motifs, themes, and multi-religious sources that contributed to the making of a new religious self-understanding based on martyrdom with no simple and straightforward source of origins and influence (cf. Hasan-Rokem 1999; also Sherwin-White 1952,

1963, 1974; de Ste Croix 1974a, 1974b). Boyarin summarizes the issue well: "This evidence suggests that, far from the complete separations implied by the usual metaphors of the 'parting of the ways,' the interaction of rabbinic Judaism and Christianity throughout Late Antiquity, and perhaps indeed, forever, was marked [as much] by convergence as by divergence, and we would do well to think, indeed, of encounters and meetings at least as much as of separations and partings" (1998, 627).

Before turning more directly to the *Martyrdom of Polycarp*, it may be helpful to summarize additional parameters of this study. First, there will be a guarded approach to thinking that conflict was an important or essential principle in the *Martyrdom*, unless the text warrants such an analysis. A controlling principle for assessing the *Martyrdom* will be the need to look at the whole picture represented by the letter, and to consider the role of Jews depicted in the text in light of that holistic focus. Mature religions frequently map out a total system of symbols (e.g., words, ideas, rituals, social groups) that depict the human condition in light of views of the sacred. These symbols are the means by which a group can address questions such as who are we, what life is about, and what the future holds. While the symbols represent essential attitudes and viewpoints, they are part of a dynamic circumstance as religions address new issues, new experiences, and new challenges. The religious symbolism in the *Martyrdom* functioned as part of a developing Christian culture defining a new people of God who were suffering and facing death for their beliefs and practices.

The *Martyrdom of Polycarp* seeks to persuade its readership not to abandon Christ or worship another god (*Mart. Pol.* 17.2), even in the face of severe persecution. It uses a master story in the form of proto-martyrology involving Polycarp,[2] who serves as the model establishing a "map" or directive for Christian living in the mid- to late second-century CE. As we shall see, Polycarp's martyrdom is "in accordance with the gospel" (*Mart. Pol.* 1.1), and he is worthy of imitation because he followed that gospel (*Mart. Pol.* 19.1). Knowing this story means knowing how Christians are to live, even in difficult situations. Boyarin's analysis that Judaism and Christianity were part of a complex dialectic of negotiated differences and sameness that included an emerging and shared concept of martyrology suggests that these two religious rivals were involved in the entwining of their ways.

One final comment on controlling parameters derives from Peter Brown in *The Making of Late Antiquity* (1978, 55). Brown proposes that the citizens of Smyrna were used to violence and death in light of the gladiators and beast hunters. Few would be impressed by Christians facing death for religious convictions. Thus, citing Polycarp's martyrdom as a witness for the gospel and noting that he was much admired by the police, the crowds, and the proconsul has the rhetorical purpose within the *Martyrdom* of drawing the *reader* into the viewpoint of the narration. One can be admired for faithfulness to Christianity, even in the face of death. Brown's view is that the process of self-definition of Christians at Smyrna was working from its own set of orientations that included claims of a new order of things involving discontinuity, challenges, and certain consequences for Christians. Taylor's caution about conflict theory is well taken, and it may be helpful to look to the *Martyrdom* as part of a conscious and deliberate process of self-shaping on the part of early Christianity. Boyarin notes that there was a gradual shift away from a proto-martyr tradition found before the Common Era, where victims refused to give up their religious integrity. These persons were executed during the emerging Christian martyrological tradition in the first centuries of the Common Era, when martyrdom became a possible response to the situation. Death was a religious experience that served group identity and group self-definition (Boyarin 1998, 606–7; cf. Brown 1978, 55).

The *Martyrdom of Polycarp* Reconsidered

In the following summary outline of the *Martyrdom of Polycarp* it is important to emphasize that the questions before us have to do with the role of Jews as outlined in the text, and what that role tells us about religious rivalry at Smyrna. The passages where Jews appear in the *Martyrdom* are highlighted below, in italics.

Summary Account of the Martyrdom of Polycarp[3]

The *Martyrdom of Polycarp* is a letter written by the church at Smyrna to the church at Philomelium and other communities of the holy and catholic church. Note the wide readership anticipated in the letter.

Introduction: Mart. Pol. 1
- The letter is the story of martyrs and Polycarp, who put an end to persecutions with his martyrdom (he was a "seal" of witnessing for early Christianity).
- Polycarp is an example of martyrdom "in accordance with the gospel" (1.1).
- He was betrayed—as was Christ.
- Imitators of Christ are those who demonstrate Christian love; they wish not to be saved alone but with all brothers.

The deliberative discourse here attempts to persuade the reader of an ultimate valuation: the martyrdom of Polycarp stands in apostolic tradition as an imitation of Christ. Note that betrayal is identified as a core feature that links Christ to Polycarp, and the reader is alerted that the party of betrayal will likely emerge in the narrative in due course. Further, the ultimate valuation of fellow-Christian martyrdom distinguishes the in-group from others and, hence, creates an identity boundary that gains a pointed quality because the hero figure was betrayed. Note Classen's agonistic principle cited above that underscores how combative and critical deliberative discourse can be.

Account of martyrdoms that preceded Polycarp: Mart. Pol. 2–4

- Blessings are pronounced on the martyrdoms that took place according to the will of God (note the importance of assigning power over all things to God, 2.1).
- Martyrs, by their deaths, are no longer humans but already angels (2.3).
- Germanicus was martyred by wild beasts and demonstrated particular courage (3.1).
- Crowds wonder at the nobility (bravery) of Christians (who are characterized as God-loving and God-fearing); nevertheless there are calls for "atheists" to be done away with; crowds demand that Polycarp be found.
- An account is given of Quintus (a Phrygian), who at first forced himself and some others to come forward on their own accord and then lost his nerve; the proconsul persuades Quintus and others to take the oath and offer sacrifice (4.1).
- The *Martyrdom* recommends that Christians not give themselves up, since the gospel does not promote this teaching (4.1).

Following Barth's thesis about ethnic identity and attitudinal boundaries, this segment of the *Mart. Pol.* suggests that a bonded fellowship is a mark of Christian identity that is recognized within the Christian community (martyrs are already angels), as well as by others (crowds recognize the bravery of Christians).

Martyrdom of Polycarp: Mart. Pol. 5–18

- Polycarp's retreat to safety in the country—*Mart. Pol.* 5
  - Polycarp retreats on the advice of others (5.1).
  - While praying, he falls into a trance three days before his arrest; he sees his pillow on fire and understands that he will be burned alive in martyrdom (5.2).
- Polycarp's arrest—*Mart. Pol.* 6–8
  - The police captain who arrests Polycarp is a man named Herod (6.2)
  - Herod, by taking Polycarp to the arena, helps to bring about Polycarp's appointed destiny; those who betray Polycarp (they

are from his own house) are destined to suffer a fate similar to that of Judas (6.2).

– Polycarp is arrested while in an upper room; he gives himself up willingly in order that the will of God be done (7.1).

– Polycarp is led into the city on an ass on a "great Sabbath day" (8.1).

– Herod and his father (Niketas) recommend that Polycarp say "Lord Caesar," offer a sacrifice, and thus be saved (8.2).

• The trial before the proconsul in the stadium—*Mart. Pol.* 9–11

– Polycarp is taken before the proconsul in the stadium and advised to "swear by the genius of Caesar," repent, and condemn the atheists (9.2).

– Again, the proconsul recommends that Polycarp take the oath and curse Christ (9.3).

– Polycarp responds, "If there is a question of who I am, listen plainly—I am a Christian" (10.1).

– The proconsul yields to the aggression of the crowds (10.2).

– Polycarp is threatened with wild beasts and death by fire, but he does not yield; he responds, "Come, do what you will" (11.2).

• The martyrdom—*Mart. Pol.* 12–18

– Reaction of the crowd—*Mart. Pol.* 12–13

– A herald announces to the crowd three times that Polycarp confessed that he was a Christian (12.1).

– *When this had been said by the herald, the whole multitude of Gentiles and Jews living in Smyrna cried out with uncontrollable wrath and a loud shout: "This is the teacher of Asia, the father of the Christians, the destroyer of our gods, who teaches neither to offer sacrifice nor to worship." They cried out and asked Philip the Asiarch to let loose a lion on Polycarp. But he said he could not legally do this, since he had closed the sports* (literally animal hunt, 12.2).

– The crowd calls for Polycarp to be burned alive, confirming the vision that Polycarp had will be fulfilled; Polycarp tells the faithful, "I must be burnt alive" (12.3).

– The crowd prepares wood and fire: *and the Jews were extremely zealous, as is their custom, in assisting in this* (13.1).

– Polycarp is prepared to endure the fire without being nailed because he is divinely empowered to do so (13.3).

– Polycarp is bound as a ram out of a great flock (14.1).

– Polycarp offers a prayer of thanksgiving. "Share in the cup of Christ…as an acceptable sacrifice," 14.2–3.

- The burning of Polycarp—*Mart. Pol.* 15–16
    - His burning is as bread-baking or gold and silver being refined; it has the smell of incense (15.1).
    - The fire does not consume Polycarp; the executioner stabs him, and a dove comes out of the wound (16.1).
    - Polycarp is one of the elect, a martyr, apostolic and prophetic teacher, the bishop of Smyrna, and his words are fulfilled in his martyrdom (16.2).
- The treatment of Polycarp's remains—*Mart. Pol.* 17–18
    - Concern is raised by Niketas (Herod's father) that if the Christians are given Polycarp's remains, they might worship him.
    - *And they said this owing to the suggestions and pressure of the Jews, who also watched when Polycarp's remains were taken from the fire—for they do not know that we shall not ever be able either to abandon Christ, who suffered for the salvation of those who are being saved in the whole world, the innocent for sinners, or to worship any other* (17.2b).
    - Christians worship Christ as son of God; they love disciples and are imitators of the Lord (17.3).
    - *When therefore the centurion saw the contentiousness caused by the Jews, he put the body in the midst, as was their custom, and burnt it* (18.1).
    - Christians take Polycarp's bones to a meeting place of Christians to celebrate the birthday of his martyrdom (18.2–3).

There are advantages in reading this section of *Martyrdom* as a whole, because it best illustrates what Eden suggests about the adversative features of deliberative discourse. Certain characteristics of Polycarp, despite the nobility of his bravery, are sequentially positioned in the presentation as a Christian response to aggression and persecution: (1) innocence that is recognized by Gentile authorities, (2) calm as a counter to the aggression of his opponents, and (3) bravery when facing death by wild animals or fire. Standing in contrast to these admirable qualities of Polycarp is the depiction of his opponents: (1) Gentile authorities express an angst in arresting Polycarp (8.2: "say 'Lord Caesar,' offer a sacrifice, and be saved"), which illustrates they are far from innocent parties, (2) Jews and Gentiles express uncontrolled vengeance and aggression, and (3) the crowd shows rage. Jews are deliberately profiled in the crowd contexts as particularly combative (contentious, uncontrollable, and applying constant pressure on the Smyrnean authorities). Note that, despite the concern that Polycarp's remains might be revered by his fellow Christians, that is exactly what happens when Polycarp's bones are taken to a Christian meeting place to celebrate his martyrdom (18.2–3).

Conclusion: Mart. Pol. 19–20

- Polycarp was the twelfth martyr in Smyrna; his status as a teacher and notable martyr is worthy of imitation because it followed the gospel of Christ (19.1).
- Marcion was responsible for the composition of the letter (20.1); Evarestus was his scribe (20.2; or Marcion was the authoritative witness and Evarestus was his reporter).

Appendixes

- A chronology is sketched: the date of Polycarp's arrest and execution (21).
- Themes are rehearsed and additional lines of succession from Polycarp are cited (22).

Martyrdom and Rhetorical Discourse

Vernon Robbins, in his *Tapestry of Early Christian Discourse: Rhetoric, Society and Ideology* (1996b, 46–65), outlines five factors of inner texture in rhetorical discourse: (1) repetitive-progressive, (2) opening-middle-closing sequence, (3) narrational voice, (4) argumentative texture, and (5) sensory-aesthetic texture. While all five features of rhetoric are evident in the *Martyrdom of Polycarp* (cf. Lieu 1996, 1998), I would like to place an emphasis on the repetitive-progression pattern that builds to a dramatic conclusion in 17.2b, affirming that Christians do not abandon Christ, who offers universal salvation, and they do not worship another god.

The repetitive-progression highlights four themes.

1. Polycarp's martyrdom is in accordance with the gospel (and other biblical) tradition.
   - This statement is specifically made (1.1).
   - He is betrayed, as was Christ (1.2).
   - All martyrdoms are according to the will of God (2.1).
   - Polycarp has a trance that lasts three days (he sees his pillow on fire, indicating he will be burned alive as a martyr) (5.2).
   - Polycarp is arrested by a police captain named Herod (6.2).
   - He is betrayed by his own followers, as Jesus was by Judas (6.2).
   - Polycarp is led into the city on an ass on a Great Sabbath (Sabbath before Passover) (8.1).
   - When he enters the stadium, a voice from heaven encourages him to be strong and be a man (9.1).

- The proconsul respects Polycarp but eventually yields to the crowds (10.2).
- Polycarp is characterized as a ram out of great flock, an oblation, and a whole burnt offering (14.1).
- As a martyr, he shares in the cup of Christ (14.2).
- The executioner stabs Polycarp, and a dove comes out of the wound (16.1).
- There is concern for Polycarp's remains (17.1–2).

2. Martyrdom is a witness.
   - This statement is made about Polycarp (1.1).
   - Germanicus, who was martyred by wild beasts, is highlighted as a witness to Polycarp (3.1).
   - Polycarp is respected by the police (7–8) and the proconsul (10–11).
   - Polycarp's martyrdom is worthy of imitation since it is in accordance with the gospel (19.1).

3. Invitations are extended to Polycarp to avoid martyrdom and thus compromise Christian worship and belief.
   - He can take an oath to Caesar and sacrifice is all that is required to avoid death (8.2).
   - He can take an oath, repentance, and condemning atheists (9.2).
   - He can take an oath and cursing Christ (9.3).

4. The Jews play a role as part of the crowd's opposition to Polycarp:
   - They are part of a larger crowd, which accuses Polycarp of being the destroyer of gods by teaching not to sacrifice or to worship (12.2).
   - They help stoke the fire to burn Polycarp (even though it was during the Great Sabbath) (13.1).
   - They register concern about Polycarp's remains, fearing Christians might worship him (17.2).
   - They are uncontrollable, loud, and contentious (12.2, 18.1).

The repetitive-progression of all four themes builds toward the primary focus of the *Martyrdom* in 17.2 that Christians do not abandon Christ, and Christian worship of Christ will not be compromised, even in the face of death. These two ideas function as fundamental principles for a developing Christian culture that promotes a new vision of the people of God. A Christian proto-martyrology is the vehicle used to profile a hero figure who best represents Christian identity and self-definition. The four themes function as parts of a larger whole that is, in fact, a claim about salvation-history. The parts are not equally weighted, although each theme has its role to play in order to complete the deliberative discourse.

Principles of Martyrdom

The details associated with gospel traditions and points of contact made with Jewish and Christian scriptures affirm that the threat of martyrdom need not evoke a denial of Christ or jeopardize Christian worship. This principle of martyrdom in accordance with the gospel blends rhetorical argument, social action, and religious belief. With reference to Barth's theory about attitudinal boundaries cited above, the *Martyrdom* selects four themes to create boundaries that distinguish Christians from other groups: (1) martyrdom is in accordance with the gospel, (2) martyrdom is a witness, (3) there will be opportunities to avoid martyrdom that, in fact, compromise Christian worship and belief, (4) there will be opponents of Christians—and among those opponents there will be Jews. The affirmation of standing in a continuum of the gospel tradition, balanced with scriptural overtones from both the Old and New Testaments, provides Christians with an identity unique to them.

The theme of witness plays a secondary role in *Martyrdom*, but it underscores the fact that proselytizing was part of the deep structure of early Christianity (Meyer 1986). The invitation to avoid martyrdom and to compromise Christian practice and belief is powerful in its simplicity. Its position in the narrative when Polycarp stands before the proconsul, together with the witness theme, allows Polycarp to declare he is a Christian (see 10.1). Boyarin notes that the confession "I am a Christian" binds the martyr to all Christians without qualification of place, time, or context and thus serves group identity and self-definition (1998, 608).

Lieu (1996; 1998, 286–87) proposes that the crowds who oppose Polycarp have a universal character. This factor corresponds to Polycarp's exalted status as teacher, notable martyr, and one worthy of imitation (*Mart. Pol.* 19.1). When the narrative focuses on specific details of the martyrdom in 12–18, Jews appear for a rhetorical purpose: they represent uncontrollable wrath (12.2), zeal for the martyrdom (13.1), and suspicions that Polycarp's remains will become a source of worship for Christianity (17.2). On all three accounts, it is hard to conceive that the narrative represents the historical situation of Jews at Smyrna. In 12.2, they are polytheistic (they are part of the crowd that accuses Polycarp of destroying "our gods") and register concern that they may not be able to sacrifice or worship according to polytheist traditions. In 13.1, their zeal drives them to stoke the fires for martyrdom, even though the execution seems to be held on the Sabbath before Pesah. It is hard to imagine why Jews in the mid-second century would be concerned about Christians worshipping Polycarp and, hence, abandoning Christ (17.2).

The profile of Jews in the *Martyrdom* functions on three levels. First, the Jewish opposition expressed by wrath, zeal, and suspicion appeals to the emotional dimension of deliberative discourse that is intended to persuade Christians to be resolved in their commitment to Christ. Second, Jewish opposition to Polycarp continues the theme of his martyrdom, paralleling the Jewish opposition to Jesus detailed in the New Testament gospels: Jewish opposition to Polycarp is in accordance with the gospel. Third, Jewish opposition to Polycarp underscores the idea that Christians are the new people of God and ignores the connection of Christianity with its Jewish origins. On this point Lieu makes a pointed and important observation:

> The tendency for the Jews to merge into or emerge out of an otherwise undifferentiated crowd of the lawless in *Mart. Poly.* (13.1; 17.2–18.1) and elsewhere is a reflection of the way this Christian self-identity oscillates between a model of the *"third* race" and a dualist contrast between the righteous and the unrighteous. Thus the charge of Jewish involvement in persecution is deeply implicated in Christian apologetics of self-identity, and, considering the dialectical relationship with Judaism within those apologetics, claiming their antiquity and heritage while denying their legitimacy, we may be surprised that it is not found more frequently. (1998, 287; cf. Perkins 1985, 222)

Assessment

The questions posed at the beginning of this study asked about the role of Jews in the *Martyrdom of Polycarp* and what that role tells us about religious rivalry at Smyrna. On the first question, the answer seems to be that they function primarily as part of the rhetorical discourse placed in a proto-martyrology. If Boyarin is correct in suggesting that martyrology is an evolving tradition in the mid-second century CE involving negotiations of differences and sameness between Judaism and Christianity, then we might expect there was the intertwining of things Jewish with things Christian that is outside of the rhetorical discourse. The specifics about Jews in the *Martyrdom*, when one follows Boyarin's thesis about intertwining, seem to result in an affirmation of conflict between Jews and Christians. However, in the overall framing of the *Martyrdom*, Jews play a minor though important supporting role in a literary endeavour struggling with self-definition that is primarily, if not exclusively, Christian. The role affirms that Jews were part of the process whereby Christians defined themselves as the people of God. Lieu is correct in saying that the universal character of the crowds is important because it focuses on the universal claim of salvation found in 17.2: Christ suffered for the salvation of the whole world. This confirms Taylor's observation that Jews in the *Martyrdom of Polycarp* should be understood as part of a larger holistic and soteriological vision of emerging Christianity.

With these first principles firmly positioned in an assessment of religious rivalries at Smyrna having to do with Jews and Gentiles, one might imagine that a case could be made that Simon's conflict theory is an important directive for understanding relations between early Christians and their Jewish contemporaries.[4] While conflict theory cannot be understood as the "big-bang" reason for explaining all relations between Jews and Christians, there are discernible socio-political contexts behind at least some instances of Jewish–Christian debate. Unfortunately, the *Martyrdom of Polycarp* does not provide easy access to those contexts because the role of Jews is so firmly placed in its deliberative discourse.

On the second question about what the role of Jews in the *Martyrdom* tells us about religious rivalry at Smyrna, the answer is delicate at best. On first blush, the proto-martyrology seems not to tell us much, and perhaps we should be satisfied with knowing what it does not tell us. Rhetorical analysis suggests that if the *Martyrdom* is an example of deliberative discourse, the depiction of Jews in it does not reflect a social and historical reality. However, returning to the observations of Fredrik Barth cited above, identity develops around a select and limited number of values and behaviours that define a group when it has close contact with another. In the first two centuries CE, the boundaries between Judaism and early Christianity were indeed ill defined. For distinctions to be made, some degree of conflict and denunciation seems necessary—and seems to be expressed in the *Martyrdom of Polycarp*. Conflict theory is an important reference for determining the relationship between Jews and Christians when they are understood as siblings (and not in filial roles). Further, both religions were building on a common biblical foundation and were developing separate identities at the same time from common scriptural foundations. Thus, rivalries between siblings seem inevitable. Similarities, as well as differences, emerged because they were offering answers to the same question while living side-by-side in Smyrna: who, in light of a common inheritance, are the people of God?

The *Martyrdom of Polycarp* is a Christian response to the question that is particularized because of persecution from the larger society. Given the intensity of such life experiences, it is rather surprising that the *Martyrdom* does not strike out even more aggressively against a traditional Christian opponent, namely, Jews. Thus, one might be inclined to conclude that in the *Martyrdom of Polycarp* religious rivalry is not particularly strong, no more so than one would expect between sibling religious traditions.

11

Among Gentiles, Jews, and Christians
Formation of Christian Identity
in Melito of Sardis

Reidar Aasgaard

Introduction

In the two first centuries CE, the struggle for Christian identity was a fundamental and vital challenge for Christians. The Christ-believers gradually grew out of their original Jewish context and gathered people of various cultural, social, and religious backgrounds. In the second century the Christians had grown in number; they had gained influence and had become more noticeable in society as a distinct religious movement. In such a period of transition and development, the need for a distinct self-understanding became ever more important (see Wagner 1994, 3–8, 11–23, 63–65, 115–38).

The attempts to construct a Christian identity followed several paths. One way of developing such an identity was to define oneself in relation to other groups. Within this strategy, the questions Who am I? and Who are we? are (at least partly) answered by defining one's standing as against others': Who are my opponents, who are my allies, and how am I to place myself in relation to them (see, for example, Sanders 1980; Frerichs and Neusner 1985; Grant 1988; Wagner 1994; Lieu 1996)? In Melito of Sardis, at his peak in the 170s, we find a very interesting example of such an attempt at Christian self-definition. Of particular interest are the ways in which he places himself in relation to the Roman world and particularly to the Jews and to other Christians, since these were the main socio-cultural groups with which he was confronted. This essay will examine how Melito appears to handle these relations, and how he strives to construct a Christian identity that was viable for himself and his church in Sardis.

Notes to chapter 11 start on page 280

The Person, Milieu, and Works of Melito

Not very much is known about Melito's person, but some interesting features emerge, nevertheless, partly from other sources, partly from his own writings.[1] Some information of relevance here is given in a letter from Polycrates, bishop in Ephesus (around 190 CE), quoted in the church history of Eusebius (265–340 CE, see *HE* 5.24.2–6). Polycrates says that Melito is now buried in Sardis and presents him as a Christian leader there: "Melito the eunuch . . . who lies at Sardis awaiting the visitation from heaven when he shall rise from the dead" (*HE* 5.24.5).[2] Eusebius adds that Melito was a bishop (*HE* 4.26.1), which can be Eusebius's own inference from Polycrates's information, but he may just as well have had independent information about Melito. Whether a bishop or not, Melito clearly was an influential figure in the Christian community in Sardis. His central social position is confirmed by the fact that he wrote a petition to the emperor on behalf of not only the church of Sardis, but apparently of the churches in Asia Minor at large. Eusebius cites this petition extensively, and we shall return to it below.

Melito seems to have been well educated—his rhetorical skills are impressive, showing a close resemblance to the rhetorical style of Asianism (Stewart-Sykes 2001, 223–28),[3] and his knowledge of the Hebrew scriptures is broad and thorough (e.g., Hall 1979, xl–xlii; Knapp 2000, 353–54, 374).[4] He also had strong bonds to Jewish tradition: Polycrates describes him as a Quartodeciman, which means that he kept Easter on the 14th of Nisan, that is, on the day of the Jewish Passover, instead of on Sunday, the Western and Roman practice.[5] Melito's own writings also show that he was deeply rooted in the Jewish world: he is, for example, familiar with the Jewish Easter haggadah (Hall 1971, 34, 45–46). He also says that he had visited Jerusalem and Palestine (*Fragment* 3).[6]

Polycrates remarks that Melito had prophetic skills. Like one of the daughters of the apostle Philip, Melito is said to have "lived entirely in the Holy Spirit" (*ton en hagiō pneumati panta politeusamenōn*), a description that indicates a status as a prophet (Stewart-Sykes 1998, 13–14).[7] Jerome (*Vir. ill.* 24.3) also confirms this status, by referring to the description of Melito by Tertullian (the church father and later Montanist, ca. 160 to ca. 220 CE) as having a reputation as a prophet: "He was thought of as a prophet by most of us Christians" (Halton 1999, 46). And in a list of Melito's writings given by Eusebius, two (now lost) works may have been about Christian prophecy: *On Christian Life and Prophets* and a treatise on prophecy (*HE* 4.26.2).[8] Thus, the impression is given of Melito as a preacher with specific skills as a Christian, and of a person somehow preoccupied with prophecy.

More, however, is known about the social and religious context in which Melito was living. Sardis, once the capital of the Lydian kingdom, was a rich and powerful city, with fifty thousand to a hundred thousand inhabitants. At the time of Melito it had been part of the Roman Empire for three centuries. It had, however, lost some of its former grandeur, partly as the result of an earthquake in 17 CE, but it was still wealthy. Its wealth grew again and reached its peak in the third and fourth centuries, after which a decline set in. It also enjoyed some privileges and a certain freedom under Roman rule, which the city and its inhabitants were under constant pressure to maintain.[9] The Roman authorities could interfere with all kinds of matters that they found of importance.[10]

Little is known about the history of the Christian community in Sardis before Melito. Lydia and the neighbouring districts had been the object of Christian mission and establishment of communities in the first century CE, partly through the ministry of Paul and other (unknown) evangelists. The church in Sardis is one of the seven churches addressed in the Revelation of John (3:1–6): here it is said to "have a name of being alive, but you are dead," and it is admonished to "wake up, and strengthen what remains and is on the point of death." Apart from this notice, nothing is related about Christians in Sardis before Melito (see MacLennan 1990, 103–105). Like several other second-century churches in Asia Minor, it seems to stand in a Johannine tradition, possibly with Palestinian roots (Stewart-Sykes 1998, 12–22).

It is possible that the church in Sardis escaped the persecutions of the early second century, which led to the martyrdom of Polycarp (Mitchell 1993, 2:37–43; Lieu 1996, 206–207). The archaeological findings bearing on Christians are almost non-existent, with only one Christian inscription from the third century, and no other earlier remains (Mitchell 1993, 2:38, with references). Whereas some scholars trace the life of the Sardis community back to the first century (e.g., Johnson 1961, 81),[11] others hold that the community, at the time of Melito, primarily had its origin in converted Jews or descendants of converted Jews (e.g., Kraabel 1971, 84). Like other Christian communities in Asia Minor, it seems to have been connected only loosely to other Christian communities and was very much dependent on its own changing conditions and practices (Mitchell 1993, 2:41; Ascough 1997). The Christians may have met in private homes or rented houses (MacLennan 1990, 96, with references). Thus, the total evidence is very meagre and indicates that the Christian community before the time of Melito was of minor importance and that its historical continuity is uncertain.

Also characteristic of Sardis was its strong Jewish community, with a history going back centuries (see Lieu 1996, 199–203).[12] Its rights to practise its religion had been confirmed by the Roman authorities already in the two centuries BCE (Binder 1999, 283–84).[13] In spite of setbacks, the community appears to have been steadily growing in size and influence (e.g., Seager and Kraabel 1983, 178–90). During the century after Melito, the Jewish community turned an old market hall into the largest synagogue known from antiquity, a richly decorated building about 85 m long and 20 m wide (Levine 2000, 242–49).[14] It is still a matter of discussion how long after the time of Melito this building was taken into use as a synagogue (Cohick 2000, 31–35), and it is also questioned whether the later Jewish wealth and influence can be used as evidence of a similar power in Melito's time (Bonz 1999, 120–22).[15] Although such backdating is risky, we have no information that supports any significant or sudden change in the position of the Jewish community in Sardis. We may thus presume that, at the time of Melito, the Jewish influence in Sardis was easily discernable or at least clearly increasing (Kraabel 1971, 77; Trebilco 1991, 52–54; Stewart-Sykes 1998, 11).[16]

The historical evidence also indicates that there were close ties between the Jewish milieu and the Roman administration of the city, with synagogue benefactors—possibly "God-fearers"—among the Gentile population (Trebilco 1991, 33–36, 43–51, 164–66, 183–85).[17] Nothing in the archaeological and written evidence tells of anything other than a peaceful everyday relationship between Jews and their polytheist neighbours (Seager and Kraabel 1983, 185–86; Hammer and Murray [chap. 12 in this volume]).[18] For example, the large synagogue was situated in the immediate neighbourhood of the forum and the city administration of Sardis (Seager and Kraabel 1983, 184; Mitchell 1993, 2:32–33).

There are also indications of everyday contact between Jews and Christians in the city. Archaeological evidence seems to show that Jews and Christians had adjacent workshops (Crawford, Hanfmann, and Yegül 1983, 161–67, especially 166; Hammer and Murray [chap. 12 in this volume]).[19] In a relatively circumscribed city such as Sardis with its strong Jewish milieu, it is most likely that Christians came into considerable contact with it, although the Christians may have been more locally marginal than the Jews (Seager and Kraabel 1983, 168, and Stewart-Sykes 1998, 9).[20] Melito's broad knowledge of the scriptures and Jewish tradition also suggests a close familiarity with the Jews and Judaism in his own social context.

In the second half of the second century, the Christian communities of Asia Minor experienced internal tensions, particularly as a result of Marcionite, Gnostic, and Quartodeciman controversies. However, most acute and challenging in Melito's environment appears to have been the Montanist movement, which had its roots in Asian Christianity. It had an enthusiastic apocalyptic character, expecting the end of the world in the near future. It also had an emphasis on some persons as particularly Spirit-led, as prophets mediating oracles from God, often accompanied by ecstasy and glossolalia (Stewart-Sykes 2001, 117–31, 227–28). Several of these prophets were women, and they also had several women as ministers (Trevett 1996, especially 151–97). Montanist prophets, such as its main figure, Montanus (fl. 170–80), would often prophesy in "I" form, claiming to mediate messages directly from God or Christ (see Grant 1988, 87–88; Trevett 1996, 80–83; Stewart-Sykes 2001, 232–38).

Phenomenologically, Montanism may be a reflection of a type of religiosity characteristic of the Lydian and Phrygian districts (Strobel 1980, 295–98; Mitchell 1993, 2:12–13, 43–49). It recruited from various levels of society and competed with and defeated "orthodox" Christian communities in many places (Tabbernee 1997, 564–69). With its more unruly nature, it was more hostile towards the surrounding world (Trevett 1996, 42, 121–29). From its starting point in Phrygia in the 170s, this "new prophecy" spread very quickly to other areas. It also came to Lydia, the neighbouring district to the west of Phrygia. There is no clear witness to Montanism in Sardis itself, but there is inscriptional and other evidence showing the presence of Montanist Christians in towns and villages nearby: to the north in Chorianon katoikia (30 km) and Thyateira (50 km); to the east in Mendechora (50 km, close to Philadelphia), Bagis (100 km), and Hierapolis, Motella, and Temenothyrae (all 120 km) (Mitchell 1993, 1:190; Tabernee 1997, 555–56).[21]

From all these places there was easy access to Sardis by roads, some of them Roman main roads (Mitchell 1993, 1:120).[22] The fourth-century bishop Epiphanius in Salamis remarks that Montanist Christians took over the Christian church in Thyateira some time between the late second and the late third centuries, very close to the time of Melito (Mitchell 1993, 2:39, cf. Epiphanius, *Pan.* 51.33). Especially in Themenothyrae, many Montanist epitaphs from the early third century are found (Tabbernee 1997, 62–86; Mitchell 1993, 2:39).[23] Thus, Melito and his community lived at the intersection between, and under the pressure of, a strong political Roman dominance in the area, an influential Jewish milieu in Sardis, and a Christian culture in Lydia and Phrygia characterized by tensions clearly visible in the growing Montanist movement.

Regrettably, little is left of Melito's works. The only complete writing is his Paschal sermon, *Peri Pascha*, which seems to have been widely read (Hall 1979, xvii–xxii).[24] Apart from the sermon, only ten or twenty short fragments survive, several of which may not be original.[25] Despite the limited evidence, it is sufficient to give an impression of how Melito tried to work out a Christian self-understanding for himself and his community. Two texts are of special importance here: his paschal sermon and his petition to the emperor Marcus Aurelius. The paschal sermon is an exposition of Exodus 12, the institution of the Passah.[26] It was probably held in a service with a large group of catechumens about to be baptized—in a liminal situation, in which issues of identity were central.[27]

Melito's petition to the emperor, Marcus Aurelius, the main part of which is preserved in Eusebius and which he calls an apology (*HE* 4.26.1; *apologia*), was written as a response to persecutions that broke out in Asia Minor, and in which many Christians were robbed of their goods (*Fragment* 1; see Hall 1979, xii, xxix–xxx).[28] Marcus Aurelius and his administration were critical attitude of the Christians, and he also visited Asia Minor in 175–76 (Grant 1988, 74–82). The reasons for the persecutions are unclear: it may have been a general dislike of the Christians by the local or central Roman authorities (Grant 1988, 93–94), or unrest because of conflicts between Christians and Jews (Kraabel 1971, 84), or even between Orthodox Christians and Montanists (Trevett 1996, 42–45; also Sordi 1962). Interestingly, the *Peri Pascha* and the petition to the emperor are very close in time, about 170–177, so they are particularly valuable as different and supplementary sources to Melito's thinking at a specific time.[29]

We shall now take a look at the texts and analyze how Melito describes his relations and those of the other Christians to Roman society and authorities, to his Jewish context, and to other Christians.

Melito and Roman Society and Authorities

The petition to the emperor is of particular interest in the attempt to understand Melito's relationship to Roman society and to Roman authorities. In the first and last part of the petition, Melito clearly attempts to gain his addressee's goodwill—it is a *captatio benevolentiae* similar to other contemporary and later apologies (Young 1999, 82–92). He appeals to the emperor's justness and emphasizes his humanity and wisdom; he accepts the authority and right of the emperor to exercise justice and to punish the guilty, even if they are Christians; he urges him to inquire closely into the issue at stake, and to become acquainted with the ideas of Christians, and to discover whether they constitute reason for punishment. In addition, he refers to the mistakes of bad emperors of the past (Nero and Domitian), but also to the clemency of Marcus Aurelius's relatives and predecessors (Hadrian and Antoninus Pius), which he is expected to exceed.

More noticeable, however, is Melito's argument in what appears to be the middle, central part of the petition:

> Our philosophy first flourished among barbarians, but it blossomed out among your peoples during the great reign of your ancestor Augustus, and became especially for your empire an auspicious benefit. For from that time the power of Rome grew to become great and splen-

did. To that power you have become a successor desired in prayer, and will continue to be so, together with your son, if you guard the philosophy of the empire which was nursed with and began with Augustus, and which your ancestors respected alongside the other cults. This also is the surest proof that it was for good that our thinking flourished together with the empire which began so well—the fact that nothing ignoble befell it from the rule of Augustus, but on the contrary everything splendid and glorious in accordance with the prayer of all…. (Eusebius, *HE* 4.26.7-8)

Several things are of interest here: Melito presents Christian faith as a "philosophy" (*philosophia*).[30] Such a description is in agreement with other Christian apologists of the second century (Young 1999, 92-99, especially 94), and clearly aims at stressing the respectability of this belief. It is not a religion of dubious origin, a superstition worthy of being condemned as a "*religio illicita*" (Grant 1988, 95). This philosophy, Melito says, first "flourished" (*ēkmasen*) "among barbarians" (*en barbarois*). *Barbarians*, which in classical literature often is used in a derogatory sense, probably here refers to the Jewish people, possibly to non-Roman peoples in general (Kraabel 1971, 83-84; Seager and Kraabel 1983, 187; Wilson 1985, 352-53).[31] Although a polemic against Jews is not very visible here, it may be present (Kraabel 1971, 84).[32] For example, earlier in the petition—possibly immediately preceding—Melito uses *barbarian* in a negative sense, when speaking of the ordinance against the Christians: it is "not fit to be used even against barbarian enemies." The mention of the "barbarian" background at least serves to throw the positive relations between the Christians and the Romans into relief. Although they earlier came from a barbarian background, the Christians now belong among the Roman peoples.

However, this philosophy only first "blossomed" (*epanthēsasa*) among the peoples under the Roman Empire.[33] Its period of blossoming coincided with the "great reign" of the first emperor, Augustus. Thus, the Christian philosophy is not an adversary of the Roman Empire. On the contrary, it has been and is an "auspicious benefit" (*aision agathon*). It has furthered the empire. And not only that, this philosophy, Melito suggests, may even be the reason this empire has flourished. It was precisely during this period that the power of Rome grew to become so splendid! In addition, Rome has, during these times, been spared from serious disasters—this even amounts to a "proof" (*tekmērion*) of the value of the Christian "thinking" (*ton kath' hēmas logon*). Here, Melito aims at giving the Christian faith (at least some of) the honour for the greatness of Rome and for its well-being in the past! He also emphasizes that the Christian philosophy already was esteemed highly by the ancestors of Marcus Aurelius. It is not a novel invention and in fact has the trustworthiness of a respectable past. Melito also states that

Marcus Aurelius has followed this up and benefited from it, and that he has been much prayed for (*euktaios*), and will be prayed for if he continues to protect the Christian philosophy alongside—to be sure—other cults. Very carefully, Melito may here indicate that even the continued well-being of Rome depends on the emperor's will to guard this philosophy.

The petition is a finely formulated diplomatic piece, and some of its very pro-empire attitude is to be attributed to the rhetorical form and genre of an official document to the emperor. Melito's intention is to present Roman–Christian relations in as favourable a light as possible. Nevertheless, the petition also reveals a thinking that, to a considerable extent, should be taken at face value. It displays a clearly expressed will to loyalty towards the emperor and the Roman authorities. But not only that, it also demonstrates Melito's optimistic perception of a close interrelatedness between the developing Christian church and Roman history in general. This way of thinking is well known from later Christian apologetic vis-à-vis the Roman authorities, but Melito is the first known to have launched the argument (Hall 1979, xxix–xxx). It does stress the value of the Christian religion for society at large, but it also appears to display a considerable self-consciousness in Melito: the future well-being of the empire may be dependent on the divine favour secured by the prayers of Christians.

The impression of Melito's pro-Roman attitudes and perceptions may also, more indirectly, find support in formulations in his paschal sermon, a text in which there should be no particular reason to focus on the relation with the Romans. In it, Melito describes in a very positive manner the response of Gentiles to the coming of Christ, whereas he sees the attitudes of Israel in a correspondingly negative light:

> But you [i.e., Israel] cast the opposite vote against your Lord.
> For him whom the Gentiles worshipped
> and uncircumcised men admired
> and foreigners glorified,
> over whom even [*kai*] Pilate washed his hands,
> you killed him at the great feast. (92)

Although these formulations may allude to passages in scripture about the Gentile nations honouring God, they nonetheless witness to a positive perception of the peoples of the Roman world: the Gentiles (*ta ethnē*), uncircumcised (*akrobustoi*), and foreigners (*allophuloi*) worship, admire, and glorify Christ. And *even* Pilate—which is one way in which the *kai* can be translated—Pilate, the Roman, was without guilt in Jesus's death.

Possibly, we can here perceive a strategy in which Melito plays the Gentile Roman world and the Jewish world off against one another. The Romans, represented by Pilate (see Matthew 27:24–25), are depicted as having clean hands, whereas Israel emerges as guilty of killing Christ (Kraabel 1971, 83–85). In this constellation, the Christians stand on the Roman side: Roman society and authorities are not the enemies but are made into the allies of the Christians.

Melito and the Jews

This leads us to Melito's relationship to the Jewish people, which must become a central issue in the discussion of his paschal sermon. His recurring and sharp polemic against Israel is renowned for its harshness, particularly in the section 72–99, a large and central part of the sermon. For example,

> It is he [Christ] that has been murdered.
> And where has he been murdered? In the middle of Jerusalem.
> By whom? By Israel.
> Why? Because he healed their lame and cleansed their lepers
> and brought light to their blind
> and raised their dead, that is why he died….
> What strange crime, Israel, have you committed?
> You dishonoured him that honoured you;
> you disgraced him that glorified you;
> you denied him who acknowledged you;
> you disclaimed him that proclaimed you;
> you killed him who made you live. (72–73)

Melito paints a very dark picture of treachery on the part of Israel against its God and Christ, his son. Although God had chosen, helped, and led the people from its very beginnings through its history, it nonetheless was ungrateful, betrayed him, and failed to acknowledge his son (e.g., 83–90).

In a climax in this part of the sermon, Israel is even accused of killing God (see Hall 1979, xliii):[34]

> he who fastened the universe has been fastened to a tree;
> the Sovereign has been insulted;
> the God has been murdered [*ho theos pephoneutai*];
> the King of Israel has been put to death by an Israelite right hand. (96)

Much has been written, partly to explain, partly to excuse this harshness. A focal point in scholarly discussions is what Melito means when speaking about Israel. Does he refer only to the Israel of the past, in the time of the "old" covenant and of Jesus (see Bonner 1940, 19–20; MacLennan 1990, 112–13; Cohick 1999, 136–37)? Or does he also speak of Israel in a more general, possibly metaphorical, sense, as a paradigm of repudiation (see MacLennan 1990, 113–14; Cohick 2000, 54, 58, 72–73)? Or does he—more or less directly—refer to the Jews of his own time, even those in Sardis (Wilson 1985, 348–49, 351; Lieu 1996, 219–20)?[35] Although Melito never uses the word *Jew* in the homily, but only *Israel* and *the people* (*ho laos*), the last opinion, nonetheless, seems the most probable.

It is very difficult to explain the ample space Melito gives to the anti-Israel polemic in the sermon without seeing it in light of the background of his local and contemporary context: a tension with, and a real or imag-ined[36] pressure from, a neighbouring Jewish community. Thus, it also func-tions as a polemic against the Jews and the Jewish religion in Sardis. And even if Melito did not intend it as such, or did not expect it to be perceived in this way (but that seems far too naive on his part), it is—considering the close, everyday contact between Jews and Christians in Sardis—likely to have had considerable impact on the minds and attitudes of his audience. To distinguish between a historical, past-time Israel and one's Jewish neigh-bour cannot have been at all easy for his audience (Wilson 1986, 93–95, 97–98; Lieu 1997, 219–20).[37] In addition, nowhere does Melito try to make such a distinction or to nuance his formulations. His message thus remains very problematic. It was, and still is, a sad instance of anti-Jewish polemic.[38]

Some efforts can, however, be made to explain—and if only partly excuse—the harsh character of Melito's rhetoric. One (less likely) expla-nation focuses on Melito's personal history: that he himself was a Jew who had converted to Christianity, and that the sharpness of his polemic reflects a protest against his own past (Stewart-Sykes 1997, 275–79). Another more likely explanation is that it is a legacy from the Christian tradition within which he stands, namely the Johannine tradition (Stewart-Sykes 1997, 279–81). More important, however, seems to be the socio-historical back-ground: the polemic of the leader of a weak and threatened minority try-ing to defend his group against the dominance of a much larger group—"the cry of the oppressed," as it were (e.g., Kraabel 1971, 83–85; MacLennan 1990, 108–11; Trebilco 1991, 31, 54).[39] Thus, Melito's words are not an instance of harshness of the strong against the weak—because these and other words were used when the relative strength between Jews and Chris-tians changed. Rather, the opposite is true. At the same time, the polemic can also be viewed as an attempt to strengthen the self-confidence of the Christians vis-à-vis their Jewish adversaries (Wilson 1985, 349).

Still another explanation, however, is that Melito in his sermon has only, or primarily, inner-Christian concerns in mind. His words are meant to strengthen a particular Christian self-understanding. Thus, not the rela-tions vis-à-vis the Jews are at stake, but the problems and needs of many Christians in Melito's own church. To this we shall return below. Finally, his animosity may also been accounted for as Melito excelling in, or even being carried off by, his own rhetorical skills, particularly in the long pas-sage 72–99 with its many pointed, antithetic, and paradoxical expressions (Wilson 1985, 349; Lieu 1996, 230).[40]

To some extent, these explanations, most of which need not exclude one another, place Melito's sermon within the context to which it belongs, although the sharpness of it still remains very problematic. Whatever the case, it is clear that Melito's polemic marks the boundaries of the Christians vis-à-vis the Jewish element, "Israel," and thus more indirectly strengthens their understanding of themselves as a distinct and privileged group.

This way of thinking becomes particularly clear in Melito's biblical hermeneutics, which he develops theologically. Here we get a clear impression of how he understands the position of the Christians in relation to their Jewish heritage. In the introduction to his sermon, the rhetorical exordium, he presents a fundamental contrast between what is "old" and what is "new." Scripture speaks about a "mystery" that is both old and new. The *old* has to do with the old covenant, with the law, and with the Passover lamb, all of which are temporal; the *new* has to do with the new covenant, with the word, and with Christ, all of which are eternal:

> Old is the law,
> but new the word;
> temporary the model,
> but eternal the grace;
> perishable the sheep,
> imperishable the Lord;
> not broken as a lamb,
> but resurrected as God....
> For the model indeed existed,
> but then the reality appeared. (4)

In his hermeneutical reflections, Melito repeatedly contrasts a Christian reading, which is spiritual, and a Jewish reading, which is literal (2–10). After having retold the story of Exodus 12 and briefly interpreted it (11–33), he develops his understanding of scripture and of the history that it tells (34–45). Here he uses the metaphor of an artisan's work: an artisan first makes a model or a sketch of what he is going to create, and then, on the basis of it, produces his final work of art. And when his work of art is finished, the model becomes inferior. It has some value in that it has served as a model and vaguely reflects, or prefigures, the finished masterpiece, but it does not have any value of itself anymore. This is also the case with the history and people of Israel: it was a prefiguration of a reality yet to come, but has now become obsolete. To use Melito's own words,

> The people then was a model by way of preliminary sketch,
> and the law was the writing of a parable;
> the gospel is the recounting and fulfilment of the law,
> and the church the repository of the reality.

The model then was precious before the reality,
and the parable was marvellous before the interpretation;
that is, the people was precious before the church arose,
and the law was marvellous before the gospel was elucidated.
But when the church arose and the gospel took precedence,
the model was made void, conceding its power to the reality,
and the law was fulfilled, conceding its power to the gospel. (40–42)

Here Melito clearly reasons along historical lines, and by way of typology.[41] Israel and the law had its importance in the past, but now is the time of the church and the gospel. And the value of scripture lies in its ability to point to the reality that it anticipates. Later in the sermon Melito gives examples, that is, of persons such as Abel, Joseph, and David (57–60), who prefigure Christ, and of words from the prophets that proclaim Christ. Throughout the sermon, Melito emphasizes the difference between the old and the new by sharply contrasting type and truth, parable and interpretation, model and reality, law and gospel.[42]

Thus, Melito's interpretation of scripture is radically typological (Knapp 2000, 362–73), with typologies partly of a christological, partly of an ecclesiological, kind. The words and events of scripture are being fulfilled with the coming of Christ and of his church. What Melito, by his strong focus on typology, seems to aim at, is to make scripture into a *Christian* scripture. It is becoming the "Old Testament," as opposed to the gradually developing New Testament. Melito is the first who is known to have used the term *Old* Covenant/Testament of the Hebrew scriptures (*Fragment* 3; see Hall 1979, xxx). The old one is still indispensable and of value, as is the history that it tells. For Melito, it is the history of how God has guided his people through the ages. Still, it has value only as a portent of what is new: Christ and the church.[43] Israel (i.e., the Jews) is now exceeded and replaced by the church.

In effect, what Melito here tries to do is to take over, to appropriate scripture. Scripture is not the book of the Jewish people, it is in reality the holy writings of the Christians. Israel has misunderstood God's actions and misread God's own testimony, scripture. Thus, Israel is dismissed as the people who rejected Christ, as well as forfeited the heritage given them in their scripture. The Christians, on the other hand, are the winners. Scripture, and the correct interpretation of it, belongs to them. And not only that, the whole history of Israel belongs to the Christians, it is *theirs*—it is a history about the coming of Christ and of the Christian church (see also Manis 1987, 400).

The radicalness of Melito's supersessionist thinking becomes visible in the way he describes central figures in the history of Israel. They were not only prefigurations, types, of Christ; for Melito, Christ was in fact present in them:

He is the Pascha of our salvation.
It is he who in many endured many things:
it is he that was in Abel murdered,
and in Isaac bound,
and in Jacob exiled,
and in Joseph sold,
and in Moses exposed,
and in the lamb slain,
and in David persecuted,
and in the prophets dishonoured. (69)[44]

Thus, if we interpret this not only as rhetoric, but also as theology, Melito here even moves beyond typology into a kind of christological "modalism" (Wilson 1985, 348, and 1986, 89, 99).[45]

In this daring way, Melito aims at appropriating not only scripture, but also the history of Israel for himself and his church. God's scriptures and God's history were in reality meant for the Christians. More than that, they in fact were about Christ and the Christians.

Melito and Other Christians

As already noted, however, Melito is not only concerned with placing himself in relation to his Roman and Jewish context, he also appears to situate himself in relation to his Christian milieu, with the tensions present in it. Read this way, the *Peri Pascha* can be interpreted as part of an inner-Christian polemic in which Melito pursues a strategy for building up a particular Christian self-understanding.

Several controversies may be reflected in Melito's writings.[46] As noted above, Melito was living in a Christian context that was deeply rooted in Jewish traditions. Seen against this background, some of his polemic very probably should be interpreted as a way of marking boundaries against the threat from Judaising forces within his own ranks (see Lieu 1996, 228-32).[47] It is intended to provide a sense of confidence and autonomy in their own standing as Christians. This can be one reason that Melito, in his interpretation of scripture, again and again stresses the superiority of the new in comparison to the old, and describes the difference in terms of a break, rather than a development. However, it has also been held that the sharpness of Melito's anti-Jewish polemic may be due to his being a Quartodeciman. Since he, as a Quartodeciman, followed the Jewish practice of dating the Passah celebration, it became even more important for him to underscore the differences between Christianity and Judaism (see, for example, Wilson 1986, 96-98). This seems rather speculative, though.

It has also been discussed whether *Peri Pascha* has an anti-docetic or anti-Gnostic agenda, but the conclusions are generally negative (Cohick 2000, 80–81). Others see an anti-Marcionite attitude in Melito, especially since he so strongly stresses the Hebrew Bible and the story it tells (Cohick 2000, 83–85).[48] This may be true, but if so, it comes to the surface to a very limited extent and in general terms.

On the basis of the general information on Melito and features in his own texts, one "front" emerges as particularly important. Melito is concerned with marking boundaries against the influence of Montanism, with its charismatic form of Christianity, and with its prophet-leaders who pleaded special charismatic gifts and revelations from God and Christ. As noted above, Montanism was a speedily spreading movement in the 170s and had already taken root in neighbouring cities. It may have been standing as a troublesome rival at the gates of Melito's Sardis. From this perspective, some of the biographical information about Melito takes on special importance, namely the descriptions of him as a prophet. As noted above, both Polycrates and Tertullian, Melito's near contemporaries (only one to three decades later), refer to his reputation as a prophet. Just as the Montanists pleaded the prophet role for some of their leaders, many "orthodox" also considered Melito to be a prophet. In addition, the list of his literary productions points in the same direction. The titles of two of his lost works indicate that they dealt with the topic of prophecy.

The attitudes towards Melito as a prophet are confirmed by the paschal sermon. Here it becomes evident that not only others, but Melito as well, place Melito in the position of a prophet, as a person mediating words from the risen Christ. This is what we see in the powerful climax of the sermon, in its final part. Here Melito first summarizes the work of Christ:

> The Lord, when he had clothed himself with man
> and suffered because of him that was suffering
> and been bound because of him that was held fast
> and been judged because of him that was condemned
> and been buried because of him that was buried,
> arose from the dead and uttered this cry.... (100–101)

Then he turns to the first person singular, speaking the words of the risen Christ, calling people to come to him:[49]

> "Who takes issue with me?—let him stand against me.
> I released the condemned;
> I brought the dead to life;
> I raise up the buried.
> Who is there that contradicts me?
> I am the one," says the Christ,

> "I am the one that destroyed death
> and triumphed over the enemy
> and trod down Hades
> and bound the strong one
> and carried off man to the heights of heaven;
> I am the one," says the Christ. (101–102)

And further on, Melito continues:

> "For I am your forgiveness,
> I am the Pascha of salvation,
> I am the lamb slain for you;
> I am your ransom,[50]
> I am your life,
> I am your light,
> I am your salvation,
> I am your resurrection,
> I am your king." (103)

This and the following passage have received very little commentary, and when they have, they have primarily been interpreted as a climax in a rhetorical sense (Halton 1970, 255), for example, as a form of speech taken from the Hebrew Bible, a "cultic epiphany" (Blank 1963, 89). This interpretation, however, is saying too little about it. More correctly, it should be viewed as a passage in which Melito presents himself as a prophet, speaking a prophetic message, a message directly from the risen Christ. He not only speaks "as if" the risen Christ were present; rather, his speech is a witness of this presence; and Christ himself is speaking (Blank 1963, 89–90; Grant 1988, 96–97).[51] As noted, Melito was part of a cultural milieu and tradition in which charismatic and prophetic gifts were highly valued. Thus, by speaking in this way, he represents and confirms this tradition and lives up to what was expected from a person who "lived entirely in the Holy Spirit" (Eusebius, *HE* 5.24.5).

At the same time, however, his prophesying can be understood not only as living up to, but as a counterweight to, the Montanist prophecy, as a way of addressing the challenges from them: here is one who speaks the word of God with the same commitment and authority as their prophets. He is in command of the same powers, he is not inferior in any way; in fact, Melito, in his position as a church leader at Sardis, is also one of the prophets (see Blank 1963, 17–18; Stewart-Sykes 1998, 227–28).

However, if we are correct in calling this part of the paschal sermon prophetic speech, it becomes important to examine the content of what he is saying. Here, two points are of particular importance. The first is that Melito uses expressions from Christian writings that were familiar and popular among the Christians of Asia Minor, particularly from the Gospel of John and from Revelation—for example, the many and characteristic "I am" sayings. Here we find a direct appropriation of many metaphors, such as lamb, ransom, life, light, resurrection, and king (cf. Matthew 20:28 and particularly Mark 10:45; John 1:29; 7:26, 41; 8:12; 11:25; 14:6; 18:37). But unlike the way in which these metaphors are used in the New Testament, Melito gives them his own rhetorical twist: Christ is their (*hymōn*) ransom, life, etc. In addition, he follows up the use of the same and similar metaphors (cf. especially John 7:26, 41; Revelation 1:8; 21:6) in the final passage, but now in the third person:[52]

> He is the Alpha and the Omega;
> he is beginning and end,
> beginning inexpressible and end incomprehensible;
> he is the Christ;
> he is the king;
> he is Jesus;
> he is the captain;
> he is the Lord;
> he is the one who rose from the dead;
> he is the one who sits at the Father's right hand;
> he carries the Father and is carried by the Father.
> To him be glory and power for ever. Amen. (105)

Thus, Melito roots his words in forms and metaphors from the new, accepted Christian writings. By doing so, he supplies his speech with the authority of the new scriptures. He speaks in the same vein as they and says nothing but what they say. He justifies his message by referring to the authority of the Christian scriptures.

The second point worth noting is the creedal-like form and content of this passage. Speaking in the first person singular, Melito reflects the main elements of early creeds, the so-called *regulae fidei*. First he summarizes Christ's life, suffering, death, and resurrection (100), then he describes their effects for those who believe: how Christ fights death and evil (101–102), and how he wins victory and salvation for them (103). Finally, he repeats the main elements of the creed, this time in more detail; now, however, he returns to the third person:

> It is he that made heaven and earth
> and fashioned man in the beginning,
> who is proclaimed through the law and prophets,
> who was enfleshed upon a virgin,
> who was hung upon a tree,
> who was buried in the earth,
> who was raised from the dead

and went up to the heights of heaven,
who sits at the Father's right hand,
who has power to save every man,
through whom the Father did his works from beginning to
eternity. (104)

Here, in the I-speech and in the final formulations in 104, Melito sums up his message and does so in the form of a creed, mentioning creation, prophecies of Christ's coming, his incarnation, crucifixion, burial, resurrection, ascension, and presence with God as eternal saviour.

A similar pattern is found in 105b (see above). Here, the role of Christ is described, and then his resurrection and presence at the Father's right hand. What Melito does in these texts, then, is to substantiate his message with the authority of the rule of faith (see Blank 1963, 17–18, 94–96). Although some scholars do not see his formulations as a rendering of a "rule of faith," their structured and strict character strongly points in the direction of such formulaic expressions, which—without necessarily being rules of faith per se—at least clearly reflect such creedal statements.[53] Another indication of this reading is the similar, but much longer, list in Melito *Fragment* 15 (Hall 1979, 82–84, especially lines 49–56). Certainly Melito's formulations do not have a trinitarian structure, but that is not to be expected, nor is it a requisite for considering them as reflections of such formulas. In this case, they focus primarily on Christ, and partly on God, which in the case of *Peri Pascha* is very natural, since here we have a sermon held at Easter and on the basis of Exodus 12.

By using (these reflections of) the rule of faith, Melito "normalizes" and regulates prophecy. He makes it ecclesiastically acceptable; he employs the gift of prophecy and prophetic speech, but within the framework of an established church and his own ecclesiastical position.[54]

Concluding Considerations

Many scholars deal with Melito's writings (especially *Peri Pascha*) as if he directs himself against only one opponent, whether Jewish, Christian, or another.[55] This essay has shown that it is not a case of "either/or" but of "both/and." Melito is, more or less directly, concerned with marking boundaries in relation to various groups at the same time.[56] He has several things on his agenda, even though some concerns and some opponents are more on his mind than others. So my aim here been to describe how Melito attempts to establish and develop a Christian identity and self-understanding in the encounter with central cultural, political, and religious groups of his milieu. The sources show how he edges his and his community's way through a multi-cultured second-century society.

First, we can see how Melito wishes to provide for the Christian church a safe and sound basis within Roman society at large, and perhaps as a guarantor for its well-being. To some extent he is successful, by playing the Romans and his own Christian philosophy off against the Jewish people. Second, we observe how Melito puts scripture and the history of Israel at the base of his thinking. However, by his typological interpretation of the words and events of scripture, he dethrones and shames Israel and the Jews, and appropriates scripture and the story it tells for Christians, and Christians alone. The new faith has superseded and replaced the old faith. And finally, we also sense how Melito tries to find a middle way between a Judaizing Christianity and a Christianity influenced by an emergent Montanist-charismatic movement. He does so by presenting himself as a prophet and by pronouncing a Christian prophecy, a prophecy, however, that is rooted in central Christian writings and traditions, about the Christ who at Easter conquered death and who now lives and is the Lord of all creation.

In the foregoing, we gain an impression of Melito's overall strategy. He strives to secure a place for himself and his co-Christians, to mould a self-understanding, an identity, that was viable in a complex society. He does so partly by allying with his opponents, partly by attacking them, partly by playing them against one another, and partly by competing with and trying to outdo them.

Aftermath and Afterthought

Not much is known about what happened to Melito and the Christian church in Sardis after the 170s. We have scarcely any remaining historical records, and the archaeological evidence is scanty. However, Christians, Jews, and polytheists seem to have worked side by side after the second century. For example, there are no signs of particular Jewish or Christian districts in the areas that have been excavated (Seager and Kraabel 1983, 187; Crawford, Hanfmann, and Yegül 1983, 161–67; cf. Hammer and Murray, chap. 12 of this volume). Two third-century Christian martyrs—Therapon and Apollonius—are known from Sardis; they seem to have fallen prey to Roman persecutions (Seager and Kraabel 1983, 187; Buchwald and Hanfmann 1983, 204n5). The remnants of a Christian basilica (ca. 340–50 CE) have been excavated 500 m southwest of the city centre, outside the city walls. It was modestly decorated and rather small (about 35 m by 18 m), especially in comparison with the synagogue (Buchwald and Hanfmann 1983, 197–99, 202–204, 206).[57] A small fourth-century chapel (about 10 m by 6 m) has been detected adjacent to an Artemis temple, 1.5 km southwest of the centre (Hanfmann 1962, 49–54; Buchwald and Hanfmann 1983, 195).[58] Also a baptistry (possibly), which may date back to the sixth century, has been located; it is in a workshop close to the synagogue (Hanfmann 1960a, 32–33).[59] Only two early graves have been identified as incontestably Christian, dating from the mid- to late fourth century (Hanfmann and Buchwald 1983, 208). The fact that so little is found in the central part of Sardis, and that what is found elsewhere is relatively modest, indicates that Christianity may never have taken firm roots in the city or at least never managed to leave its stamp on the city as a whole.[60]

We may ask why the church of Sardis after Melito has left so few traces in the historical records. It may be the result of earthquakes and economic depression that struck Sardis in late antiquity and early Byzantine times (Bonz 1993, 145–48; cf. Muir, chap. 9 in this volume). It may be the result of the impact of the Jewish community, which apparently flourished in the centuries after Melito, a community that may also have received the support of the Roman authorities at the cost of the Christians (Stewart-Sykes 1998, 23–24, with references). Since the Jewish milieu was so wealthy in the centuries after Melito and after the empire had been "Christianized" by the end of the fourth century, and since the synagogue was in use even in the beginning of the seventh century, this also has been taken as indication of a coalition of Jews and polytheists against the Christians (Seager and Krabel 1983, 186). It has been suggested that the Christians took over the synagogue after a time (Botermann 1990, 120–21), but the arguments are far from satisfactory. It is more likely that the Jewish community prevailed and swallowed up the Christians, who, as noted, may have had strong Jewish sympathies (Stewart-Sykes 1998, 23–25).[61] The Christians could have been weakened by internal rivalries, perhaps between Quartodeciman and "orthodox" Christians (MacLennan 1990, 106–7). Or they may have ended up in a disorganized Montanist-like enthusiasm. We do not know the reasons. Nor do we know whether or to what extent Melito's strategies contributed to the fate of this Christian church.

We may be critical about some of Melito's approaches and opinions. He held views that have proven to be problematic indeed. But whatever we may think about them, and wherever his strategies may have led his church, we cannot but be impressed by his commitment to shaping a Christian self-understanding and identity, and by the strategic boldness he displayed doing so, in challenging the social, cultural, and religious second-century world in which he was living.

12

Acquaintances, Supporters, and Competitors
Evidence of Inter-Connectedness and Rivalry among the Religious Groups in Sardis

Keir E. Hammer and Michele Murray

Introduction

In his 1996 article "Multiculturalism at Sardis," John Crawford presented his analysis of the relationship among Jews, Christians, and polytheists, based on the *realia* from the Byzantine shops in Sardis. Crawford, who was involved in the excavation of the site, is the only one to have written a paper on the evidence gleaned from these shops, and his main premise, that Jews and Christians lived, worked, and worshipped side by side without apparent animosity, has been regularly cited but never fully probed. While we agree with Crawford on the whole, we think that the evidence from the shops should be further examined and its possible connotations explored.

We will not examine all of the shops that Crawford has designated as either Christian or Jewish (although we do think a more thorough examination of these designations would be a useful exercise in the future); instead we will focus on those shops that contain evidence most relevant to this paper. One cannot, however, examine the Byzantine shops without at least acknowledging the massive synagogue that provided the backdrop to a number of these shops. Thus, we will also briefly examine some of the evidence from the synagogue.

Initially, the relevant details from the shops will be presented along with the relevant synagogue details. We will then draw on this evidence in a tentative exploration of ways in which to interpret the *realia* from this area of ancient Sardis. Ultimately, our analysis will be divided into two main sections: (1) a re-examination of Crawford's claims that the evidence does not reveal any "competition" among Jews and Christians but that it does reveal animosity of Jews and Christians towards polytheists, and (2) an

Notes to chapter 12 start on page 284

extension of his analysis of the religious affiliation of some of the shops and his conclusions regarding the connection between Jews and Christians based on this evidence.

We do not suggest that every possibility was active in Sardis simultaneously, but we do think that this multi-faceted approach offers insights into an understanding of religious rivalries in the context of the Sardis shops. Two key questions that underlie our analysis are (1) does the existence of cooperation among specific religious groups necessarily eliminate the possibility of competition among these same groups? and (2) what are some ways that one can explain and understand the interrelationships among religious communities in the ancient world?

The Evidence from the Shops and Synagogue[1]

The Shops[2]

The Byzantine shops in Sardis, built as part of a reconstructive project around 400 CE, back onto the centrally located bath-gymnasium complex as well as the synagogue in the southeast corner of this complex. Built on the south side of the complex, the shops border the main avenue of Sardis, which served as a key thoroughfare for the city (today the Izmir-Ankara highway runs just south and parallel to the main avenue). This building project further included the paving of the main avenue with marble and the installation of colonnaded sidewalks covered with mosaics on both sides of the avenue.

Excavators divide the shops into two groups: east and west. All shops west of the main hall of the gymnasium complex are indicated by numbers preceded by *W*, all those east of it are indicated by numbers preceded by *E*. The *realia* found inside the shops and residences are understood by Crawford to reveal the occupants' professions and their religions. The western shops run from W1 to W15 and back onto the bath-gymnasium complex. Of these fifteen shops, four have been identified as Christian (W1, W2, W8, W9). The eastern shops run from E1 to E19. Shops E1 through E5 also back onto the bath-gymnasium complex, while E6 through E19 back onto the synagogue. Between E18 and E19 lies a southern entrance to the synagogue. Of the fifteen shops on the eastern side, six have been identified by Crawford as Christian (E1, E2, E3, E4, E5, E18) and six as Jewish (E6, E7, E8, E12, E13, E14). None of the other shops yielded enough evidence to identify the religious affiliation of their occupants.

A pair of shops, W8 and W9, is considered to have formed a single unit: a commercial dye shop. What came to be designated as the dye vat was at first thought to be some type of religious structure, because of the size of its religious symbols. The vat was constructed from two reused marble gravestones that have been marked with two very large Latin crosses. Crawford indicates that such a practice of marking reused polytheist objects with crosses made them acceptable to Christians (1996, 41).[3] What is most interesting here is the placement of the crosses in relation to the doorway: the crosses faced the doorway (to the south) and were directly in line with it.

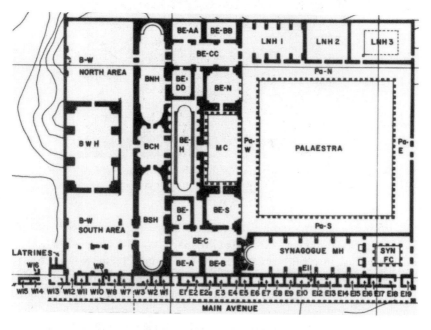

Plan of bath-gymnasium complex, as excavated in 1974. ©Archaeological Exploration of Sardis/Harvard University.

Shops W1 and W2 were also paired, according to Crawford, to form a Christian restaurant. The religious symbols found in this shop include a terracotta ampulla with a Latin cross, a copper alloy ring with a Maltese cross, and a Latin cross graffito. A furniture support in the form of Attis was also found with its face removed. Crawford considers that the removal of Attis's face indicates an animosity by the Christian occupants towards this polytheist image (1996, 42–44).

Shop E3 is labelled as a Christian residence. The Christian evidence comes from a prominently placed cross on the outside wall. A Latin cross (with a looped *rho*) can be found on a reused marble block that forms part of the outside wall, just to the left of the doorway, but the cross would have been clearly visible from the colonnade (Crawford 1996, 41).

Balloon aerial photograph of the bath-gymnasium complex at Sardis, W. and E. Myers. Courtesy of the Archaeological Exploration of Sardis.

E5 is also considered a Christian residence (Crawford 1990, 56). A sizeable cross, along with elaborate Christian iconography, was discovered on a large flask inside this residence. The iconography seems to be eucharistic, with rabbits[4] nibbling on leaves and branches that are growing from the cross; on the reverse, geese can be seen eating grapes. Samples from the flask indicate that it was likely not from the area,[5] and Crawford speculates that it was brought back from a pilgrimage (1990, 56). Building E5 was the only shop in which a silver coin was found, indicating that the resident was a wealthy Christian and thus able to make a pilgrimage. Also found in this shop was a lion-shaped brass lamp, considered one of the most attractive and interesting pieces in Sardis (Crawford 1990, 56). The lion grasps a shell in its mouth to hold the wick, and Crawford believes that "on the basis of comparisons to marble and bronze statuettes, terracottas, coins and a silver group...the lion once carried a statuette of Cybele on its back" (1990, 56). A crude patch on the back of the lamp provides further evidence for the removal of Cybele from this lamp, which Crawford interprets as an act of antagonism by the Christian owner (Crawford 1996, 42).

Shops E6 through E8 are labelled by Crawford as a Jewish dye establishment (1990, 60). Evidence for Jewish occupancy comes solely from E7, which contained two amphoras inscribed with the Greek *Iakovos* (genitive of the name Jacob). More important, two menorahs were etched onto the inside of the doorframe and would have been noticeable to those exiting the establishment.

The Byzantine shops as restored along the south side of the bath-gymnasium complex in Sardis, 1973. Courtesy of the Archaeological Exploration of Sardis.

E12 and E13 were also combined to form a Jewish establishment that specialized in glassware vessels and window panes.[6] Stairs in E12 led to an upper floor.[7] This establishment offers a most interesting connection between Jewish and Christian symbols and Crawford found its religious affiliation to be the most difficult to identify (1996, 41). Upstairs in E12, which was also considered part of the shop, not a residence (Crawford 1996, 41), two marble fragments were found with partial menorahs etched onto them.[8] Further, three names were found separately (in Greek) on three pottery vessels: one vessel from E12 contained the name *Ioannes*, and two vessels in upper E13 contained the names *Sabbatios* and *Theoktistos*. On the basis of the names (although he does admit that *Ioannes* and *Theoktistos* were also common for Christians)[9] and the menorah fragments, Crawford eventually classified this as a Jewish shop (1996, 41). Part of what made the religious identity difficult was the discovery of what Crawford describes as "a puzzling bronze object" (1990, 79), found among the evidence from the lower floor of E13, and initially identified as a censer or robe holder but then labelled as a weighing device. The most enigmatic aspect of this piece is that the top of it is decorated with a Maltese cross, which, as Crawford observes, "seems out of place in a supposedly Jewish Shop" (Crawford 1990, 79). Crawford identifies the shop as Jewish because "since

the shop's menorah plaque was larger, and therefore probably more important, than the small, less noticeable cross on the weighing device," so the
shop owner "must have been Jewish" (1996, 42). The presence of the weighing device with the cross (a symbol that could have been easily removed)
indicates for Crawford that the Jewish occupant did not take offence at
this Christian symbol (1996, 42).

The final shop, E18, also provides a connection between Jews and
Christians. Crawford suggests that the data found in E18 were more consistent with a residential than a commercial function (Crawford 1990, 98).
Inside this residence were two items with Christian symbolism: a plate
fragment with a partial stamped Greek cross monogram and an elaborate
copper-alloy lamp with a cross decoration and a lid shaped like a dolphin.
Crawford considers the dolphin to be a Christian symbol and relates it to
the acronym *ICHTHUS* (1996, 41).[10] While E18 did not contain any Jewish symbols, its placement in the row of shops and its location relative to the
synagogue are especially intriguing. This is the only shop identified as
Christian that backs directly onto the synagogue; it was located immediately
beside the short entrance leading from Main Avenue to the synagogue,
separated by a wall one brick thick. A further connection between E18 and
the synagogue is by way of the vertical drainpipe at the back of the shop,
which was linked to a water channel from the synagogue.

The Synagogue[11]

The Sardis synagogue has been explored extensively, and, while not wanting to duplicate the discussion, we do want to introduce some evidence
from the synagogue, given its connection to our discussion. The synagogue,
built directly into the southwestern corner of the bath-gymnasium complex
between 330 and 340 CE, runs lengthwise from east to west. It has an
extremely large (at least in comparison to other synagogues thus far excavated) main hall (60 m long and 20 m wide) and a sizeable forecourt (25
m long and 20 m wide) at its eastern end. The forecourt, with a primary
entrance to the east and a smaller entrance to the south, provides the only
access into the main hall. The height of the main hall is estimated to have
been between 9 m and 16 m (16 m if there was a clerestory on top) and probably seated around a thousand people. At the western end of the hall was
a broad apse and, in front of the apse, a huge marble table. The table supports are still intact and are decorated with Roman eagles clutching thunderbolts. Flanking this table were two pairs of lions, with each pair consisting
of two lions back-to-back as if standing guard. Seager notes the possible connection between these lions and the image of Cybele in Sardis when he
writes, "Perhaps [they were] associated with the image of Cybele origi-

nally!" (Seager and Kraabel 1983, 170). Another massive lion was found just outside the synagogue's forecourt and may have been one of yet another pair of lions, with this pair occupying a key position outside the synagogue.

The forecourt had a peristyle roof, which was covered around the outside but open in the middle so that the sun could shine into the court and onto the fountain below. The court was colonnaded on all four sides by what had probably been two-storey columns, although only one storey has been restored.[12] Serving as a centrepiece of the forecourt was a large fountain consisting of a marble crater with volute handles fed by an elaborate system of pipes under the floor. Around the fountain lay an intricate, multi-coloured floor of stone mosaics set in complex, geometric patterns. Although simply furnished, the impressive and beautiful forecourt would likely have caught the attention of non-Jews passing by and, if the court was accessible to Gentiles,[13] certainly by those who entered.

Both the forecourt and the main hall contain inscriptions, most of which are in Greek. Over eighty inscriptions concerning gifts of interior decorations and furnishings were found inside the synagogue and forecourt (either in mosaic on the floor or carved in marble plaques). These inscriptions reveal key details about the synagogue members and donors: a number of the Jewish congregants were of high social status and strongly connected to the polis. Many are given the title "citizen of Sardis." Eight are identified as members of the city council (*bouleutēs*), and other occupations and positions are acknowledged (Noakes 1974, 245; Trebilco 1991, 43–51). In the forecourt, one especially interesting mosaic inscription reads, "Aurelios Eulogios, God-Fearer [*theosebēs*] Redeemed His Vow (Pledge)."[14] Perhaps this is a donation by a Gentile.[15] Overall, the inscriptions provide strong connections between the members of the synagogue and the life of the polis.

Evidence of Jewish–Christian Competition in Sardis

Crawford suggests that the evidence from the shops demonstrates that "actual relations between Christians and Jews were not as hostile as literary sources claim" (1996, 44). We agree that the extreme hostility previously assumed to exist between Jews and Christians based on literary sources (e.g., Melito's *Peri Pascha*) needs to be re-evaluated,[16] but we also think that Crawford's emphasis on a non-hostile environment could be clarified by evidence from the shops.[17] Upon initial examination, the evidence seems to support such a non-hostile environment between Jews and Christians. No Jewish or Christian symbols were defaced, there is evidence for some very close interactions, and in at least one case, Jewish and Christian symbols are found in the same shop. Nonetheless, a closer examination of the evidence yields a more nuanced view.

When we examine the evidence from the perspective of what might be seen as an "aggressive" or "explicit" display of religious symbols in public areas, it takes a slightly different twist. The idea that the size, location, and design of religious buildings affected how a city's citizens and visitors perceived them and could expand religious boundaries into the public realm (i.e., they could "dominate" certain portions of the city and highlight the importance of a god or religion to the people) has been acknowledged in various forms.[18] Extending this function to publicly displayed religious symbols is not an implausible task, given the recognized symbolic nature of these displays.[19] If we acknowledge this as a possibility, we notice what could be evidence of "competition" between the Christian and Jewish groups in Sardis. The "bold" display of Christian symbols is what first stands out when examining the religious symbols in the Byzantine shops.

E3 provides the strongest and most obvious display of religious symbols in public view. E3, considered a residence by Crawford, displays on its outside wall a Latin cross large enough to be visible from the colonnade. We need to keep in mind that this row of shops was parallel to the main avenue of Sardis and would have accommodated much local traffic as well as visitors entering and exiting the city. There is no obvious reason to display the cross on the building's exterior. If, for example, the cross was meant as a means of "spiritual protection" (e.g., from evil spirits), why not simply place the cross on the inner doorframe (on both sides, for that matter) so that it could protect the owner while reassuring him with its presence? When placed on the outside of E3, the cross would have announced a Christian presence to those involved in daily activities in this area, to those shopping in this complex, to those going to the synagogue, and to visitors travelling along the main road.

Crawford notes that travellers might have taken shelter under the colonnade and watched those in their shops do their work. Further, those conducting business in or around the shops would have had opportunity to glance inside or even enter some of these shops. Any religious symbols of a significant size, displayed near the entrance of the shops, would have been unavoidable for many of these people. Once again, we find evidence of the prominent display of Christian symbols, this time near a shop entrance. The dying vat in shops W8 and W9 would have been noticeable from the colonnade, perhaps even from the street, and they most certainly would have been unavoidable for anyone entering the establishment. The very large Latin crosses inscribed on the gravestones used in the creation of the vat faced the doorway (south) of W8 so that those inside and outside the establishment could view them. As noted above, the crosses were so large that they were initially thought to be some kind of religious structure by the excavators and would have been impossible to ignore. The vat could have been built so that the crosses faced west (mainly towards the inside of the shop), but instead was built so that the crosses were directly in line with the front entrance. This appears to have been a purposeful tactic on the part of the occupants. At least it was a possible indication that Christians were announcing their presence in a manner that could be interpreted as an attempt to "compete" for religious space within the city.[20]

Jewish symbols were much scarcer than Christian symbols, and those found were in less noticeable locations. On first glance, this appears to fit the theory that any signs of competition came from the Christian side. Not only were there fewer shops identified as Jewish (ten Christian, six Jewish), but also in the six shops considered to have been occupied by Jews, the religious symbols used to identify them come, in fact, from only two of the shops (the connection of these two shops to others is what raised the number of shops identified as Jewish to six). E12 and E13 were eventually labelled as Jewish, because partial menorahs were found on the upper floor of E12 (we will say more about this evidence below).[21] The shop composed of E6, E7, and E8 was labelled as Jewish on the basis of a name inscribed on two amphoras found in E7 and, more important, on two menorahs etched onto the inside of the door jamb of E7. These menorahs, the most prominent evidence of Jewish presence in any of the shops, would have been visible only from the inside when leaving the shop. The evidence of a bold or "competitive" display of Jewish symbols seems almost non-existent, especially in comparison with the Christian symbols.

We would argue, however, that the synagogue, upon which many of the shops backed, plays an integral role in any discussion of the competition for public space by means of religious displays. In fact, the synagogue's design and placement fits well with the above-mentioned theories on the implications of a religious structure's location, size, and architectural design. Although we do not necessarily agree with all the conclusions of Kraabel on the presence of the synagogue,[22] his discussion of the synagogue evidence reveals some telling information about the synagogue as a prominent religious display.[23] Kraabel notes that most of the other Diaspora synagogues that have been excavated are about the size of a private dwelling, and even the significant Dura synagogue lies behind a walled complex. He surmises, "In view of its central location, its size, and its embellishments, it is hard to avoid the conclusion that the building was intended to be a showplace of Judaism" (Seager and Kraabel 1983, 188). The location of the synagogue, as well as its size and prominent visibility above the shops, could be interpreted as a "competitive" display of Jewish presence.

Not only was the synagogue prominently displayed, but the forecourt of the synagogue, which was, as Kraabel phrases it, "more attractive than efficient," could be viewed by the passerby from the roads on the eastern and the southern sides. During the day, sunlight would have illuminated the central fountain and highlighted the colourful mosaic flooring. Those passing by (and perhaps entering, if the forecourt was open to the public, as is speculated) would certainly not have missed such an attractive and expensive display.

Obviously the evidence is never as clear as one would like, but we need to be careful not to miss what could be signs of competition in the public arena from both the Christian and Jewish communities. The boldly placed Christian symbols would not have gone unnoticed, and the elaborate and extensive synagogue dominated the main avenue of Sardis. Crawford's valid recognition of Jewish and Christian tolerance needs to be balanced with the signs of underlying competition.

Evidence of Jewish and Christian Connections with Polytheist Sardis

We also want to clarify Crawford's conclusions on the relationship between the polytheists and the Jews and Christians. Crawford contrasts the fact that none of the Jewish or Christian symbols were mutilated or defaced with the mutilation or destruction of some polytheist objects. We want to balance Crawford's emphasis on the evidence of "antagonism" towards polytheist objects by Jews and Christians with the connection between Jews and polytheists and between Christians and polytheists.

First, let us look at the polytheist evidence found in what have been labelled as Jewish or Christian settings. Crawford cites evidence of the defacing and destruction of polytheist objects from two Christian "shops" and from the synagogue. In W1-W2, considered a restaurant, were three signs of Christian symbols: a cross on an ampulla, a cross on a copper-alloy ring, and a cross graffito. The furniture support in the form of Attis was also found in this restaurant. The face of this support appears to have been removed by the Christian occupant. Further, E5, regarded by Crawford as a Christian residence, contained a large flask marked with a sizeable cross and elaborate Christian iconography. In this same residence was found the lion-shaped brass lamp with a crude patch on its back. The patch is probably what is left of an image of Cybele, who rode on the lion's back. Finally, Crawford notes that the synagogue contained two reused pieces of material, one an Artemis-Cybele relief and the other a monument of Cybele. Both of these materials were reused in such a way as to obscure the gods' images (e.g., one was face down as part of the floor).

Two comments bear on this evidence: (1) we should distinguish between purposely defacing an image out of animosity and choosing not to display the image of "another deity," and (2) defacing something that has become one's possession and defacing a public image in the polis. In light of these two distinctions, the evidence at Sardis provides much less direct evidence of antagonism than Crawford has proposed. For example, in the case of the reused material in the synagogue, while the hiding or removing of the image of a polytheist god certainly does indicate a dislike of displaying such an image, it does not specifically indicate antagonism. We do not doubt that, given their common teaching on images of other gods (i.e., idols),[24] Jews and Christians alike would take strong exception to displaying polytheist images. We want to caution, however, against creating antagonism purely for the drama of the situation. When examining Jewish, Christian, and polytheist evidence, scholars have traditionally created a scenario in which there are clear-cut "good guys" and "bad guys."[25] We would suggest a more nuanced scenario in which antagonism (of various degrees) and cooperation existed side by side.

While we do not have space here to delineate all the ways in which Jews and Christians demonstrated connections to their polytheist neighbours, perhaps some examples will suffice. Harland has recently questioned the model of a declining polis and argued that inscriptional evidence indicates an ongoing vitality in the polis rather than a decline. Indications are that religious groups, including Jews and Christians, were very active in the life of the polis (Harland 2000, 99–121; 2003, 89–112, 213–37). Harland cites especially the model of social networks of benefaction. Although he does not provide specific evidence from Sardis, we can tentatively generalize that such models may well have been active in the Christian community of Sardis.[26]

Evidence from the Sardis synagogue also reveals a connection between the Jewish community and polytheist life in the polis. The most interesting connection is the large lion (possibly one of a pair) found just outside the forecourt of the synagogue (pairs of lions flanked the eagle table inside the synagogue's main hall). Kraabel considers this use of the lion image to indicate the strength of the Jewish community: it was able to maintain its own identity while assimilating polytheist objects based on its own history.[27] Certainly we do not want to return to the argument that Jews were deliberately syncretistic,[28] but we do want to note the connection between the Jews and their polytheist neighbours. Lions were an important part of the imagery of the polytheist community in Sardis.[29] Cybele functioned as one of the key figures in the city during the early Byzantine period, and lions were regarded as her sacred animal and came to represent her (Vermaseren 1977, 14–15; Hanfmann and Ramage 1978, 20; Crawford 1996, 42). Given the important connection of the lion to the polytheist cult in Sardis, it is not difficult to see the image of a lion outside the synagogue, in full view of all who pass by, as perhaps something more than a mere assimilation of the image of the Sardis lion into the Jewish context. Perhaps one can understand the lions flanking the eagle table in the synagogue's interior as an assimilation, but the large lions on the main avenue just outside the synagogue would be more likely connected to the lion images associated with the city of Sardis and with Cybele than to the lion as it was assimilated into the Jewish context. These lions seem to reflect the Jewish community's significant connection to its polytheist context (cf. Murray, chap. 13 in this volume).

The inscriptions found in the synagogue, moreover, indicate that key positions within the polis were held by Jews, and that Gentiles may have contributed to the Jewish community. The Jews are described as citizens of Sardis, and at least eight had occupied positions on the city council. Furthermore, at least one of the inscriptions, in the forecourt, may indicate the connection of a Gentile "God-fearer" to the synagogue. The combination of the evidence from the lions and from the inscriptions reinforces the probability that Jews and Gentiles in Sardis were both interested in and cooperative with one another, despite what appear to be signs of antagonism.

What is most interesting about Harland's study (noted above) is that, within this model, he proposes that one can find signs of co-operation and competition (2003, 266–67). He notes that inter-city competition may have resulted in a stronger cohesion among the inhabitants of a certain polis, while at the same time, competition for benefaction and participation in civic networks within the city could have produced rivalry among some of the groups within that city. We suggest that the evidence from the Byzantine shops and synagogue at Sardis mirrors this combination of co-operation and competition.

Evidence for the Complexities of Jewish-Christian Relations in Sardis

We now shift our attention to a more focused analysis of the evidence for interaction between Jews and Christians, with a specific look at the archaeological data recovered from two particular shops. Our intention is to extend Crawford's analysis of Jewish–Christian relations in Sardis by exploring alternative interpretations of the possible interconnectedness among certain members of both communities. In order to gain a fuller appreciation of the various options, we will integrate the archaeological data with some of the literary evidence associated with Sardis and its environs. We begin our analysis with an overview of the pertinent *realia* discovered in E12, E13, and E18, and an investigation of the implications of such data for Jewish–Christian relations.

Archaeological Evidence: Shops E12–13 and E18

As noted above, E12–13 present intriguing evidence connecting Jews and Christians. Some of the items relevant to our interests include the flat-bottomed jar with the name *Ioannes* that came from the upper storey, and the two marble fragments incised with partial menorahs (Crawford 1990, 78). Two other names found in graffiti in the upper-storey deposit of E13 were *Sabbatios* and *Theoktistos*. While all three of the names were used by Jews during the Byzantine period, Crawford notes that *Ioannes* and *Theoktistos* were frequently used by Christians as well, and a saint *Sabbatios* even existed in the Greek Orthodox Church (1996, 79). Thus, the names found in the inscriptions are of sufficient ambiguity to complicate the religious identification of the occupants of these shops. The situation is rendered all the more perplexing by the discovery of the weighing apparatus whose top is decorated with a cross. Crawford acknowledges that this find adds to the confusion about the religious identity of the occupants: "So were the people who operated this shop Jewish or Christian?" he asks (1996, 41).

His analysis of the evidence, including his judgment that the menorah was more important because it was larger than the cross, leads Crawford to identify the occupant of E12–13 as Jewish. What most intrigued Crawford was that the Jewish occupant of this shop did not remove the Christian cross from the weighing device. It would have been easy to do, so why didn't he? (1996, 42). In response to his question, he refers to information gleaned from personal conversation with the late Israeli archaeologist Nachman Avigad, who suggested to him that "such a quotidian object as a lamp would not arouse either interest or antagonism in the user, and could therefore fit unobtrusively in almost any context." Crawford concludes that "the same was probably true of our bronze object" (1990, 79). Thus, the scenario presented by Crawford is that of a Jewish merchant who did not mind using a Christian weighing tool (whether he understood its symbolism or not). It is this type of evidence that he employs to substantiate his argument that Jews and Christians "respected each other's religious symbols and therefore probably each other" (Crawford 1996, 42).

We do not disagree with Crawford's general argument. Certainly, archaeological evidence at Sardis indicates that the relationships among certain Jews and Christians were close; indeed, Jewish and Christian merchants were trading side by side in the shops alongside the synagogue, in the commercial centre of the fourth-century CE city. We would further agree with Crawford that the religious symbols uncovered in E12 and E13 show that the occupant could very well have been Jewish. But this is the only possibility proffered by Crawford. In our view, it is advisable to explore additional interpretations of the evidence. For example, the shop's occupant might have been a Jew who not only did not mind using a weighing tool bearing a Christian symbol, but actually embraced Christianity in some fashion. Thus, in this scenario, perhaps he did not remove the cross from this object because he did not wish to remove this Christian symbol!

Certainly the evidence for Crawford's conclusion needs to be examined. He draws a parallel between the discovery of the Christian weighing device on the first floor of E13 and the discovery by Nachman Avigad of a third- or fourth-century CE lamp bearing the monogram *ChiRho* in a Jewish catacomb at Beth She'arim (Crawford 1996, 41; cf. Avigad 1976, 188).[30] Avigad's argument that utilitarian objects of daily use—such as lamps—could "fit unobtrusively in almost any context" is, in our view, more convincing when applied to his own discovery at Beth She'arim. Even he acknowledges that the *ChiRho* symbol is a "surprising" find in a Jewish setting, but then he suggests that it was likely that "the Jewish buyer of this lamp did not notice the symbol or did not understand its significance." The reason, he suggests, is that "at that time, the first half of the fourth century CE, this symbol was still relatively new and perhaps did not disturb the sensibilities of Jews as the sign of the cross would later on" (Avigad 1976, 188). Crawford argues that the Jewish merchant in Sardis shop E12–13 likewise would not have cared about the cross symbolism, although there is a difference between the symbol of the cross and the use of the *ChiRho* monogram. It seems more likely that a third- or fourth-century CE Jew might not recognize the meaning of the *ChiRho* and thus make use of a lamp. It seems less likely, however, that a fourth-century CE Jew used an object bearing a prominent cross without knowing or caring that the cross was a Christian symbol. The use of a cross in a Jewish context may be more significant than Crawford allows. While there is a paucity of evidence for Christian Jews living in Asia Minor in the fourth century,[31] this paucity might be an accident of discovery (or rather, lack thereof). At present, little more can be said about this option.

Another, perhaps more compelling, hypothesis to consider is that the occupant of E12–13 was a Christian. As noted earlier, in his analysis of the religious association of the shop resident, Crawford considers the size of the evidence found. He decides that since the menorah was larger, it bore more significance than the cross, hence the resident was Jewish. A different aspect of the evidence to consider is *where* the two objects were found. The weighing device was discovered in the first floor, while the menorah was found in the upper-storey deposit. Of the two locations, likely the first floor was the more public area, where the occupants interacted with their patrons. The second floor, while accessible by stairs and perhaps still a part of the shop, was more hidden away from the view of most patrons. Thus, one could argue that the Christian symbol was potentially more publicly displayed, and perhaps pointing to the occupant's commitment to Christianity. This could have been a Gentile Christian who was secretly interested in Judaism, hence the incised menorah placed upstairs rather than downstairs. As will be discussed below, several canons from a church council held in Asia Minor in the fourth century CE reflect that certain ecclesiastical leaders in the region were aware of Judaizing practices and sought to eradicate such behaviour from within their churches.

Sardis shops backing onto the synagogue. Photo by Michele Murray, used by permission.

Data found in shop E18, located at the easternmost part of the colonnade, provides further intriguing evidence for Jewish–Christian relations at Sardis. As noted above, E18 is the only shop identified as Christian that backs directly onto the synagogue, and is located just west of one of its entrances. E18 is identified by Crawford as Christian (1996, 41) because the only religious symbols found inside are Christian: an intricately decorated bronze lamp with an ivy leaf-shaped handle guard decorated with a cross, a lid with a knob in the shape of a jumping dolphin (1990, 98, figs. 567, 568, 570), and a plate fragment with a stamped cross monogram.

The location of E18, at the far eastern end of the colonnade next to the entrance to the synagogue and sharing a wall with the synagogue surrounded by Jewish shops and residences, situates it deep within "Jewish territory." If Crawford has correctly identified the religious identity of its occupant, this is evidence that supports his argument that Jews and Christians were tolerant of one another. In our view, however, more can be said about the evidence found in E18 and its implications for Jewish–Christian relations in Sardis.

That a Christian would inhabit a shop so far into "Jewish territory" raises questions about the Christian's relationship with the Jewish community. Perhaps this evidence points to the existence of an actual interconnection among certain members of each community. Literary evidence associated with Sardis and its environs from the fourth century CE and earlier suggests that Christians and Jews not only tolerated and respected one another, but that boundary lines between the communities were crossed. Let us turn briefly to two different literary sources: the fourth-century CE Laodicean canons, and the second century CE *Peri Pascha* of Melito, bishop of Sardis.

Literary Evidence: The Laodicean Canons and Melito's Peri Pascha

At Laodicea, a city of Asia Minor located near Sardis, a group of Anatolian bishops held a council in 364 CE (within the time that the new commercial centre of Sardis would have been thriving). The main duty of the council was to introduce harmony and order into the Christian communities, and formal decisions or "canons" taken by this particular ecclesiastical council are still preserved. The phenomenon of Gentile Christian Judaizing—that is, Gentile Christians combining a commitment to Christianity with adherence in varying degrees to Jewish practices, without viewing such behaviour as contradictory—was making its influence felt within the Christian church in regions of the Roman empire during the fourth century, and certain of the Laodicean canons presuppose Judaizing tendencies among Christians.[32] In Canon 29, Christians are instructed not to "Judaize" by resting on the Sabbath; instead, they are to work on that day and to rest on Sunday (Canon 29 in Parkes 1969, 175). Furthermore, they are to read the Gospels as well as the Jewish scriptures on the Sabbath (Canon 16). As Simon suggests, the "authors of the canons are thinking of those Christians who, in conforming to the Synagogue pattern, read nothing on that day but the Old Testament, and perhaps did their reading together with the Jews" (Simon 1986, 329). Christians are instructed not to share in Jewish festivals, nor are they to receive gifts associated with such festivals from Jews (Canon 37). Apparently, some were participating in Passover Seders with their Jewish neighbours, for Canon 38 specifically forbids Christian acceptance of unleavened bread from Jews as well as their taking part in Jewish "impieties." One of the troubling aspects of Gentile Christian Judaizing, from the perspective of church leaders, was that these Christians blurred the dividing lines between Christian and Jewish communities and thereby challenged the Christian sense of a distinctive self-identity.[33] As Parkes observed long ago, "These regulations taken together certainly leave a strong impression that even in the fourth century there were not only Judaic practices in the Church in Asia, but that there was actual religious fellowship with the Jewish inhabitants" (1969, 175-76; Simon 1986, 329).

Parkes's assertion could be applicable to Sardis, particularly given the connection between Jewish and Christian symbols reflected in the archaeological evidence found in E12-13 and E18. Intimate contact between Jewish communities and non-Jewish communities—a situation that appears to have existed in fourth-century CE Sardis—is considered to be one of the causes of Judaizing (Murray 2004, 11-26). Melito's *Peri Pascha,* which probably was written in Sardis in the late second century CE, may provide further insight into the relationship between Jews and Christians living in Sardis.[34] While this document predates the archaeological evidence on which this essay is mainly focused by approximately two centuries, we would argue that Melito's words offer clarification on the history of the relationship between Sardis Jews and Christians, and thus may be useful for interpreting the later archaeological data.[35]

Melito, bishop of Sardis, was a Quartodeciman who lived about 120-185 CE during the reign of emperor Marcus Aurelius (161-180 CE).[36] Quartodecimans, apparently populous throughout Asia Minor by the late second century CE, celebrated Easter on the same date as the Jewish Passover, the 14th of Nissan. Their manner of observance had Jewish overtones, for they held a Seder in the same way as the Jews, and their leaders were familiar with the Jewish customs of Passover (Werner 1965, 200).[37] Melito's attitude towards Judaism, however, was far from positive. His contention was that Judaism and its law were defunct, replaced by the church and the gospel, and that the Jews were fully responsible for the death of Jesus.

For Melito, the Jewish people no longer held a special position before God. If any uncertainty remained, Melito dispels it unequivocally with characteristic forthrightness: "The people was made void [*ho laos ekenothe*] when the church arose" (line 278). The implication is that Christians had secured the position formerly held by the Jews. Judaism served a purpose for a time, but it was a mere foreshadowing of the superior religion yet to come (lines 235-40). While Melito's evaluation of Judaism was not entirely negative, his positive comments pertain only to Israel's past. Israel's present, in his view, is futile and hopeless.[38]

According to Melito, the Jews were responsible for every aspect of the crucifixion of Jesus: they prepared sharp nails and the false witnesses (line 555); they fed him vinegar and gall (line 557); they "brought forth scourges for his body and thorns for his head" (lines 559-60). Finally, Melito tells them, "You killed your Lord at the great feast" (line 565). The Jews killed "him whom the gentiles (*ta ethnē*) worshipped and the uncircumcised (*akrobustoi*) admired and foreigners (*allophyloi*) glorified" (lines 673–75).[39] Melito is the first Christian writer unambiguously to accuse the Jews of deicide: "God has been murdered" by them, he declares (line 715–16; Werner 1966, 191–210).[40]

What impelled Melito to strike out against the Jews in such an uncompromising way? The answers to this question are found by trying to understand the context in which Melito wrote and the circumstances he faced as a Christian living in Asia Minor in the middle of the second century. Kraabel made the argument, based on evidence from the location and size of the Sardis synagogue, that Melito's bitter attack responded to the fact that the Jews were in a wealthier, more prestigious position than the fledgling Christian group he represented in Sardis (1971, 83ff.), and suggested that the "Jews' attitude might have been one of hostility toward 'apostates' or one of openness; either way, in the face of such a large and powerful Jewish community Melito felt forced to adopt the stance demonstrated in the *Peri Pascha*" (Kraabel 1971, 84). In a more recent publication Kraabel clarifies that the *Peri Pascha* "does not mean a Jewish–Christian conflict in late second century Sardis; there is no evidence from the Jewish side for that.... There is no firm evidence that Sardis Jews were even aware of Melito, or that a direct hostility on their part provoked his attacks" (1992e, 264; see also Norris 1986, 16–24). Noakes argues that "the intensity of Melito's polemic against Israel surely testifies to the antagonism between the Jewish and Christian communities in Sardis" (1974, 246).

While it is correct that Melito's words reflect hostility towards Jews, we suggest that Melito inveighs against the Jews in order to create distance between communities that were, in fact, *too closely intertwined* (cf. Aasgaard, chap. 11). Perhaps the anti-Jewish polemic that Melito expounds in his homily was prompted not by Jews, but by Gentile Christians within his own community who were interested in Judaism.[41] Wilson suggests that while some of the Christians in Sardis may have been converts from Judaism, "there may also have been traffic in the other direction" (1995, 253). This may have manifested itself in the form of Gentile Christian Judaizing, or, even more disturbing to a leader of a church, perhaps the outright conversion of Gentile Christians to Judaism.[42] Melito's attempt to establish boundaries between Jews and Christians could have been in reaction to an environment in which Christians were exposed, and attracted, to Judaism. As Quartodecimans, the Gentile Christians of Melito's community were already in the habit of fusing their Christian practices with Jewish customs once every year at Passover; adopting additional Jewish rites might have seemed quite natural to them. Melito's manner of juxtaposing positive assessments of the behaviour of Gentiles with negative evaluations of the behaviour of "Israel" might have been an attempt to discourage Gentile Christians from adopting other Jewish customs by denigrating the Jews and discrediting Judaism.

When the archaeological data uncovered in E12–13 and E18 are supplemented with literary evidence, it is possible to explore a fuller spectrum of interpretations of those data. The Laodicean canons reveal that certain Gentile Christians in Asia Minor continued to be attracted to Judaism during the fourth century CE, and even participated in certain Jewish customs, such as resting on the Sabbath and hearing the Jewish scriptures on the Sabbath, perhaps in the company of their Jewish neighbours. Melito's animosity towards Jews, reflected in his *Peri Pascha*, can be understood as a reaction to Judaizing among Gentile Christians in Sardis stemming from a closely intertwined relationship among certain Jews and Christians in the late second century CE.

Conclusion

In this paper we set ourselves a twofold task: (1) to reconsider Crawford's conclusions on the relationship between Jews and Christians and between the Judeo-Christian and polytheist communities, and (2) to extend his analysis of the *realia* uncovered in the Sardis shops in combination with literary sources from the region, exploring the implications of such evidence for the issue of Sardis Jewish–Christian relations in particular. In the first section, by undertaking a closer scrutiny of the evidence from the shops and the synagogue, we discovered traces of underlying rivalry among Jews and Christians and contended that Crawford's assertion of tolerance needs to be tempered by acknowledgment of underlying competition. Furthermore, we detected Jewish and Christian connections with polytheist Sardis, which balance Crawford's postulation that only antagonism existed between the monotheistic and polytheist communities. With this analysis, we argue for a more nuanced scenario than that presented by Crawford, one in which a combination of degrees of opposition and co-operation existed concurrently between the Jewish and Christian communities, and between the Judeo-Christian and polytheist communities.

In the second section, we investigated alternative interpretations of the archaeological evidence taken exclusively from the shops yielding intriguing data connecting Jews and Christians. In our view, more can be said about these interconnections than has been offered by Crawford. While we do agree that there was tolerance in Sardis between the Jewish and Christian communities, when we probed some of the relevant literary sources, we discovered evidence that strengthened our contention that additional interpretations of the interaction among members of these two groups ought to be explored. Specifically, after first raising the possibility of the presence of Jewish Christians, we posited the more compelling scenario of the phenomenon of Gentile Christian Judaizers. The combination of literary evidence and archaeological data discloses grounds for a wider spectrum of interconnection among Jews and Christians living in Sardis.

BROADENING THE CONTEXT

13

Down the Road from Sardis
Adaptive Religious Structures and Religious Interaction in the Ancient City of Priene

Michele Murray

Introduction

In the Roman civic environment, no less than in our own modern cities, construction was a natural part of life. The building of new structures, and the remodelling of older ones, was an integral part of the fabric of ordinary urban society. L. Michael White has effectively drawn attention to the importance of taking notice of the adaptive religious structures of the Roman world; he argues convincingly that analysis of the various stages of renovation of ancient buildings imparts important social evidence on the status and circumstances of religious communities (White 1990).

Amid all of the archaeological evidence reflecting renovation of religious buildings, particularly interesting is evidence of architectural modification of the private home for cultic use and the involvement of patrons and benefactors in this process. Among the archaeological discoveries in ancient Priene, a city situated on the Ionian coast of Asia Minor between Ephesus and Miletus, was an adapted private house located in the domestic quarter of the city. The first excavators of the site, a German team led by Theodor Wiegand, identified the structure as a Christian *Hauskirche* and dated it to the fourth or fifth century CE.[1] The building is now properly identified as a synagogue, dated to the second or third century CE, which was constructed by remodelling a private home.

What makes this synagogue discovery particularly intriguing is its juxtaposition with two other religious structures: a *temenos* identified as belonging to the cult of Cybele, and a sanctuary to the deified Alexander the Great. Both of these religious sites, like the synagogue, are located on renovated private property; consequently, all three were dependent on the benefaction of patrons for the acquisition and use of the property. Each of

---

Notes to chapter 13 start on page 290

these remodelled dwellings is found along West Gate Street, one of the main roadways of the city. The location of these buildings just inside the city wall, however, places them decidedly on the outskirts of the urban centre of Priene, in a location typical of many Greco-Roman voluntary associations. After a brief overview of the history and setting of the ancient city of Priene, I will present and analyze the relevant archaeological evidence as recorded in the original 1904 excavation reports on the city and other more recent archaeological reports.[2] My analysis will proceed in the following order: (1) the *temenos* of Cybele, (2) the shrine to Alexander the Great, and (3) the synagogue. I will then focus the discussion on the status of the Jewish community in Priene, as well as the interaction among Jews and Christians in the city, based on the archaeological *realia*. I will also note that despite the obvious differences in their wealth and the size of their synagogues, the Jewish communities at Priene and Sardis resembled one another in their positive coexistence with the citizens of the polis and the respective Christian communities in each (cf. Cohick 1999, 127).

Priene: The Setting of Its Ruins

The present site of the archaeological ruins of Priene beside the village of Turunclar, Turkey, is not the original site of the city. It was forced to move from its older (uncertain) location because of the accumulation of clay deposits from the Maender River. In 350 BCE the new city was constructed on its present site, located on a slope at the foot of a rock cliff among the lofty Mycale Mountains. At this time, Priene was closer to the sea than it is presently, and maintained a small port called Naulochos (see Bean 1966, 197–218; Akurgal 1970, 185–206).

This new town was still being built when Alexander the Great arrived in 334 BCE. Discovering that the principal temple of the city, the temple to Athena, was still unfinished, Alexander supplied the finances for the building of the rest of the structure. One of the rewards for his generosity was the honour of dedicating the temple, which is recorded in an inscription now housed in the British Museum (Stoneman 1997, 29).[3] The architect of the temple to Athena, Carian Pytheos, later wrote an architectural manual that used this very temple at Priene as the ideal model for Ionic temple construction (Bean 1966, 200). Other temples, such as ones dedicated to Demeter and Kore and to Zeus Olympios, also date to the early days of the city's existence and are located in the heart of the city centre.

In 129 BCE, Priene became part of the Roman province of Asia Minor. The combination of its location near the more economically vibrant city of Miletus to the south, and the gradual accumulation of clay deposits in its own harbour, were detrimental to the city's economic growth, hence Priene remained comparatively small (Trebilco 1991, 55). One of the consequences of this relative obscurity is that massive Roman buildings were not built on top of earlier structures, so Priene offers a striking example of Hellenistic architecture and of the grid type of town-planning associated with the Hippodamian system. Main streets, which run east and west, are intersected at right angles by lanes running north and south, and each block commonly contains three or four houses. The streets and houses of Priene are among its best preserved and most attractive features, and it is to the three private dwellings on West Gate Street that we now turn.

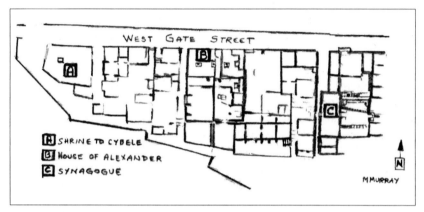

Diagram of West Gate Street, Priene. Drawing by Michele Murray, used by permission.

The Shrine to Cybele

On the south side of West Gate Street, among the private homes in the last plot inside the west gate of the city wall, a small shrine was found in an asymmetric five-sided courtyard.[4] A sacrificial pit, square in shape and of sizeable dimensions (approximately 1.5 m long by 1.5 m wide, and 1 m deep), was discovered in the western area of the courtyard. The pit was filled with ashes, bone splinters, and pieces of clay vessels; these remains also were found scattered about in the courtyard (Wiegand 1904, 171; Schede 1964, 101).

The shrine was identified as belonging to Cybele, because a marble statue of this popular Phrygian goddess was discovered there. The statue is of a woman (missing her head and arms) who is sitting on her throne wrapped in a heavy robe with a crouching lion serving as her footstool (Wiegand and Schrader 1904, 172, image 164; Schede 1964, 101, image 122 on p. 104). Wiegand and Schrader refer to a second statue, whose feet are resting on a richly decorated footstool, but which is missing a head, torso, and arms. They specifically state that a lion is not to be found either at the woman's feet or on her lap, but that she nonetheless should be identified as Cybele (1904, 172).[5] German archaeologist Martin Schede, in the 1964 edition of his *Die Ruinen von Priene* (first edition, 1934), provides a later report on the excavations at Priene. He presents a picture of a second, well-preserved terracotta found in the area of the courtyard (not mentioned by Wiegand and Schrader) that shows Cybele in the manner typical of Hellenistic-Roman representations of her: she sits on a throne flanked by lions and wears a heavy, flowing robe and a tall crown, and she seems to be holding a small animal (perhaps a lion cub) in her lap (Schede 1964, 104, Abb. 123).

The cult of Cybele, "Mother of the Gods" (*Magna Mater*), was the first of the Near Eastern religious cults to be received officially into Rome, sometime in the third century BCE (Livy 29.10–14 in Ferguson 1987, 264). She is associated with frenzied public processions, and in particular, with the Galli priests. These priests would emasculate themselves as an offering of blood in ecstatic devotion to the goddess, probably as a means of purification or atonement, and they would typically wear female clothes and let their hair grow long (Ferguson 1987, 267). The lion, the much-feared king of the beasts, is depicted as subject to this goddess of the wild forests and savage mountains (Vermaseren 1977, 14). When Cybele is enthroned, the lions are usually portrayed as her sentinels, and she shows her authority over them often by allowing one to lie passively on her knees like a gentle lapdog or by letting it serve as a humble resting place for her feet (Vermaseren 1977, 15).

The shrine to Cybele in Priene seems to have been a simple, modest one; no inscriptions or coins were discovered in the courtyard. Wiegand and Schrader argue that the location of this shrine so close to the western gate of the city wall probably means that Cybele was considered a protector-goddess whose district was the territory around this western gate. They suggest that this was indeed a state-supported cult, and that in comparison with these other shrines, the Cybele shrine was more sophisticated and reflected greater power and significance than the others (1904, 172). Schede, on the other hand, asserts that Cybele generally was most popular among the poor and probably was not supported on a governmental level in Priene (1964, 101).

Evidence of widespread devotion to Cybele throughout the Greco-Roman world points to an eclectic variety of devotees, from peasants and woodcutters to businessmen working in seaports, whose expression of devotion ranged from modest terracotta statues to more expensive marble representations (Turcan 1996, 57). The location of the Cybele shrine in a private, residential area of Priene, in my view, points towards the participation primarily of the urban poor, including slaves and freedmen, who were living in homes on the outskirts of the city. The lack of embellishment of this *temenos* militates against Wiegand and Schrader's assertion, although the frieze on another temple in Priene—that of Athena Polias, which depicts Cybele riding on a lion—implies some form of state acknowledgment of the cult (Vermaseren 1977, 31).

This setting is typical of voluntary associations and small cults throughout the Hellenistic and Roman period. Using private homes was a means of introducing religions of the Greek East into the Roman world (White 1990). An individual of sufficient means would allow a part of his or her property to be used for cultic purposes in return for a position of honour and esteem in the religious community. In this case, part of a courtyard, which may have belonged to the house next door, was converted into a place of worship to Cybele. This house-based shrine located in a peripheral residential district stands in contrast to the grandiosity of the main public temples of Priene, located in the heart of the city centre. Similarly, many Jewish, Christian, and Mithraic house-based religious structures typically were established on the periphery of the urban centre, often near the city walls (see White 1990, 1997; Richardson 1998b, 373-84).

The House of Alexander

The neighbouring block of homes east of the Cybele shrine is the site of another residence-based place of worship. Here, according to Wiegand and Schrader, was discovered a "strangely built shrine," which they refer to as the *hieros oikos* (1904, 172). This structure was adapted from what was a typical private home of the Hellenistic period (1904, 173), consisting of a large courtyard, surrounded by several smaller rooms, accessible from a side alley leading from West Gate Street on the western side. To the north is the main room of the sanctuary: it is a long room of "impressive" dimensions with three pillars and two naves.[6] On the eastern side of the courtyard are three small rooms, and along the southern part of the courtyard are two larger rooms that are angled to fit along the rock (1904, 172).

The various connections between the house shrine and the adjacent dwelling suggest that the two may have belonged to the same owner. Wiegand and Schrader were convinced that the shrine was built later than the adjacent house. They observed that the eastern wall of the *hieros oikos* does not possess a façade; instead, it leans against the western wall of the adjacent home (1904, 174). One of the southeastern rooms of the shrine does not have its own end wall either, but is built on the southwestern corner of the adjacent house. In addition, neither of the two rooms to the south of the *hieros oikos* has its own end wall but, instead, uses the western wall of the adjacent home for this purpose (1904, 174).

The house shrine clearly was considered a sacred place. In the lane, lying very close to the entrance gate, was found an ashlar (belonging to the left doorpost) that bears an inscription declaring that none shall enter this "holy sanctuary" except those wearing white clothing (1904, 174; also Schede 1964, 101).[7] Perhaps this stipulation, in addition to its connotations of purity, was an attempt to efface the hierarchical structures of society or at least convey a common sense of belonging, by having all members of this association wear the same colour.

The earliest excavators were not certain who was worshipped here, but more recent analysis has identified this as a shrine to the deified Alexander the Great. Among the marble works of art discovered in this sanctuary was a well-preserved statue bearing features of *"unverkennbare Aehnlichkeit"* (unmistakable likeness) to Alexander the Great's portrait presented on coins from Lysimachos (1904, 180).[8] The statue comprises the head (0.09 m) and torso of a man (0.28 m in height; missing is the entire left arm, the lower right arm, and the rest of the lower body), and reflects stylistic characteristics typical of the Hellenistic period.[9] Also discovered was a fragment belonging to the left hand of this statue, which reveals that Alexander carried a sword in his left hand (Wiegand and Schrader 1904, 182). Wiegand and Schrader suggest that the statue ought to be dated not long after the lifetime of Alexander, so "fresh and direct" is the execution of the statue (1904, 182; Schede 1964, 106).

The shrine's identification as a sanctuary dedicated to the deified Alexander the Great is strengthened by the discovery of an inscription stating that a sacred place devoted to Alexander existed in Priene, and that it was restored in 140 BCE for 1,000 drachmas donated by wealthy inhabitants of the city; no other possible site has so far been found (Schede 1964, 106; Bean 1966, 216).[10] Alexander allegedly stayed in Priene when he fought against Miletus in 334 BCE. The house in which he lived likely was renovated into a shrine dedicated to him after he left the city—or perhaps more accurately, after he died. While there is evidence that Alexander was invested with divine honours during his lifetime, and that he may have considered himself to be more than a human being, worship of the deified Alexander occurred with more frequency after his death (Ferguson 1987, 191; Plutarch, *Life of Alexander* 27).[11]

On the site itself, the pedestal stones of three bases are still aligned against the northern wall of the portico *in situ*: one semicircular, one round, and one square. It appears that at one point in its history statues were placed side by side on each of the pedestals (Wiegand and Schrader 1904, 175). Wiegand notes that a second door was built later in the southern wall, after the room of the *hieron* had been separated into two by a cross-wall.[12] In the northeastern corner of the *hieron* is a podium (1.20 m high by

2.15 m wide) made of rough stone and lime, that runs along the north and
east walls. Scattered around the podium, pieces of marble and terracotta statuettes were found; these statues probably were displayed on top of the
podium. Two little steps in the front lead up to it (0.70 m by 0.40 m wide),
while a third step (0.55 m wide) was found at the southern part of the
podium (Wiegand and Schrader 1904, 176; Schede 1964, 101).

It is clear that cultic rites were performed at this site; the protection and
patronage of Alexander were sought through the offering of sacrifices. In front
of the podium, between the two steps, two legs of a table were discovered.
In addition, the surface of the table, made of marble and measuring 1.57 m
by 0.95 m, was found next to the legs. The table legs are decorated on the
front surface with four flutes; Wiegand describes the legs as in the shape of
lion paws (1904, 176). Between the table legs and in front of the podium was
a natural crevice in the floor, approximately 1.50 m long, 0.60 m wide, and
1.50 m deep (1904, 176). Schede suggests that the table probably stood over
this crevice and was used for offering sacrifices; the blood would then flow
into the crevice (1964, 106). Wiegand and Schrader, on the other hand, dis-
miss the idea that the crevice was used as a sacrificial pit, asserting that
"there is not sufficient reason" to draw such a conclusion (1904, 176). They
do assert, however, that the marble table was used for sacrifices and offerings.
Because the table lacked a rim around its surface (which would collect the
blood), they suggest that the offerings made were dry (1904, 176).

A similar sacrificial table was found in the room adjacent to the north-
east corner of the courtyard; this table was discovered collapsed on itself
(Wiegand and Schrader 1904, 177).[13] According to Wiegand, "The way in
which the main room with two naves does not stand on its own and thereby
dominate the space, but instead is surrounded by smaller rooms which
surround the courtyard on three sides, was unusual in that it bears no
resemblance to a temple" (1904, 178). Wiegand and Schrader suggest that
this "was not the place of a public, state cult but rather the private installation of the fertility cult; not a real temple but rather a *'heiliges Haus'*"
(1904, 178). The largest room was likely used for setting up cult images and
for larger communal feasts, with the smaller rooms used for simpler festivities (1904, 178). This was a private home that had been converted into a
multi-purpose facility for cultic ritual practice, as well as communal eating
and drinking, all of which were activities typical of voluntary associations
(Wilson 1996, 12).

The Synagogue

We move farther east along West Gate Street to the next adaptive religious
site, a structure initially identified as a house church, but now (correctly)

as a synagogue.[14] The synagogue, located in the block next to the *heiliges Haus* of Alexander described above, was created from what was originally a rather simple Hellenistic private house with an *oecus* and *prostas*. Through physical alterations made to the courtyard, the house was transformed into a modest synagogue in the second or third century with a main assembly hall and an entry hall from the side street (White 1997, 327–32).[15]

As White notes, the three central phases of physical adaptation consist of (1) the creation of a new entrance by knocking out the old walls of the three small chambers (a shop, a latrine, and a duct) and the building of a main entrance that accessed the main room of the synagogue through a forecourt from the side lane;[16] (2) the laying of two rows of stone slabs aligned east-west along the floor, which "probably served as a stylobate" (only one column fragment was found), as well as the installation of benches and steps (White 1997, 330–31); (3) the construction of the square niche, which would have been visible directly from the entrance to the synagogue. White notes that this niche was created by "knocking out a portion of the party-wall with the adjacent building" and that the niche, which probably functioned as a Torah shrine, actually projected *into the adjacent structure*" (1997, 331, emphasis mine). White logically suggests that this renovation indicates that "the Jewish community had come into possession of all or most of the houses and buildings in the block" (1997, 331).

The main room of the synagogue, measuring approximately 10 m east-west by 14 m north-south, was the principal place of community assembly: a bench runs along its northern wall, where men and women presumably sat together.[17] The main room is surrounded by smaller rooms—formerly the domestic quarters of the house—which probably were used by the Jewish community for various functions, including a hostel, a custodian's chamber, or a school (Trebilco 1991, 55; White 1997, 332; Kraabel 1979, 502).[18] Four items discovered in the building prove it was a synagogue: (1) A relief of a menorah, flanked by peacocks[19] and a *lulab*, was found in the floor of the synagogue in front of the Torah niche (Wiegand and Schrader 1907, 481), (2) a large pillar with the "weathered" remains of a roughly chiselled menorah (Wiegand and Schrader 1907, 481, although they do not mention that the drawing is incomplete), (3) a Torah niche on the east wall, and (4) a large ablution basin.[20] No Christian symbols have been found. How long the synagogue was in use, or when it fell into disuse, is not known. Trebilco understands that the discovery of the Torah niche, the reliefs bearing Jewish symbols, and the basin for ablution in this synagogue reflect a community for which the Torah and purity rules were important, and that this community belonged to the "mainstream of Jewish faith and practice of the period" (1991, 56).

The Status of the Jewish Community at Priene

In discussions about the synagogue in Priene there is the propensity to argue that the Priene Jewish community consciously attempted to conceal the synagogue and to hide itself away from public recognition. This argument is based on an interpretation of the archaeological remains of the synagogue, particularly its location in the residential area of the city, and the fact that the main entrance to the building opens onto a side alley, and not from West Gate Street. Comparisons between the Priene synagogue and the Sardis synagogue have tended to focus on the dissimilarity in size and wealth of the two communities, and have contributed to the understanding that the Priene synagogue was deliberately inconspicuous. Trebilco, for example, notes the "striking" contrast between the Priene synagogue and the one at Sardis in size and location (1991, 55); he suggests that the Jewish community at Priene was "small and undistinguished" (1991, 57). Trebilco further observes that the Priene structure lacks "signs of obvious prosperity and influence that are to be found at Sardis" and that it "was on a side street and was not easily identified as a synagogue" (1991, 55). Kraabel contends that "because of the Jews' minority status, the Diaspora synagogue may be concealed or at least deliberately inconspicuous, e.g., Dura, Ostia and probably Priene. But that is not always the case, e.g., Sardis and possibly Stobi" (1979, 501). The implication is that the general environment in the city was un-friendly, even hostile, to minority groups, and that, for reasons of security, the Jews of Priene sought to hide the existence of their place of worship.

This argument must be challenged. While it is accurate to say that the entrance to the synagogue in Priene was not from the main West Gate Street, the construction of the entrance to the synagogue on the side street might have been motivated by reasons other than an attempt to conceal or disguise the synagogue. The placement of this entrance might be connected to the fact that West Gate Street, as the main thoroughfare of the city, probably was full of activity and noise. Entering the synagogue from a side alley would enable worshippers to remove themselves from the clamour of the main road and would provide a quieter, reverential atmosphere more suitable to entering a religious building. The private nature of the synagogue structure is consistent with the architectural practice of other religious sanctuaries in the city: we have observed already that the entrance to the shrine to Alexander was likewise from a private alley off West Gate Street.

The physical alterations made by the Jews to the private home, furthermore, were of a sufficiently substantial nature to have been noticed by others, perhaps even from the main street. White admits that the original home was modified in the interior, but notes that "razing the shops and rebuild-

ing the walls of the court had to attract public notice" (White 1990, 67). In
the construction of the synagogue, the Jewish community encroached on surrounding structures. The creation of the Torah niche, which broke through
the shared wall and jutted into the adjacent building, was particularly intru-
sive and might indicate that members of the Jewish community owned the
neighbouring houses. As White suggests, "The renovation project suggests
a larger and more visible Jewish community," one whose "status was not generally threatened" (White 1990, 67). The remodelling of the synagogue site
is consistent with what we observed at the other two cultic sites.

We have already discussed the fact that the cults of Cybele and Alexander were situated in private residences; likewise, this synagogue arose in a
private setting in which, like the other two adaptive religious structures, a
patron was involved. An individual would have provided the property at
Priene, likely through a private donation, and perhaps the initial owner
continued to live in some of the rooms surrounding the assembly hall, as
host and on-site provider of the community. This is the situation reflected
in a well-known inscription from Stobi that indicates that a wealthy home-
owner, Polycharmus, donated some of his property to the Jewish community with the stipulation that he and his family could continue to live in the
upper level of the house above the synagogue (*CIJ* 694; see White 1997,
354-55). Polycharmos apparently acted as the community's patron and
benefactor, the "father of the synagogue [*patēr en synagōgēs*]," a position he
held side by side with the local patriarch (White 1990, 78-79).

The Jewish community at Priene probably initially met together in the
home of one of the more prominent members of the community. Then,
sometime in the second or third century, the decision was made to alter the
home to better suit the needs of that community, and substantial changes
were made to the building. What prompted these changes? Probably the
growth of the community—the house was too small, so a larger meeting
room with the appropriate religious accoutrements (such as Torah niche,
menorah reliefs, basin for ritual ablutions) was added.[21]

Jewish–Christian Rivalry or Attraction in Priene?

As mentioned earlier, Wiegand and Schrader identify the synagogue building as a *Hauskirche* (1904, 480ff.). They suggest that this adaptive structure,
located next to the sanctuary to Alexander the Great and only a couple of
houses east of the sanctuary where worship of Cybele occurred, was yet
another example of what they observe to be the Christian pattern of establishing churches next to pagan shrines in Priene.[22] They believe that they
have discovered evidence for the "interesting transition from the older, simple type of house church to the younger basilica-type," but were initially sur-

prised by the "remarkably" small square niche in the eastern wall (1904, 480; as noted earlier, this is now properly identified as a Torah niche). They conclude that this was a church niche "in which there was room for only one cleric" and that this was "the remainder of the not-quite developed type of house church," which they date to the fourth or fifth century CE (1904, 480). The discovery of the lightly chiselled menorah relief (mentioned earlier) found in front of the niche did not discourage them in their identification of the structure as Christian: this relief, they suggest, decorated the back wall of the church (1904, 481, image 586 [see photo, next page]).[23] As noted earlier, the presence of this menorah relief in this household building is one reason later scholars recognize that the structure was in fact a synagogue and not a house church.[24]

Wiegand and Schrader seem aware that their identification of the building is somewhat unusual, but they explain only briefly why they identify it as a house church, and not a synagogue: "In Italy, one would assume from the discovery of such a relief that it comes from a synagogue, especially since the sign of the cross is missing. In Asia Minor, such a sharp distinction does not seem possible" (1904, 481). They then state, "In the *Grossenkirche*, for instance, a candelabra relief (image 582) was found" (1904, 481). The *Grossenkirche* to which these excavators refer is a Byzantine basilica-style church located in the heart of the city centre, next to the theatre. Discovered on its floor were tombs, inscribed stelae from the nearby temple to Athena, and a seven-armed candelabra (Wiegand and Schrader 1904, 481). Apparently, the "logic" behind Wiegand and Schrader's identification of the household sanctuary as a "house church" was as follows: the basilica building beside the theatre was clearly a Christian church, and since the Christians *there* placed a menorah symbol in their sanctuary, likewise the household sanctuary bearing a menorah was a Christian church.

An important question that arises from this discussion is how one interprets the discovery of the menorah relief in the Byzantine church. Surprisingly, there has been little commentary on this point. While discerning motivation from archaeological *realia* is admittedly problematic, exploring various interpretations of the evidence may offer insight into religious interaction among Jews and Christians in Priene. The relief itself is impressive: a seven-branched menorah flanked by an *ethrog* (a citrus fruit) on the left and a *lulab* (a palm branch) on the right, as well as by a difficult-to-identify, right-angled object whose identity has been much debated, but is deemed by most at present to be a *shofar* (ram's horn).[25] Underneath the branches and on either side of its shaft lies a rolled-up Torah scroll.[26] The typical explanation for finding a menorah in the large church is that it was "spoil from a Jewish site" (White 1997, 328), perhaps even originally from the synagogue itself (Sukenik 1934, 43; Levine 2000, 249). White notes that the "slab was dadoed along the bottom edge probably for setting into a channel or slot for a stand" (White 1997, 328), and so it was likely displayed publicly in the church.

Menorah etched into stone, Priene, *in situ*. Photo by Michele Murray, used by permission.

The suggestion that the menorah is "spoil" presupposes that the Christians using the Byzantine church had plundered a Jewish site (perhaps the synagogue itself) and had taken the menorah as an aggressive act of antagonism towards Jews. This interpretation attributes an anti-Jewish impulse and an act of overt religious rivalry to Christians in Priene: displaying the menorah in the church would have asserted the superiority of Christianity over Judaism generally, or more specifically, over the Jewish community in Priene. One would imagine that displaying such a well-known, decisively Jewish symbol in the Byzantine church would express the understanding that Christianity was the culmination of Judaism, the inheritor even of Jewish symbols, and that the Jews were defeated and Judaism moribund. Certainly there is evidence for anti-Jewish action on the part of Christians in the early Byzantine period. For example, an increasing number of synagogues were destroyed or converted into churches from the late fourth century onward (e.g., the synagogue at Callinicum in 388; another in Mago, Minorca, in 418; the conversion of a synagogue to a church in Edessa ca. 436 [Simon 1986, 224ff.]). There is a reference in the fifth century Theodosian code to the "widespread burning of synagogues" (*Codex Theodosius* 16.8.21 in Parkes 1985, 236) and, in the sixth century, John of Ephesus boasts that on his journey through Asia he turned no less than seven synagogues into churches (Parkes 1985, 263). The discovery of a menorah in the church might reflect a similar anti-Jewish attitude, and if correct, it would reflect a scenario in which there was explicit, overt competition by the Christians with Judaism in Priene.

While this is a plausible interpretation of the menorah relief in the *Grossenkirche*, it is not the only one. Another option that ought to be considered is that the display of the menorah in the church was motivated by a *positive* attitude towards Judaism. Displaying the menorah in the church would then be an expression of appreciation or even attraction towards Judaism. There is plentiful literary evidence for such attraction in earlier Christian literature from Asia Minor: Ignatius in his letters to the Philadelphians (6.1; 8.2) and Magnesians (8.1; 9.1–2; 10.3);[27] Melito's discussion of Judaism in his *Peri Pascha* probably is a reaction to what was too close a connection between Jews and Christians in Sardis.[28] The fourth-century council held by Anatolian bishops in the Asia Minor city of Laodicea issued canons that oppose a very real Christian interest in Judaism, such as attending Jewish festivals, the observing the Sabbath, participating in Passover Seders, and other activities (Canons 29, 16, 37, 38 in Parkes 1985, 175; see also Simon 1986, 383).[29] Within Asia Minor, there is evidence for Christian interconnection with and attraction to Judaism and for a certain fluidity in Jewish-Christian boundaries and identity.[30] The possibility that the discovery of the menorah in the church (a structure admittedly dated slightly later than much of the literature just cited) might reflect a pro-Jewish attitude on the part of the Christian community of Priene cannot be dismissed out of hand.

Conclusion

Analysis of the archaeological remains of three adaptive religious sites juxtaposed along West Gate Street, on the outskirts of the city of Priene, reveals that each began its existence in the private household setting, and was dependent on the benefaction of a patron—someone of sufficient means, interest, and generosity to give over a part of his or her property. This was a step that would have promoted stability by providing members with a consistent place for gathering—a "headquarters"—for religious worship, and would have enhanced group cohesion. We observed that successive modifications were then made to the private courtyard (in the case of the *temenos* of Cybele) or domestic building (in the case of the House of Alexander and the synagogue) so that the space would better suit the needs of the cult. In our three examples, the modifications included the creation of a sacrificial pit in a courtyard (the shrine to Cybele), the building of a podium and tables for sacrificial purposes (the House of Alexander), the installation of columns (the House of Alexander and the synagogue), the introduction of statues and reliefs bearing pertinent religious symbols (all three sites), and the construction of a niche and a basin (the synagogue). These modifications sometimes went to the extent of encroaching onto neighbouring property (e.g., in the case of the synagogue and the shrine to Alexander the Great).

We discussed the status of the Priene Jewish community in particular, and argued that the "private" entrance into the synagogue was not indicative of the community's attempt to conceal their place of worship, but that, as with the side-alley entrance into the Alexander the Great shrine, it provided a more appropriate approach for devotees to their sanctuary. Indeed, the nature of the architectural adaptations made to the private home reveals that the Jewish community possessed a public presence in that region of the city. Our investigation of the misidentification of the synagogue as a house church by its original excavators raised the question of how a menorah relief discovered in the Byzantine church beside the theatre came to be there; two possible answers to this question that explored alternative ways of understanding Jewish–Christian relations in Priene were offered.

This investigation of the archaeological *realia* along West Gate Street in Priene provides a glimpse into the nature of religious interaction in that city. Our analysis of the archaeological data revealed the existence of autonomous communities, each transforming its domestic space to suit its own needs, seemingly without obstruction. The emerging portrait of Priene is of a small urban centre composed of independently thriving communities pursuing its particular religious interests in an environment of coexistence and diversity.

14

Urbanization in the Roman East and the Inter-Religious Struggle for Success

Jack N. Lightstone

Introduction: Focus and Objectives

From the inception of the work of the CSBS's seminar on religious rivalries and the struggle for success, participants have profited conceptually, theoretically, and methodologically from the definition of the seminar's focus by Leif Vaage (1995). First, Vaage insisted from the outset that inter- and intra-religious rivalries should not, and could not, be analyzed as a distinct issue within a *sui generis* realm of religious thought, institutions, and identity. The realm of religious self-definition and religiously informed social formation in the late Roman world usually presupposed the significant, close-at-hand "other" in a complex, multi-faceted social landscape that had become increasingly large, complex, and diversified. Moreover, a greater number of social actors in that landscape were mobile.

Hence, Vaage's second major point. While the rhetoric and discourse serving preaching, apologetics, or polemics often described or caricatured the social, ritual, or theological traits of the other in "ideal" terms—as the "ideal" or "mythical" foil to "us" and, therefore, as people with whom to shun social and religious concourse—day-to-day separation from, and shunning of, "the other" was in fact socially impossible and patently undesirable. Therefore, it is essential to understand how diverse and often competing religious communities inhabiting the same social landscape managed their social relationships in order to effect the dual objectives of maintaining both their intra-group socio-religious identity and solidarity, and the requisite level and types of social interaction with "others" that underpinned the social, economic, and political conditions upon which the welfare of all depended.

It is precisely within Vaage's framework that the meaning and place of the discourse and rhetoric of inter- and intra-religious rivalry has become

---

Notes to chapter 14 start on page 293

"problematized" in new and significant ways. Concretely put, it is no longer self-evident what is going on when a Christian presbyter or bishop demonizes Jews and polytheists in speech or treatise in one moment, in full knowledge that he and the members of his community will necessarily do business with them in the next, and then participate with Jews and polytheists in some important civic celebration, which often has religious overtones. (Indeed inversely, the polytheist Roman emperors sponsored regular sacrifices at the Jerusalem Temple in their name to the Jewish God, and polytheists and early Christians were regulars among the pilgrims to the Temple.) It is no longer sufficient to say that Christian characterizations of Jews or polytheists as the demoniacally "other," or rabbinic characterizations of polytheists as morally no better than animals, are merely polemic or caricature, or that they represent the language of social labelling. All this raises the question about the meaning of such characterizations in context—a context of complex social interaction, even mutual interdependence, in addition to social differentiation and avoidance.

This leads to another particular insight that seminar members gained from Peter Richardson's contributions to our joint work (Richardson 2002)—an insight that seemed to hit me like a bolt of lightening, although I cannot understand why it did not previously so impress itself upon me. As Richardson described the physical layout and material evidence of urban archaeological sites, I attained a new-found realization of how crowded and dense was the physical stage for the inter- and intra-religious social relations about which Vaage talks. The groups "struggling" for success in competition with, or in the face of, one another truly lived cheek by jowl. As Richardson has repeatedly brought to our attention, the material loci for specifically Christian, Jewish, and polytheist activity and ritual took place virtually next door to one another in neighbouring churches, temples, and synagogues, with the civic space and institutions of the basilica and forum equally close—all tightly surrounded by dwellings.[1]

With this image in mind, the cogency of Vaage's understanding of the seminar's focus, as well as his conceptual and methodological exhortations, is all the more apparent. It is clear because most of the evidence for the topic of our seminar comes from and reflects the social reality of life in and around the cities of the late Roman period. In our evidence, village and country life figures less significantly, principally in the narratives of the Synoptic Gospels and in evidence from late second- and early third-century Galilee and southern Syria. However, even here the literary evidence, at least, is probably the production of city dwellers, and in the case of second- and third-century Galilee and southern Syria, largely revolves around the assimilation of villages and the countryside into city centres in whose administrative sphere the villages were now officially placed. As for understanding earliest Christianity, Wayne Meeks has unassailably shown the relevance of understanding the urban setting as the social stage and staging place for expansion (Meeks 1983).

So it becomes increasingly relevant to say more about what happened in and to cities in the imperial Roman world. Let me begin by placing into some comparative context what is commonplace knowledge about Roman republicanism, that is, before the advent of the imperial order under Augustus. At the heart of Roman republicanism was a social mapping of the world around one unique urban centre, Rome itself. All lines of power and authority in the surrounding villages and towns of the countryside converged there. The wealthy rural landowners migrated to the city seasonally, and in most cases permanently, to join the senatorial/curial class, all the while maintaining their rural fiefdoms as the principal (officially, the only) legitimate social and economic basis for their noble status. The rural Roman tribes came to the city to vote with the urban tribes in order to annually name magistrates for Rome and its territory (in the singular).

Thus, well before the imperial period, the Roman way of mapping social order onto their world was one of constitutional urbanization, seen as an ongoing process rather than a once-and-for-all outcome. As republican Roman hegemony expanded in Italy, Roman governance of its expanded territory was conceived as, and legally and administratively achieved by, extending Rome as an urban centre. Thus, all of Italy came to be defined as part of the territory of the city of Rome, in effect, Rome's "countryside." Free Italians became Latin-rights citizens of Rome. The most wealthy of Italy's prominent families and its ancient tribal nobility became "new" men among Rome's upper-class ranks. Someone no less illustrious than Pompey was from such a Johnny-come-lately northern Italian family.

While the city of Rome may be a cousin to the ancient model of the Greek polis, both constitutionally and socially, Roman urban republicanism differed from the classical Athenian model. These differences are key to understanding the particularly Roman approach to urbanization in the east during the imperial period. Roman republicanism was as much the result of the nobility overthrowing the ancient Roman monarchy as it was the result of democratic principles. Socially and constitutionally, fairly rigid class stratification was integral to all aspects of Rome's conception of the "city." Without trying romantically to imply that the Athenian model produced or enshrined a democratic classless society of (free) persons, the formal and historical gulf between Athens and Rome in this respect was enormous. Roman republicanism may have eliminated kings constitutionally, but not socially, since some Roman republican families proudly asserted their royal ancestry. However, Roman republicanism enshrined socially, politically, and legally the status and power of nobility and lesser aristocratic classes.

Another important distinction between Athens and Rome is the differing shared cultural perceptions of the "mapping" of space. The republican Roman conception of *the* city's territory significantly departs from the classical Greek notion of *a* city's territory. For the latter, a city's territory was the immediate agricultural hinterland from which its need for (primarily) food would be met. For republican Rome, its territory was much more than that; it was the legal and cultural map for the extension of its security, power, authority, wealth, clientele, and ultimately the *dignitas* of its most prominent citizens (and by remove, the *dignitas* of all Roman citizens). Roman republican cultural geography was capable of mapping massive areas as the city's territory, and this countryside contained quite large towns. Rome and its territory completely outstrip not only in size but also in conception the city-states of classical Greece, or the "Greek" cities of the Hellenistic empires in the east after Alexander.

This second difference has an interesting upshot. With respect to the Hellenistic polis in particular, the city was the city, and the country was the country, aside from a relatively small rural hinterland that belonged to the polis. In effect, in the model of the polis, a vast part of the countryside belonged to no city at all. The rural folk were left to organize themselves along traditional tribal and clan lines of social organization, unless they had been conquered, in which case they might be ruled as a subject people.[2] In the Roman republican conception, a vast countryside was "naturally" part of the city. As mentioned, the countryside of *the* city could itself contain not only villages but quite large towns. The inhabitants of these large towns would be socially and legally country folk; the Latin-rights citizens among them would be members of a "rural" tribe. To put matters glibly, in the Athenian model, urbanization (that is, the spread of the "city" as a form of social mapping and social organization) could happen only by replication elsewhere. In the republican Roman model, urbanization in this sense happened by extension.

A major turning point in the history of the Roman republic, and no doubt an underlying impetus for the formation of the Roman principate, occurred when it became impossible to extend the legal-administrative hinterland of the city of Rome to include the far reaches of an ever-expanding empire beyond the Italian peninsula. Yet the process of "Roman" urbanization by extension was the long-established cultural model for mapping order onto chaos to create a viable world. If the Roman empire could not be one large "city"—the city of Rome and its territory—it could be a series of subject Roman urban colonies and clones of "the city" of Rome. In essence, in the imperial period the emperor and Senate adopted a model of urbanization that was a compromise between Athens and Rome on the specific question of how to extend the city (of Rome) to relatively far-flung reaches. A specifically "imperial-type" urbanization was a major feature of Roman imperial policy, from Britain to northwestern Mesopotamia. To anticipate matters somewhat, conceived as a tool for the imposition of Roman law and for the Romanization and civilizing of the peoples of the empire (in order to ensure political and economic stability for Rome itself), urbanization gradually effected radical transformations of social relations in the various regions of the empire, even where the Hellenistic polis was already well established. Among these transformations was the reformulation of lines of power, authority, deference, merit, and honour—elements integrally related to social structure at large and to religion, and to intra- and inter-religious competition and co-existence.

The remainder of this article undertakes a brief survey of the foremost features of urbanization in the Roman empire over the first several centuries CE, with special attention to the Roman east (section 2), and commences a discussion of the possible relevance of these transformations to understanding inter- and intra-religious relations (section 3). The reader is warned, however, that this article is very much still a work in progress and quite preliminary. Its aim is to fill in, if only partially, the context of this volume's focus on religious rivalries and the struggle for success in the late Roman world.

It is not this article's aim in section 2 (next), nor its claim, to make an important contribution to the study either of urbanization during the imperial Roman period or to the assessment of scholarship in this field. For this reason, the reader will forgive me the following: while I have consulted many modern scholars in preparing section 2 of this article, the article is unabashedly dependent upon the significant corpus of one: the late A. H. M. Jones.[3] Insofar as I might claim to bring some scholarly originality to the subject matter, it is perhaps in section 3 that I have achieved this goal. In section 3, I try to offer some of my own musings on how Roman-style urbanization in the east may have affected Jews' and Christians' social and political status and participation in the larger community on the one hand, and affected their intra-group social formations on the other.

Roman Imperial Urbanization in the East

A number of core opinions and conclusions pervade Jones's work on the ancient and late antique city. We begin with some preliminary comments about Jones's views and conclusions. First, his depiction of the history of urbanization in antiquity from Alexander is shot through with a distinct value judgment. He views the emergence and spread of autonomous, constitutional city governance as the primary expression and means of "civilizing" the lands of the eastern Mediterranean and of developing social, economic, and cultural systems that move beyond those characteristic of more "primitive" forms of tribal, semi-nomadic, or agrarian village life, from Thrace through Egypt and Cyrenaica to northwestern Mesopotamia. Neither the theocratic nor monarchical city states or kingdoms, which characterized much of the Levant and Syria before Alexander and which to some significant degree persisted (the Hellenistic cities aside) in the centuries that followed, could produce the type of cultural and social elevation among city dwellers, let alone among the peasantry, that constitutional "democratic" city governance achieved.

Second, while the transplantation of the polis east and north of Greece and the Ionian coast may be attributed to Alexander and his successors, only a minute proportion of the population of Hellenistic kingdoms, Jones stresses, were subsumed under constitutional urban governance, for several reasons. Relative to the area in question and their populations, the total number of constitutional cities was insignificant. In a related vein, the rural territories given over as "territory of the city," and therefore subject to its constitutional rule, were quite small, because the Hellenistic urban model permitted little else. Finally, the Hellenistic kings, influenced by the model of the Oriental kingdoms that they displaced, tended to define all land not under constitutional city governance as the "king's land" and therefore defined its population as more or less serfs of the king.

Third, Jones vociferously asserts that it was the Roman conquest of the lands east of the Adriatic, and not Alexander's conquest, that in stages from Pompey to Diocletian achieved the massive urbanization of the population by bringing city and rural dwellers alike under largely autonomous, constitutional governance of one polis or another. To put matters simplistically, during approximately three centuries (a time span slightly longer than the Hellenistic era), almost all of the rural territory of the eastern Roman Empire was carved up and given over to one "city" or another, and almost all cities that had not yet achieved constitutional city governance were afforded some form of it, except for those larger towns that became part of some city's "countryside."

Fourth, the slide into social, economic, and eventually cultural decay in the Byzantine Empire—in Jones's view, not mine—correlates with the slow demise of the institutions of constitutional city governance from Diocletian to Justinian.

Fifth, Jones maintains that this demise of the institutions of city governance has most to do with the economic, social, and therefore moral collapse of the local nobility of constitutional cities, whom the rigidity of the class structure in the empire placed in what, over the long haul, was an impossible situation.

Sixth, Jones views the spread of Greek as a correlative sign of the civilizing of the east. To Jones, "Grecization" is the result of urbanization. Yet he readily admits that, by the end of the Byzantine period, native languages, particularly in the Levant and Egypt, are patently alive and well; this he takes as a sign of the "lack of success" of urbanization.

The Progression of Urbanization in the Roman East

For the purposes of this essay, I focus on Jones's account of the period from Pompey's conquest of the eastern Mediterranean to the reign of Diocletian.[4] While Rome may indeed have viewed the promotion of the polis in the east as part of a process of Romanization (at least Romanization in a Hellenistic mode), Jones gives far more weight to a different motive. Perhaps Pompey, but especially Augustus, recognized the incompetence of the senatorial class to effectively administer the eastern provinces, each of which was large and populous enough to comprise a major empire in its own right. And while the equestrian class, because of its traditional business involvements, offered more administrative experience, its talents, too, paled before the task. The utter foreignness (socially, culturally, etc.) of the populations of these lands would have rendered direct administration by Romans all the more difficult. And no senatorial or equestrian governors or praetors ever gained significant experience in any locale, because of the limited duration of administrative tenure—usually one year. Since, according to Jones, Rome's interest in acquiring vast eastern territories was more economic than ideological—the oft-cited motive of Alexander—any system that made the indigenous peoples rule themselves, subject to Roman hegemony in each province, appeared preferable.

Despite the peppering of "cities" across these eastern lands (outside of Greece, Macedonia, and Ionia, of course), the Hellenistic kingdoms of the eastern Mediterranean adopted a model of highly centralized hierarchical administrations. Where such centralized governments and their bureaucracies were still in "good working order," they were maintained under the hegemony of the Roman governor and his limited number of staff. Where an indigenous monarch (or rival) could be trusted to run such an administration and to remain loyal to Rome, he or she ruled under the suzerainty of the ranking Roman official as the emperor's representative. Among the strongest and healthiest of such central hierarchical systems "found" by Pompey were those in eastern territories that were, or had previously been, under Ptolemaic rule. These include especially Egypt and Cyrenaica, Nabatea, Idumea, Judea, Samaria, Galilee, and southernmost Syria until the expansion of the Seleucid kingdom under Antiochus III (the Great). Antiochus III maintained these administrative forms after he wrested control from the Ptolemies of southern Syria, Galilee, Samaria, Judea, Idumea, and Nabatea—as did the Hasmoneans and the Herodians. Rome did the same until the reigns of Hadrian in the first quarter of the second century and of Septimus Severus at the end of the second century. As I shall explain later, nothing just stated contradicts or is contradicted by the fact that nearly thirty cities in this region enjoyed autonomous, constitutional government in the first century CE (see Tcherikover 1964, 83–134; 1970, 90–116).

The foregoing claims by Jones are of crucial importance for my particular interest in the Levant. With some few, even if notable, exceptions, Roman-style urbanization (which I shall describe shortly) did not happen in a wholesale manner in southern Syria, Galilee, Samaria, and Judea or in the semi-desert regions to the immediate east and south until Hadrian (117–38) and especially Septimus Severus (193–211). Nor was urbanization applied across the board to the remainder of the once Ptolemaic holdings in the Levant and North Africa until Diocletian a century later.

Where was Roman urbanization, then, first effected in the Roman imperial east? According to Jones, where Rome (that is, Pompey) found already weakened, ineffectual, centralized government administrations, Pompey, and Augustus following him, carved up vast tracts of land and populations into "city territories," assigning the direct administration of each to a city or major town in its midst; where constitutional government did not exist, they granted to these cities constitutional, republican self-governance (under Roman suzerainty, of course). This system of urbanization would assign many villages (and some reasonably sized towns[5]) holus bolus to a nearby or sometimes quite distant "city."[6] Moreover, Jones points out that, depending on the density of large towns in any one region, city territories might be anywhere from several to several dozen kilometres in radius to a massive 120 kilometres in radius. And the cities to which these territories were subject might be as developed as Antioch on the Orontes, or as an adobe caravan way station in some primitive outback between Damascus and the Euphrates.

In sum, according to Jones, Roman urbanization in the east took place in two great and distinct stages, depending upon the pre-existent state of affairs at Pompey's (and his immediate successors') arrival. *Mass* urbanization either (1) took place during the careers of Pompey and Augustus over the middle decades of the first century BCE on into the first century CE, or (2) was effected between Hadrian and Diocletian roughly between the mid-second and late-third century CE. During the interim of almost two hundred years between Pompey and Hadrian, little changed in major urbanization, although individual towns gained and lost city status throughout the period, depending upon the constant political and military struggles with which Rome had to contend in regions of the east.

Finally, in light of the above, it is important to distinguish two quite different senses of the term *urbanization* in the Roman imperial Levant. The first is a general commonsensical meaning of the term: the establishment of a large town and the populating of its precincts, often by moving people into it from the surrounding rural areas. The second sense, which is the chief concern of Jones and of this article, is a more restricted, particular one: the establishment of a large town or the transformation of the status of an existing one to create a polis with its own constitution and its own rural territory. Therefore, to focus on Galilee, when the Herodians "re-established" Sepphoris and later built Tiberias virtually from scratch, they were urbanizing in the first sense but not the second. Sepphoris and Tiberias served as administrative centres for their respective "toparchies" in the context of a highly centralized, hierarchical administration of the type inherited from the Ptolemies. The basic "cellular" unit in such a system remained the rural village led by its headman (*kōmarchēs*), whatever council of local rural notables advised him, and the village scribe (*kōmēgrammateus*). Many such non-polis cities, like Sepphoris and Tiberias, would have been granted the status of "city" (in the second sense) by Hadrian, and if not, then by Septimus Severus, at which time vast parts of what had been the toparchy countryside (including villages and towns) would have been given them as their city territories. With this transformation, the new cellular unit was the city itself, and each was independently subject in legal terms only to the emperor (or his provincial delegate). What this transformation might have meant for rural village culture, social structure, and institutions we shall return to later.

The Demise of the "Cities" in the Byzantine Period

It is a firm view of Jones that after Diocletian's reforms, the "cities" of the empire began a slow decline. By Justinian's reign, they were all but moribund. By implication at least, Jones understood the massive centralized bureaucracies of the Byzantine empire to be unequal to the task of filling the void. A little over a century later, the easternmost parts of the empire fell to the Muslims. Cities west of the Muslim-Byzantine frontier had long fallen into constitutional and cultural decay, and what remained of the Byzantine empire continued on under a largely centralized administration.

It is important to note to what Jones attributes the demise of the cities in eastern Mediterranean. The Roman city in particular placed a heavy financial burden on its elected magistrates. City magistrates were expected to be particularly generous in supplying revenues for maintaining the city's infrastructure and for underwriting the civic events that were such an important aspect of community life, social solidarity, and social identity (at least until the outright Christianization of the urban population). In addition, few cities were "free" in the sense that they were absolved of paying tribute or bloc levies to the central imperial treasury. The city's magistrates were ultimately personally responsible for the city's payments. This situation was difficult enough for constitutional cities in Asia Province and other parts of Asia Minor in the late republican period, when cities had little in the way of rural territory and rural population under their authority.

In the centuries following Pompey, however, when Roman-style urbanization in the east placed relatively vast rural areas, rural populations, and their villages not only under the authority, but also into the care and responsibility, of their "city" magistrates, few but the most wealthy could bear up under the privileges of civic office. People began actively avoiding public office, despite (all too late) attempts from Diocletian and his successors to reorganize the constitutional structure of magistracies. I can only imagine from Jones's account that, as constitutional civic reorganization reduced the number of magistrates that had to be found from a dwindling pool, the financial risks to the individual assuming magisterial office must have thereby increased steadily over the long haul. In short, Jones's representation of the state of affairs, which Diocletian at once addressed and to which he inadvertently contributed, indicates that immediate solutions precipitated a downward spiral over a more protracted time to an inevitable result.

Civic "Freedom"

Much of Jones's account of the history, development, and demise of "city" governance in the eastern Roman world seems coloured by the value he places on "freedom," of which he sees the ancient constitutional cities as the chief guarantors and promoters. This seems to be for him a corollary of what he deems the civilizing effects of the spread of the constitutional city in the ancient world. Therefore, Jones often takes pains to point out that after Alexander, the Hellenistic kings, the Roman republic, and finally the Roman Empire all undertook to whittle down the definition of civic freedom. Formally and informally, the power and authority of the king's, the Senate's, and finally the emperor's military and administrative representatives were imposed in various ways upon the individual constitutional city.

I shall not describe in detail the ways and means of achieving this end, but I shall mention two about which Jones writes because they illustrate so well the value Jones places upon a certain definition of constitutional civic freedom. For Jones, the classical Athenian model is the ideal. The power to elect officials in assembly is equally vested in all men (literally) of the city (including those in its hinterland) who are not slaves. Moreover, the city establishes and modifies its own constitution. Larger political units comprised leagues of cities.

By contrast, as mentioned earlier, the city of Rome in the republican period was not a copy of Athenian democracy, but an oligarchy. Moreover, when Rome's power extended over Italy (and then beyond), other towns were legally part of Rome's (rural) territory. They were not free cities in league with Rome. In the imperial period in the east, Roman urbanization established oligarchic civic constitutions, and more often than not, Roman authorities gave to the city its constitution and laws.

Laws and Courts

Jones reminds us that the formal definition of an "autonomous" constitutional city is one governed by laws of its own making. According to Jones, for a polis to have *its* laws imposed upon it diminishes a core element of the civic institution. In only two limited instances during the imperial period was this not the case, namely with *colonia* and *municipia*. The former is a city created by transplantation of bona fide Romans. The second is a polis created by giving its citizens (who are not slaves) *Roman* citizenship and, consequently, full Latin rights. *Colonia* and *municipia* had all the rights and privileges of homeland Latins and Italians, as well as their responsibilities. They were also subject to the very same laws as obtained in Rome and the Italian peninsula. Jones reminds us that, in fact, only a handful of cities in the eastern empire were either *colonia* or *municipia*; technically, other constitutional cities were governed by their own laws.

Jones, then, is clear that in the imperial period constitutional cities had government *by laws of their own making* only in theory. This was so not only because Rome gave to cities their constitutions, but also because a consistent trend from the beginning of the imperial period was for Roman officials and envoys to arrogate increasingly to themselves the adjudication of cases, rather than permit the trying of cases by constitutionally chosen juries of civic citizenry under city constitution. This slow but steady usurping of control over judicial proceedings paralleled the ever-increasing application of Roman rather than city law in the courts, with the inevitable long-term result that, over several centuries, local city law came ever increasingly to align itself with Roman law—although with local variation, accounted for by preserving antecedent local and Hellenistic legal traditions. Thus, when in 212 CE the *Constitutio Antoniniana* made Roman law the law of the entire empire (just as it made all freemen Roman citizens), what resulted would not have been experienced as entirely revolutionary. And when, concurrently, Roman citizenship was given to all inhabitants of the empire who were not slaves, in effect making all cities by definition *municipia*, little changed in practice (and tribute was still exacted from cities previously subject to the levies, that is, from almost all cities in the empire).

Financial Administration of Constitutional Cities

Cities with constitutions were technically "free" to tend to their own internal affairs and municipal development, subject to the provisions already mentioned (e.g., increased Roman control of the courts and payment of tribute, if a city was not one of the lucky few absolved of this burden). As Jones reminds us, chief among the responsibilities of the "autonomous" city was to develop and maintain the municipal infrastructure (including roads other than military trunk roads through its territory). As in Rome itself, this requirement was effected by a combination of financing from the civic treasury (by levies the citizenry imposed upon one another collectively) and especially by the munificence of local magistrates who wished by their generosity to win honour from co-citizens for themselves in life and after death for their heirs.

The repair of sewers and roads was less likely to achieve this latter end than the building of new and magnificent temples, theatres, basilicas, and the like. Hence, there was a tendency to start development of new monumental projects without necessarily being able to conserve enough funds to maintain or repair existing and basic infrastructure. The result was a combination of threat of decay of basic infrastructure and constant danger of bankruptcy of the civic treasury.

The Roman emperors and their representatives were highly sensitive to these issues. The central imperial government relied on the cities to maintain civic infrastructure and roads. Jones reminds us that a bankrupt city could not pay its tribute or meet its other treaty obligations to the Roman emperor. Therefore, a growing tendency throughout the imperial period was for the emperor to appoint "curators" and "auditors" to verify and oversee city finances. These were at first envoys from Rome of senatorial rank. As (the perceived) need for them increased, members of the equestrian class were sent to occupy these posts. By the mid-second and third centuries, Rome relied heavily on trusted locals to fulfill this role of financial oversight, thereby incorporating these locals into the superior classes of the imperial central government.

One cannot mention city finances without incurring a question about tax farming, among the most hated institutions of the late Republican and early imperial periods. Jones is unequivocal in claiming that the first several centuries of imperial rule in the east saw the steady abandonment of this hated system in favour of direct taxation based upon census data. Wherever city government existed, the city was entrusted with the collection of the tax bill for its inhabitants, including the rural peoples in the city's territory. In addition to imperial tax levies, cities required monies for civic responsibilities and functioning. Therefore, some taxation for the city treasury added to the financial burden of the inhabitants. As previously mentioned, the latter was never sufficient, and from Hellenistic times, wealthy citizens of the city were expected to donate generously to the maintenance and the development of the city's infrastructure.

Civic Responsibilities

As is already intimated in the foregoing sub-section, the "city" bore a number of responsibilities. Some were imperial services, that is, responsibilities to the central imperial government. Provision of food, of ships and other transport, and of beasts of burden to imperial militia and engineers posted or working within the city and its territory figured heavily among them. Billeting militia and imperial and government officials (no doubt, in a manner to which they were accustomed) fell to the city as well. Billeting legionnaires seemed a hateful task, made socially less difficult for some cities by constructing permanent housing facilities for transient Roman militia.

Civic (as opposed to imperial) services included provision of basic physical infrastructure and civic institutions, as mentioned above. Cities maintained and developed streets, roads, sewers, water supplies, and the like. The life of the city required a public marketplace (forum and cardo), meeting halls for administrative and judicial bodies and officials (basilica, treasury), places of entertainment and of sacred games (theatre, odeon, stadium, hippodrome), centres of civic religious and celebratory activity (temples, monuments), and sites for training and for education (gymnasium). Responsibility for provision of basic infrastructure included not only the town proper but extended to the villages of the city's territory and the roads that interconnected them. As mentioned, only the construction and maintenance of the main imperial-military trunk roads were the imperial government's responsibility (although the emperor might himself choose to act as benefactor to a city for some monumental project).

Civic Enfranchisement and Institutions of Civic Governance

Democracy, freedom, and self-government, and therefore civilization, are for Jones the legacy of the classical Greek city. Jones virtually idealizes the polis on the model of classical Athens. He is fully aware that the ideal, wherever it was installed, was in practice always somewhat tarnished. Slaves and many freedmen were not citizens. Rarely were resident aliens or their descendants enfranchised, even in the classical Greek polis. In theory, if not in historical origins, the citizens of the polis were a grouping of *indigenous* households, clans, and tribes who came together for the mutual benefit and protection that an established constitutional relationship and supporting institutions could provide. Authority and power were ultimately vested in the assembly of the people (that is, the citizens), who chose annually from among their number members of the governing council (*boulē*), and magistrates as well as chief priests (the latter sometimes, but not always, for life—indeed sometimes on a hereditary basis for life).

As for universal enfranchisement, and universal eligibility for judicial and legislative bodies and for related magistracies and liturgies, in Jones's view, the ancient city underwent a slow, steady, and denaturing process from Alexander to Justinian, despite the valiant efforts of the emperors up to and including Diocletian to save the city as the basic institution of governance and social order. Given our focus on urbanization in the Roman imperial period in the east, let us go directly to the situation of the first several centuries CE.

Citizenship in imperial cities in the east was a complex issue as a result of the overlay of different practices and the migration of peoples of different legal status from Alexander's time to the imperial era. Until the *Constitutio Antoniniana* of 212 CE, which granted Roman citizenship to all inhabitants of the Roman Empire (other than slaves), Roman citizenship was the privilege of a small minority east of Italia proper. But being a citizen of one's city did not entail or confer Roman citizenship, nor, for that matter, vice versa. Basically, before 212 CE there were four types of constitutional cities and citizenry:

1. Cities founded by Greek-Macedonian colonists, in which citizenship in the city (but not Roman citizenship) was limited primarily to the alleged descendants of the Greek-Macedonian founders

2. Cities founded by Latin colonists, in which primarily the colonists and their descendants were citizens of the city (*colonia*) as well as Roman citizens

3. Towns that were given city status either in the Hellenistic or Roman period, in which primarily the *indigenous* inhabitants and their descendants were citizens of the city (but not of Rome)

4. Towns or constitutional cities whose inhabitants or citizens (and their descendents thereafter) were given Roman citizenship (therefore becoming *municipia* with full Latin rights), usually because of some extraordinary service rendered to Rome

This rather variegated situation combined with Roman-style urbanization (i.e., the assignment of large rural territories to cities to administer) and increased mobility across the empire to form an even more complex state of affairs. All peoples who for a variety of reasons might be considered by those in the city who were citizens to be either "subject," "conquered," or "alien," had no enfranchisement, nor did their descendants. Thus, for example, indigenous peoples in the city's rural territories or in the cities themselves, where the founders of the constitutional city were Greek-Macedonian or Latin colonists, had no enfranchisement (as subject or conquered people, e.g., native Egyptians in Alexandria). Freedmen also had no enfranchisement. People who had migrated for one reason or another to the city or its territory had no enfranchisement. Therefore, in any city and its territory there were both rich and poor, serf and (economically and cultural speaking) upper class, foreigner and aboriginal who were not enfranchised. They were not part of the assembly of the people, until the *Constitutio Antoniniana*. (It is not difficult to imagine the potential social upheaval and "anomie" that the *Constituto Antoniniana* would have caused.)

As mentioned, Jones appears to idealize the classical Greek polis in which all indigenous peoples of the city and its territories voted by tribe in the assembly of the people. They elected from among their own number a city council and magistrates to attend to finances, infrastructure, defence, diplomacy, laws, and justice. The council or magistrates appointed persons to perform the liturgies. The latter usually obligated those so "honoured" to pay out of their own pockets (without the benefit of treasury or taxation) to organize and finance certain civic functions and celebrations (religious and civil). I have mentioned that Jones sees the developments of the late fourth century BCE to the sixth century CE as the relentless tarnishing of his ideal. Already during the Hellenistic period, the wealthy had an ever-increasing monopoly on council membership, magistracies, and liturgies.

With the advent of the Roman empire in the east, however, there developed a definite civic "curial class," which tended to constitute a true aristocracy much as did the Roman senatorial/curial class. They and only they came to be members of the council and appointees to magistracies and liturgies. Moreover, now only the council nominated persons to civic office. The assembly at first was relegated to ratifying a slate of nominees of the council to these offices. Later, by the mid-second and early third centuries, even ratification by the assembly was dispensed with. Ironically, as the emperor's central government came to play a more active and direct role in the supervision of the city's financial affairs and jurisdiction, and as diplomacy and defence were by definition no longer the purview of the city, city officials (now a hard-and-fast class of urban nobility) were confined to exercising authority over (and therefore standing surety for) civic and territorial infrastructure and the responsibilities of the liturgies.

Jones points out that at first the desire of wealthy holders of magistracies and liturgies to immortalize their family names produced extravagances in games and monumental building projects, leaving ongoing maintenance to a rapidly depleting civic treasury. By the second half of the second century and beginning of the third, council membership was still sought and guarded jealously. But civic magistracies and liturgies were steadily becoming an unhappy duty to be periodically borne rather than a coveted honour to be sought. Often the authority of the provincial governor or his local representative had to be exercised to secure a nomination to a magistracy for ratification by the council. Jones suggests that one reason for the creation of *Constitutio Antoniniana* might have been to greatly expand the pool of wealthy persons to take up magistracies and liturgies, since before the *Constitutio Antoniniana* the many wealthy individuals who were ineligible for citizenship for one of the many reasons adduced above could not be appointed to civic councils, magistracies, and liturgies. Ultimately, Jones makes a rather sweeping judgment: he believes that the narrowing of the responsibilities of civic officers to what for him appear almost menial matters, by contrast to great issues of political, military, and foreign affairs, contributed to the slow demise of city leadership.

Education

I must give institutions of education in the city of the eastern Roman empire special attention. The Roman imperial cities of the east inherited from the Hellenistic era the gymnasium as *the* cultural-educational institution. Besides membership on and appointment to the city council and curial boards of magistrates and liturgies, which dealt with finance, taxation, imperial services (like the post), and civic services (like water supply), the organization and governance of the city's gymnasium was a principal responsibility of the curial class. The gymnasium provided both physical training and leisure-related activities appropriate to various age categories as well as basic, advanced, and "continuing" education for (primarily wealthy) citizens of the city. Its constituent age-appropriate bodies were conceived as "assemblies," "clubs," or "societies" (*synodos, synedrion, gerousia, systema*) governed by gymnasium councils and council "rulers." In many cities, within the gymnasium was a society of "elders," which constituted the most exclusive aristocratic club of the city. The city council regularly appointed magistrates to head the one or several gymnasia of the city, an assignment that placed a heavy financial burden on the incumbent. It seems that the imperial distrust of clubs and societies, a distrust so well documented in the correspondence of Pliny the Younger, to name just one source of evidence, did not include the clubs and societies interior to the gymnasium.[7]

Implications of Roman Imperial Urbanization in the East for the Inter- and Intra-Religious Relations

Let me begin section 3 with a theoretical or conceptual framework that might guide us to salient issues. All human communities must create a *grid* that categorizes and differentiates the physical and social landscape and that establishes the *rules*—for social interaction, the exchange of goods and services, rights, responsibilities and privileges, deference and honour—which make possible human society within any physical environment, be it town or desert. The cogency of any system of grid and rules for those living in their socially constructed world lies in a number of socio-psychological mechanisms (see Douglas 1973, and the entries "Self-evidence" and "In the Nature of Things" in 1975a, 1975b). Through these mechanisms, the community's grid- and rule-system is experienced by its inhabitants as largely given rather than contrived, ordained rather than mere convention.

I shall not here describe in any detail the elements that constitute these socio-psychological mechanisms, but principal among them is the shared experience of structural homologies and consistencies in the many realms and spheres of life that together make up the grid- and rule-system. These spheres include what we would normally think of as the social, economic, and political realms, but also encompass the sphere of religion and the realm of the gods.

It is a paradoxical corollary of the foregoing that this sense of givenness, with which any grid- and rule-system must be experienced, is *always* in the process of being undermined principally by what one might call "complexification" (to coin an ungainly neologism). Complexification calls for modification of the grid- and rule-system by the adjustment or increased differentiation of categories making up the grid, so that revised rules may be established. Alternatively, complexification may be handled by rejection, that is, the defence of the existing categories and attendant rules in the face of an evident, implicit challenge to them. Adjustment takes time: first, for the complexification to be "felt" or to "register"; second, for one or another of the adjustment strategies to be "identified" and implemented by the relevant players; third, for the initial strategy to be tested; fourth, for it to infiltrate the system. The time factor is one of the several reasons why a community might, alternatively, choose to exclude or expel those elements that call their grid- and rule- system into question. If those so excluded arrive the following month with an army or an edict from the emperor, the players in question may quickly conclude that adjustment would prove the better course.

If adjustment, as opposed to exclusion, happens too radically or too quickly in aspects of the grid- and rule-system that are too central, then the sense of givenness upon which the system depends is undermined. If adjustment does not happen quickly enough, then the cogency of the grid- and rule-system may be felt to be in question because of its evident failure to describe and adequately regulate the new complexity. Once again, the temptation for a community to defend the current grid- and rule-system by exclusionary means is great if there is no evident threat of strong and effective retaliation. And once again, it is evident that the element of time is an essential issue in any grid- and rule-system's handling of complexification. This is so because the maintenance of the requisite sense of givenness has to do with the cultural management of collective memory, especially when important aspects of the system have been adjusted. To recollect collectively that the grid- and rule-system has changed in important ways is to recognize that the system is not "given-like." Thus, traditional societies seem to have a strong collective commitment to repress recognition of major change.

The cities of the eastern Roman empire are, at one and the same time, a physical representation and artifact of collective grid- and rule-making—that is, in their architecture and physical infrastructure, as well as a non-physical operationalization of such a grid- and rule-system—in their civic social and religious institutions, and in their civic laws, customs, and rituals.

The arrival of Rome on the scene in the east effected change, and therefore complexification. Its appearance required adjustments or exclusionary tactics. Rome's arrival may have been experienced by some as opportunity—the opportunity to create new complexification, or to renegotiate the modalities and terms of old adjustments. In light of the foregoing and the substance of section 2, permit me to make several observations.

(1) Rome imposed a model of the "city" in the east that differed substantially from the Hellenistic model previously in place. It produced a rigid class society creating a local, essentially hereditary, nobility to whom was given honour, responsibility, and the enormous financial burden of running their civic "corner" of the empire under the watchful eye and control of the imperial, senatorial, equestrian, and imperial-bureaucratic classes, all of whom outranked and lay outside the civic classes. The duties of this civic nobility and the city council (*boulē*), to which they became bound by birth and wealth, essentially eclipsed the power of the city's assembly of the people, which in effect ceased to exercise any legislative power by reason of enfranchisement.

(2) Roman imperial urbanization in the east redefined the relationship between the countryside and the city. Members of the rural wealthy classes could not exercise the power and privileges or win the honour they thought appropriate to their social and economic stature without migrating to the city that ruled their territory. There they became active members of the city's curial class and became absentee landlords of their rural holdings.

On the other hand, many (and sometimes quite large) towns and villages were politically and legally "countryside" to a city. Their formal modes of social and political organization had no constitutional civic standing. Ironically, town and village assemblies (often called *ekklēsia*), councils (usually called a *gerousia*, rather than the *boulē*), and magistracies did provide for local rural services, including some basic infrastructure, markets, fairs, and festivals. However, perhaps because these village institutions were so low on the political scale and because the imperial bureaucracy was content, through urbanization, to rid itself of direct supervisory authority over the "countryside," the members of these villages or even large towns were not caught in the iron rigidity *at the local level* of the class structures of the city.

Why might this be so important to us? In Palestine and adjacent areas, we have every reason to believe that Jews, Christians, Samaritans, and polytheists (mostly ethnic Syrians) inhabited both city and countryside alike. Certainly, in these regions Jews, Samaritans, and polytheists were mostly rural by all indication. Elsewhere in the eastern Roman Empire Jews, Samaritans, and Christians (when Christianity arrived on the scene) were mostly urban dwellers.

(3) The imposition of the Roman urban model on the east occurred at two distinct times. The first was in the period from Pompey to Augustus. The second was in the period after Trajan and Hadrian, particularly in the period of the Antonines and Severi at the end of the second and the beginning of the third centuries. Egypt, Palestine, southern Syria, and adjacent areas experienced Roman constitutional urbanization during this second period. As mentioned in section 2, this does not mean that cities did not exist or that cities were not built in these areas during the earlier imperial period. It means rather that until the second half of the second century CE, the Ptolemaic/Seleucid-like form of direct monarchical governance of town and country was maintained, except in constitutional cities (like those of the Decapolis) that dotted the landscape. In these cities, the decurial class quickly developed, as it did elsewhere in the empire. Thus Jews, Christians, and polytheists (of which there were very many) in Palestine and adjacent areas found themselves urbanized (in the Roman sense) late in the game, with different players long established and with quite different models of "adjustment" already in evidence from areas "Romanized" two hundred years or so earlier.

(4) While it seems evident, I think it may be very important to consider that organized Jewish communities in the Diaspora had developed forms of governance and of Jewish polity before the first and second waves of Roman-style urbanization. There were no such Christian forms at all during the first wave, only at the time of the second one. This must have rad-

ically affected the relative *marges de manoeuvre* of Christians and Jews in relation to polytheists in the Roman imperial cities.

(5) Over the first two and a half centuries of the Common Era, the arenas in which to acquire, and rules for winning, honour within the city and its territory shifted considerably, when first, the curial noble class formed as an exclusive and privileged group, and later, it began to fracture as an arena from which to escape, either by finding a way to ascend above it to the lower equestrian or senatorial ranks or to descend below it in order to find new venues for winning honour. For winning honour is always in accordance with rules that are social-venue specific, and venue shifting is more difficult the more rigid the class structure.

(6) Again an obvious point: being a Jew or Christian did not in itself peg one to any one place in the rigidly class-differentiated city. In theory, one could be a Jew or Christian and be a member of just about any class or sub-class in the city, whether slave, disenfranchised freeman, city citizen, Roman citizen, city decurion, imperial civic servant, or (and by the end of the third century) perhaps a member of the equestrian or senatorial class in the east. However, this being said, while individual Jews could be a member of any class, Jews *as a group* tended to be classed as resident aliens in cities outside of Palestine and adjacent areas by reason of being an ethnic national group. Christians *as a group* could not be so classified, yet they seemed from very early on to organize themselves in the city much as Jews did.

I suggest that this posed an immense problem, because for Christians and Jews civic institutions of civic society, class structure, law, economy and markets, and religion produced a confusion of contrary norms and grid categories with which persons who were non-Jews and non-Christians did not usually have to contend. The rigid map of class and the rules for moving from one to another, insofar as movement was possible at all, were designed expressly to fit a "polytheist" identity and to fix polytheist, and their progeny, within a particular socio-legal category in a particular city (i.e., of his or her *origo*).

To give an example, a Jew could become a decurion (and some few did), but certain magistracies necessarily involved participation in or direct financial support for polytheist worship (which most Jews would undoubtedly deem unacceptable). But to be a decurion and yet decline the burden of magistracies would not prove acceptable for long to a curial class bearing collectively a considerable financial load in order to maintain their "honour." And once one was a decurion, one could not honourably (or later legally) leave the city's curial ranks (whether upward or downward) unless truly extraordinary circumstances obtained.

(7) Closely related: with the establishment of the rigid classes and means of acquiring or maintaining "honour" within each class, how does

a Jew or Christian win and maintain honour within either the Jewish or Christian social institutions, if it is socially desirable for the individual and his or her community that the honour be recognized by the inhabitants of the city at large?

The seeds of many possible papers are latent in these seven points. Permit me to prefigure just one of them by offering some observations specific to the organized Jewish communities in urban settings outside of Palestine and southern Syria, that is, in the Greco-Roman Diaspora. (The situation within Palestine will be necessarily considerably more complex.) When the Hellenistic kings founded constitutional cities by granting civic constitutions to existing large towns, for the most part the free indigenous population together with recently arrived Greeks and Macedonians formed its enfranchised citizenry. Persons classed as foreigners or resident aliens were not citizens. But it would seem there was considerable leeway in who would be classified as resident aliens. In not a few locales there seems to be at least circumstantial evidence that some "long-resident" Jewish families, on a case-by-case basis, were classified among the citizenry. Later, often more numerous Jewish immigrants to these same cities would not be citizens, just like other "foreign" elements who arrived in order to take up permanent residence. Some of the latter might be granted civic enfranchisement only by reason of some extraordinary service.

Hence, some Jews as individuals probably claimed membership as citizens of the city, perhaps became members of the *boulē* (which was not yet a hereditary curial nobility), and they may even have been elected to magistracies or appointed to liturgies, if their personal religious scruples allowed them to participate in associated rites and games. But as Jews they were not citizens, since Jews as a collective social category were most often classed outright as foreigners and as resident aliens.

It is clear, however, that in most urban centres the Jews as a community organized themselves in formal fashion. They gathered or organized to worship, to study and to read their revered national texts, to educate their children, sometimes to share meals, to organize services for the destitute and ill, to provide registrarial/archival services (for births, marriages, wills, business contracts, etc.), and to adjudicate cases among themselves (unless one or another of the litigants wished to take the case before non-Jewish courts). As Richardson argues, the physical evidence of the earliest synagogues in the Diaspora is consistent with the synagogue building's functioning as the venue for assembly for a range of communal activities (Richardson 1996a). At the other end of our historical spectrum, John Chrysostom in Antioch gives evidence of the synagogue as the venue not only for formal communal prayer, but for judicial and other services (medicines, potions, and amulets; see Meeks and Wilken 1978).

The organized Diaspora Jewish community (sometimes referred to as *synagōgē, laos, synodos*, and sometimes *katoikia*) possessed councils (usually called *gerousia* as opposed to *boulē*) of rulers or elders. These bodies had responsibilities and provided services to the members of the community. Oversight, and probably surety for, these services and responsibilities were borne directly by magistracies bearing various names (*archontes, gerousiarchēs, archisynagōgos*). Evidence from the Roman period indicates that Jewish communal council membership and magistracies had become virtually dynastic, the prerogative of a local Jewish nobility (see Lightstone 1984; Levine 1998b, 2000).

In sum, while individual Jews may have been citizens of the city, and in some instances rose to the class of councilmen and magistracies, the Jewish community as a community of resident aliens seems to have been organized like a city within the city by the Roman period. In light of the points outlined earlier and with a view to the conceptual and theoretical claims proffered at the beginning of this section, how could this system be accommodated after Roman-style urbanization within the now very rigid, vertically organized, class-based, grid- and-rule system of the Roman imperial city?

The answer in some respects seems to be that accommodation to the new Romanized civic context was difficult. Take, for example, Alexandria, for which the literary evidence is most complete. From Augustus to Claudius there seems to have been periodic, serious, and sometimes violent controversy over issues related to where Jews and Jewish communal organizations fit within the constitutional city of Alexandria. The evidence demonstrates a clear Roman position: Jews as Jews are not citizens of Alexandria, and therefore Jews (as individuals) should cease to aspire to places in social classes that are above them, namely Alexandrian citizenship proper (Tcherikover 1964, 270–93; 1970, 296–332; Tcherikover and Fuks 1957–64, 1:1–110, 2:25–107). Rather, they are to be content with the rights and privileges that they have long possessed, presumably as a community.

But to be content with the latter meant precisely what? Presumably Jews in Alexandria (and in other Romanized cities) had their rights confirmed to organize as earlier described. However, it is no longer evident what legitimate formal place such forms of organization occupied within the Roman city's grid- and rule-system. Richardson (1996a) asks whether synagogues were licit *collegia* (legally tolerated voluntary associations). On this point, he appeals to the "literary inscriptions" preserved by Josephus in *Antiquities* 14.187–262. To be sure, these literary inscriptions instruct the "people, council and magistrates" of Roman cities in the east to afford the Jews certain privileges associated with their communal life and religious observances, in accordance with their ancestral laws and traditions. However, these "inscriptions" make no reference to any specific forms of social-communal organization of the Jewish community or to their legal status and place in the city's constitutional structure.[8] Perhaps Richardson is correct that they are *collegia* despite Rome's deep distrust of most voluntary associations, as witnessed in Pliny the Younger's correspondence with the imperial office. There is, however, another probable hypothesis.

As I read Jones on the effects of Roman-style urbanization on village and town institutions (which were now part of some cities' constitutional jurisdiction and responsibilities), I was immediately struck by the similarity between Jones's description of the forms of (re)organization of these villages and towns and everything I have ever known or thought I knew about the formal characteristics of Jewish communal organization in the cities of the Diaspora. To me, Jewish communal organization (synagogue/ assembly, council of notables, rulers chosen from among the council members for various functions, delimited powers to adjudicate cases by courts set up by the council, some degree of communal services, etc.)—even the terminology most commonly used (e.g., *gerousia* instead of *boulē*)—seems to resemble village or town organization within a constitutional city's territory. Moreover, as described by Jones, villages usually continued to worship their own village/rural deities and celebrate associated festivals and rites particular to themselves. In addition, inhabitants of the nearby villages regularly came to the city to sell their produce and wares, and otherwise participate in the economic life of the city, on market days and during fairs. Finally, the social and cultural distance and difference between city folk and country dwellers might reasonably be perceived as an apt analogy for the social and cultural oddities of an ethnic minority. Since the assemblies of the people by *origo*, so basic to the earlier Hellenistic notion of city and enfranchised citizenship, largely disappeared in Romanized cities in the east, the Jewish community and its members, perceived as village-like societies within the city's territory, would seem to be *in practice* no more or less enfranchised than any other group who were not of the urban decurial-class.

Therefore, the Jews as a community struck me as being organized, and having many of the socio-cultural features of, a "village" or a "city." On subsequently re-reading Tcherikover (1964 and 1970) on Jewish communities and Greek cities (which I had not done for more than two decades), I found buried in one sentence in a single paragraph (in his 1970 edition of *Hellenistic Civilization and the Jews*, pages 297-98) the outright assertion that "legally" the organized Jewish communities of the first-century Diaspora cities were "villages" and most specifically *katoikia* (communities of Greek, Macedonian, and later Roman-legionnaire immigrants that had been settled as "rural" villages and towns, but not as "cities"). These,

Tcherikover asserts, the organized Jewish communities resembled legally in every way.

What did this mean for the "struggle for success" for Jewish communities in the cities of the eastern Roman Diaspora? To a significant degree it meant the struggle to maintain a *legal status* that had bona fides for the urban world in which the Jews lived—in this case, as a "village" (or if one prefers Richardson's view, as a licit voluntary "association") of the city. But maintaining legitimate legal status is only one aspect of the matter. Far more important is the fact that it permitted Jews as a community to inhabit a legitimate social category in the perceptions of their urban co-inhabitants. This would afford the Jews, as a group, a "normal" place within the rigid world of the eastern Roman city. As inhabitants of a "village," Jews were *pagani*, and like all "rurals" after Roman-style urbanization, they could claim a perfectly normal and legitimate status within the city's territory. It seems to me that this social categorization was workable, whatever the degree of wealth that some Jews, just as some village notables, amassed and dispensed to the benefit of "village" infrastructure, and the Jewish community's notables won legitimate and normal "honour" in their "village," but not among the decurial class of the city. The Jewish community and its notables had a legitimate place in the "normal" minor leagues, as it were, in their "village." Moreover, no amount of "struggle for success" would ever get the Jewish notables, with some few exceptions as noted, a place in the more elevated major league that comprised the aristocratic members of the city's *boule*. Indeed, to return to a point made earlier, this too, in effect, was exactly what the Edict of Claudius asserted (parallel, separate institutions, somewhat inferior, and certainly, before the *Constituto Antoniniana* in 212, not co-citizens of the city as a group; Techrikover and Fuks 1957–64, 2:36).

If (or perhaps more likely, where) Jewish communities were understood to be licit voluntary associations, rather than villages, the lines of social categorization and demarcation would not have been so clean at all. For "member of a voluntary association" was not a social, and even less a legal, category that could be easily and cleanly differentiated from other social pigeonholes that constituted "the city." No wonder, given the rigidity of the Roman imperial social system, that voluntary associations as a whole were suspect entities and that Jewish communities, if and where perceived as voluntary associations, regularly had their rights and privileges questioned or withdrawn, thereby requiring imperial authorities regularly to order municipal assemblies, councils, and magistrates to afford Jews these rights and privileges (see Richardson 1996a).

If we understand the Jewish community as fitting socially and legally into the urban landscape as something like an ethnic (rather than native) "village" of foreign nationals (*peregrini*), it is easy to appreciate the danger that Judaizing *Gentiles*, especially enfranchised or curial Gentiles, represented. In the Roman city, as opposed to the Hellenistic one, class status fixed levels of social responsibility. And as the first several imperial centuries wore on, flight from class responsibilities (but not class honours), especially among the curial class, was viewed as undermining the viability of city life and its infrastructure. I am not saying that a Judaizing Gentile (or even a converted) decurion thereby escaped the curial class. Clearly, to do so was difficult, because imperial laws made it so. Rather, the danger lay at the level of social perception and symbolization. Judaizing, even (or especially) without conversion, represented a degree of social mobility or "boundary blurring" completely antithetical to Roman-style urbanization, since greatly increased class rigidity and class-boundary impermeability were its defining characteristics in comparison to the Hellenistic era. Bad enough that Jews did not worship the city's deities or the divine emperor (which could to some degree be assimilated to adhering to more ancient "aboriginal" village deities and their cult), worse still that urban Gentiles should worship a foreign god, perhaps to the exclusion of the city deities and the divine emperor. Indeed "anti-Semitic" vilification by Greek and Latin authors often seems engendered by Gentile (not Christian) Judaizing (e.g., Gentiles lighting Sabbath lamps, refraining from work on the Sabbath, and observing Jewish fast days).

In sum, the Jewish community for Jews might be safely classed as a "native village" within the city's territory. However, when Judaizing Gentiles appeared to join the Jewish community, the community then appeared to look more like a far more dangerous voluntary association, and these Judaizing urban Gentiles seem to blur and undermine the sense of the evident "givenness" of the highly structured and differentiated urban social map.

What does all this make urban Christians within the grid- and-rule system of the Roman city? In effect, they would represent an even greater challenge and danger to the classificatory system upon which the city stood than did Gentile Judaizers. Far more so than Gentile Judaizers, Christians (like the Jews) rejected outright the city's deities and cult, tended (like the Jews) to abhor civic festivals and games, and (like the Jews) organized themselves as communal assemblies. Yet they did not join the Jews (that particular *sui generis* urban-village class). Indeed, Gentile Christians as Christians were of no particular class, and certainly did not constitute a *sui generis* one within the urban social landscape. Nor were they *peregrini* by definition, as was the Jewish community as a whole. Thus, their very existence as an organized group could be an affront to civic society in a way that the Jews as a community of ethnic resident aliens was not.[9]

Worse still, Gentile urban Christians *claimed* explicitly to be a kind of resident alien class (a kind of neo-Judaic ethnos in a "spiritual" manner rather than a "fleshy" one). I cannot imagine this postion as being anything less than a direct challenge to the Roman imperial civic class structure, which by the late first century was the very basis for Roman imperial administration. Moreover, it was a direct challenge to the legal and social principle of *origo* (i.e., city-tribe of origin by ancestral descent) that was at the very heart of Roman-type urbanization. (Witness Luke's use of *origo* as the pretence to get Joseph and Mary back to Bethlehem in order to establish Joseph and Jesus' Davidic origins.)

Christian writers appear to be quite sensitive to these issues of the place of the Christian community within the city, and the apologists in particular walk a thin line in this regard, because they must both answer Christian's critics and uphold the basis for Christian communal organization. Consider what can be read only, in my view, as an attempt by Tertullian (*Apol.* 42) in large part to place Christians within the framing categories of civic life.

> [We Christians] live with you, enjoy the same food, have the same manner of life, and dress, the same requirements for life....We cannot dwell together in the world without the marketplace, without butchers, without your baths, shops, factories, taverns, fairs, and other places of business. We sail in ships with you, serve in the army, till the ground, engage in trade as you do; we provide skills and services to the public for your benefit. (trans. R. M. Grant 1980, 28)

Tertullian chose to defend Christians by providing a list of aspects of civic life. As with all apologies, Tertullian's argument is somewhat weak if it is intended to convince anyone other than Christians themselves. For he is of necessity highly selective in his account of the spheres of civic life in which Christians "are like everyone else," when in fact he and his readers know that in significant ways they are not.

Chapter 5 of the *Letter to Diognetus* proffers an even clearer example of Christian apologetics dealing with the ambiguous social location of Christians within a typically Roman urban social system.

> For Christians cannot be distinguished from the rest of the human race by country or language or customs. They do not live in cities of their own; they do not use a peculiar form of speech; they do not follow an eccentric manner of life...they live in Greek and barbarian cities alike, as each man's lot has been cast, and follow the customs of the country in clothing and food and other matters of daily living[;] at the same time they give proof of the remarkable and admittedly extraordinary constitution of their own commonwealth. They live in their own countries, but only as aliens. They share in everything as citizens,

and endure everything as foreigners. Every foreign land is their father-land, and yet every fatherland is a foreign land….It is true that they are "in the flesh," but they do not live "according to the flesh." They busy themselves on earth, but their citizenship is in heaven. They obey the established laws, but in their own laws, they go far beyond what the laws require. (trans. E. R. Fairweather, in C. Richardson 1953, 216–17)

The author of *Diognetus* explicitly plays on the ambiguity that Christians are full "citizens" who "take their full part as citizens" of the city (since he cannot mean Roman citizenship), yet they are organized as if they were "transients" (aliens). Their transient-like nature, however, is not due to the fact that elsewhere in another earthly local they would be in their (ter-restrial) homeland. Rather, they are transients on earth because their home-land is heaven. So they are aliens who cannot be accused of being aliens from elsewhere. Since they go to their heavenly homeland only after they have played their roles as earthly citizens in their home cities, they cannot be understood as shaking off their *origo*.

In sum, the forcefulness of the arguments of Tertullian and the author of *Diognetus* betrays the perceived weakness of the Christian position as good, well-heeled urban dwellers in their cities of origin. Consequently, and it seems odd to say this, Christianity, while having made significant inroads in the Roman world, was not a very popular choice for inhabitants of the Roman Empire in the first several centuries (the persecution of Chris-tians is less the cause of this unpopularity, than a reflection of it). By the beginning of Constantine's reign, Jones estimates that about 10 percent of the population of the empire was Christian.[10] By comparison, at the time of Pompey and Julius Caesar, Jews represented about 10 percent of the empire's population and 20 percent of the eastern half, and 30 percent in Alexandria.[11] Since outside of Palestine, southern Syria, and Egypt Jews were concentrated in the cities of the eastern empire, their numbers in urban settlements must have made them a significant proportion of the popula-tion of cities and towns.

Turning now to Palestine, Idumea, Transjordan, and southern Syria and Golan, the situation is necessarily far more complex, so much so that I can make only a start. The situation is made complex by a number of factors. First, as Jones informs us, full Roman-style urbanization happened relatively late in this region, in the latter part of the second century and the first half of the third century CE (just as it did in Egypt). This does not mean that there were no constitutional cities in these areas. Obviously there were, among them Ashkelon, Ptolemeis (Acco), and Caesarea Maritima.[12] Rather, the distinction that Jones's analysis permits us to make is the following: here the Romans, until the second half of the second century CE, merely perpetuated the Hellenistic model. Some cities and towns had been granted constitutional autonomy, others had not and were subject to direct central imperial rule. Moreover, the countryside and small towns and villages were not given over to the cities as their territory, but were ruled directly by the central imperial government machinery until truly Roman-style urbanization took place.

Second, inter- and intra-religious communal relations and the effects of urbanization on them could not but be affected radically by the disproportionately high Jewish population in the remains of their homeland. Third, and closely related, the vast majority of Jews in this region probably lived in rural, not urban settings (the case for virtually all inhabitants of their homeland in the Roman Empire), unlike the situation of Jews in the Diaspora. Fourth, Jews would have had a disproportionately high influence on the fate and success of Christianity in both rural and urban settings in this region, in comparison to the situation elsewhere in the eastern empire. Fifth, I would venture that in this region there were a higher number of rural Christians in the first several centuries than would have been the case elsewhere in the empire.

Sixth, a massive population shift occurred in this area as a result of the two major Jewish rebellions. Jews who survived the aftermath of the Bar Kokhba rebellion migrated out of the area of Jerusalem and the Judean hills in large numbers to the coastal plain, Lower and Upper Galilee, and Golan. In addition, Rome encouraged significant polytheist (largely ethnic Syrian) settlement in Judea and throughout the area. In truth, Syrian polytheists (including Phoenicians) were already a major element of the population in the coastal towns and obviously in southern Syria and Transjordan (where they joined polytheists of Idumean and Nabatean origins). As a result, ethnically and religiously, the region was a checkerboard by the late second century CE. One could talk of "Jewish" cities, towns, and villages and "Gentile" cities, towns, and villages. No doubt each contained as well some often-significant proportion of "the other" as a minority. It may also be the case that by Hadrian's time (that is, just before or at the onset of Roman "urbanization" of the countryside), some rural villages here and there in this region were predominantly Christian. This possibility is significant in that pre-urbanized villages, ruled directly by the central government, were the "cellular administrative unit" (as opposed to cities) of these regions. Consequently, traditional village forms of organization (local village headman and a council of village elders constituting a type of rural aristocracy) handled matters and infrastructure about which the Roman central government was neutral or onto which the central imperial authority devolved traditional village governance out of convenience. In other words, traditional rural and village forms of self-governance (although not having constitutional status as autonomous) remained not only strong, but were in effect sanctioned by the imperial administration, until the second half of the second century.

In this rather more complex situation, it is easy to surmise that urbanization in the second half of the second century would have been experienced as a major upheaval of a delicately balanced social situation. What would it mean for Jewish villages and small towns, in which traditional forms of self-organization, deference, honour, etc., held sway, to become legally the "territory" of a "polytheist" constitutional city? Similarly, what was a Jewish "city" to do with a polytheist or Christian urban minority and with towns and villages in its territory that may have been predominantly polytheist or Christian? With all rural territory now subdivided and redistributed to their respective cities, as opposed to directly administered by the central imperial authority, how could the matters of Jewish legal concern that Romans everywhere in the empire since the time of Pompey and Caesar had devolved to the Jewish communities be regulated and coordinated in the land of Israel? The relative density of the Jewish population in this region, despite the major presence of Gentiles, meant that there was a level of social, religious, cultural, and economic intercourse among Jews, now administratively subdivided under various city jurisdictions, that required a degree of coordination and regulation that was unlike anything that the Jews of Ephesus needed to coordinate with the Jews of Halicarnassus, let alone with those of Tarsus. Indeed, post-Pentateuchal Judaic law required certain coordinated activities within the "Land of Israel" specifically (e.g., calendar, Sabbatical year, tithing of produce, to name just a few).

I strongly suspect that the "creation" of the Jewish patriarchate in Palestine at the end of the second century represents Rome's attempt to respond to the situation just described brought about by the Roman-style urbanization of Palestine. As I read Jones on the differentiation and respective responsibilities, power, authority, and class status of the urbanized classes, including the urban decurion class, on the one hand, and their immediate "betters," namely, the lowest echelon of the imperial central bureaucratic class, on the other, I have become increasingly convinced that Judah the Patriarch and his progeny (with respect specifically to the Jews of Palestine and immediately adjacent areas) had been elevated to, enjoyed the class privileges and honour of, and acted with the levels of authority and across-urban-territorial responsibilities proper to, a member of the provincial imperial bureaucratic class, which socially and legally "escaped the chains" of *origo* in their home city and acted in many instances to coordinate matters across city jurisdictions. The early rabbinic guild of masters presumed to ride on the coattails of the patriarch, who effectively used his power to "elevate" members of the rabbinic class to the imperial provincial bureaucracy over which he had specific jurisdiction. The stories in third- and fourth-century rabbinic sources—whether historically accurate or fabricated is immaterial—of the patriarch's "appointment" of, or withholding of appointments from, members (only) of the rabbinic guild to jurisdictional functions hither and yon in Palestine, as well as stories of the regularized displays of deference by decurions visiting the patriarch's "court" make best sense within the context I have just proposed (Lightstone 2001, 177–200 and notes; Levine 1985). Likewise, it is in this context that one can best make intelligible the story of rabbis in Tiberius asking the patriarch to defend their (alleged) exemption from contributing tribute to the "crown" levied by the imperial office and collected by the no doubt vexed and insistent city magistrate who, as is the norm, is responsible for making up the total amount personally and financially (Levine 1985).

In sum, what I am suggesting is that the patriarchate came into its own near the end of the second century as a means for the Roman imperial government to deal with peculiarities of the region that were the result of demographics. These peculiarities had been more easily managed before wholesale imposition of Roman-style urbanization in Palestine. However, with the imposition of the latter, the only legal means available was to raise a Jewish official to a class level well above the urban curial class and bestow upon that official powers and privileges properly held by Roman imperial officials. Therefore, in some respects, the patriarch's powers and privileges would be reminiscent of those of the Herodian family's tetrarchies, that is, as ethnarchs who acted as suzerain sovereigns of territory under Roman subjugation, although, of course, such a position was politically and legally an impossibility in the region in the second half of the second century. This is no doubt what was behind at least one Palestinian Christian writer, Origen (in *Africanus* 20, 14), of the early fourth century derisively describing the Palestinian Jewish "ethnarch's" behaviour as illegitimately monarchical in nature (see Levine 1979, 1996; Goodblatt 1994).

The Roman-style urbanization of Palestine in the latter part of the second century and the beginning of the third helps us understand the establishment (or, if you will, the transformation) of the Jewish patriarchate. Urbanization also sheds light on the correlative formation or transformation of the rabbinic guild of masters. Moreover, it helps us better understand numerous third- and fourth-century rabbinic passages in Tosefta and the Palestinian Talmud that deal with formal urban responsibilities in Palestine among its Jewish residents. As mentioned, the distinction between Jewish and Gentile cities figures heavily. In addition, the sources consider the questions of when one's status has changed from a transient to temporary and finally to permanent resident for the purposes of bearing the financial responsibility for civic infrastructural and social services. Clearly some notion of *isopoliteia* (correlative rights of citizenship and permanent residency) between neighbouring city territories underlies these concerns. Such issues are well attested among the polytheist cities and residents of eastern Roman cities and provinces.

The position of Christians in the finally urbanized social and political landscape of Palestine must have been precarious. If whole rural villages of "native" Palestinian Christians existed, and I suspect that they did, they might have enjoyed some security as "villages" within the city territory, with their own village headman (*kōmarchēs*), assembly, and council of elders. But those Gentile Christians in the urban settings of polytheist Palestinian cities would have had the same challenges as their co-religionists elsewhere in the eastern Roman Empire. Christians in Jewish cities would probably have been viewed and treated as heretics, particularly if their ancestry was Jewish. Perhaps this last-mentioned urban situation stands behind the treatment of the "two-powers" heretics and sectarians in late second- and third-century Jewish sources.

Conclusion

There is no elegant way to end this article, when it has but scratched the surface of the topic. Suffice it to say that the matter rightly deserves more attention and far deeper analysis. This fact alone, which I hope the article has demonstrated, shows only too well the difficulties resulting from the fact that social historians of the Roman world and social historians of early Christianity and ancient Judaism interact too little. Too few among us are well enough versed in the sources and evidence that pertain to both for the period of interest to us. Of course there are notable exceptions. The situation is better for the Byzantine period, at least as regards Roman history and the history of Christianity, where the subjects themselves converge, as demonstrated so ably by Peter Brown (1978; 1981; 1992; 1995; 1996). For the history of Judaism, the situation does not improve in the least as one looks at the Byzantine period. It is simply too easy to read the rabbinic sources without significant recourse to the Roman ones, largely as the result of the overwhelming force—at once a help and a hindrance—of the medieval rabbinic exegetical tradition. This article's subject matter suggests, then, that we would profit greatly were we to include more Roman historians for our explorations into the interactions among religious groups in antiquity.

CONCLUSION

15

Religious Coexistence, Co-operation, Competition, and Conflict in Sardis and Smyrna

Richard S. Ascough

Introduction

During the first three years of the CSBS's Religious Rivalries seminar, the focus was on the city of Caesarea Maritima, the results of which have been published by Terry Donaldson as *Religious Rivalries and the Struggle for Success in Caesarea Maritima* (2000). In summarizing the situation at Caesarea Maritima, Donaldson picks up on John North's analogy of the marketplace to describe the coexistence and competition among the diverse "merchants of religion" in that city (2000, 6). A vast array of religious "wares" were available, and, as in the bustling casbahs of the Middle East today, these wares were hawked to all and sundry, their strengths promoted and their competitors' flaws revealed. Donaldson, in his conclusion to the book, organizes the religious "marketplace" nicely into four categories, all conveniently alliterated with the letter *c*: coexistence, co-operation, competition, and conflict.

What is striking about Donaldson's list is the predominance of evidence within the first two categories of coexistence and co-operation, and the slim evidence available for the last categories of competition and conflict.[1] As William Arnal notes in his review of the book, "What *I* found most striking about his survey was the degree to which the inter-religious contacts in Caesarea were not conflictual" (2001, 430, his emphasis). And of the seven points Donaldson lists under "competition," three have to do with competition among adherents of similar or related religious groups. The overall picture gives a surprising lack of *clear* evidence for sustained conflict with "outsiders" and the very clear evidence, spanning a few centuries, for like religious groups competing with one another (see Ascough 2000). It is worthwhile, then, to see if this

---

Notes to chapter 15 start on page 295

pattern is repeated in Sardis and Smyrna. To do so, we will use Donaldson's four-*c* rubric as a way of plotting some of the seminar's findings from these cities.[2]

Sardis

There are a considerable number of interesting instances of religious coexistence at Sardis that are explored in the essays in this book. In some instances the evidence indicates that devotees of various deities lived alongside one another: "Archaeological evidence points to Jews, Christians, and polytheists living, moving, and working in close proximity and cooperatively, manufacturing and selling a large variety of goods, including metal tools, utensils, glass vessels, and jewellery" (Neufeld, chap. 3, 31; cf. Aasgaard, chap. 11). The archaeological remains from the Byzantine shops in Sardis suggest that Jews and Christians were living, working, and worshipping side by side without apparent animosity (Hammer and Murray, chap. 12). The existence of the synagogue within the bath-gymnasium complex points to a willingness in the third century to share sacred and social space across belief systems (Ascough, chap. 4).[3]

Melito, a second-century Christian homilist of Sardis, writes to Marcus Aurelius to advocate co-operation between the Christians and the Roman emperor (Neufeld, chap. 3; Wilson 1995, 255). From Melito's point of view, the emperor Marcus Aurelius would do well to become acquainted with the Christian "philosophy." He expects that, should the emperor do so, he would find little reason to punish Christians as Christians. Christians not only support the empire; Melito intimates that the well-being of the empire is tied to the emperor's willingness to protect the Christian philosophy (Aasgaard, chap. 11). Although it is not clear whether anything resulted from this argument, it is noteworthy that this Christian would advocate coexistence.

Other evidence, however, attests to a degree of acknowledgement of the religious commitments of others and a willingness to be involved even marginally in the religious systems of the "other." We find in Sardis decrees allowing Jews to meet regularly and to collect money for Jerusalem, which Gaston suggests might indicate the existence of a *politeuma* (Gaston, chap. 2), a distinction granted to the Jewish population of a city that allows for self-rule. What is striking is that the Jewish community is recognized and its practices approved. Indeed, by the third century CE we find inscriptional evidence suggesting that at least eight Jews are members of the city council at Sardis (Kraabel 1992d, 229). Beyond that, evidence indicates the existence of "God-fearers" among the Gentile population (Aasgaard, chap. 11; Trebilco 1991, 33–36).

Perhaps not as neatly as we would like, there is a sense in which the book of Revelation reflects some willingness to coexist among the various groups through its use of astrological imagery.[4] In examining Revelation chaps. 4 and 12, Tim Hegedus notes that, remarkably, these passages "demonstrate the use of astrological imagery to express Christian meaning" (chap. 6, 85). Even if Revelation's use is rather unsophisticated, it "shows little or none of the suspicion of astrology that would become so fixed in later Christian polemic against astrology" (Hegedus, chap. 6, 85). Nevertheless, the author's Christian appropriation of the imagery fails to *displace* the traditional polytheist imagery.

John Marshall examines Revelation 12:1 in more detail and suggests that the imagery embraces both the patriarchs and the zodiac, reflecting "an instance of a complex of thinking" about both that is "broadly distributed in ancient Judaism." The author of Revelation is "shoring up a boundary across which there should be no commerce and finding passage across the boundaries that would be dissolved in the age to come" (Marshall, chap. 7, 87). His exploration shows that Christians, Jews, and polytheists, while not completely aligned with one another, were using similar imagery in their respective religious discourses. To suggest that this is a rivalry is to overplay the nature of the evidence and to buy into the scholarly tendency towards binary oppositions (e.g., Judaism versus Hellenism; orthodoxy versus heresy). What we have in Revelation is an instance of correlation of images across a spectrum of religious traditions.

Along with these instances of religious coexistence, we have evidence for some co-operation among religious groups in Sardis. For example, Melito (and others) were Quartodeciman—celebrating Easter on the day the Jews celebrated Passover (14 Nisan), no matter what the day of the week (Neufeld, chap. 3). The practice of Christian Sabbath observance and the sharing in Jewish festivals is condemned in Canon 27 of the Laodicean canons, perhaps with Sardis (among other cities of Asia Minor) in mind, given the proximity of Laodicea and Sardis (Hammer and Murray, chap. 12), suggesting that there was further co-operation in festive dates between Christians and Jews. Presumably, such keeping of common festival and Sabbath days had a noticeable impact on the commerce and work habits in the city.

While it would be striking if coexistence and co-operation were the complete picture of religious life at Sardis, such is not the case. There are a number of instances of competition and conflict among the religious groups of the city. While some examples are minor, others indicate a greater degree of animosity. We begin with the more minor examples.

While there is little evidence of Jews in competition with polytheists (according to Gaston, chap. 2), the possible existence of God-fearers is suggestive of polytheists choosing to adhere to the Jewish community for their primary religious expression, indicative, perhaps, of their rejection of a former way of life (Ascough, chap. 4). Furthermore, despite the seemingly benign coexistence of Jews and Christians, the bold display of Christian symbols (such as a Latin cross on the exterior of the outside wall of a residence) may be interpreted as evidence of competition for public recognition. Although there is less evidence for the public display of Jewish symbols, the location, scale, and design of the synagogue might indicate the Jewish community's participation in this competition for public recognition (Hammer and Murray, chap. 12).

Muir's essay challenges the sweeping conclusions of Rodney Stark (1996) about the role of healing in the spread of Christianity. While admitting that helping the sick and poor was a specialty of the Christian movement, Muir shows that Christians were not the only group whose charitable work would have provided opportunity to bring in new members, for "there would have been competition from the Asclepius cult, other healing cults, magicians, and sometimes even physicians" (Muir, chap. 9, 140). Even so, the evidence seems to point to Christian charity being mostly "in-house," with only a ripple effect into the wider community.

Competition among members of associations is also evident. Associations compete with one another for patrons and benefactors, as seen in multiple inscriptions from groups connected to a single extended household (Harland, chap. 5). In one specific instance, an inner group of Zeus worshippers are prevented from participation in an older, well-established cult of Sardis (Ascough, chap. 4; Harland, chap. 5).

The evidence of conflict is perhaps slightly stronger. For example, we might point to the reuse of the Temple of Artemis as a fourth-century CE Christian chapel or Christian and Jewish defacement of polytheist images (Ascough, chap. 4). In the case of the latter, while the reuse and defacement of polytheist religious items in the synagogue may indicate conflict (so Ascough, chap. 4), Hammer and Murray rightly caution that "we should distinguish between purposely defacing an image out of animosity versus choosing not to display the image of 'another deity'" (chap. 12, 184–85). The reuse of the lion statues may indicate assimilation (so Seager and Kraabel 1983, 184) or perhaps more likely "the Jewish community's significant connection to its polytheist context" (Hammer and Murray, chap. 12, 186). Indeed, the reuse and defacement of items in the private sphere falls into a different category altogether, for, as Hammer and Murray point out, there is a clear distinction between "defacing something that has become one's possession versus defacing a public image in the polis," where the latter would be to make a public statement of challenge to the "other."

Two third-century CE Christian martyrs and local persecutions (Neufeld, chap. 3) indicate some aspects of conflict within the city, as does the earlier sermon of Melito (ca. 170–80) against the Jews (although he refers only to "Israel" and "the people"). Melito's accusation against the Jews of deicide (the first unambiguous such reference among Christian writings; see Wilson 1995, 246–50), and particularly his supersessionist viewpoint, mitigates the idea of "co-operation" based on Melito's Quartodeciman practices (the texts are detailed by Aasgaard, chap. 11). Although it is unclear that the Jews even knew of Melito, and thus whether he really counts as an example of "conflict" (so Gaston, chap. 2; Hammer and Murray, chap. 12), Aasgaard suggests that the close physical proximity between Jews and Christians at Sardis would likely "have had considerable impact on the minds and attitudes of his audience" such that Christians would look upon and perhaps treat their Jewish neighbours differently in daily contact (Aasgaard, chap. 11, 165).

Nevertheless, Melito's rhetoric more likely indicates inner-Christian conflict. Hammer and Murray raise the possibility that the conflict arises from some Christians being overly interested (in Melito's view) in Judaism. This point is developed by Aasgaard, who suggests that the key concern for Melito's anti-Jewish polemic is not primarily aimed at the Jews of Sardis per se or even the Judaizers but the Montanists of Asia Minor. Melito presents himself as a prophetic counterpart to Montanist prophecy: he is the prophet who is rooted in and aligned with the Christian scriptures. Melito develops the anti-Jewish polemic from Jewish and Christian scriptures in order to legitimate himself as a true prophet. These texts tell the *Christian* story. Thus, while Melito's *Peri Pascha* can be placed in relationship to the Roman world and to the Jews, it is primarily in its relationship to other Christians that its rhetoric functions to construct a viable Christian identity for Melito and his church at Sardis.

Yet Stephen Wilson has raised the possibility that the *actual* Jewish-Christian conflict at Sardis necessitated Melito's travelling to Jerusalem to obtain precise information about the number and arrangement of the books of the Jewish Bible. This trip "indicates a lack of contact with the Jews in Sardis, perhaps due to mutual hostility which discouraged the informal exchange of information—the sort of hostility in fact that, from the Christian side, comes to expression in the homily itself" (Wilson 1995, 253; see further the summary of four approaches to Melito's view of Judaism in Cohick 1999).

It is clear that the actual evidence for competition and conflict between religious groups at Sardis remains illusive and obscure, although still present. What stands out, however, as it did with Caesarea Maritima, is the amount of coexistence. This is not to say that there is no evidence for competition and conflict. However, at least some of that evidence points to the locus of competition and conflict resting within the seminar's designated categories of "Christians, Jews, and 'Others'"; so, for example, competition is seen among Zeus worshippers or between associations, while conflict is evidenced in Christians debating their own self-identity.

Smyrna

Turning to Smyrna, we again will use the four *c*'s as our interpretive rubric. Here the evidence for coexistence and co-operation is more scant than for Sardis. Indeed, only one significant piece of evidence was explored by the seminar. Drawing upon the work of Daniel Boyarin (1998), Wayne McCready concludes "that Judaism and Christianity were part of a complex dialectic of negotiated differences and sameness that included an emerging and shared concept of martyrology [that] suggests that these two religious rivals were involved in the entwining of their ways" (chap. 10, 146). The rivalry that is behind the rhetoric of the *Martyrdom of Polycarp* thus reflects that between siblings, not foes, as each group seeks to establish its own separate identity in contrast to, but hence dependent upon, the existence of the "other."

Evidence for religious competition at Smyrna is much greater than for coexistence and co-operation. Along with the competition between Christian groups and other healing religions such as that of Asclepius (as Muir noted for Sardis; see above), we also have associations vying with one another for pre-eminence within the city. Thus, associations could become benefactors to the city, in order to enhance their public reputation above that of another association, as may be seen in the list of donors to civic institutions in *ISmyrna* 697 (ca. 124 CE; Harland, chap. 5). We see claims for pre-eminence through the phrase "before the city" (*pro poleōs*) by two contemporaneous (II CE) groups, one worshipping Demeter Thesmophoros and the other aligned with Dionysos Breseus (Harland). An association might also align itself with civic dignitaries or the emperor in order to enhance its reputation above others, as did the *mystai* of Dionysos Breseus (Harland). Aelius Aristides of Smyrna makes clear that in his view "it was in associations devoted to Sarapis, more so than any others, that participants truly experienced communion with their god" (Harland, chap. 5, 63).

According to Gaston (chap. 2), there is no evidence of Jews in competition with polytheists, although there is an enigmatic reference to *hoi pote Ioudaioi*, a phrase that might be understood as "former Jews" (i.e., now "lapsed" or converted to a different religion) or "Jews formerly of Judea." These possibilities are discussed by both Gaston (chap. 2) and Harland (chap. 5), both of whom read it in the second sense as referring to residents of Smyrna who once lived in Judea.

In the Christian sphere, Ignatius of Antioch writes two letters from Smyrna in which he treats issues relating to Judaism. However, in both cases it is unclear whether the warning is against Jews or, more likely, reflects an inner-Christian debate over the traditions (dates and practices) inherited from Judaism (Neufeld, chap. 3). Ignatius writes to the Philadelphians, warning them against living according to Torah (6.1). He also writes to the Magnesians, "Therefore, having become his disciples, let us learn to live according to Christianism [*christianismos*]. Whoever is called by another name more than this is not of God....It is impossible to speak of Jesus Christ and to Judaize. For Christianism did not put its faith in Judaism [*ioudaismos*], but Judaism in Christianism" (*Mag* 10.1.3, LCL). Earlier, he warns the Christians against living according to Judaism (8.1–2) but later connects this type of living to issues of dates: "no longer living for the Sabbath [*sabbatizontes*], but for the Lord's Day" (Neufeld, chap. 3).

James Knight argues that we need to take seriously the *worship* of the goddess Roma as part of the religious makeup of ancient cities rather than marginalize Roma as somehow an act of political diplomacy and not "real" religion. Thus, the presence of a temple to Roma in Smyrna (and elsewhere) provides the backdrop for understanding the imagery of the book of Revelation (Knight, chap. 8). Through the image of the harlot as Rome (Revelation 12), Revelation represents a challenge to the conventional Roman politico-religious ordering of the world—a vision in which God and the Lamb rule the cosmos (Knight). While this might be understood as religious competition, the reference in Revelation 2:9 to "the slander on the part of those who say that they are Jews and are not, but are a synagogue of Satan" indicates to some scholars "the bitter opposition" between Christians and Jews (Hemer 1986, 76).

However, the various investigations of the Rivalries seminar, while not denying the presence of some Christian–Jewish–polytheist conflict at Smyrna, suggests rather that much of the information is unclear, at best. This issue is perhaps best illustrated in the various approaches to understanding the story of the martyrdom of Polycarp, bishop of Smyrna, in the mid-second century CE. The *Martyrdom of Polycarp*, Ascough (chap. 4) suggests, indicates polytheists' accusations against Christians. Gaston (chap. 2) intimates that the text reflects Christian anti-Jewish rhetoric: *Martyrdom of Polycarp* tells of Polycarp's death in a way that recalls Jewish involvement in Jesus's death and is written from an anti-Semitic standpoint. On the other hand, Neufeld suggests that this reflects not Christian–Jewish conflict but an inner-Christian conflict, perhaps about dates and calendars (Neufeld, chap. 2).

McCready (chap. 10) argues that the rhetoric of the *Martyrdom of Polycarp* reveals it to be part of a developing Christian identity aimed at internal consumption by Christians, rather than dialogue with interlocutors. Although the text has as one of its four themes a message that there will be opponents of Christians, some of whom will be Jewish, the three other themes are primarily focused on bolstering the faith commitment of the Christians themselves. McCready admits that while "there are discernible socio-political contexts behind at least some instances of Jewish–Christian debate...the *Martyrdom of Polycarp* does not provide easy access to those contexts because the role of Jews is so firmly placed in its deliberative discourse" (chap. 10, 155).

Neufeld regards the story of the martyrdom of Pionius (ca. 250) as of dubious historical reliability (chap. 3). It reflects a Christian disdain for learned polytheists and chastises the Jews for gloating about Christian apostasy, cautioning Christians that the Jews killed Jesus. But it is unlikely, suggests Neufeld, that this rhetorical flourish can be trusted as an actual portrayal of the social reality at Sardis.

In sum, an analysis of religious groups at Smyrna indicates more evidence for competition and conflict among them than evidence for coexistence and co-operation—the opposite of what we found in Sardis (and in Caesarea Maritima). Nevertheless, a close examination of the evidence in the essays in this volume has shown us that in many, but not all, cases it is a matter of competition and conflict among members within a particular group designation. Thus, associations vie with other associations for public recognition, or Christians engage one another over the proper use of their Jewish heritage as a means of self-definition.

Conclusion

The Rivalries Seminar's studies of Sardis and Smyrna have confirmed what Donaldson pointed out after the study of Caesarea Maritima: the eventual triumph of Christianity across the Roman Empire in the fourth century "should not be taken to mean that there was necessarily a conscious competition for the soul of the empire in the second" (2000, 2). Although there are some examples of conscious competition and conflict, more predominant in the Sardis and Smyrna studies is religious coexistence. What examples there are of competition and conflict are at least equally divided between inter-group and inner-group conflict. This latter finding was one of the most striking aspects to come to the fore in the course of the seminar's work and is clearly reflected in the essays in this volume.

NOTES

Chapter One

1 Also, some of the papers presented in the seminar were published else-where, e.g., Broadhurst 1999; Beavis 2000; D'Angelo 2003.

2 In earlier periods Sardis was called Hyde. See Homer, *Il.* 20.385; Strabo 13.4.6.

3 On the widespread knowledge of the Croesus stories through the second century CE see Hemer 1972.

4 Arrian, *Anabasis* 1.17.3–6; Diodorus Siculus 9.33.4; Herodotus 1.141; Theophanes, *Chronogr.* I 474B; but see Hanfmann, Robert, and Mierse (1983, 131) who suggest that there is little to confirm that this temple was ever actually built.

5 Twelve cities in Asia Minor were ruined by the earthquake, but Sardis was hit the hardest.

6 Pliny, *Hist. Nat.* 2.86.200; Seneca, *Naturales quaestiones* 6.1.13; Suetonius, *Ceas.*, "Tiberius," 48.2; Tacitus, *Ann.* 2.47. I am grateful to Dietmar Neufeld for pointing me to some of these sources.

7 Recent archaeological finds have shown that Ramsay's rather dismal view of the conditions in the city from the first century CE to the Turkish period was wrong (Ramsay 1994, 269–70, but originally published in 1904).

8 This is true for Asia Minor more generally. It was also in the second century that the imperial cult became closely associated with local deities at various sites in Asia Minor. See Ramsay 1994, 88–89; cf. Johnson 1975, 83.

9 The prosperity of Sardis continued until it was destroyed by the Persians in 616 CE; see Foss and Scott 2002, 615, 617.

10 See Greenewalt, Ratte, and Rautman 1990; Tassel 1998; Greenewalt and Rautman, 1998, 2000; Greenewalt, Cahill, Stinson, and Yegül 2003.

11 See in particular Pedley 1972; Hanfmann and Waldbaum 1975; Hanfmann and Ramage 1978; Buttrey 1981; Yegül 1986; Crawford 1990; Schaeffer, Ramage, and Greenewalt 1997; Ramage and Craddock 2000. The earlier

253

Princeton University excavations (1910–14, 1922) also produced a number of volumes, including Bell 1916; Butler 1925; Buckler and Robinson 1932. Hanfmann (1980) surveys the fragmentary archaeological evidence for aspects of urban life at Sardis in the fourth century BCE. Of particular interest is his assessment of the data for religious architecture, but it is too early for the scope of the "Religious Rivalries" seminar.

12 The city was probably actually rebuilt by Antigonus and Lysimachus around 290 CE (Aune 1997, 160). Later coins show the Smyrnean Nemeseis appearing to Alexander with plans for the refounding of the city (Ramsay 1994, 183).

13 Various dates are given for this event. Cadoux (1938, 239) dates it to 26 CE; whereas Aune (1997, 175) and Broughton (1938, 709) put the date at 29 CE.

14 Wreaths or crowns were used in a number of contexts in antiquity and could indicate such things as the conferral of honour, victory or achievement, celebration (e.g., a wedding crown or at banquets), or cultic or religious occasions. In cultic or religious settings there were a number of functions for wreaths: they were sometimes placed on a statue of a deity as a symbol of sovereignty and divinity or worn by functionaries during prayers, sacrifices, and processions (Aune 1997, 174–75). For more uses and an elaboration, see Ramsay 1994, 187–88; Aune 1997, 173–75.

15 Aune (1997, 158) suggests that "garland" is a better rendering of *stephanos*, since *diadema* ("diadem, crown") is found elsewhere in Revelation.

16 See Calder 1906; Cadoux 1938, 171–73; Hemer 1986, 59.

17 Again, I am indebted to Dietmar Neufeld for pointing me to these ancient sources.

Chapter Two

1 It is possible that parts of the *Sibylline Oracles* are from Asia Minor, but there is no indication that some are from our cities, and the nature of the genre makes them difficult to use for our purposes.

2 It seems likely that Jews are to be found in Sardis (= Sepharad) as early as Obadiah 20, but that is not directly relevant for present purposes.

3 The scholar most skeptical about the decrees is Moehring 1975, 3:124–58. Barclay (1996, 262–64) is hesitant. Much more receptive are Tcherikover (1970, 306–309), Smallwood (1976, 127–43), Rajak (1985), Trebilco (1991, 8–19), and Richardson (1996a:90–109, esp. 95–96; 1996b, 269–70).

4 On sacrificing in a synagogue, see Binder 1999 and Levine 2000.

5 There is some confirmation of at least the third in Philo, *Legatio* 311–16.

6 On the debate surrounding the nature of the term *politeuma*, see Lüderitz 1994.

7 "Sabbath" is mentioned by name in other decrees: Josephus *Ant.* 14.242, 245, 258, 263.

8 See the complementary studies of Collins (1983, 137–74), Mendelson (1988, 51–75), and Sanders (1992, 190–240). See also Hammer and Murray, chap. 12 in this volume.

9 On the significance of the discovery, see especially the publications of A. Thomas Kraabel, many of which are conveniently reprinted in Overman and MacLennan 1992.

10 Lieu (1996, 6–7) finds that the century-long separation between the two does not allow the later to explain the earlier.

11 See further Aasgaard, chap. 11 in this volume.

12 See most recently Wilson 1995, 241–56.

13 He asserts the same thing about Sardis; Thompson 1990, 124.

14 Frend 1965 is a prominent example.

15 See Parkes 1969, 121–50.

16 I have used the text and translation of Musurillo 1972.

17 "Destiny had given him the same name" (6.2).

18 Later the Sabbath before Passover would be called Shabbat Ha-Gadol, but that has no connection. Besides, Polycarp was said to have been martyred on 23 February (21).

19 See also McCready, chap. 10 in this volume.

20 For what it is worth, it is said that when Rabbi Meir went to Asia and found no Megillah there, he wrote one out by memory (*Meg.* 18b).

21 So Kraabel (1982, 455): *Ioudaioi* = Jews in Judea. In the light of Wilson (2000, 354–71), I am no longer so sure of the correctness of Kraabel's translation, but I still find it marginally most probable.

22 "The evidence for positive relations between various cities and their Jewish communities from the second and third century CE onwards is quite strong. These clues suggest that the paucity of references to hostility in the literary sources between the cities in Asia Minor and their Jewish communities from II CE onwards is significant and that some sort of peace was arrived at" (Trebilco 1991, 184).

23 The situation of the Sardian Jews was then just the opposite of Rodney Stark's conception of Hellenistic Judaism as an insecure, anxiety-ridden marginal fruit ripe for picking by the triumphant church (1996, 49–71).

24 A recent book to that effect is Taylor 1995.

Chapter Three

1 See in this volume Hegedus (chap. 6), Marshall (chap. 7), and Knight (chap. 8).

2 Ignatius, bishop of Antioch, while en route to Rome to be martyred (117 CE), spent some time in Smyrna, where he was welcomed by Polycarp, the bishop of Smyrna.

3 See McCready, chap. 10 of this volume.

4 See further, Aasgaard, chap. 11 of this volume.

5 In this connection it is useful to ask, in the words of Lieu, "What is the rhetorical function of Jews and Judaism in the early texts (Ignatius, Polycarp, Meltio)? How does this rhetorical function relate to the historical, theological and social framework within which these texts arose and functioned? And, how did these texts help constitute the framework for later text?" (Lieu 1996, ix).

6 See further, Hammer and Murray, chap. 12 of this volume.

7 The translation of this and the following quotations from the letters of Ignatius are taken from the LCL.

8 See further, Gaston (chap. 2) and McCready (chap. 10).

Chapter Four

1 Since there is no one good way to refer collectively to these "other" religious groups, for ease of use I will refer to them as "polytheist" religions, in no way meaning this use to be pejorative.

2 The following is summarized from McDonagh 1989, 257 and Hanfmann 1983, 119–21.

3 Ramage (1987, 30) points to a large votive relief depicting Artemis and Cybele being worshipped together: each has her own representative adornments (a deer and a lion, respectively), thus showing that they "kept their distinct and individual identities."

4 See *ISardBR* 8, lines 132–39 (2 BCE). Zeus Polieus is not to be confused with the very different Zeus Sabazios, a priest resident at Sardis in Hellenistic times (Hanfmann 1983, 132). The head of another Zeus has been possibly identified as Zeus Lydios and reflects "evidence for a revival of interest in local divinity in the second century A.D. which would correspond to the revival of interest in the local Sardian goddess or Kore" (Métraux 1971, 159).

5 The statue of Artemis is now lost. Ramage (1987, 31) describes the fragment of the statue of Zeus found at Sardis.

6 Hanfmann (1983, 120) suggests that earlier the Artemis temple may even have been home to statues of Tiberius and Livia.

7 The Pactolus River was a source of gold for Sardis in antiquity. According to legend, the gold was carried downstream from Phrygia because Midas once bathed in its upper reaches; McDonagh 1989, 252.

8 See Hanfmann and Ramage 1978 no. 256; for a description see Ramage 1987, 27. The lion was the symbol of Sardis (Ramsay 1994, 260).

9 In older literature this image is often mistakenly assumed to be Kore; e.g., Ramsay 1994, 266–67.

10 Robert 1975; Horsley 1981, 21–23; Herrmann 1996, 329–35. See also Herrmann (1996, 21–29) for other inscriptions testifying to the *therapeutai* of Zeus at Sardis, esp. *ISardBR* 22.

11 During the reign of Artaxerxes II Memnon.

12 Gschnitzer (1986) argues against this interpretation, suggesting that *Baradateō* should be taken as a genitive (it is the normal Ionic form).

13 Horsley (1981, 22) points out that this is "a product of the breadth of the dominion of the Persian empire."

14 Edwards (1996, 32; cf. Briant 1985) thinks it is more likely that the text reads current concerns into the past. Either way, it is the "current" concern that interests us.

15 In a brief paragraph Horsley begins the process of comparing this group with features of early Christian groups. However, this comparison warrants further exploration. An obvious beginning point is Robert's article "Une nouvelle inscription grecque de Sardes: Règlement de l'autorité perse relatif à un culte de Zeus" (1975). As Kraabel observes, "Robert has fully discussed the importance of the text for the religious history of Sardis; his account should be consulted by all who are interested in that subject" (1992d, 254).

Also note Herrmann 1996, 329–35, esp. 334–35, and the issues and bibliography there.

16 The same image also appears on coins from other Lydian cities at that time; Kraabel 1992d, 254.

17 For a description of the iconography of the god, see Johnson 1968, 544. The cult of Sabazios extended from central Asia Minor through Greece and Italy, and as far northwest as modern Belgium (Johnson 1968, 543). Its popularity in Lydia likely was connected to its being the official cult of the Pergamene kings.

18 Johnson (1961, 82) points out that the connection with Zeus "is not surprising, since elsewhere in Lydia Zeus-Sabazios inscriptions appear." Sabazios has also been connected with Men, Dionysos, and the Great Mother (Johnson 1961, 82). For a list of the variants on Sabazios's name, see Johnson 1968, 543.

19 Kraabel (1992d, 254) admits that he is most interested in discussing the influence of "paganism" on Judaism at Sardis but has "said nothing of possible *influences* of Sardis Judaism on Sardis Gentile piety, and yet, given the number and strength of the Jews, that cannot be excluded" (his emphasis).

20 On the goddess Roma, see further Knight, chap. 8 of this volume.

21 It probably incorporated the earlier cult of Roma into it; Ratté, Howe, and Foss 1986, 65–70.

22 For a detailed discussion of the relevant inscriptions from this time, see Herrmann 1995.

23 For the text of this inscription, see Hermann 1995, 32–33 (and plate 4, 1–2). This statue base was dedicated at the time of Claudius.

24 The obverse shows the genius of Sardis, a veiled woman, kneeling in supplication before Tiberius. See the brief discussion with drawings in Ramsay (1994, 268–69).

25 This is the only temple found at Sardis, apart from the temple of Artemis and fragments from the Hellenistic Metroon of Cybele, found in the synagogue. Ratté, Howe, and Foss (1986, 45n1) list other temples known from the literature but without physical remains uncovered: temple of Zeus Olympios founded by Alexander; temple of Hera; temple of Athena Nikephoros; sanctuary to Dionysos (ca. 150 CE); shrines to Apollo; shrines to Men; temples of Attis, Demeter, and Kore; temple of Asklepios; temple of Roma; and temple of Augustus. An inscription seems also to mention a *Hadrianeion*, suggesting a second-century CE temple to the emperor (Hanfmann 1983, 145). Hanfmann (1983, 145) speculates that this might be the first temple of the imperial cult awarded to the city and thus the occasion of their becoming *neōkoros*. However, this assessment must be changed in light of the finding of the earlier pseudodipteral temple. Worship of a particular emperor, and even a temple to him, need not necessarily indicate neokoros status (Ratté, Howe, and Foss 1986, 65).

26 A statue of Lucius Verus, co-emperor with Marcus Aurelius, seems to have stood on the pedestal.

27 The image of Antoninus Pius was "of almost exactly the same colossal dimensions" as the image of Zeus Polieus placed earlier in the temple of Artemis (Ramage 1987, 31).

28 The title *prōtēs Ellados* also appears in *ISardBR* 64, 68, 69, 70. The title is partially restored in all of the inscriptions, but the various legible letters make the reconstruction fairly certain.

29 The emperor of the third neokorate remains unidentified (Ratté, Howe, and Foss 1986, 45n1).

30 See further, Hammer and Murray, chap. 12 in this volume.

31 A dedicatory inscription dates the decorative scheme to 211–12 CE.

32 Kraabel (1992d, 246) suggests that by using the lion statues in their synagogue the Jews of Sardis are "actually associating themselves in some way with this traditional Sardis image" rather than simply drawing on the biblical image of the "lion of Judah"; cf. reference to themselves as *Sardianoi*, "citizens of Sardis" (Kraabel 1992b, 280). But see Crawford 1996, 42–44.

33 The chapel "was evidently thought of as hallowing the sanctuary of Artemis and providing a chapel for the large cemetery nearby" (Pedley 1992, 984, citing Hanfmann 1983, 195).

34 Cf. *CCCA* 1.460; for a description of the relief see Mitten 1966, 51–55; Hanfmann and Ramage 1978, 43–51; Ramage 1987, 27.

35 See *ISardRobert* 2; *ISardBR* 95, 96; Kraabel 1969, 82–83; Kraabel 1992d, 248.

36 For a general discussion of the problem, see Donaldson 1997, 65–69; Ascough 1998b, 16–20. See further, the works of McKnight 1991; Feldman 1993b; Goodman 1994; and Carleton-Paget 1996.

37 On the voluntary associations more generally, see the papers from a previous CSBS seminar collected in Kloppenborg and Wilson 1996.

38 It is interesting that, despite the general lack of material from Smyrna when compared to Sardis, at last count Harland lists more than twice as many association inscriptions from Smyrna (38, 17). See Harland's essay in this volume.

39 For example, a series of four inscriptions from the second and third century CE found in the temple of Sylvanus at Philippi (*CIL* III 633) indicate that a number of members of the association contributed to the building and furnishing of the temple. An association from Knidos (*IKnidos* 23, II BCE) lists a number of people who have "freely chosen to assist the association," including the amounts of their donations. All of the donors are of servile status and cannot be assumed to be wealthy patrons of the association. The money collected is not designated for any specific reason and presumably is to be used to support the general operation of the association, particularly in their social gatherings.

40 See *IG* II² 1327 (Piraeus, 178/77 BCE) wherein a treasurer is honoured because, among other things, he "organized the original collection of the common fund." Other associations had "common funds"; see *IG* II² 1263 (Piraeus, 300 BCE); IDelos 1520 (II BCE). The most obvious means for gaining funds is through membership dues, either upon initiation (*IG* II² 1298; 1368; *IG* V/1 1390) or upon attendance at each meeting (*IG* II² 1339; *IG* XII/1 155; *CIL* 2112; *IDelos* 1519; 1521; *P.Mich.Tebt.* 243; *P.Cairo.dem.* 30606). These membership dues would pay for association expenses or special projects.

41 For a list of known deities worshipped at Smyrna, see Bilabel 1920, 212. A more complete description is provided by Cadoux 1938, 202–27.

42 Ramsay (1941, 90–91) links the duplication to the geographic feature of the twin peaks, both at Smyrna and at Dionysopolis.

43 During Tiberius's reign, the entire city of Smyrna was declared to be a place of refuge, but the physical location was reduced by the Senate in 22 CE to the Temple of Aphrodite alone.

44 "A deity of unique type worshipped by the Aiolians of Smyrna and later by their Ionian successors was Boubrostis, a personification of ravenous hunger....She had a temple at Smyrna, and the Ionians used her name in cursing their enemies" (Cadoux 1938, 224–25).

45 Cf. *ISmyrna* 601, 622, 639. See also the Dionysiac Artists' inscriptions; *ISmyrna* 598, 599.

46 Possibly simply "an image."

47 The site of the temple is not known; Cadoux 1938, 212.

48 See the depiction of the river god Meles on a coin of Smyrna, reproduced in Ramsay 1994, 191, fig. 20.

49 Unfortunately, the location of this temple remains unknown.

50 Cadoux (1938, 240) states, "For some unexplained reason the term is not actually found on her coins before the time of Caracallus."

51 Various dates are given for this event. Cadoux (1938, 239) dates it to 26 CE; Broughton (1938, 709) and Aune (1997, 175) to 29 CE.

52 Tacitus (*Ann.* 3.63) recounts that during Tiberius's reign the Roman senate stipulated that bronze tablets were to be set up inside temples in the major cities of Asia that would serve as a warning not to allow religion to become a cloak for inter-city rivalries.

53 Cadoux (1938, 259n1) notes that the connection of this inscription with Smyrna is not certain.

54 Head 1911, 594; see Cadoux 1938, 203 for further details.

55 *ISmyrna* 623, 591. It is unclear whether this latter inscription is referring to Hadrian (so Cadoux 1938, 203) or Nero (so Chapot 1904, 431).

56 E.g., Acts 5:31, 13:23; 1 Tim. 1:1, 2:3, 4:10; 2 Tim. 1:10; Titus 1:3–4; 2 Pet. 1:1, 11; Jude 25.

57 See also *ISmyrna* 665, 666, 667, all from the III CE.

58 Cf. Herrmann 1996, 340–41. Harland has tackled this issue in terms of imperial religion and associations at Ephesus (1996).

59 More generally on civic pride in Greco-Roman antiquity see Ascough 1998a, 96–100.

60 The following is a summary of Cadoux 1938, 264–70.

61 An obscure deity or hero known at Ephesus and Miletus.

Chapter Five

1 I use the term *associations* to refer to small, *unofficial* groups (of usually ten to fifty members) that met regularly for social and religious purposes (excluding more official groups, such as gymnastic organizations and boards of temple-functionaries that served in an ongoing, daily manner in a given

sanctuary). The traditional view, which speaks of three types of associations based on *purpose*—occupational, burial, and cultic (e.g., Waltzing 1895–1900), is problematic in that virtually all groups, including guilds, served a variety of religious, social, and funerary purposes (see Kloppenborg 1996, who deals with the difficulties of the old typology and points us in a more useful direction for understanding the types of associations; see Harland 2003, 25–87 on the various types and purposes of associations). Moreover, issues of membership composition and social network sources are quite useful in making sense of the types of associations found in Asia Minor. Basically, associations in this region could draw their membership from pre-existing social network connections associated with (1) the family/household, (2) common ethnic or geographic origins, (3) common occupation, (4) common neighbourhood, or (5) common cultic interests (encounters at the sanctuary of a favourite deity). Though a particular group could certainly draw on more than one of these sources, there are cases in which the principal network source for a particular group is quite evident; furthermore, many groups' expression of self-identity corresponds to the social network base in question (see Harland 2002a; 2003, 25–53).

2 On "Baccheion" see *IEph* 434, *IDidyma* 502, *IGBulg* 1864 (Bizye, Thracia), *IGR* I 787 (Heraklea-Perinthos), *IG* II² 1368 (Athens).

3 For the former, compare *IG* VI 374 (an association of Agrippiasts at Sparta) and *CIJ* 365, 425, 503 (a synagogue of Agrippesians at Rome). On the synagogues, see Leon 1995, 140–42, and Richardson 1998a, 19–23.

4 *SEG* 46 1524 (I CE); cf. *TAM* V 932 for another guild of slave-market merchants at Thyatira. All translations are mine, unless otherwise noted.

5 *TAM* V 972 (ca. 50 CE); cf. Buckler 1913c, 296–300, nos. 2–3; Harland 2003, 143–47 (on the dyers at Thyatira).

6 *TAM* V 975 (I CE); see Harland 2003, 146, fig. 25, for the family tree.

7 Traditionally (following Jean Baptiste Frey in *CIJ* 742), *hoi pote Ioudaioi* has been understood as "former Jews" in the "religious" sense of apostates: "Jews who had acquired Greek citizenship at the price of repudiating their Jewish allegiance" (Feldman 1993a, 83, citing Smallwood 1981, 507). Those who understand it as such cite no other inscriptional evidence for this interpretation. Moreover, it seems that broader assumptions about whether or not Jews could actually participate in such ways within the *polis* without losing their Jewish identity play a significant role in the decision to interpret the phrase as apostasy. Kraabel, who is followed by others, challenges this translation and suggests the possibility that the term means "people formerly of Judea" (Kraabel 1982, 455; cf. Fox 1986, 481; Trebilco 1991, 175; *ISmyrna* 697 [notes to line 20]). He does not cite inscriptional evidence to back up this use of the term *pote* specifically to refer to a group of immigrants, however. He bases his interpretation on the fact that this type of monument erected in connection with benefactions from various groups to the *polis* would be an unlikely place to make a public renunciation of faith. Ross Kraemer (1989) builds on Kraabel's suggestion and pursues further evidence that suggests the term could indeed be used as a geographical indicator. Margaret

Williams (1997, 251–52) contests Kraabel's suggestion, arguing that conspicuous Jewish apostasy did occur and "foreign residents are *never* described as 'formerly of such and such a region'" (italics mine; she is, in fact, wrong, unless she is still focused on the word *pote*). She makes no positive arguments for how we should translate this phrase in the inscription (apparently resorting to the unfounded apostasy theory).

There is good evidence for the geographical (not "[ir]religious") understanding of the phrase. A lengthy inscription recording various benefactions to the *polis* would be, as Kraabel (1982, 455) states, an unlikely place to make a public statement of apostasy, and there are no other attested epigraphical parallels to it. The announcement of one's former religious status not only as an individual but as a group would also be peculiar; the clear proclamation of one's geographical origins (with its obvious accompanying religiocultural implications), however, is common in inscriptions. Moreover, it seems more plausible that the term *Ioudaioi* should be understood in a geographical sense: this refers to "the former Judeans" (an immigrant association of Judeans). Even though it is clear that *Ioudaioi* had geographical (alongside cultural) connotations to the ancient hearer, the difficulty here is that we have no other *exact* parallels to this specific usage of *pote* in the known cases of ethnic or geographic based associations of foreigners specifically. It is important to point out, however, that there is no consistently employed form of self-designation by such groups in Asia, such that we cannot speak of deviations. Often groups simply designate themselves "the Alexandrians," "the Phrygians," "the settlement of Romans," "the association of Asians," "the Samothracians," without any further clarification or use of a preposition, for instance. Perhaps more important, there is, in fact, a similar phrase used on inscriptions to designate *former geographical origins* for an individual or several individuals, which closely parallels the case at Smyrna in many regards; namely, the use of *prin* (instead of *pote*) as in the phrase "when Aurelius, son of Theophilos, formerly of Pieria, was secretary [*grammateōs Aurēliou Theophilou tou prin Pieriōnos*]" (*NewDocs* I 5 = Mitchell 1999, 131, no. 51 [Pydna, Macedonia]; cf. *IG* IV 783.b.4; *IG* X/2 564 [Thessalonica]; *SEG* 27 293 [Leukopatra]; all III—early IV CE). I am grateful to John S. Kloppenborg for pointing me to these inscriptions.

8   For discussion of associations and diplomatic relations with emperors, see Millar 1977, 456–64, and Harland 2003, 155–60, 220–23.

9   Meiggs (1960, 321–23) rightly doubts strict enforcement of such laws in the second century, citing plenty of evidence for multiple memberships in the guilds at Ostia. Imperial legislation along these lines did gradually develop towards the compulsory guilds of the late empire, when governmental control of *collegia* reached its peak. In the first two centuries, governmental involvement or interference in the life of associations was very limited and sporadic (see Harland 2003, 161–73). For discussion of imperial legislation on associations, see Waltzing 1895–1900 and Radin 1910. Early research tends to uncritically assume consonance between law and reality, however.

10 Robert (1975; cf. *NewDocs* I 3) convincingly suggests the Persian character of this cult (in its IV BCE form), identifying Zeus with Ahura Mazda; this makes better sense of why the mysteries of native Phrygian deities, Sabazios (cf. *IPhrygR* 127 = *CCIS* II 6, 39, 43 [initiates of Zeus Sabazios near Philomelion]) and Agdistis (cf. *ILydiaKP* III 18 = *LSAM* 20 = Barton and Horsley 1981), and the Cappadocian deity, Ma, were strongly discouraged. The situation and implications when the inscription was later republished in the Roman era, however, would be different.

11 "Sacred/most sacred": *IEph* 636 (silversmiths); *IKyzikos* 97 (guild of marble-workers), 291 (sack-bearers/porters); *IHierapJ* 40 (guild of wool-cleaners), 41, 342 (guild of purple-dyers); *SEG* 36 1051–53 (associations of linen-workers, sack-bearers/porters devoted to Hermes); *IGLAM* 656 ("tribe" of leather-tanners at Philadelphia); *ISmyrna* 652 (synod of Breiseans devoted to Dionysos). "Emperor-loving": *IEph* 293 (initiates of Dionysos); *IMiletos* 940d (goldsmiths in the theatre). "Great": *IEph* 4117 (*collegium* of imperial freedmen [*Kaisarianoi*]). "Worldwide": *SEG* 36 1051 (guild of linen-workers at Miletos). This last was a favourite among guilds of performers and athletes.

12 See *PKöln* 57 and *NewDocs* I 1 for several invitations to such banquets in Egypt, in which Sarapis himself is the host who bids his guests to attend.

13 For other uses of the phrase "before the city" in connection with Dionysiac and other associations see *IEph* 275, 1257, 1595, 3808a, 4337 (cf. Merkelbach 1979; *NewDocs* VI 32). Somewhat ironically (in light of the situation at Smyrna), at one point, the Dionysiac initiates and Demetriasts at Ephesus joined together to form a single association, using this phrase of pre-eminence in reference to the united group (no. 1595; II CE). Cooperation also regularly found its place in association life. The phrase *pro poleōs* (without the article) is used at Ephesus as an additional title for Artemis, pointing to her prominence as patron deity (*IEph* 276, 650).

Chapter Six

1 A current example of this approach is the work of Roger Beck of the University of Toronto who in numerous publications has demonstrated the central role of astrology within the Roman mystery cult of Mithras.

2 See the description of the planetary characteristics in Bouché-Leclercq 1899, 88–101; Barton 1994, 111–13.

3 Both authors note the contradictions inherent in the astrological view of Saturn: the picture of Saturn as an old man hardly accords with the planet's common association with fecundity and generation.

4 See the description of the zodiacal signs in Bouché-Leclercq 1899, 130–49. The mythological connotations of the signs are conveniently summarized in G. P. Goold's introduction to his LCL edition of the *Astronomica* (Goold 1977: xxiv–xxx).

5 Festugière refers in particular to the astrological doctrine of "aspects," i.e., the angular (opposition, square, trine, and sextile) relationships that could be established between the zodiacal signs (cf. Ptolemy, *Tetrabiblos* 1.13); see Bouché-Leclercq 1899, 165–77n1; Barton 1994, 99–102.

6 Cumont describes these as "oeuvres nébuleuses et abstruses qui devinrent en quelque sorte les livres saints de la foi...en puissance des étoiles" (Cumont 1929, 152). The book of Nechepso opened with a nocturnal divine revelation brought by a heavenly voice (Bouché-Leclercq 1899, 576–77n1).

7 See the discussion of Greek views of the Persian magi in Beck 1991, 511–21.

8 *De Abstinentia* 4.8; the text is found in van der Horst 1984, 20–22. This report, attributed to the philosopher Chaeremon by Porphyry, reflects an idealized description of Egyptian clergy (van der Horst 1984, x, 56n1); nevertheless, there is no reason to doubt that, as the text indicates, the functions of the priests and *hōroskopoi* overlapped.

9 *Stromateis* 6.4 depicts the *hōroskopos* holding a clock and palm in his hand and the astrological teachings of Hermes Trismegistus always in his mouth.

10 Earlier, Vettius Valens had expressed a similar view (Cumont 1929, 159; Barton 1994, 59).

11 Seeking to know the emperor's allotted life span was seen as evidence of ambition to the throne and was, therefore, repeatedly outlawed.

12 Ambrosiaster, *Quaestio* 115.50–51; Augustine, *Enarratio in Psalmos* 40.3; cf. the sophisticated combination of astrological and Christian beliefs in the *Book of the Laws of Countries* of Bardaisan of Edessa.

13 This is the argument of my book (Hegedus 2004); see also Hegedus 2003.

14 This seems to be the scholarly consensus on the date and location of the text (Collins 1992, 701).

15 See further, Hemer 1986, 57–77 on Smyrna, and Hemer 1986, 129–52 on Sardis.

16 For example, it is doubtful that the image of the Son of Man in Rev. 1:12ff. refers to some sort of constellation (Malina 1995, 52, 67–70). Apart from a brief and biased report by Epiphanius (*Panarion* 16), we know nothing about "Pharisaic astrology" (Malina 1995, 78). Except for the allegorizers of Aratus and the Peratae discussed by Hippolytus (*Refutatio* 4.46–50; 5.12–17), an allegorical reading of the heavens was not "rather usual in the astronomics of those deviants labelled as 'heretics'" (Malina 1995, 73). There is no evidence that the "giants" of Jewish legendary tradition (based on Gen. 6:4) were "responsible for stone structures of gigantic proportion (Mediterranean dolmen and menhir, like Stonehenge) and [that] their skeletons are still found at times (dinosaur remains identified as the bones of giants)" (Malina 1995, 64). Aries's turning its neck backwards was understood to mean that it was looking back towards Taurus (Manilius, *Astronomica* 1.264) rather than that its neck was broken (Malina 1995, 53, 111). It is also unclear what the real benefit is of translating *angelos* as "sky servant" or *pneuma* as "sky wind" (Malina 1995, 61–63, passim). A further problem with Malina's book (1995) is its contention that Revelation should be interpreted exclusively in cosmological terms (see the review by deSilva 1997).

17 Regulus is actually a modern name, though it was called *stella regia* in antiquity (Pliny, *Natural History* 18.235, 271). Leo was also the astrological sign of royalty (Bouché-Leclercq 1899, 139, 139n2, 438–39).

18 Boll bases this on Mesopotamian star lore; the "scorpion men" of Mesopotamian lore are the warrant for his identification of the creature with a human face as Scorpio.

19 Beck also points out that the passage in Firmicus Maternus is complicated by the mention of two more royal stars in *Mathesis* 6.3. Whether these are located in Taurus or Gemini (and, hence, likely equivalent to Castor and Pollux), these two other stars complicate the fourfold schema that is the basis of Boll's reading of the four living creatures.

20 Most recently by Malina 1995, 99.

21 While Boll does emphasize the close association between Pegasus and the constellation Aquila (1914, 38–39), he does not identify the eagle of Rev. 4:7 with Aquila because of its proximity to Scorpio (1914, 37n1).

22 As well, Scorpio is the astrological house of Mars; Bouché-Leclercq 1899, 185.

23 For another example of the positive use of Aquarius in a Christian context (as an image of Christ and Christian baptism), see Zeno of Verona, *Tractatus* 1.38.

24 This connection between the book of Revelation and the Jewish festivals was more central to Farrer's earlier study of Revelation (Farrer 1949).

25 Farrer (1964, 117) acknowledges the anti-calendrical order of the living creatures but, again, does not offer an explanation.

26 According to Farrer (1964, 98–99), the first living creature in Rev. 6:1–2 is the lion, since it speaks "with a voice of thunder," like a lion's roar. In 6:3–4 the second creature is the bull, "a beast of slaughter," which heralds "the bearer of the sword." The third creature at this point in the text is not Aquarius, however. Rather, since 6:5–6 seems to refer to economic inflation, Farrer sees the living creature of v. 5 as Libra "the constellation of the scales, the sign of scarcity...in the very claws of the Eagle's zodiacal equivalent, the Scorpion" (Farrer elaborates on this further on p. 100). Finally "the Man (Aquarius) presides over the death of the year...so let him stand for *the* death (the pestilence)" in Rev. 6:7–8. This latter order (Leo, Taurus, Eagle/Scorpio, Aquarius) is also found in Farrer's astrological reading of those who are "sealed" from the twelve tribes of Israel in Rev. 7:4–7 (1964, 107). However, it is unclear from Rev. 7:4–7 itself why an astrological reading of this passage is even warranted.

27 Contra (Farrer 1964, 92, 17); nor is it at all clear that the figure of the beast in Rev. 13–19 is to be identified as "Behemoth" and so to correspond with Taurus the bull (Farrer 1964, 144, 151, 162–66).

28 Contra Farrer 1964, 172–75.

29 The traditional attribution of the four living creatures to the writers of the canonical Gospels was first made by Irenaeus, *Adversus Haereses* 3.11.8.

30 Cf. Hesiod, *Theogony* 381–92. The zodiac is explicitly described as a crown in a later astrological text; while this text dates from the Byzantine period, it contains "astrologiae formam qualis Romana aetate praevalebat" (*CCAG* 5/2:134.4).

31 *Regina caeli* is the term used by Lucius in Apuleius's *Metamporphoses* (11.2) to address the goddess who turns out to be Isis. Isis's sovereignty over fate

is then affirmed in 11.6, since she is able to prolong Lucius's life beyond its allotted span. Her rule over the stars is also mentioned in aretalogies from Cyme, Ios, and Andros.

32 *De Nuptiis Mercurii et Philologiae* 1.75. A more mundane parallel is Diogenes Laertius's description of a hat "with the twelve *stoicheia* woven on it" (*Vitae* 6.102 [LCL]).

33 Gundel 1972, 628, no. 49 (Jupiter); 629, no. 51 (Heracles); 625–26, no. 42, 44, 44a (Helios wearing a balteus with zodiac); 649, no. 129 (mosaic with Sol on quadriga). Jupiter was often portrayed on coins as surrounded by the zodiac; see Gundel 1972, 668–70; Cook 1914, 752–53. A mosaic from Sentinum depicts a young man encircled by a zodiac (see the photograph of plate 8 in Godwin 1981, 45); the young man may be Sol (*TMMM* 2.419). Godwin claims that the mosaic derives from a Mithraic "temple," but in the view of Cumont (*TMMM* 2.257), followed by Vermaseren (*CIMRM* 686), it came rather from a Serapeum.

34 Wernicke 1897, 1467–68.

35 Godwin 1981, 168, plate 139 (Dionysus and Ariadne); Gundel 1972, 632, no. 59 (Helios and Selene); Gundel 1972, 669, no. 188 (coin with Helios and Selene).

36 Other synagogue mosaics are listed in Gundel 1972, 650–51, nos. 132–34.1; see also Charlesworth 1977, 193–98; cf. Gen. 37:9, where the sun, moon, and eleven stars bow down to Joseph in a dream. As well, there are "twelve rays" (*dōdeka aktines*) under the feet of Judah in *Testament of Naphtali* 5.4; the latter is part of a larger passage (5.3–6) featuring astrological imagery (Levi seizes the sun, Judah the moon; Levi becomes like the sun, Judah like the moon; a bull appears with eagle's wings on its back), which is comparable to that in Revelation.

37 She was also associated with the moon goddess Selene; Collins 1976, 71.

38 Gundel (1972, 628–29, no. 50) and Godwin (1981, 113, plate 75) suggest that the goddess in the zodiac is Cybele; Glueck (1965, 108–10, plates 46, 48, 396) sees her as Tyche-Atargatis.

39 Patterson describes the woman's crown of stars in Rev. 12:1 as "a slightly depaganized version of the zodiac which encircles Selene" on the Argive stele, and he writes that the figure of Selene on the Argive stele and the woman of Rev. 12 "provide a graphic representation of the universal Queen of Heaven" (Patterson 1985, 442–443).

40 Not all such representations were of benevolent goddesses. The head of Medusa could also be portrayed in this manner (Gundel 1972, 670, no. 195 [coin] and 676–77, no. 213 [gem]).

41 Also the seven stars surrounding Selene on the Argive stele (Patterson 1985, 440).

42 The temple dates from the first century CE.

43 For example, the Pyramid texts describe the voyage of the sun-god Re across the heavens in the barque of the sun (Lesko 1991, 118–19).

44 We would expect the number twelve to be retained as representing the zodiac, in any case (Boll 1914, 103).

45 Ps-Eratosthenes, *Katasterismoi* 9 says that there are many ways that people understand Parthenos (i.e., Virgo): some say she is Demeter because she has an ear of grain but others view her as Isis. This motif was also appropriated in Christian usage: Boll cites a portrayal of Mary and her child with ears of grain (Boll 1914, 115n1).

46 Boll adds, "Diese Ähren sagen genugsam, dass hier die als Jungfrau im Tierkreis versternte Isis abgebildet ist...."

47 A sixth-century Persian translation of the Teucros passage adds the ears of grain that are characteristic of Virgo and adds that the child is called Jesus by some (Boll 1914, 115).

48 On Isis as the "goddess of many names" see Plutarch, *De Iside et Osiride* 53 (Griffiths 1970, 202–25), Apuleius, *Metamorphoses* 11.2 (269.14–270.2), *POxy* 1380 (which identifies her with over fifty deities), and the general discussion in Witt 1971, 111–29.

49 The use of the same verb in 12:18 (the dragon standing on the seashore) is entirely different.

50 A similar allusion to Gen. 3:15 is evident in the description of the relationship between Draco/the devil and Engonasin/Adam in Hippolytus's report concerning the Christian allegorizers of Aratus (Marcovich, *Refutatio* 4.47.1–5, 131–32).

51 Cf. the frequent opposition between God and a dragon (identified as Rahab, Leviathan, Behemoth, etc.) in the Hebrew Bible; the passages are listed in Charles 1920, 317–18. Such "combat myths" between two deities, one of which is often a monster or dragon, were widespread in ancient Mediterranean cultures. For a discussion of such myths as the background to Rev. 12, see Collins 1976, 57–100.

52 Cf. the identification of the constellation of the dragon in the Persian zodiac as a crocodile (Boll 1903, 327). The crocodile was connected with Typhon, according to Plutarch, *De Iside* 50.

53 In Plutarch's *De Iside* 21 the Bear is said to be Typhon's "soul," just as the Dog Star/Sothis is the "soul" of Isis. According to Griffiths's comment on this text (1970, 373), the equation of Seth and the Great Bear was well established in ancient Egypt.

54 According to Vettius Valens (*Anthologiae* 1.2) Hydra's head is at the claws of Cancer, and its tail is at the claws of Scorpio. A scholium on Aratus's *Phaenomena* 443 states that Hydra contains three signs: Cancer, Leo, and Virgo; another says that Hydra's head is in Cancer, its middle in Leo, its last part in Virgo, and its tail ought to be over the head of Centaurus so that its end is under Libra; cf. the image of the dragon bearing six of the zodiacal signs on its back in *CCAG* 5/2:134.4–5. Similarly, the dragon is said to be 180 degrees long (six signs, or half of the zodiacal circle) in a work by the seventh-century CE Syrian bishop Severus Sebokt (Nau 1910, 254).

55 As in the beast with ten horns, with another growing alongside, and three being plucked out, in Dan. 7:7–8:24, or the beast with seven heads, ten diadems, and ten horns in Rev. 13:1.

56 Ovid's version of the myth of the Snake, Raven, and Cup in *Fasti* 2.243–66 mentions that the three were catasterized together, as does Ps-Eratosthenes.

57 In Revelation see 6:13, 8:10, 9:1; according to Farrer (1964, 71) the angel of the church at Ephesus is addressed as a fallen star in Rev. 2.5 ("Remember then from what you have fallen").

58 It is also presumably evident in Seneca's description of the fall of the stars in *Thyestes* 827–74, with its detailed listing of the constellations. This passage is remarkably similar to *Sibylline Oracles* 5.512–31 (cited below).

59 Charles (1920, 319) incorrectly claims that the woman gives birth on the earth.

60 Translated by Adela Yarbro Collins in OTP 1.405; see also *2 Macc.* 5.2–4; Josephus, *Bell.* 6.5.3.

61 *Astronomica* 2.238; at 4.202 he claims that those born under her will not be "fecundus," adding "quid mirum in virgine?"

62 Cicero discusses the various equivalencies of Venus and Minerva in Cicero's *De Natura Deorum* 3.59.

63 Apuleius, *Metamorphoses* 6.4 (Juno addressed as the virgin Dea Caelestis, worshipped at Carthage).

64 Cumont 1958, 1249–50.

65 *CIL* 7.759 is dedicated to Virgo along with Caelestis, Magna Mater, Ceres, and Atargatis; see Yates 1975, 34.

66 On Isis as Ilithyia, see Boll 1903, 210, 212; the two together are the objects of prayer in Ovid, *Amores* 2.13.

67 "Veneris virginis—si tamen Veneri placuit aliquando virginitas...."

68 "Quam totam vanitatem aboleri et extingui utique ab illo oportuit, qui natus est virgine...."

69 Also briefly mentioned in Virgil, *Georgics* 2.474 and Ovid, *Metamorphoses* 1.149–50 (where the goddess is named Astraea). Dike was identified with the constellation of the Virgin already in Hesiod, *Works and Days* 256.

70 The Latin text reads:
    magnus ab integro saeclorum nascitur ordo.
    Iam redit et Virgo, redeunt Saturnia regna,
    iam nova progenies caelo demittitur alto.
    Tu modo nascenti puero, quo ferrea primum
    desinet ac toto surget gens aurea mundo,
    casta fave Lucina; tuus iam regnat Apollo.
    The name Lucina was applied to Diana and Juno in the context of childbirth (Cicero, *De Natura Deorum* 2.68). The return of Virgo at the destruction of the world (understood in the Stoic sense of periodic renewal) is also referred to in Seneca, *Thyestes* 855.

71 In light of this text, Boll asks whether the references to Virgo and Lucina (the goddess of childbirth) in Virgil's fourth Eclogue might not be more closely connected than scholars have traditionally thought (Boll 1914, 105n1, my translation).

72 Constantine seems to have based his comments on the Latin original of the poem (Barnes 1981, 75). Mary's perpetual virginity is also affirmed in this section of the speech.

73 Lactantius, *Divinae Institutiones* 7.24. On the difference in approach of Lactantius and Constantine to Virgil's fourth Eclogue, see MacCormack 1998, 24–26.

74 On Lactantius's use of Virgil's fourth Eclogue elsewhere, see Courcelle 1957, 294–95.

75 See the drawing of Virgo in Bouché-Leclercq 1899, 140.

76 Exod. 19:4; Deut. 32:11–13; Isa. 40:31; 1 Enoch 96.2; *Testament of Moses* 10.8–9 (which parallels Israel rising on the necks and wings of an eagle with being placed in the heaven of the stars).

77 It is unlikely that it is an allusion to Rome, considering the negative portrayal of Rome as "Babylon" in Rev. 17–18. The entry for Aquila in Ps-Eratosthenes, *Katasterismoi* 30, refers to the eagle that carried Ganymede up to Zeus. Manuscripts of Aratus portray Zeus himself sitting on the eagle (Boll 1914, 113n5); an example is given in *Sphaera* 115. Within Revelation, a parallel image to the eagle bearing the woman is the horse bearing Christ (Rev. 19:11); astrologically, the horse corresponds to Pegasus (i.e., the constellation Equus), which bore Bellerophon (identified with the constellation Heniochus/Auriga, the Charioteer, cf. Manilius, *Astronomica* 5.97–100).

78 Cf. 1 John 3:9, and the Pauline notion of the heavenly Jerusalem as the "mother" of the Church in Gal. 4:26.

79 Farrer's view of the woman as representing the female figures of the biblical salvation history is a version of this type of approach (Farrer 1964, 142–43).

80 Cf. the term *sign* (*sēmeion*) in Rev. 12:1.

81 *Patrologia Graeca* 61, 737 (*Chairi kecharitōmenē, ouraniou stachous atheristos aroura*); for other examples of the identification of Mary with Virgo, see Gundel 1950, 20–28.

82 The inscription continues with a sexual reference "and no mortal has ever lifted my mantle." Another version of the inscription is recorded in Proclus's commentary on the *Timaeus* 21E; cf. the mention of "Isis, who they say is the origin of the world from whom all sprang and through whom all exist" in Athenagoras, *Legatio* 22.8; also Isis's self-predication as ruler of time in Apuleius, *Metamorphoses* 11.5.

83 Cf. Rudolf Bultmann's acknowledgement of the need for a historical "*dass*" (i.e., the "that" of Jesus's historicity) as a basic minimum to anchor the Christ of faith within history (Bultmann 1955, 66; 1964, 20, 25).

Chapter Seven

1 Leigh Gibson and Richard Ascough have provided helpful criticism that has improved this paper.

2 "Options" is a weak gesture to the asymmetry of the rivalry under examination. Even embracing the characterization of plural Judaisms in the ancient world, Judaisms were, largely by virtue of the ethnic element of the religion and its very high valuation of exclusivity, one of the most cohesive religious options in the ancient world. On the other hand, the zodiac and astrology was one of the most diffuse religious structures in antiquity. Perhaps predictably rivalry is felt and expressed more intensely on the Jewish side.

3 The consideration of Revelation as a Jewish (rather than Christian) text is crucial to my approach. See Marshall (2001) for the argument and the stakes involved in such an approach to Revelation.

4 See especially Collins 1976; 1984a; 1988.

5 More succinctly, she writes, "In the context, the twelve stars can represent *only* the zodiac" (1984b, 1264, emphasis added). Similarly, Collins claims that the twelve stars in Rev. 12 called to mind the zodiac for the earliest readers (1984b, 1265–66).

6 In reaction to the pioneering work of Hermann Gunkel (1895), several commentators strove to integrate ancient Near Eastern mythologies into their interpretation of Rev. 12, most notably Bousset (1906), Boll (1914), and Loisy (1923). For the aftermath of Gunkel and history of exegesis of Rev. 12, see Charles (1920, 1:310–14), Prigent (1959), Feuillet (1963, 91–97), Vanni (1980), Böcher (1988, 68–75),and Chevalier (1997, 329–58). Recently, though in very different modes, Malina (1995) and Chevalier (1997) have sought to make an effective reintegration of astrology and astronomical speculation as the focal point of the interpretation of Revelation. Each goes much further in this effort than even Collins (1984b), but neither has found a substantial following. A much less influential group of scholars of Revelation favour an interpretation of the stars as the patriarchs of Judaism: see most recently Prigent (2001, 293).

   Charles (1920, 1:300) identifies the twelve stars with the zodiac and later (316) with the patriarchs, but only after having suggested that the crown of stars (and several other elements) are "superfluous" and not the creation of John, but merely detritus left over from polytheist materials adapted to this context. Beckwith (1919, 623) suggests that the twelve stars "may possibly" allude to the patriarchs, but "ultimately" go back to the zodiac. In the context of the vogue for source theories for Revelation that reigned through the late nineteenth and early twentieth centuries, commentators typically appealed to the exigencies of combining and adapting source materials to explain (away) what Apocalypse appeared to be a dual reference to the patriarchs and the zodiac, rather than exploring a trajectory in Judaism that might actively make such an identification.

7 After her description of the origin of the twelve stars image, Collins writes, "These particular motifs in Revelation [seven stars, seven spirits, twelve stars] show that the author of Revelation was aware of certain Hellenistic astral traditions and was able to view them in a positive light and adapt them for his own purposes" (1984b, 1274). She notes that this is also true for several Jewish apocalypses.

8 See Boll (1914, 99n1) and Collins (1984b, 1264) for the use of the singular *astēr* to refer to a constellation of stars.

9 "And Israel blessed his son before he died and told them everything that would happen to them in the land of Egypt, and made known to them what would come upon them in the last days; and he blessed them and gave Joseph two portions of the land"; cf. the much more extensive testamentary blessing in Gen. 49:1–28.

10 Charlesworth calls *Jub.* 12.16–18, in which Abraham's efforts to predict rainfall in the coming year by means of astral observation are rebutted, "the major passage in the Pseudepigrapha that condemns astrology" (1977, 188). See Charlesworth (1978, 384n2) for an abbreviated catalogue of opposition to astrology in Second Temple Judaism.

11 As a note to his translation, "omens of," Rabin indicates "Alternative readings 'the chariot of' or 'the wheel of' (with reference to the Zodiac)" (Rabin in Sparks 1984, 36n3).

12 *Jubilees* is quite vague about the actual substance of Arpachshad's sin, offering no more explanation than contained in *Jub.* 8.3.

13 Reuben, ninth month, *Jub.* 28.12; Simeon, tenth month, *Jub.* 28.13; Levi, first month, *Jub.* 28.14; Judah, third month, *Jub.* 28.15; Dan, sixth month, *Jub.* 28.18; Naphtali, seventh month, *Jub.* 28.19; Gad, eighth month, *Jub.* 28.20; Asher, eleventh month, *Jub.* 28.21; Issachar, fifth month, *Jub.* 28.22; Zebulun, seventh month, *Jub.* 28.23; Joseph, fourth month, *Jub.* 28.24; Benjamin, eighth month, *Jub.* 32.33; Dinah, seventh month, *Jub.* 28.23.

14 The only exception is a very abbreviated reference to the dreams of Gen. 37 in *Test. Zeb.* 3.3. The treatment of Joseph's visions in *Test. Jos.* 19 is substantially corrupted by obvious Christian interpolation or composition, and the divergent expansion of Joseph's visions in the Armenian version—in contrast to the Armenian's usual contraction of materials—shows the intense reworking that this section of the *Testaments* has undergone in the course of its transmission and translation; see Stone 1975; Sparks 1984, 592n4.

15 E.g., *T.Sim.* 2.6–5.1; *T.Zeb.* 2.1–7; *T.Dan.* 1.4–9; *T.Gad.* 1.4–3.3.

16 See *T.Lev.* 16.1; *T.Jud.* 20.1; cf. *T.Iss.* 4.4; *T.Zeb.* 9.7. This list is illustrative rather than exhaustive.

17 Expressed in verbal forms of euthynō: *Test. Sim.* 5.2; *Test. Jud.* 26.1.

18 Cf. 1 Enoch 5:4 "But you have *changed* your works" (trans. Black and Vanderkam, 1983, emphasis added). As Nicklesburg makes clear, fixity and change stand as tokens for discussing righteousness and sin in 1 Enoch 1–5 (2001, 157–58).

19 Marinus de Jonge forcefully revived the notion of an essentially Christian provenance for the *Testaments* (1953) and has been the major proponent of this view in the last half of the twentieth century; see also de Jonge 1960; 1987; 1991.

20 Treating the relation of the *Testament of Naphtali* to the *Hebrew Naphtali* document, Hollander and de Jonge suggest that "at least in the case of the visions, the Hebrew text, though late, is nearer to the original than the Greek Testament" (1985, 26).

21 *Nai*/amēn (1:7), *Abbadōn*/*Apollyōn* (9:11), *Diabolos*/*Satanas* (12:9, 20:2).

22 Most famously the solution to the 666 gematria of Rev. 13:18 advocated by Charles (1920, 1.266–67, credited to Charles's associate Smith and also reached independently by four nineteenth-century scholars; see Charles 1913b, 47); see Bohak (1990) for Revelation 17:10 and 21:17.

23 I have articulated this position in a larger exploration of John's eschatological vision (Marshall 2001, 185–89).

24 See Gager (1972, 134–61; 1994) for more detailed exposition of this text and this tradition as well as the notes of Morton Smith, the translator of *PGM* XIII; see also Smith 1984.

25 Nonetheless, Schwartz's very helpful discussions of the zodiac exclusively are devoted to synagogue material remains either in inscriptions or mosaics (Schwartz 2001, 243–63).

26 Most recently Levine (2000) and Schwartz (2001); see also Feuchtwang (1915), Goodenough (1953–68), Foerster (1987), and Weiss and Netzer (1996).

27 See Goodenough (1953–68, 10:27–41). The basic data for the Dura synagogue are available in Kraeling (1956).

28 Goodenough (1953–1968, vol. 11, fig. 27); Kraeling (1956, plate 59).

29 Kraeling (1956, 349) on Num. 21:6, Goodenough (1935, 209) on Exod. 15:27.

30 Goodenough (1953–68, 10:30–31).

31 The inscriptions are dual, naming both sign and month.

32 See Feuchtwang (1915), Goodenough (1953–68, 8:196–206), and Charlesworth (1977). These three authors provide helpful starting points for this section.

33 The Soncino edition renders *mzl* as "planetary influence," but it can also indicate constellations or specifically the signs of the zodiac.

34 "Thus says the Lord: Do not learn the way of the nations, or be dismayed at the signs of the heavens; for the nations are dismayed at them" (NRSV).

35 Mingana (1917–18). In 1978, James H. Charlesworth reintroduced a portion of the Rylands Syriac MS 44 to the scholarly world with a revised estimation of the manuscript's other, more substantial, astrological text: *The Treatise of Shem*. Redating this text to the aftermath of the battle of Actium (1978, 379–81), Charlesworth argued for its significance as a witness to a very positive ancient Jewish appropriation of astrology. In 1977, he made the sweeping claim that "the only preserved Jewish pseudepigraphical document that consistently advocates astrology is the virtually unknown *Treatise of Shem*" (1977, 190). While a very narrow understanding of pseudepigraphy—narrower than that of Charleworth's pseudepigrapha collection (1983)—may justify the exclusion of the Asaph fragment from the category "pseudepigrapha," it is equally unabashed in its embrace of astrology. By neither mentioning it nor translating it in his 1978 article, Charlesworth allowed it to remain as ignored as the *Treatise of Shem*, which he so diligently resuscitated. (Both the 1977 article and the 1978 article refer to one another as "in press." It seems that the presses turn more swiftly in Cambridge than in Manchester.)

36 The most obvious hints from Gen. 49 concern Reuben and Judah. Reuben: "Reuben, you are my first-born, my might, and the first fruits of my strength, pre-eminent in pride and pre-eminent in power. Unstable as water, you shall not have pre-eminence because you went up to your father's bed; then you defiled it—you went up to my couch!" (Gen. 49:3–4). Judah: "Judah is a lion's help; from the prey, my son, you have gone up. He stooped down, he couched as a lion, and as a lioness; who dares rouse him up?" (Gen.

49:3–4). Less obvious, but quite justifiable are Dan, Zebulun, Dinah, and Ephraim and Manasseh. Dan figured as the Scorpio: "Dan shall be a serpent in the way, a viper by the path, that bites the horse's heels so that his rider falls backward" (Gen. 49:17). Zebulun as Cancer, the crab: "Zebulun shall dwell at the shore of the sea" (Gen. 49:13). Dinah is not mentioned in Jacob's blessing, but she saves any of the other patriarchs being cast as the female Virgo. Ephraim and Manasseh are only hinted at in Gen. 49:22, which describes Joseph as a fruitful bough, echoing Gen. 48:4, where Jacob also pronounces Joseph fruitful and gives a double share of inheritance to Joseph so that Ephraim and Mannaseh inherit as sons of Jacob rather than grandsons; thus, they stand ready as for the role of the twins—Gemini; see also the joint account of their birth, though not specifying they were twins, in Gen. 41:50. Requiring even more interpretive agency are Asher, Naphtali, and Gad. Gen. 49:20 says of Asher, "Asher's food shall be rich, and he shall yield royal dainties." Perhaps this functioned as a cue to align Asher with the generosity of Libra. Naphtali is, according to Gen. 49:21, "a hind let loose, that bears comely fawns." For this description, the (female) goat Capricorn is an apposite correlation. Gad is described in Gen. 49:19 as a raider—"Raiders shall raid Gad, but he shall raid at their heels"—and Asaph follows this closely. Mingana suggests that the enigmatic Kirek is a corruption of "Crotus" (1917–18, 89). With three signs remaining and most of the clues offered by Gen. 49 tracked down, the identifications of Issachar as Aquarius, Simeon as Aries, and Levi as Pisces are not readily explicable on the basis of the Genesis text.

Chapter Nine

1 I benefited from discussing areas (Ignatius, patronage) of this paper with my colleague Ritva Williams (Augustana College, Illinois) and wish to acknowledge her assistance.

2 Whittaker 1979 finds that "universal charity was the commonly accepted ideal of the ethics of later antiquity" and that neither polytheists nor Christians could claim to be unique in pursuing humanitarianism; see also Dodds 1965, 136n4; Grant 1977, 96–123, 124–45; Mullin 1984; González 1990; Hamel 1990, 222–38; Praet 1992–93.

3 This phrase, which I use in my title, comes from Polycarp, *Phil.* 6.1.

4 For example, Yamauchi 1980, 55 (Smyrna 100,000).

5 Strabo *Geography* 14.1.37; discussed in Hill 1999, 40–41, who provides a detailed assessment of Smyrna's water system; also mentioned in Ramsay 1904, 262.

6 Ancient writers: Philostratus *Life of Apollonius* 4.8–10, *Lives of the Sophists* 25; Apollonius of Tyana, *Letters* 38–41, 51, 75, 75a, 76; Plutarch, *Precepts of Statecraft* 825D. Modern writers: Magie 1950, 599–600; Rostovtzeff 1957, 2, 8, 117; MacMullen 1966, 183; Hanfmann 1983, 144; Hemer 1986, 146; Thompson 1990, 154–56. See Bonz's assessment of inflation in Sardis (1993, 146–48).

7 Magie 1950, 663; Boak 1955, 26; Johnson 1961, 87–88. These plagues are identified by Stark as critical to the growth of Christianity.

8 The following sources give general information on the spread of the plague in Asia Minor. Although they do not speak specifically of Sardis or Smyrna, we may infer that the plague was in those locations. Roman armies under Lucius Verus (brother of and co-ruler with the emperor, Marcus Aurelius) were repelling a Parthian attack on the southeastern provinces of the empire, 165 CE (Rostovtzeff 1957, 213; Gilliam 1961; Littman and Littman 1973, 243; McNeill 1976, 103–04; Boak 1977, 318–19). Inscriptional evidence describes troop movements through Asia Minor at the time of the plagues (Johnson 1961, 87–88; Mitchell 1993, 133). The plague flared up again in the reign of Commodus, 189 CE (Gilliam 1961, 225–51).

9 The issue of various calamities in Asia Minor is surveyed in Hill 1999.

10 In Philostratus's *Life of Apollonius* 4.4, 10, the philosopher (fl. late first century CE) is called in as oracle to deal with a plague in Ephesus. Philostratus's biography of Apollonius was written in the early third century. Gilliam 1961, 234n35, describes an inscription from Tutludja in southern Mysia that mentions a plague (*nouson*). Plagues are mentioned in the book of Revelation; see discussion below.

11 Pedley 1972, 8, 11, 24; Ramsay 1924, 179, 183; Cadoux 1938, 190, 194; Magie 1950, 580–82, 663; Rostovtzeff 1957, 146–47, 600; MacMullen 1966, 180, 184, 249–54; Hanfmann 1983, 144; Hill 1999; cf. Garnsey 1988, 256.

12 Ramsay 1924, 182–84; also Robinson 1924, 5–20; 1925, 253–62; Hemer 1986, 4.

13 Cf. Garnsey 1988, 19, 32.

14 Ancient writers: Philostratus *Life of Apollonius* 4.5; Aristides *Or.* 48.39. Modern scholars: Ramsay 1904, 266; Cadoux 1938, 245, 266, 279; Behr 1968, 76; Pedley 1972, 64; Hanfmann 1983, 3, 141–44; Hemer 1986, 134, 144. The best known earthquake was in 17 CE; see Strabo 12.8.18 and Tacitus, *Ann.* 2.47, both in Pedley 1972, nos. 219–20). Aristides gives evidence of one in the late second century.

15 Here I have chosen not to discuss Jewish charitable activity, although I will note that there we would see a bounded religious-social group that operated in ways similar to early Christianity.

16 Pergamum is about 75 km from Sardis and linked to it by a Roman military road going from north to south along the coast (leading to Ephesus, the provincial capital). Sardis is about 75 km from Smyrna and linked by a similar road running east–west; Mitchell 1993, map 7; Cadoux 1938, 149; Foss 1976, 1.

17 Mitchell (1993a, 204) describes a coin celebrating (or promoting) the concord between Smyrna and Pergamum: obv. wreath of Caracalla; rev. Asclepius (of Pergamum) standing before enthroned Cybele, ca. 215 CE— *PERGAMENON SMURNAION OMONOIA A ES GEMINOU.*

18 In fact, there may have been two temples to Asclepius in Smyrna: one at the gymnasium (Aristides, *Or.* 47.17, 19), and one at the harbour (Aristides, *Or.* 50.102); see discussion in Cadoux 1938, 205.

19 Cadoux 1938, 179, 191, 205–06, citing *IGR* IV 1414.

20 Cadoux 1938, 205, citing Philostratus, *Soph.* 2.26.

21 Cadoux 1938, 206, citing *CIG* 3158.

22 Cadoux 1938, 203, citing *CIG* 3159. Cadoux notes that according to Aristides, Asclepius was worshipped at Smyrna as Zeus Asclepius (1938, 205; *Ors.* 42.4, 47.45, 78; 49.7; 50.46).

23 Cadoux 1938, 205, citing *CIG* 5974.

24 Moving outside Sardis and Smyrna, we know that Asclepius was worshipped at Thyateria (north of Smyrna and Sardis) and honoured with games (Walton 1894, 71, 112; Buckler 1917, 106–7; Keil 1923, 252–53). There are many inscriptions concerning the cult throughout Asia Minor (Walton 1894, 110–12 [various locations]; Ramsay 1904, 370 [Ariandos]; Buckler 1914–15, 181 [Keryzeis]; Buckler 1917, 106 [Teheni]; Keil 1923, 252–53 [various locations]; Mitchell 1993a, 133 [Pessinus, Aezani]; Mitchell 1993b, 14 [various city states, including Ancrya]). There is also coin evidence of the cult throughout the region (Gilliam 1961, 243; Walton 1979, 107–17; Buttrey 1980). There is evidence of particular reverence to Asclepius in Laodicea (Yamauchi 1980, 145). Finally, a Christian tradition records an interesting story of a conflict between the Asclepius cult and Christianity (Lebreton and Zeiller 1942, 1205).

25 Ramsay 1904, 365; Mounce 1977, 109. Outside our time period but demonstrating continuity, we have a Byzantine inscription of a propitiatory confession to Artemis; Buckler 1932, 97–98 nos. 95, 96.

26 Inscription: Gilliam 1961, 234; cf. Ramsay 1904, 263–64. On Aristides, see below.

27 Ramsay 1898–99, 13; Buckler 1914–15, 169–183; Robert 1964, 23–30; Kraabel 1978b, 25; Hemer 1986, 146; Mitchell 1993b, 12, 20.

28 Buckler 1914–15, 169–71; 1932, 96–98; Robert 1964, 27; Kraabel 1978b, 25.

29 Elsewhere I have written about Aristides, the disease-haunted and passionate devotee of Asclepius (Muir 1995, 362–79), so I will only summarize aspects of his career here and refer readers to that article and its bibliography, especially works by Behr (1968, 1973, 1981, 1993).

30 See the interesting discussion of social interaction among the convalescents by Remus 1996, and the analysis of Aristides at the Asclepieion by Jones 1998.

31 E.g., *Or.* 50.95; see Behr 1968, 105–6.

32 However, Gilliam (1961, 230n19) sees evidence in Aristides's appeals after the earthquake that the plague of 165 CE was not serious in Asia Minor, especially in Smyrna: "If the earthquake had been a second great disaster and if serious depopulation following a plague already existed, [Aristides] might have mentioned the fact in his appeals for aid."

33 Aristides, *A Letter to the Emperors concerning Smyrna* 12, cited in Hill 1999, 43.

34 Also *Or.* 33.6, 48.39, 50.9, 51.25; Behr 1968, 96–97, 166–68.

35 *Ors.* 48.45–50, 45.33–34 (*To Sarapis*). The Isis cult in Smyrna is discussed by Behr 1968, 21.

36 *Or.* 48.7, also 47.22, 48.50, 49.43; Behr 1968, 25.

37 In *Or.* 47.17, 19 Aristides mentions a temple of Asclepius in the district of the gymnasium, with a statue of the god. Is this the same temple mentioned by Pausanias (1.26.9) as being "by the sea"?

38 As is typical for a Greco-Roman city, there were bath-gymnasia in Sardis; see Hammer and Murray, chap. 12 in this volume. Note, however, that a bath is not always a healthy site: since people often used public baths when they were ill, there was a likelihood of the transmission of infectious diseases (Yamauchi 1980, 69–74). Bonz 1993, 142, speculates that a city the size of Sardis may have had as many as three large-scale bath-gymnasia (Ephesus having at least four).

39 Buckler 1932, 63; Cadoux 1938, 143; Magie 1950, 583–83; Rostovtzeff 1957, 148–49, 599.

40 On Christianity in Sardis, see Johnson 1961, 81–90. On Christianity in Smyrna, see Cadoux 1938. Christianity in these cities is discussed by Neufeld, chap. 3 of this volume. On Christianity in Asia Minor, see von Harnack 1908, 2:326–69; Lebreton and Zeiller 1942 passim; Johnson 1975; Hanfmann 1983, 186; Thompson 1990, 116–32; Mitchell 1993b, 3–10, 11–51.

41 In addition to below, see the following: Rom. 16:5, Epaenetus, first convert in Asia, now in Rome. 1 Cor. 16:19, churches of Asia send greetings. 2 Cor. 1:8, the "affliction" suffered by Paul in Asia (here, probably rejection or challenge to Paul's authority, so Acts 21:27; 24:19). Acts 20:4 mentions Tychicus and Trophimus from Asia. Tychicus is mentioned in Eph. 6:21, commended in Col. 4:7, also 2 Tim. 4:12 and Titus 3:12. Trophimus (one from Asia, one from Ephesus—the same person?) Acts 21:9; 2 Tim. 4:20.

42 Betz 1979, 224–25, 228, and nn51–53, 59, 93. Paul laconically notes that it was *on account of* (*hoti di*) an illness or weakness of the flesh (*asthenian tēs sarkos*) that he first preached among the Galatians (4:13). He continues that the Galatians did not reject him but received him "as an angel of God." Betz 1979, 224 (with examples in n46) notes the Hellenistic *topos*, "It is the sign of real friendship to provide unlimited help at the moment of great need, in particular illness."

43 Betz 1979, 224, esp. n48, suggests a common background between Paul and the Galatians; see perhaps Gal. 4:12.

44 Rom. 1:1; 1 Cor. 7:21–22; 9:19; Gal. 1:10. Part of this reference here is attributable to Paul's rhetorical contrast between the freedom to which the Galatians were called (no longer being under obligation to fulfill Torah) and the "slavery" that Paul's opponents were endorsing (renewed Torah observance). Paul, therefore, advocates a different kind of slavery: voluntary community love enacted in mutual service.

45 In this maxim, Paul draws on a Hellenistic *topos*, notes Betz 1979, 298. Confusingly, but not unusual in Paul's discourse, he seemingly contradicts himself soon after by suggesting that each person must carry his own load (6:5)!

46 Betz 1979, 309, equates "doing good" with the "fruit of the Spirit."

47 On doing good to one's neighbour, see also Gal. 6:10, 1 Thess. 3:12, Rom. 15:2.

48 See Betz's discussion, 1979, 311.

49 A similar list of gifts of the Spirit in Rom. 12:6–8 includes service (*diakonian*) and showing mercy (*eleōn*) but does not mention healing. However, in Rom. 15:19 (see also 2 Cor. 12:12) Paul speaks of doing acts "by the power

of signs and wonders, by the power of the Spirit of God," and we might assume that charismatic healing would be at least a portion of these actions. The phrase "signs and wonders" (*sēmeia kai terata*) is frequently used in Acts (2:43, 4:30, 5:12, 6:8, 8:6, 14:3, 15:12) in reference to mighty acts by the apostles, mostly healings and exorcisms. A list of leadership roles for an Asia Minor community does not mention healing (Eph. 4:11). The Galatian list of the fruit of the Spirit (5:22–23, *karpos tou pneumatos*) speaks of community attitudes rather than abilities or actions. That being said, we might suppose that attitudes such as love (*agapē*), kindness (*chrēstotēs*), and goodness (*agathōsynē*) could manifest themselves in charitable acts; on the last, see Betz 1979, 287–88.

50 Smyrna is on a main north–south road that connects Ephesus with Pergamum, and is about 60 km from each centre.

51 Arnold 1989, 5, 14–16, 18. Arnold notes that magic amulets were discovered between Smyrna and Ephesus bearing Jewish characteristics (1989, 16); see also Thompson 1990, 118–19. Arnold 1989, 16, also notes Ignatius's only use of *magic* in *Eph*. 19.3, "With this [birth of Christ] all magic was dissolved." Ephesus was the centre of the cult of Artemis, whose function as a saviour god sometimes included healing (Arnold 1989, 20–28, 39). There were also Asclepius and Sarapis-Isis cults at Ephesus (Arnold 1989, 35).

52 So Nock (1925, 94): "There can be...no doubt that the demonstration by cures, exorcisms, and the like of the superior nature of this power [*dynamis*] was a most effective cause of conversions"; see the discussion below on the apocryphal Acts.

53 Perhaps we see veiled references to magic, in 5:11's injunction to take no part in the unfruitful works of darkness or the reference to the cosmic powers of this present darkness in 6:12.

54 Eph. 4–5 has a dualistic view of separation between "the world" and the church; especially note the warfare imagery in 6:10–17.

55 1 Tim 3:12 *diakonoi*, 3:11 *gynaikas*. The latter may mean women deacons in this context rather than simply wives or women. In either interpretation, we may assume that the women are serving some kind of diaconal function since their qualities are set out in this job description; see Dibelius and Conzelmann 1972, 58.

56 We encounter references to widows again in the epistles of Ignatius and Polycarp, and groups of continent women may be behind the apocryphal Acts, all discussed below.

57 The writer seeks to place limits on the visitations (5:13); also see the discussion of the widows' activities in Dibelius and Conzelmann 1972, 75; Bassler 1984; Thurston 1989, 36–54. What should be kept in mind is that the discussion of widows in 1 Tim. is prompted by the controversy over how much charitable support the *ekklēsia* should extend to them; see Winter 1988.

58 The *Didascalia Apostolorum*, an early third-century church order (Connolly 1929), likely from Syria, sets out ecclesiastical job descriptions. Concerning widows, it notes that widows should not act on their own authority but strictly follow the bishop's directives (*Did. Ap.* XV). They are not to teach,

fast, dine with, or take donations from others; and they are not "to lay hands on and pray over any one without the command of the bishop or deacon." Deaconesses are given the primary task of teaching and ministry to other women (*Did. Ap.* XVI.iii.12).

59 The extent of references to specific local circumstances has been debated in scholarship; see discussion in Scobie 1993. In particular, the following statement by Scobie is apposite: "Recognition of such references does add a new dimension to our understanding of the letters and of how they were written. What they do is to present us with a picture of John as a *pastor* who was intimately acquainted with his people—with their successes and failures. Or perhaps one should say that they present us with a picture of John as a *prophet* who believed that his message was divine in origin yet who, like the prophets of the OT, directed it to a very specific local situation" (1993, 622). Ramsay 1904 and more recently Hemer 1986 find many local references.

60 So Mounce 1977, 31–37.

61 See Thompson's extensive discussion of relations between Christians and non-believers in Asia Minor, 1990, passim, especially 120–21.

62 Note the contrast to Laodicea in Rev. 3:17.

63 Also Scobie 1993, 614; Hermer 1986, 58–59 notes that the seer may be drawing upon a long-standing motif in Smyrnaen traditions of the "suffering city." When one considers the letters to the other churches in Revelation, there seems to be little evidence of matters relevant to this paper.

64 See discussion of the apocalyptic imagery in *Epistula Apostolorum* in Hill 1999 (below).

65 Mounce 1977, 154–55, identifies the red horse and rider as symbolizing civil disorder, anarchy, and rebellion—internecine conflict rather than invasion.

66 Rev. 6:6 refers to the inflated food prices that result from the shortages of famine; another reference to famine is 18:8; see Dickey 1928, 410; Mounce 1977, 155–56.

67 In Rev. 9:3–6 the torture of the locusts is like a disease; in 9:20 afflictions are called plagues. These images deliberately recall Exodus imagery (Bauckman 1977, 228; Mounce 1977, 193–95). Other references to plague are 11:6, 15:1, 8, 16:2, 11, 18:4, 8, 21:9.

68 Rev. 6:12; 8:5; 11:19; note that the shaking of the earth is a standard motif for theophany or upheavals of the eschaton. We know that Asia Minor is a prime earthquake region; see discussions in Bauckham 1977, 224–33; Mounce 1977, 161–62.

69 We see this same dualistically tinged reference to the outside world in 1 Peter 2:12. Missionary-teachers might preach to non-believers, but they do not accept charity from them; see the issue of hospitality in the apocryphal Acts, discussed below.

70 The apocryphal Acts are legendary stories about the apostles. The Greek texts date from the mid-second to mid-third centuries, and they are from various Hellenistic centres (Greece, Asia Minor).

71 Also argued by Davies 1980, 17–28, and Perkins 1995, 126. See also Nock 1925, 94.

72 Achetemeier 1985, 171–73; Gallagher 1991; Perkins 1995, 126–29. Gallagher 1991, 16, notes that out of twenty-nine conversion stories in the five principal apocryphal Acts, twenty are described as being the result of a miracle and two more are "miracle-tinged."

73 Davies 1980, 15, argues for the historical value of these admittedly legendary accounts, noting that "in writing pious fiction, people model the imaginary world about which they write on the real social world in which they live." This suggests a rhetorical mirroring process of the kind I have outlined.

74 See Gallagher 1991; Stoops 1992. For example, in *Acts of Andrew*, Andrew heals, resurrects, and preaches, and many are converted (Schneelmelcher 1991, 119–22, 123, 127, 135).

75 There is a lacuna in the text that may recount further activities of John in other western Asia Minor cities; see Schneelmelcher 1991, 192.

76 In *Acts of John* 19–25, the apostle cures the wife of Lycomedes, a wealthy praetor. He also resurrects Lycomedes. The couple converts. In *Acts of John* 30–36, John heals the old women of the city in the amphitheatre, in a most striking combination of preaching, healing, and theatrical spectacle. The "entire city" is assembled to watch. In *Acts of John* 46–47, we see the resurrection and conversion of a priest of Artemis. In *Acts of John* 48–54, John resurrects a father who was killed by his son. The father converts. John then admonishes the remorsefully self-castrated son, who also converts.

77 See Riddle 1938, 141–54; Meeks 1983, 191–92.

78 In a case similar to that of Ignatius's tour, Lucian notes that the Sophist-cum-Christian Peregrinus received charity from Asian Christians: "People came even from the cities in Asia, sent by the Christians at their common expense, to succor and defend and encourage the hero. They show incredible speed whenever any such public action is taken; for in no time they lavish their all" (*Peregrinus* 13.1–7 LCL).

79 Schoedel 1985, 238–39, notes that Ignatius has a complex understanding of grace. Here it refers to "a whole pattern of life and thought bestowed on the church by God or Christ." Thus, actions (in particular, ethical obligations) are entailed in the concept.

80 Although this passage draws from a standard early Christian rhetorical list of unfortunates, it may still reflect a social reality; see the discussions in Osiek 1981, 370–71; Schoedel 1985, 239–40.

81 The usual translation is "prisoner" and "the released one," perhaps referring to formerly imprisoned confessors (so Schoedel 1985, 239). But these words can be understood as metaphors for lame or paralyzed and then healed; see Luke 13:16 and the comment by Lightfoot 1992, 306, *dedemenou*, lit. "the bound," and *lelumenou*, lit. "the loosed" (cf. Mark 7:35). Those who had been healed had been "released" from the affliction that had imprisoned them.

82 This translation is from Schoedel 1985, 238.

83 Schoedel 1985, 238, notes that the theme "observe and avoid" in *Smyrn.* 6.2, 7.2 is a traditional polemic; see, for example, Rom. 16:17 and Titus 1:16, where false teachers are unmasked when their actions are considered, for they are unfit for any good deed; Lohse 1971, 29.

84 Schoedel 1985, 241, citing Tertullian *Apol.* 39.16–19; Hippolytus *Trad. Apost.* 26; Justin *Apol.* 1.67.6; see also Ignatius, *Pol.* 4.1–3, especially reference to the common fund (*koinou*); also Shepherd 1940, 151; Schoedel 1980, 33.

85 Schoedel 1980, 33; 1985, 240; Maier 1991, 155.

86 See *Smyr.* 2.1: "[Christ] truly suffered just as he also truly raised himself, not as some unbelievers say that he suffered in appearance."

87 Shepherd 1940, 144, noting *Smyrn.* 6.1, the faction's concern with "heavenly powers and the glory of the angels and the visible and invisible archons."

88 The tight ecclesiastical bonds of the Asia Minor churches, evident in the concern for Ignatius (von Harnack 1908, 1: 189, 191) is noted in Lucian, *Peregrinus* 13.1–7.

89 Schoedel 1985, 261. This is along the lines of his advice to the Smyrneans to "suffer together" in *Pol.* 6.1.

90 Schoedel 1985, 69; 1980, 53–54: "The pagans in the immediate environment of the churches are potential converts and in spite of their treachery must be repaid with good and be treated in a spirit of brotherhood."

91 Lightfoot 1992, 332 translates *astheneis* as "the sickly."

92 See discussions in Lightfoot 1992, 332; Phillips 1930, 80; Osiek 1981, 373. Schoedel notes again the standard list of unfortunates (1987, 21).

93 On the role of deacons in distributing charity, see Cranfeld 1966 and Lampe 1966.

94 Valée 1999, 82, citing Eusebius *HE* 5.3.4, 5.14–18 and Epiphanius *Panarion* 48. In Eusebius, *HE* 5.16.18, Apollonius talks of Maximilla's "predictions in which she prophesied wars and anarchy" (conditions, however, that Apollonius disputes). Apollonius accuses the Montanists of exploiting the poor, not helping them: "For we will show that those whom they call prophets and martyrs gather their gain not only from rich men, but also the poor, and orphans, and widows" (*HE* 5.18.7).

95 Acts 21:8–9; Eusebius, *HE* 3.39, citing Papias.

96 This passage is from Irenaeus, *Haer.* 5.33.3–4 (ANF 5.562–63) and can also be seen in the collated "Fragments of Papias" in ANF 1:153–54. Irenaeus's connection to Asia Minor is strong: he was born in Smyrna and knew Polycarp; see *Haer.* 3.3.4.

97 Telfer 1936, 229–230; MacMullen 1984b, 59–61; Mitchell 1993, 53–57. Gregory Thaumaturgus lived ca. 210–60 CE. Legendary stories about him were collected in a panegyric by Gregory of Nyssa (ca. 331/40–395 CE).

98 *Synaxarium ecclesiae Constantinopolitanae* May 26, col. 711ff. (ca. 257); cited in Foss 1976, 117; see also Thecla's healing tradition, note the discussion in the apocryphal Acts section.

99 Argued convincingly by Brown 1992, 71–117.

Chapter Ten

1 See Cameron 1991, 7, for comments about early Christian writers using rhetoric for long-term self-definition.

2 See Burrus 1994; Castelli 1995, 1996; and Boyarin 1998, 593–94 for features of a full-fledged martyrology that includes not being charged with a specific

crime other than being a Jew or Christian, martyrdom as fulfilling a religious expectation, and erotic factors associated with martyrdom.

3 Following K. Lake in *The Apostolic Fathers*, vol. 2 (1913); all English translations are from Lake's edition.

4 Conflict theory does not require a Jewish mission to the larger Gentile world as a necessary condition (cf. Baumgarten 1999, 476). Stephen Wilson, in *Related Strangers: Jews and Christians 70–170 C.E.*, notes that disagreement between Jews and Christians is a slippery and ill-defined matter (1995, 284). Part of the difficulty has to do with ancients determining an authoritative voice to speak for each religion in its emerging definition. The *Martyrdom* is but one voice in Christianity, which had mostly to do with addressing persecution and martyrdom imposed by Roman authorities. In moves similar to the gospel traditions, the *Martyrdom* sought to take the edge off the role of Gentile opposition by denigrating Jews.

Chapter Eleven

1 See the summary by Neufeld, chap. 3 of this volume. See also Hall 1979, xi–xii, for a brief and concise presentation of Melito's life and works, with important references. In the following, the Greek text and translations of Melito are from Hall 1979. The life and situation of Melito have been the object of many (daring) theory constructions during the last two decades. The recent monograph by Cohick represents in several ways a deconstructive take on such positions. She presents many valuable caveats against such theories and calls for a new start in research on Melito; see Cohick 2000, 147–53. In my opinion, however, she is overly critical of some of the traditional scholarly positions. Similar criticism is voiced by Taylor 1995.

2 *Eunuch* (*ton eunouchon*) probably does not mean that he was a eunuch physically, but that he lived in celibacy; cf. Hall 1979, xi.

3 See also the thorough analyses of his style and rhetoric in Wifstrand 1948, 201–19, esp. 217; Halton 1970, 249–55.

4 However, Cohick 2000, 151, is far more reserved on Melito's familiarity with scripture.

5 This is the position of most scholars. For a presentation of the Quartodeciman position, see, for example, Blank 1963, 26–41; Stewart-Sykes 1998, esp. 25–29. The view has, however, recently been challenged by Cohick, who argues that the homily only reflects traditional Christian exegesis of the biblical material, with no Quartodeciman interests; see Cohick 2000, 22–31 (esp. 30–31), 148–49. I agree with her that the *Peri Pascha* does not seem to be coloured by any Quartodeciman interests; however, Melito may nevertheless have been a Quartodeciman, but without making a point of it in the sermon.

6 Preserved in Eusebius, *HE* 4.26.13–14; see Hall 1979, xxx, 65–67.

7 However, Stewart-Sykes (1998, 5) also takes this observation to mean that he was a bishop; it speaks of "Melito's governance of the church in the Holy Spirit."

8 *To peri politeias kai prophetōn* and *logos autou prophēteias*. Trevett 1996, 40, appears to interpret them as anti-Montanist works; Stewart-Sykes suggests

that the latter may be a collection of Melito's own prophecies (1998, 13n58). The books may also have been about the Hebrew Bible: see Hall 1979, xiii–xiv.

9 For a thorough presentation of the history of Sardis, see Mitten 1966; Hanfmann 1983; for brief presentations, cf. Kraabel 1995, 100–3; Stewart-Sykes 1998, 8–11; cf. also Ascough, chap. 1 in this volume, and references there.

10 For example, part of a *senatus consultum* regulating the expenditures of high priests has been found in Sardis, and the same has been found in Italy and Gaul; see Mitchell 1993, 1:110.

11 MacLennan 1990, 103–4, rightly criticizes Johnson.

12 See also MacLennan 1990, 99–102; Mitchell 1993, 2:31–33, 36–37; Kraabel 1995, 105–6, 120; for a rather critical survey of scholarly contributions on the strength and influence of the Jewish community, see Cohick 2000, 64–68.

13 Roman edicts directed to Sardian Jews indicate this confirmation.

14 See Hammer and Murray, chap. 12 in this volume. See also Mitten 1966, 63–66; Seager and Kraabel 1983, 168–78; Botermann 1990, 103–20; Trebilco 1991, 40–43; Kraabel 1995, 102–106; Lieu 1996, 203–206. The synagogue survived until the sixth, probably the seventh century—in 616 CE the whole city, including the synagogue, was destroyed by an earthquake (see Muir, chap. 9 in this volume).

15 Bonz also offers an alternative reconstruction of the development of the Jewish community, questioning the strength of the community at the time of Melito; see also Cohick 1999, 126–27.

16 Bonz 1993 (esp. 152) holds that Sardis in general experienced an economic depression in the second half of the third century, and that the Jewish community thus could buy the building at a "reasonable price." She takes this as evidence of the wealthy and well-organized character of the Jewish milieu in Sardis. However, as Lieu (1996, 228) and others have reminded us, one should be very careful in order not to project from the strength of Melito's polemic to the strength of the Jewish community.

17 See also Kraabel 1971, 77 (with note 4), 83–84; Stewart-Sykes 1998, 9–10, with references; Levine 2000, 248.

18 The only exception is Melito's *Peri Pascha*.

19 Many of the workshops are from late antiquity, however.

20 I agree with them, against MacLennan 1990, 109.

21 Most of the inscriptions are, however, from the third century and later, mainly the fifth and sixth century. Except in Phrygia, very little Christian inscriptional material survives from earlier times; see Mitchell 1993, 2:37–39.

22 For an impressively thorough presentation of material, see Tabbernee 1997, esp. 51–104 (180–224 CE), but also 135–212 (225–74 CE).

23 According to Mitchell, the evidence of Themenothyrae may indicate early third-century rivalries between Montanists and orthodox Christians there. Farther north, in the upper Tembris valley, there is rich evidence for a particular type of inscription called "Christians for Christians" inscriptions (248 to ca. 350 CE), which may be from Christians closely related to Montanists; see Gibson 1978; Mitchell 1993, 2:40, 42; Tabbernee 1997 (but cf. 555).

24 For example, there are preserved fragments of translations into Latin (epitome), Syriac, Coptic, and Georgian, and the writing is mentioned by Clement of Alexandria and Eusebius. Cohick is very critical about both the proposed authorship and setting of *Peri Pascha*, and in a thorough argument holds that it is unlikely that it is written by the Melito of Sardis mentioned by Polycrates and Eusebius; she also maintains that the homily does not reflect a Quartodeciman position; cf. Cohick 2000, 11–87, 147–49. The information indicating that it is Melito of Sardis who is the author of the homily is so compelling that the burden of proving the contrary is on Cohick's side. Although there obviously are reasons to be critical towards some of the information given by Polycrates and Eusebius (e.g., Melito's Quartodeciman stance), she is, in my opinion, far too critical on these points and does not give sufficient reason to invalidate their testimony.

25 For a discussion and evaluation of the authenticity of each fragment, see Hall 1979, xxviii–xxxix; also Cohick 2000, 39–51.

26 For summaries and commentaries on the sermon, see esp. Blank 1963; Lieu 1996.

27 It has recently even been argued that the text is not a sermon, but in fact the liturgy of the Quartodeciman Paschal service; see Stewart-Sykes 1998, xi, 206. Although it is possible that this is the case, in my opinion it is doubtful and does not affect my considerations in this article. On baptism as a ritual of status transformation, see Ascough 1994.

28 See also Hall 1979, 62–65; Young 1999, 81–82. Some (e.g., Kraabel 1971, 79) hold that it may have been addressed to Marcus Aurelius's adoptive brother and early co-emperor, Lucius Verus. However, this seems unlikely; see Stewart-Sykes 1997, 272–73n10.

29 Hall 1979, xxii, dates *Peri Pascha* to between 160 and 170, which is also possible, but does not have any significant impact on my discussion and conclusions in the following.

30 And as a *logon* (1.33), a term with long traditions within, for example, Stoicism.

31 Wilson (1986, 100) has a more friendly explanation: *barbarians* refers to the empires that preceded Rome and is employed in a positive manner, in order to underscore the antiquity—and consequently distinguished character—of Christianity.

32 However, Stewart-Sykes 1997, 273, disagrees on this point.

33 Lieu 1996, 183–84, holds that, by his choice of words, Melito tries to downplay the flourishing (*ēkmasen*) as against the blossoming (*epanthēsasa*) in Roman times, and this may, in fact, be the case.

34 It is surprising to note that in a fragment (probably of another homily) discovered in a Georgian homiliary and published as late as in 1972, we find many similarities in style and content with the passage of 72–99, but entirely lacking the polemic against Israel; Melito *New Fragment II*; cf. Hall 1979, xxxix, 86–95.

35 Wilson (1985, 350) holds that Melito, in *Peri Pascha*, is consciously contrasting the Christian Easter celebration with current Jewish Passover practices.

36 It is a central point in Lieu (1996, e.g., 234–35) that such a pressure might be more of an idea in Melito's head than a reality.

37 I here agree with them, against Taylor 1995, 73, and Cohick 2000, 73–74.

38 I share this position with many other scholars; see, for example, Blank 1963, 84–86, Skarsaune 1997, 44–46, and Cohick 2000, 77, also 52–54, 77–80.

39 This is, however, a position that has been strongly criticized and problematized in the last decade; see, for example, Stewart-Sykes 1997, 271–75; Cohick 2000, 64–74. It has even been suggested that Jews took part in the Roman persecution of the Christians; see Hansen 1968, 93–99; Manis 1987, 400–1. For a criticism of this position, see Taylor 1995, 82–87, and Cohick 2000, 70–74.

40 It has also been suggested that Melito could have been atypical of Christian attitudes towards Jews in Sardis (Seager and Kraabel 1983, 187–88). This position remains speculative and seems improbable. It is not likely that Melito would be so out of touch with the general attitudes of his co-Christians in Sardis. The reception history of *Peri Pascha* also tells that it won much sympathy. It was spread rapidly and translated into several languages (Hall 1979, xvii–xix; Stewart-Sykes 1997, 281–82).

41 See Knapp 2000, 348–52, for a succinct presentation of typology as an exegetical approach in the second century.

42 Stewart-Sykes 1998, 14–16, points out the many similarities between the use of typology in John and in *Peri Pascha*.

43 See Knapp 2000, 369–73. The very strong contrast between the old and the new signals a problem in Melito's theology: he risks degrading the Hebrew Bible and subordinating it totally to the message of the New Testament—a risk that he shares with Marcion.

44 Melito also has passages very similar to this elsewhere in *Peri Pascha* (57a, 59–60) and in the long *Fragment 15* (70 lines); see Perler 1970, 263–64.

45 For a more detailed discussion of this passage, see Perler 1970, 256–65.

46 Cohick 2000, 152–53, emphasizes theological concerns as primary in *Peri Pascha*: the sermon is intended to further a focus on what is "new" in Christ (christology), and its polemic against Israel is not part of an anti-Jewish polemic, but of an inner-Christian discussion of how to understand the relationship between the "old" (the history of Israel) and what is "new" (the role of Christ). Clearly, putting emphasis on (the more theoretical aspects of) its theology is warranted—also in order to clear the table for new perspectives on the text. But leaving out the possible cultural and religious contexts of it is saying too little, for plausible settings need to be constructed in order to be able to understand it properly.

47 This is also the view of other scholars, e.g., Kraabel 1971, 84, and Wilson 1985, 350; for a criticism of this position, see Cohick 2000, 68–70.

48 See also Blank 1963, 16–17, 18–19; Lohse 1970, 179–88; Hall 1979, xli; Wilson 1985, 351–52; 1986, 98–99; Lieu 1996, 216, 21–34.

49 Blank 1963, 92, describes Christ's call here as a *logos protreptikos*, in which he summons people to turn to him and to receive baptism and salvation.

50 *To lytron* (manuscript A) or *to loutron* (manuscripts B and C, which would then refer to baptism; so Blank 1963, 93).

51 Stewart-Sykes (1998, 13–14; 2001, 227–28) also argues briefly in favour of such a view.

52 It is not accidental that the Gospel of John and Revelation, with their many "I" sayings, are the writings that Melito most frequently cites or alludes to; they were central in second-century Christianity in Asia Minor; cf. also Blank 1963, 90. It is also worth noting that Melito's use of Matthew, the most Jewish Gospel, is equally frequent. For Melito's use of the New Testament writings and its apocryphal writings, see, e.g., Beskow 1984, 70–71; Lieu 1996, 233 (with references).

53 Hall views them rather as a "collection of customary phrases or topics in which the faith could be summarized at the speaker's discretion" (1979, xliii).

54 For a general discussion of the development from prophecy to preaching in second-century Christianity, see Stewart-Sykes 2001, esp. 272–73. My view of Melito's role in this process corresponds well with his.

55 See the thorough survey of the various scholarly views given by Cohick 2000, 52–87.

56 This position runs contrary to that of Taylor 1995, 140–41, although I generally agree with her criticism of the tendency of many scholars to overdetermine texts theologically.

57 The so-called church EA. Its location outside the city walls may be to the result of its being built on a martyr's grave, but that is not certain.

58 The so-called church M.

59 Two Byzantine churches (twelfth to thirteenth centuries) have also been located; see Kraabel 1971, 78n8.

60 This is the position of Kraabel in Seager and Kraabel 1983, 185–88, but cf. Buchwald and Hanfmann 1983, 203. I follow Kraabel, against Buchwald. Stewart-Sykes (1998, 23–25) also shares Kraabel's view.

61 Stewart-Sykes's view is that they became Judaized, and he adduces parallel material from Syrian areas to substantiate his claim (1998, 23–25).

Chapter Twelve

1 For a range of diagrams and images we encourage the reader to consult Crawford, Hanfmann, and Yegül 1983; Crawford 1990.

2 Crawford, Hanfmann, and Yegül (1983) and Crawford (1990, 1996) are our sources for the shop evidence, and to save space, we will provide only parenthetical references for their interpretive comments on the evidence.

3 In support of his statement, Crawford cites the fact that the Temple of Artemis in Sardis was marked with crosses and surmises that this evidence demonstrates that Christians marked pagan materials with crosses to make them acceptable for reuse. Foss (who is cited by Crawford) indicates that this issue is actually much more complicated. Foss notes, "A well known law by Theodosius II provided that remaining temples be destroyed and purified by the sign of the cross" (1976, 49) and that "this law…did not provide for the conversion of temples into churches, as is sometimes maintained" (1976, 159n128). The law of Theodosius II in fact does not refer to the reusing of

pagan places but only to the purifying (exorcising?) and destroying of these pagan places. The law (16.10.25) states, "We command that all their fanes, temples, and shrines...shall be destroyed by the command of the magistrates, and shall be purified by the erection of the sign of the venerable Christian religion" (Pharr 1952, 476). Contrary to what Crawford seems to think, reused pagan items are not even part of the discussion. It is possible that the marking of pagan items with crosses for apotropaic purposes had been the practice of Christians, and Theodosius II then assimilated this practice into his law concerning pagan temples, but ultimately, we do not have a definitive reference to the practice by Christians of marking pagan items with crosses for reuse.

4 Hanfmann (1983) seems to raise a question about the identity of these as rabbits in the caption for fig. 244: "Terracotta flask (*ampulla*) with rabbits (?) eating green shoots issuing from the cross," but Crawford (1996, 41) seems sure about the identification.

5 Crawford notes that "its clay lacks the mica typically associated with Sardian clay" (1996, 41).

6 There appears to be some question about the connection between these shops and their functions. Crawford writes, "The fact that E13 was connected with E12, and that numerous glass fragments were found in both Shops, would seem to suggest that the two Shops formed a single unit which sold glass objects. However, the pottery, weighing devices and layer of red-orange material in the upper story and yellow material in the vats and basins in the lower story would suggest a dye shop. It is possible that the Shop had both functions, or cooperated with the dye shops in the area" (1990, 79). Moreover, in a much earlier summary of these shops, Crawford indicates that it was shops E13–14 that were connected (Crawford, Hanfmann, and Yegül 1983, 166). Possibly the latter is merely an oversight, since both subsequent publications link E12 with E13 (Crawford 1990 and 1996). The exact function of the shop is still unclear.

7 Although all of the shops had upper floors, only E4, E5, E7, and E12 had stairs; most occupants probably accessed the second storey with ladders (Crawford, Hanfmann, and Yegül 1983, 163).

8 Whether this evidence constitutes fragments from a single menorah plaque or from two separate plaques is uncertain. See Crawford, who records that "Hanfmann noted that although Th. [0.025 cm—estimated span of outer groove] and treatment with multiple claw chisel are the same, one has a larger, flatter carved channel, so 2 carved slabs may be represented" (1990, 82).

9 It is interesting to note that in his book, which predates his article by six years, Crawford assumes *Sabbatios* and *Theoktistos* are Jewish names, and this, he says, "corroborates the theory of Jewish ownership based on the discovery of the menorah plaque in E12" (Crawford 1990, 79). Not until his later article does he acknowledge the possibility that these could be Christian names.

10 From the Greek word for fish, this acronym stands for Jesus Christ, Son of God, Saviour (*Iēsous CHristos THeou hUios Soter*), and was used to symbol-

ize Jesus and Christianity by the early church. The dolphin also was considered a symbol of salvation since it was believed to save people at sea (Ferguson 1961, 15).

11 Seager and Kraabel (1983) are our source for the synagogue evidence, and to save space, we provide only parenthetical references for their interpretive comments on the evidence.

12 Seager and Kraabel (1983, 169) note that a two-storey forecourt would have been in keeping with the scale of the main hall.

13 If the forecourt's fountain is the "Fountain of the Synagogue" (*krene tou synagogiou*) mentioned in an inscription listing public fountains in Sardis, then it would have been accessible to the public (Seager and Kraabel 1983, 169 and 281n8).

14 See Hanfmann 1983b, fig. 254.

15 The exact meaning of *Theosebes* is much disputed, especially by Kraabel (1981), who doubts the existence of the category of "God-fearers" as Gentiles who attached themselves to Diaspora synagogues but did not fully convert. Overmann (1992, 145–52) offers some significant points of weakness in Kraabel's theories. Moreover, as Murray notes (2004, 13), "A number of Gentiles observed a variety of Jewish customs and traditions and attended synagogue services without converting fully to Judaism. Inscriptions from Aphrodisias, Sardis and Miletus identify a group of people with exclusively Greek names as [*Theosebes*] or god-fearers (Reynolds and Tannenbaum 1987:48–67; Siegert 1973:109–64; *CIJ* 228, 748)." We seem to have possible evidence here of such a Gentile "God-fearer."

16 See Aasgaard, chap. 11 in this volume.

17 At this point we are seeking to clarify Crawford's emphasis by exploring possible indications of competition between Jews and Christians, whereas later in the paper we will seek to evaluate how the two communities may have been connected.

18 De Polignac (1994, 3) states, "According to the classical picture of the city, the territory of the city is understood as the 'space of the citizens.' ...Among the large number of cult places which are scattered over it, ranging from a simple altar...to a monumental temple, some manifest *particularly openly* the authority whose exercise each city determinedly reserved to itself" (emphasis ours). Although de Polignac's emphasis is upon the singular authority of the city, his central point concerns how certain structures can openly manifest authority, and as such, the importance of a religious site within a certain area (cf. de Polignac 1995). Further, a religious structure's location, size, and architectural design are considered symbolic of the perceived order of reality (see Norberg-Schulz 1975, esp. 81–115; Lloyd and Mueller 1980, 184–85; Wright 1994, 40–41).

19 Hanfmann (1983a, 166), among others, recognizes the symbolic nature of these religious symbols. We might also draw a limited connection to "monumentalizing"—the significance of erecting monuments. Although those who examine the significance of monuments deal primarily with epigraphy, some of the general insights could be applied to publicly displayed religious

symbols. The visual message of monuments assumes a "sense of audience" (MacMullen 1982, 246; Woolf 1996, 23) and provides information about the individuals or groups who erected those monuments and how they perceived their place within society (Woolf 1996, 29). The public display of religious symbols can be connected to similar motives and perceptions, although perhaps in a much more limited sense. For more details on the significance of monumentalizing see Harland, chap. 5 of this volume.

20 Assigning motivation can be problematic, but, given the fact that we have two strong examples of the public display of crosses and that other options for displaying these symbols were certainly available, we must at least acknowledge the possibility of intent.

21 Although the three names inscribed on some pottery contributed to the identification of these shops as Jewish, it was the menorahs that convinced Crawford (1990, 78; 1996, 41–42).

22 The premise behind Kraabel's works appear to stem from his ThD dissertation in which he concluded that Sardis was a logical place for Jewish missionary activity, given the age and status of the Jewish community (1968, 201ff, 242.). Discussion of his conclusions is beyond the scope of this present work.

23 Seager (Seager and Kraabel 1983, 168–70) confirms Kraabel's description of the prominence of the Sardis synagogue in terms of its location, size, and architecture.

24 See, e.g., Ex. 20:3–5; Deut. 5:7–9, 29:16–28; Ezek. 6:4–7; Isa. 45–48; 1 Cor. 5:9–10, 10:6–7, 14; Gal. 5:19–21; Eph. 5:5; Rev. 9:20.

25 The fact that this situation is not so clear-cut should be obvious after examining the stances taken by Kraabel and Crawford. Crawford pits Jews and Christians against pagans (1996, 42), while Kraabel pits Jews and pagans against Christians (Seager and Kraabel 1983, 186). Both extremes have their inherent weaknesses.

26 We are aware that several problems exist in such a straightforward generalization: (1) Harland's analysis covers only the first to third centuries CE, while our work focuses on the late fourth and the early fifth centuries CE, and (2) the Christian community at Sardis may actually have not been well involved in the polis (in contrast to other Christian communities in Asia Minor). Unfortunately, space does not permit a fuller analysis of these issues, although we would argue that it is realistic to project some of Harland's findings into the later periods.

27 For example, the image of the lion occurs at various points in ancient Jewish literature: the tribes of Dan (Gen. 49:9) and Judah (Deut. 33:22) are described as "lions," as is all of Israel (Num. 23:24; 24:9); Judah the Maccabee is also pictured as a lion (*1 Macc.* 3:4–6), as is the Messiah (*4 Ezra* 12:31–32). Kraabel (1992a, 281) also contends that the lion is popular as well in Jewish art and other literature.

28 This older consensus, as outlined by Kraabel (Seager and Kraabel 1983, 178), considers the Jews in the Diaspora to be a "ghetto people," without power or a place to belong, whose only hope of survival is to compromise

themselves in the Gentile world and allow themselves to be assimilated into Gentile society. Bonz (1990, 343–59) provides a balance to Kraabel's view.

29 In Greek literature, lions are associated with Sardis (Seager and Kraabel 1983, 184), and their prominence in Sardis during the Lydian and Persian eras prompts Hanfmann to state that "the Lydians suffered from a regular *leontomania*" (Hanfmann and Ramage 1978, 20; see also 15, 21–23). The altar of Cybele in Sardis—which survived until at least the fourth century CE—was surrounded on four corners by lions (Hanfmann and Ramage 1978, 96; Ramage, Goldstein, and Mierse 1983, 37; Crawford 1996, 42). The lion is also thought to be a symbol of Sardis (Ramsay 1994, 260).

30 Crawford (1996, 41) refers to "a third–fourth century lamp with a cross on it at a Jewish catacomb at Beth She'arim." This description is somewhat misleading, since what is actually incised on the handle of the lamp is the Christian monogram *ChiRho* (Avigad 1976, 188).

31 Justin Martyr knew of the existence of Jewish Christians either in Asia Minor or Rome in the second century CE (*Dialogue* 47). In the fourth century CE, Epiphanius refers to Jewish Christians and distinguishes different groups of them, such as the Nazareans (*Heresies* 29) and the Ebionites (*Heresies* 30), but he does not describe these Jewish Christians as living in Asia Minor. While he does describe Cerinthus as a Jewish Christian living in Asia Minor, the historical value of his comments is doubtful (see Klijn and Reinink 1973, 8–19).

32 The phenomenon of Gentile Christian Judaizing was not a new development in fourth-century Asia Minor. Paul addresses Judaizing behaviour among Gentile Christians in Galatian churches in his letter to those communities (Gal. 2:3, 5:2–12, 6:12–15; see Murray 2004, 27–39); Gentile Christian Judaizers might be the targets of obscure accusations embedded in letters addressed to Smyrna and Philadelphia in the book of Revelation (Rev. 2:9, 3:9; see Gaston 1986a, 33–44; Wilson 1995, 162–63; Murray 2004, 73–82). In the early second century CE, on his journey through Asia Minor on his way to Rome, Ignatius, bishop of Antioch, writes letters to communities in Magnesia and Philadelphia expressing his disapproval of Gentile Christian Judaizers. In *Mag* 10.3, for example, he explicitly discourages Judaizing: "It is monstrous (*atopon*) to talk of Jesus Christ and to practice Judaism (*ioudaizein*). For Christianity did not base its faith on Judaism, but Judaism on Christianity, and every tongue believing on God was brought together in it" (LCL translation; see also *Mag.* 8.1; 9.1–2; *Phld* 6.1; 8.2; see Gaston 1986; Wilson 1995, 163–65; Murray 2004, 82–91); see also Neufeld, chap. 3 of this volume. Strong evidence of Judaizing Gentile Christians is found in Justin Martyr's *Dialogue with Trypho* (chap. 46, 47; see Wilson 1995, 165–66; Murray 2004, 91–99), although whether this document reflects an Asia Minor or a Roman environment is an issue open to debate.

33 As has been pointed out on numerous other occasions, the vehemence with which John Chrysostom lashes out against Gentile Christian Judaizers in his sermons from the years 386 and 387 CE is the consummate example of the degree to which such behaviour was perceived to be undermining Christian identity (Wilken 1983).

34 On Melito and Sardis, see further Aasgaard, chap. 11 in this volume.

35 The translation and critical text used here is that of Hall (1979). The following discussion of Melito is a much condensed argument from Murray's
book on Gentile Christian Judaizers (see Murray 2004, 101–16).

36 Eusebius describes Melito, the bishop of Sardis (*HE* 4.25), as a champion
of the Quartodeciman view as a celibate ascetic and one of the luminaries of the church living "entirely in the Holy Spirit, and who lies in Sardis
waiting for the visitation from heaven when he shall rise from the dead"
(*HE* 5.24). He was a talented and prolific writer. Tertullian calls him an
elegant and most eloquent spirit (*elegans et declamatorium ingenium*;
quoted in Jerome, *De Viris Illustribus* 24). Eusebius provides a long list of
his works (*HE* 4.25), but most of Melito's writing has been lost, except for
a fragment from his *Apology*, which was addressed to the emperor, and the
Peri Pascha.

37 In contrast to churches in Asia Minor, Roman congregations and other
churches in the western part of the empire celebrated Easter one week after
the Passover on Sunday, the day of the resurrection of Jesus. This difference in practice generated much dispute and tension among the propo-
nents of each view (Eusebius, *HE* 4.23–24).

38 As Wilson observes, "Insofar as the attributes of Judaism have continuing
value it is by absorption into the Christian reality alone" (1995, 246).

39 In line 676 Melito claims "even Pilate washed his hands," which is a view
consistent with the apologetic tendency, evident already in the Gospels, to
exonerate Pilate (and, therefore, the Roman government) and blame the
Jews. This positive portrayal of Pilate reflects a positive attitude towards
Rome, one that is also evident in Melito's *Apology* to Marcus Aurelius in
which he implies that the success of the Roman Empire was a natural out-
growth of the infiltration of Christianity into the empire (*HE* 4.26).

40 As Wilson notes, "The notion that the Jews were responsible for the death
of Jesus had a long pedigree in Christian thinking, stretching back at
least to the early accounts of Jesus's Passion. Prior to Melito, however, no
one had made the accusation with such boldness and dramatic skill, and
no one had transformed the 'crime' of the Jews from responsibility for
the death of Jesus to responsibility for the death of God" (1995, 248).
Melito's virulent polemic against the Jews does not distinguish between
Jews of Jesus's time and those living during his own time, nor does he
make a distinction between the leaders of the Jews and the rest of the
Jewish people, as is found in the Gospels, for example. For Melito, the
term *Israel* refers to all Jews without distinction, making his denunciation
all the more destructive.

41 Intriguingly, at one point in his life, Melito made a journey to Jerusalem.
Eusebius, our only source for information on Melito's trip, allegedly quotes
from one of Melito's letters to "his brother in Christ," Onesimus, who had
"repeatedly asked for extracts from the Law and the Prophets regarding the
Saviour and the whole of our faith, and…also wished to learn the precise
facts about the ancient books, particularly their number and order" (*HE*

26.7). This journey to the east raises several questions: Why did Melito undertake such a trip? Where did he go in Palestine? This information, unfortunately, is not supplied (at the time, of course, Jerusalem was a pagan city). Melito describes his friend Onesimus, who presumably was of Gentile origin, as a devoted Christian, striving "with might and main to win eternal salvation" (*HE* 26.7). Was Onesimus a member of Melito's congregation in Sardis? Why was Onesimus interested in the ancient books in the first place? Were there many others like him who were interested in learning about the Hebrew Jewish scriptures?

42 Justin Martyr was aware of precisely such a phenomenon in the middle of the second century CE. In his *Dialogue with Trypho* 47.4 he refers to Gentile Christians who denied Jesus and "passed over [*metabainō*]" into life under Jewish law.

Chapter Thirteen

1 Initial excavation of Priene began in 1895 and was led by German archaeologist Karl Humann. When Humann became too ill to continue his directorship, he asked Theodor Wiegand to replace him. Wiegand and Hans Schrader published the earliest excavation reports in *Priene: Ergebnisse der Ausgrabungen und Untersuchungen in den Jahren 1895–1898* (Berlin: Georg Reimer, 1904).

2 All of the quotations from Wiegand and Schrader (1904) and Schede (1964) in this paper are my own translations. I would like to thank my colleague Sophie Boyer for her assistance with them, also Pat Coyne and Daniel Miller for reading a draft of the paper and providing helpful comments.

3 Apparently, Alexander also had wished to leave a lasting memorial commemorating his visit at Ephesus by restoring that city's temple of Artemis, but the Ephesians refused his offer, tactfully stating, "It was not right for one god to dedicate a temple to another" (Strabo 14.1.22 in Stoneman 1997, 29).

4 The earliest excavators assert that the western half of the city in the first century CE was thinly populated and served as a quarry (Wiegand 1904, 478).

5 Unfortunately, they do not provide a photo of the statue, which they describe as approximately 0.8 m high (1904, 172).

6 The room measures 19 m by 9.2 m; Wiegand and Schrader consider these dimensions to be of impressive size, since the *cella* of the Temple of Athena measures only 14 m by 9 m (1904, 173).

7 The entrance door from the western lane was 2.25 m wide; the ashlar was 1.09 m high (1904, 174).

8 Wiegand and Schrader acknowledged this statue to be one of Alexander the Great, but they did not suggest that this site was a shrine to him.

9 The statue, with the triangular-shaped head, apparently resembles another head of Alexander portrayed in the large mosaic representing the Battle of Issus and kept in the Naples museum (Akurgal 1970, 206).

10 My sources are rather vague on exactly where this inscription was discovered; none explicitly stated that this inscription was found in Priene, though this seems the most logical place to have uncovered it.

11 Alexander certainly was considered to be a god in Egypt; he was acknowledged as pharaoh and portrayed as such on temple reliefs (Stoneman 1997,
82). Stoneman is of the opinion that Alexander viewed himself as the son of
the god Ammon, and that "it seems highly likely" that at a certain point in
his career he did consider himself to be divine: "And he did indeed receive
cult in Athens and in some cities of Asia Minor in the last years of his life"
(1997, 82–83). Priene might well be one of those Asia Minor cities; Stoneman does not provide names of the ones he has in mind.

12 The crosswall was not part of the original building because it was not stuc-
coed like the other walls (Wiegand and Schrader 1904, 175).

13 The floor of this room was covered in a mosaic of black and white stone, with
no recognizable pattern (Wiegand and Schrader 1904, 177).

14 Wiegand and Schrader's misidentification of this structure is discussed
below.

15 In his 1990 volume, White proposes the second century as the date for the
renovations (1990, 67). He states that "it is not altogether clear how the
house was used in the early Roman period, but there seems to have been
some renovations introduced both in the court area and in the house proper"
(1997, 329–30). Kraabel asserts that the synagogue "in its present form is
probably from the time of the Roman Empire, but there is no reason that a
Jewish community could not have existed there earlier" (1978b, 491).

16 The street level had risen by this stage, and the three rooms were covered over
or filled in at this point (White 1997, 330). The significance of the side
entrance to the synagogue is discussed below.

17 Bernadette Brooten notes that "no suggestion has been made of a women's
gallery or women's section, and there is nothing in the ruins to indicate
such a thing" at Priene (1982, 125).

18 White suggests that the renovations made in the second or third centuries CE included the conversion of the southernmost of the two smaller
rooms to the north of the synagogue into a paved court, and that "these
renovations suggest that the north quarters lost most, if not all, of their
domestic function," though he does not explain exactly why this is so
(1997, 330).

19 Sukenik (1934, 43) describes them simply as "two birds"; no discussion of
the details of this intriguing art piece is offered by White (1990, 1997).
Within the pagan world, peacocks were considered a symbol of immortal-
ity, from a legend that their flesh was incorruptible and the tail could per-
petually renew itself. In the *Physiologus*, a third-century anthology of unusual
tales about both real and mythical figures, it is stated that whoever ate an
entire peacock would live forever—Augustine apparently tried three times but
was not successful (Apostolos-Cappadona, 1995, 274). Within the Jewish
environment, depictions of peacocks are found both in Israel and the Diaspora. In fact, Goodenough asserts, "The peacock appears in such important
places in the Jewish remains that it was clearly a part of the current symbolism adopted by Jews" (Goodenough 1953–69, 8:52). Examples of the usage
of peacocks in Jewish settings include, among others, the depictions found

on arches, ceilings, and tombstones of Catacomb Torlonia and Catacomb Vigna Randanini, and on either side of the Torah shrine in the mosaic in the synagogue at Beth Alpha, as well as in the mosaic floor of the North African Naro (Hammam Lif) synagogue (Goodenough 1953–69, 8:52; for the latter, Levine 2000, 260–61, fig. 57). Interestingly, the peacock is a ritually clean bird according to Jewish laws of kashrut, and its head is mentioned in *b.Shab.* 130a as a special culinary treat. The meaning of the symbol of the peacock is not, however, discussed in rabbinic literature; Goodenough probably is correct to propose a Jewish borrowing of this pagan symbol and that it symbolizes eternity (1953–69, 8:58).

20 Kraabel (1979, 490) and Trebilco (1991, 55) erroneously describe an additional menorah relief decorated with rolled Torah scrolls as if it were another item found in the synagogue, when in fact this particular relief was discovered in a Byzantine church (see discussion below).

21 A similar progression is found in the construction of the synagogue at Dura Europos. As at Priene, the synagogue in that city is located in a block of private homes along the western wall of the city. It underwent three construction phases; in the last two the structure was used as a synagogue. The early synagogue originally was adapted from a typical private home in 150–200 CE by making internal renovations, and then underwent another more major renovation in about the middle of the third century into a larger synagogue (White 1990, 74; 1997, 272–87). Of the six Diaspora synagogues thus far excavated, five were adapted from private homes architecturally characteristic of the local area: Priene, Stobi, Delos, Ostia, and Dura Europos (White 1990, 63).

22 Wiegand and Schrader observe, "It is the rule in Priene to build churches and chapels next to pagan shrines and to drive off demons through the burial of holy men inside the churches," and they identify Christian buildings beside pagan religious structures in several different locations, e.g., "east of the Athena Temple, southeast of the Asklepios Temple and *east of the hieros oikos on West Gate street*" (1904, 478–79; emphasis added).

23 Wiegand and Schrader (1904) present a sketch of the menorah relief found in the "house church" in Abb. 586 on p. 481. White provides the measurements from his own visit of the site: the menorah is 0.53 m wide by 0.53 m high (extant) and "appears to be on a jamb or wall slab" (White 1997, 328n71).

24 V. Schultze (1926) recognized it as a synagogue, then Sukenik (1934) and Goodenough (1953–69; see Kraabel 1979, 489–90). About Martin Schede, Kraabel observes the following: "Interestingly, the most recent survey of Priene, M. Schede, *Die Ruinen* (1964), continues the Wiegand-Schrader identification, which the Jewish evidence from the site has proved incorrect" (1979, 489–90). While I did not find that Schede mentioned a house church per se, what he seems to have done is ignore that structure altogether, although he does discuss the Byzantine church. It is interesting to note that Schede, who was at one point president of the *Deutsches Archaeologisches Institut*, applied on May 14, 1937, for membership in the Nazi party. (The

application can be viewed at <www.area-archives.org/germany.htm> [last viewed December 22, 2004, *ed.*]. It is from the Berlin Document Center [Bundesarchiv Berlin], from the personal file of M. Schede.) Perhaps his Nazi leanings prevented Schede from acknowledging the presence of the synagogue in Priene.

25 Sukenik called it a *shofar*. Goodenough thought it was "some kind of circumcision knife" (1953–69, 2:77), but later changed his mind (1953–69, 13:215).

26 Goodenough observed that whereas there are Torah scrolls depicted with menorahs on reliefs from Rome, this Priene relief "is the only plaque of its kind which shows the ends of Torah scrolls thus tucked under the branches of a menorah" of which he was aware (1953–69, 2:77). Lee Levine observes that use of Jewish symbolism, particularly the menorah, but also the *shofar*, *lulav*, and *ethrog* are "common phenomenon of Diaspora and Palestinian synagogues" (2000, 285).

27 See the essay by Neufeld, chap. 3 in this volume.

28 See the essays by Aasgaard (chap. 11) and Hammer and Murray (chap. 12) in this volume.

29 Rutgers furthermore observes, "Several laws in the *Codex Theodosianus* testify that for many Christians who were not theologians and did not have the *otium* either to ponder extensively over the question of how to perceive the continuing flourishing of Judaism in relation to the Church's claims to primacy or to get upset about all sorts of petty definition problems, boundaries were not always clearly etched," and he perceives the Laodicean canons of the fourth century as supporting "the impression left by the Theodosian Code" (1992, 115).

30 It is somewhat ironic that while Wiegand and Schrader incorrectly identified the religious structure in the third block of West Gate Street as a house church, in their explanation of how they arrived at such an identification they were correct when they suggested that a close interconnection existed among Jews and Christians in Asia Minor. For further discussion of this relationship, see Murray 2004.

Chapter Fourteen

1 See Hammer and Murray, chap. 12 in this volume.

2 For example, the notion that even the rural landed nobility, let alone the peasants, of rural Hellenistic Egypt were thereby members of the ruling nobility and citizenry respectively of the polis of Alexandria would have turned the stomach of even the most liberal-minded citizen of that polis (see, e.g., Tcherikover and Fuks 1957–64, 1:1–110, 2:25–107; see also Philo *Legatio* 166ff., 205; *Flaccus* 17, 29, 28, 92ff.). And the initial Territory of Alexandria, vouchsafed to it at its founding, was taken away from Alexandria early in the Ptolemaic period.

3 Jones's first major work on Roman cities was published in 1937 under the title *The Cities of the Eastern Roman Provinces* (*CERP*; a second edition was published in 1971). For the second edition, Jones enlisted nine of the most eminent scholars in the field "to correct the errors, [and] supply the omis-

sions" evident in the first edition, as well as to "bring the bibliography up to date." Both the first and second editions of *CERP* are monuments to painstaking detail, notation, and erudition. The first edition of *CERP* forms the basis for part 1 of Jones's *The Greek City from Alexander to Justinian* (1940; repr. 1966). After Jones's death in 1970, P. A. Brunt reprinted several of Jones's notable papers in a volume entitled *The Roman Economy: Studies in Ancient Economic and Administrative History* (Jones 1974). Two of these essays bear specifically on our topic: "The Cities of the Roman Empire: Political, Administrative and Judicial Functions" (first published in 1954), and "The Economic Life of the Towns of the Roman Empire" (which first appeared in 1955). With respect to cities in the Byzantine period, another work of Jones may be added to the list: *The Later Roman Empire, 284–602* (1964).

4 I have not referenced specific sections of Jones's work, since, as before, I will attempt to collate and summarize the *grands lignes* that emerge from the previously mentioned works taken as a whole. In justification of this approach, it is my considered opinion that with respect to these *grands lignes* Jones remained consistent with the first edition of *CERP* until his death.

5 As a dramatic example, Syrian Antioch was for some short time during the late Roman period assigned as "country-side territory" to another Syrian city—this as punishment for anti-imperial activities by its inhabitants.

6 As we shall discuss later in this paper, this transformation of the place of the countryside and its villages represented a major cultural challenge to traditional village systems of formal and informal social organization, power and authority, deference and influence, and norms for the assignment of honour.

7 See Cotter 1996. Also, I recall that one of the several disputes between the Jews and Macedonian-Greeks in first-century Alexandria involved an appeal to Rome about certain Jews' claims to be members of the gymnasia of Alexandria. The dispute had to be settled by the emperor Claudius himself, as attested to in a papyrus published by Tcherikover and Fuks (1957–64, 2:36; see also 1:1–110, 2:2–107).

8 Williams (1998) argues against the hypothesis that Jewish communities were organized as *collegia*.

9 Something resembling the very beginnings of such an argument may be found in Goodman (1997, 25).

10 Confirmed by more recent studies by Stark (1996, 4–13, incl. table 1.1) and Hopkins (1998, 192–94, incl. fig. 1).

11 By the estimates of Baron 1937, 167–71; Grant 1973, xi; see also Avi-Yonah 1984, 19; MacMullen 1984b, 109–10; Wilken 1984, 113–14; Wilson 1995, 21, 25.

12 Tcherikover (1970, 90–116) provides a list of nearly thirty cities that had civic constitutions in the mid-first century CE in the southern Levant.

Chapter Fifteen

1 For a summary, see Ascough 2003.

2 We should also note that the only direct evidence we found for religious rivalry between the two cities was their competition in 29 CE for the title of *neokoros*, which Smyrna eventually won (discussed briefly in Ascough, chap. 4, and Knight, chap. 8).

3 Such coexistence is also evident in Priene, as shown by Murray's essay on the existence alongside one another of a synagogue, a *temenos* of Cybele, and a sanctuary to the deified Alexander the Great in the second or third century CE (chap. 13).

4 Both Sardis and Smyrna are named among the seven intended recipients of Revelation. Thus, our summary here under "Sardis" is also applicable for Smyrna. I treat Revelation here primarily because of the astrological star-imagery in the letter to Sardis in Rev. 3:1.

WORKS CITED

Achtemeier, Paul J. 1985. Jesus and the disciples as miracle workers in the apocryphal New Testament. In *The book of Revelation: Justice and judgment*, ed. Elizabeth Schüssler Fiorenza, 149–86. Philadelphia: Fortress.

Akurgal, Ekrem. 1970. *Ancient civilizations and ruins of Turkey: From prehistoric times until the end of the Roman Empire*. 2nd ed. Istanbul: Haşet Kitabevi.

Alcock, Susan E., and Robin Osborne, eds. 1994. *Placing the gods: Sanctuaries and sacred space in Ancient Greece*. Oxford: Clarendon Press.

Alexander, G. G., ed. 1926. *Cambridge legal essays written in honour of and presented to Doctor Bond, Professor Buckland, and Professor Kenny*. Cambridge: W. Heffer and Sons.

Amand, David. 1945. *Fatalisme et liberté dans l'Antiquité Grecque*. Louvain: Bibliothèque de l'Université de Louvain. Repr., Amsterdam: Hakkert, 1973.

Anderson, G. 1994. *Sage, saint and sophist: Holy men and their associates in the early Roman Empire*. London: Routledge.

Apostolos-Cappadona, Diane. 1995. *Dictionary of Christian art*. New York: Continuum.

Applebaum, S. 1974. The legal status of the Jewish communities in the Diaspora. In *Jewish people in the first century: Historical geography, political history, social, cultural and religious life and institutions*, ed. S. Safrai and M. Stern. Vol. 1. Assen: Van Gorcum.

Arnal, William. 2001. Review of *Religious Rivalries and the Struggle for Success in Caesarea Maritima*, ed. Terence L. Donaldson. *SR* 30:429–30.

Arnold, Clinton E. 1989. *Ephesians: Power and magic*. Cambridge: Cambridge University Press.

Arnulf, Arwed. 1989. Die Deckelinschrift des Berliner Kindersarkophags: eine sardische Zweitverwendung eines stadtromischen Sarkophagkastens. *JAC* 32:139–50.

Ascough, Richard S. 1994. An analysis of the baptismal ritual of the Didache. *StLit* 24:201–13.

———. 1997. Translocal relationships among voluntary associations and early Christianity. *JECS* 5:223–41.

———. 1998a. Civic pride at Philippi: The text-critical problem of Acts 16.12. *NTS* 44:93–103.

———. 1998b. *What are they saying about the formation of Pauline churches?* Mahwah and New York: Paulist.

———. 2000. Christianity in Caesarea Maritima. In *Religious rivalries and the struggle for success in Caesarea Maritima*, ed. Terence L. Donaldson. ESCJ 9. Waterloo: Wilfrid Laurier University Press.

———. 2003a. The Canadian Society of Biblical Studies' Religious Rivalries Seminar: Retrospection, reflection, and retroversion. *SR* 32:155–73.

———. 2003b. *Paul's Macedonian associations: The social context of Philippians and 1 Thessalonians*. WUNT II/161. Tübingen: Mohr Siebeck.

Athanassiadi, Polymnia, and Michael Frede, eds. 1999. *Pagan monotheism in late antiquity*. Oxford: Clarendon Press.

Attridge, Harold W., and Gohei Hata, eds. 1992. *Eusebius, Christianity and Judaism*. Detroit: Wayne State University Press.

Aune, David E. 1997. *Revelation 1–5*. WBC 52A. Dallas: Word Books.

———. 1998. *Revelation 17–22*. WBC 52C. Dallas: Word Books.

Avigad, Nachman. 1976. *Beth She'arim: Report on excavations during 1953–1958*. Jerusalem: Masada Press.

Avi-Yonah, Michael. 1971. Synagogue architecture. *Encyclopedia Judaica* 15:595–600.

———. 1984. *The Jews under Roman and Byzantine rule*. New York: Schocken.

Baldwin, Barry. 1982. Continuity and change: The practical genius of early Byzantine civilization. In *City, town and countryside in the early Byzantine era*, ed. Robert L. Hohlfelder, 1–24. New York and Boulder: East European Monographs and Columbia University Press.

Barclay, John M. G. 1996. *Jews in the Mediterranean Diaspora: From Alexander to Trajan (323 BCE–117 CE)*. Edinburgh: T. & T. Clark.

Barnes, T. D. 1981. *Constantine and Eusebius*. Cambridge, MA: Harvard University Press.

———, ed. 1994. *The sciences in Greco-Roman society*. Edmonton: Academic Printing and Publishing.

Baron, Salo W. 1937. *A social and religious history of the Jews*. Vol. 1. New York: Columbia University Press. Repr. Philadelphia: Jewish Publication Society, 1952.

Barrett, A. A. 1978. Polemo II of Pontus and M. Antonius Polemoa. *Historia* 27:437–48.

Barth, Fredrik. 1969. *Ethnic groups and boundaries: The social organization of culture difference*. Boston: Little and Brown.

———. 1981. Ethnic groups and boundaries. *Process and form in social life*, ed. Fredrik Barth, 198–227. London: Routledge and Kegan Paul.

Barton, M., ed. 1966. *Anthropological approaches to the study of religion*. London: Tavistock.

Barton, S. C., and G. H. R. Horsley. 1981. A Hellenistic cult group and the New Testament churches. *JAC* 24:4–41.

Barton, Tamsyn. 1994. *Ancient astrology*. London: Routledge.

Bassler, Jouette M. 1984. The widow's tale: A fresh look at 1 Tim 5:3–16. *JBL* 103:23–41.

Bates, George. 1971. *Byzantine coins*. Sardis monograph 1. Cambridge, MA: Harvard University Press.

Bauckham, Richard. 1977. The eschatological earthquake in the apocalypse of John. *NovT* 19:224–33.

———. 1993. *The theology of the book of Revelation*. Cambridge: Cambridge University Press.

Baumgarten, A. I. 1999. Marcel Simon's *Versus Israel* as a contribution to Jewish history. *HTR* 92:465–78.

Bean, George E. 1966. *Aegean Turkey: An archaeological guide*. London: Benn.

Beauvery, Robert. 1983. L'Apocalypse au risque de la numismatique: Babylone, la grande Prostituée et le sixième roi Vespasien et la décesse Rome. *Revue biblique* 90:243–60.

Beavis, Mary Ann. 2000. "Pluck the rose but shun the thorns": The ancient school and Christian origins. *SR* 29:411–23.

Beck, Roger. 1977. Cautes and Cautopates: Some astronomical considerations. *JMS* 2:1–17.

———. 1991. Thus spake not Zarathustra: Zoroastrian Pseudepigrapha of the Greco-Roman world. In *A History of Zoroastrianism*, ed. Mary Boyce and Frantz Grenet, 490–565. Leiden: Brill.

Beckwith, Isbon Thaddeus. 1919. *The Apocalypse of John: Studies in introduction with a critical and exegetical commentary*. New York: Macmillan.

Behr, Charles A. 1968. *Aelius Aristides and the sacred tales*. Amsterdam: Hakkert.

———, trans. 1973. *Aristides*. LCL. Cambridge, MA: Harvard University Press.

———, trans. 1981. *P. Aelius Aristides: The complete works*. 2 vols. Leiden: Brill.

———. 1993. Studies on the biography of Aelius Aristides, trans. Charles A. Behr, in *ANRW* II. 34.2:1140–1233.

Bell, Harold. 1916. *Sardis XI/1: The coins*. Leiden: Brill.

Benko, S. 1971. Pagan criticism of Christianity during the first two centuries A.D. *ANRW* II.23.2:1055–1118.

Benoit, André et al., eds. 1978. *Paganisme, Judaïsme, Christianisme: Influences et affrontements dans le monde antique: Mélanges offerts à Marcel Simon*. Paris: de Boccard.

Beskow, P. 1984. *Om påsken*. Skellefteå: Artos.

Betz, Hans Dieter. 1979. *Galatians: A commentary on Paul's letter to the churches at Galatia*. Philadelphia: Fortress.

———. 1986. *The Greek magical papyri in translation, including the Demotic Spells*. Chicago: University of Chicago Press.

Bilabel, Friedrich. 1920. *Die ionische kolonisation, Untersuchungen über die grundungen der Ionier, deren staatliche und kultliche Organization und Beziehungen zu den Mutterstadten*. Leipzig: Dieterich.

Binder, Donald D. 1999. *Into the Temple courts: The place of the synagogues in the second Temple period*. Atlanta: Scholars Press.

Bird, Frederick B. 1983. A comparative study of charity in Christianity and Judaism. In *Truth and compassion: Essays on Judaism and Religion in Memory of Solomon Frank*, ed. Howard Joseph, 5–29. Studies in Religion Supplements 12. Waterloo: Wilfrid Laurier University Press.

Black, Matthew, and James C. Vanderkam. 1983. *The book of Enoch: A new English edition*. SVTP 7. Leiden: Brill.

Blank, J. 1963. *Meliton von Sardes Vom Passa: Die älteste christliche Osterpredigt*. Freiburg: Lambertus.

Blasi, Anthony J., Jean Duhaime, and Paul-André Turcotte, eds. 2002. *Handbook of early Christianity and the social sciences*. Walnut Creek: AltaMira Press.

Boak, A. 1955. *Manpower shortage and the fall of the Roman Empire in the west*. Ann Arbor: University of Michigan Press.

Boak, A., and W. Winnigen. 1977. *A history of Rome to AD 565*. New York: MacMillan.

Böcher, Otto. 1988. *Die Johhanesapokalypse*. 2nd ed. Erträge der Forschung 41. Darmstadt: Wissenschaftliche Buchgesellschaft.

Boeckh, Augustine. 1828–77. *Corpus inscriptionum graecarum*. Berolini: Georg Reimeri Libraria.

Bohak, Gideon. 1990. Greek-Hebrew Gematrias in 3 Baruch and in Revelation. *JSP* 7:119–121.

Boll, Franz Johannes. 1894. *Studien über Claudius Ptolemäus: Ein Beitrag zur Geschichte der Griechischen, Philosophie und Astrologie*. Leipzig: Teubner.

———. 1903. *Sphaera: Neue Griechische Texte und Untersuchungen zur Geschichte der Sternbilder*. Leipzig: Teubner.

———. 1914. *Aus der Offenbarung Johannis: Hellenistiche Studien zum Weltbild der Apokalypse*. Repr. Amsterdam: Hakkert, 1967.

Boll, Franz, Carl Bezold, and Wilhelm Gundel. 1966. *Sternglaube und Sterndeutung*. Stuttgart: Teubner.

Bonner, C. 1940. *The homily on the Passion by Melito Bishop of Sardis and some fragments of the apocryphal Ezekiel*. Philadelphia: University of Pennsylvania Press.

———. 1943. A supplementary note on the opening of Melito's homily. *HTR* 36:317–39.

———. 1949. The text of Melito's homily. *VC* 3:184–85.

Bonz, Marianne P. 1990. The Jewish community of ancient Sardis: A reassessment of its rise to prominence. *HSCP* 93:343–59.

———. 1993. Differing approaches to religious benefaction: The late third-century acquisition of the Sardis synagogue. *HTR* 86:139–54.

———. 1999. The Jewish community of ancient Sardis: Deconstruction and reconstruction. In *Evolution of the synagogue: Problems and progress*, ed. Lynn H. Cohick and Howard C. Kee, 106–22. Harrisburg, PA: Trinity Press International.

Borgen, P., V. K. Robbins, and D. B. Gowler, eds. 1996. *Recruitment, conquest, and conflict: Strategies in Judaism, Christianity, and the Greco-Roman world*. Atlanta: Scholars Press.

Boring, Eugene M. 1989. *Revelation*. Louisville: John Knox Press.

Bormann, Lukas, Kelly Del Tredici, and Angela Standhartinger, eds. 1994. *Religious propaganda and missionary competition in the New Testament world: Essays honoring Dieter Georgi*. NovTSup 74. Leiden: Brill.

Botermann, H. 1990. Die Synagoge von Sardis: Eine Synagoge aus dem 4 Jahrhundert? *ZNW* 81:103–21.

Bouché-Leclercq, A. 1899. *L'Astrologie Grecque*. Paris: E. Leroux. Repr. Bruxelles: Cultures et Civilisation, 1963.

Bousset, Wilhelm. 1906. *Die Offenbarung Johannis*. 6th ed. Göttingen: Vandenhoeck and Ruprecht.

Bowersock, G. W. 1965. *Augustus and the Greek world*. Oxford: Clarendon.

———. 1969. *Greek sophists in the Roman empire*. Oxford: Claredon.

———. 1995. *Martyrdom and Rome*. Cambridge: Cambridge University Press.

Bowersock, G. W., C. P. M. Jones, and Louis Robert. 1994. *Le Martyre de Pionios, prêtre de Smyrne*. Washington, DC: Dumbarton Oaks Research Library and Collection.

Boyarin, Daniel. 1994. *A radical Jew: Paul and the politics of identity*. Berkeley: University of California Press.

———. 1998. Martyrdom and the making of Christianity and Judaism. *JECS* 6:577–627.

———. 1999. *Dying for God: Martyrdom and the making of Judaism and Christianity*. Stanford: Stanford University Press.

———. 2001. Justin Martyr invents Judaism. *CH* 70:427–61.

Boyce, Mary, and Frantz Grenet, eds. 1991. *A history of Zoroastrianism*. Leiden: Brill.

Braaten, Carl E., and Roy A. Harrisville, eds. 1964. *The historical Jesus and the kerygmatic Christ*. New York: Abingdon.

Briant, P. 1985. Les iraniens d'Asie Mineure après la chut de l'empire achéméide. *DHA* 11:167–95.

Broadhurst, Laurence. 1999. Rhetoric and reality in Melito's homily. Paper presented at the CSBS Religious Rivalries Seminar, Lennoxville, June 3, forthcoming in *Rhetorics and realities in early Christianities*, ed. Willi Braun. ESCJ; Waterloo: Wilfrid Laurier University Press, 2005.

Brooten, Bernadette. 1982. *Women leaders in the ancient synagogue*. Chico: Scholars Press.

Broughton, T. Robert S. 1938. *Roman Asia Minor*. Vol. 4 of *An economic survey of ancient Rome IV: Africa, Syria, Greece, Asia Minor*, ed. Tenney Frank, 499–916. Baltimore: Johns Hopkins Press.

Brown, Peter. 1978. *The making of late antiquity*. Cambridge, MA: Harvard University Press.

———. 1981. *The cult of the saints: Its rise and function in Latin Christianity*. Chicago: University of Chicago Press.

———. 1992. *Power and persuasion in late antiquity: Towards a Christian empire*. Madison: University of Wisconsin Press.

———. 1995. *Authority and the sacred: Aspects of the Christianization of the Roman world*. Cambridge: Cambridge University Press.

————. 1996. *The rise of western Christendom: Triumph and diversity, AD 200–1000*. Oxford: Blackwell.

Brown, Raymond E. 1979. *The community of the beloved disciple.* New York: Paulist.

————. 1993. *The birth of the Messiah.* Rev. ed. New York: Doubleday.

Brugsch, Heinrich Karl. 1891. *Egypt under the Pharaohs: A history derived entirely from the monuments.* London: J. Murray.

Buchwald, Hans, and George M. A. Hanfmann. 1983. Christianity: Churches and cemeteries. In *Sardis from prehistoric to Roman times: Results of the archeological exploration of Sardis 1958–1975*, ed. George M. A. Hanfmann, 191–210. Cambridge, MA: Harvard University Press.

Buchwald, Hans et al., eds. 1992. *The churches of Sardis: Archaeological exploration of Sardis.* Cambridge, MA: Harvard University Press.

Buckler, W. H. 1914–15. Some Lydian propitiatory inscriptions. *The annual of the British School at Athens* 21:169–83.

————. 1917. Lydian records. *JHS* 37:88–115.

Buckler, W. H., and W. M. Calder, eds. 1923. *Anatolian studies, presented to Sir William Mitchell Ramsay.* London: Manchester University Press.

Buckler, W. H., and David. M. Robinson. 1912. Greek inscriptions from Sardes I. *AJA* 16:11–82.

————. 1913a. Greek inscriptions from Sardes II. *AJA* 17:29–52.

————. 1913b. Greek inscriptions of Sardes III. *AJA* 17:353–70.

————. 1913c. Monuments de Thyatire. *RevPhil* 37:289–331.

————. 1914a. Greek inscriptions from Sardes IV. *AJA* 18:35–74.

————. 1914b. Greek inscriptions of Sardes V. *AJA* 18:321–62.

————. 1932. *Sardis VII: Greek and Latin inscriptions, Part 1.* Leiden: Brill.

Budde, Gerard. 1931. Christian charity: Now and always. *Ecclesiastical Review*, 9th series, 5 (85): 561–79.

Bulloch, Anthony, Erich S. Gruen, A. A. Long, and Andrew Stewart, eds. 1993. *Images and ideologies: Self-definition in the Hellenistic world.* Hellenistic Culture and Society 12. Berkeley: University of California Press.

Bultmann, Rudolf. 1951–55. *The theology of the New Testament.* 2 vols. New York: Charles Scribner's Sons.

————. 1964. The primitive Christian kerygma and the historical Jesus. In *The historical Jesus and the kerygmatic Christ*, ed. Carl E. Braaten and Roy A. Harrisville, 15–42. New York: Abingdon.

Burrell, Barbara, 1980. Neokoroi: Greek cities of the Roman east. PhD diss., Harvard University.

Burrus, Virginia. 1986. Chastity as autonomy: Women in the stories of the apocryphal Acts. *Semeia* 38:101–18.

————. 1994. Word and flesh: The bodies and sexuality of ascetic women in Christian antiquity. *JFSR* 10:27–51.

Butler, Howard Crosby. 1922. *Sardis I: The excavations part I: 1910–1914.* Leiden: Brill.

————. 1925. *Sardis II: The Temple of Artemis.* Leiden: Brill.

Buttrey, Theodore V. 1981. *Greek, Roman, and Islamic coins from Sardis.* Cambridge, MA: Harvard University Press.

Cadoux, Cecil J. 1938. *Ancient Smyrna: A history of the city from the earliest times to 324 A.D.* Oxford: Blackwell.

Cagnat, R., J. Toutain, P. Jovgvet, and G. Lafaye. 1906–27. *Inscriptiones graecae ad res romanas pertinentes.* Paris: Leroux.

Caird, G. B. 1984. *A commentary on the Revelation of St. John the Divine.* 2nd ed. London: A. & C. Black.

Calder, W. M. 1906. Smyrna as described by the orator Aelius Aristides. In *Studies in the history and art of the eastern provinces of the Roman Empire, written for the Quartercentenary of the University of Aberdeen by seven of its graduates,* ed. William M. Ramsay, 95–116. Aberdeen University Studies 20. Aberdeen: University of Aberdeen.

Cameron, Averil. 1989. Virginity as metaphor: Women and the rhetoric of early Christianity. In *History as text: The writing of ancient history,* ed. Averil Cameron, 171–205. London: Duckworth.

————, ed. 1989. *History as text: The writing of ancient history.* London: Duckworth.

————. 1991. *Christianity and the rhetoric of the empire: The development of Christian discourse.* Sather Classical Lectures 53. Berkeley: University of California Press.

Carleton-Paget, James. 1996. Jewish proselytism at the time of Christian origins: Chimera or reality? *JSNT* 62:65–103.

Carney, T. F. 1975. *The shape of the past: Models and antiquity.* Lawrence, KN: Coronado Press.

Carson, R. A. G., and H. Mattingly. 1923–62. *Coins of the Roman Empire in the British Museum.* 6 vols. London: The British Museum.

Case, S. J. 1928. *Studies in early Christianity.* New York: Century.

Casson, Lionel, and Martin Price, eds. 1981. *Coins, culture and history in the ancient world: Numismatic and other studies in honor of Bluma L. Trell.* Detroit: Wayne State University Press.

Castelli, Elizabeth A. 1995. *Visions and voyeurism: Holy women and the politics of sight in early Christianity.* Berkeley: Center for Hermeneutical Studies.

————. 1996. Imperial reimaginings of Christian origins: Epic in Prudentius's poem. In *Reimagining Christian origins: A colloquium honoring Burton L. Mack,* ed. Elizabeth A. Castelli and Hal Taussig, 173–84. Valley Forge: Trinity Press International.

Castelli, Elizabeth A., and Hal Taussig, eds. 1996. *Reimagining Christian origins: A colloquium honoring Burton L. Mack.* Valley Forge: Trinity Press International.

Chapot, Victor. 1904. *La Province romaine proconsulaire d'Asie, depuis ses origines jusqu'à la fin du Haut-Empire.* Paris: Bouillon.

Charles, R. H. 1913a. *The Apocrypha and Pseudepigrapha of the Old Testament in English.* Oxford: Clarendon Press.

————. 1913b. *Studies in the Apocalypse.* Edinburgh: T. & T. Clark.

————. 1920. *A critical and exegetical commentary on the Revelation of St. John.* 2 vols. New York: Scribners.

Charlesworth, James H. 1977. Jewish astrology in the Talmud, Pseudepigrapha, the Dead Sea Scrolls, and early Palestinian synagogues. *HTR* 70:183–200.

———. 1978. Rylands Syriac MS 44 and a new addition to the Pseudepigrapha: The Treatise of Shem. *BJRL* 60:376–403.

———. 1983. *The Old Testament Pseudepigrapha*. New York: Doubleday.

Chevalier, Jacques M. 1997. *A postmodern revelation: Signs of astrology and the Apocalypse*. Toronto: University of Toronto Press.

Chevallier, R. 1974. Cité et territoire: Solutions romaines aux problèmes de l'organization de l'espace; Problématique 1948–1973. *ANRW* II.1: 649–788.

Christie, N., and S. T. Loseby, eds. 1996. *Towns in transition: Urban evolutions in late antiquity and the early Middle Ages*. Aldershot: Scholars Press.

Clark, Gillian. 1993. *Women in late antiquity: Pagan and Christian lifestyles*. Oxford: Clarendon.

Classen, C. J. 1995. Rhetoric and literary criticism: Their nature and their function in antiquity. *Mnemosyne* 48:513–35.

Cohen, Henry. 1880–92. *Description historique des monnaies frappées sous l'Empire romain*. 2nd ed. 8 vols. Paris: Rollin and Feuardent.

Cohen, Shaye J. D. 1987. Pagan and Christian evidence on the ancient synagogue. In *The synagogue in late antiquity*, ed. Lee I. Levine, 159–81. Philadelphia: The American School of Oriental Research.

———. 1989. Crossing the boundary and becoming a Jew. *HTR* 82:13–33.

———. 1990. Was Judaism in antiquity a missionary religion? In *Jewish assimilation, acculturation and accommodation: Past traditions, current issues and future prospects*, ed. Menahem Mor, 14–23. Lanham, MD: University Press of America.

———. 1996. Judaism without circumcision and rhetoric without reality in Ignatius. Paper presented at the Annual Meeting of the SBL, New Orleans, Louisiana, November 26.

Cohick, Lynn H. 1998. Melito of Sardis's *PERI PASCHA* and its "Israel." *HTR* 91:351–72.

———. 1999. Melito's *Peri Pascha*: Its relationship to Judaism and Sardis in recent scholarly discussion. In *Evolution of the synagogue: Problems and progress*, ed. Lynn H. Cohick and Howard C. Kee, 123–40. Harrisburg, PA: Trinity Press International.

———. 2000. *The* Peri Pascha *attributed to Melito of Sardis: Setting, purpose, and sources*. BJS 327. Providence: Brown University.

Cohick, Lynn H., and Howard C. Kee, eds. 1999. *Evolution of the synagogue: Problems and progress*. Harrisburg, PA: Trinity Press International.

Cohn-Sherbok, Dan, and John M. Court, eds. 2001. *Religious diversity in the Greco-Roman world: A survey of recent scholarship*. Sheffield: Sheffield Academic Press.

Collins, Adela Yarbro. 1976. *The combat myth in the book of Revelation*. HDR 9. Missoula: Scholars Press.

———. 1984a. *Crisis and catharsis: The power of the apocalypse*. Philadelphia: Westminster.

————. 1984b. Numerical symbolism in apocalyptic literature. *ANRW* II.21.2: 1221–87.

————. 1986. Vilification and self-definition in the book of Revelation. *HTR* 79:308–20.

————. 1988. Early Christian apocalyptic literature. *ANRW* II.25.6: 4665–711.

————. 1992. Revelation, book of. *ABD* 5:694–708.

Collins, John J. 1983. *Between Athens and Jerusalem: Jewish identity in the Hellenistic Diaspora*. New York: Crossroad.

Connolly, R. Hugh, ed. 1929. *Didascalia Apostolorum*. Oxford: Clarendon Press.

Conze, A., and C. Schuchhardt. 1899. Die Arbeiten zu Pergamon. *MDAI(A)* 24:164–240.

Conzelmann, H. 1978. *Bemerkungen zur Martyrium Polycarpus*. Göttingen: *NAWG* Ph-H Klasse.

————. 1992. *Gentiles, Jews, Christians: Polemics and apologetics in the Greco-Roman era*. Minneapolis: Augsburg Fortress.

Cook, Arthur Bernard. 1914. *Zeus: A study in ancient religion*. Cambridge: Cambridge University Press.

Cook, J. M. 1958/59. Old Smyrna, 1948–1951. *ABSA* 53/54:1–34.

Corbier, Mireille. 1991. City, territory and taxation. In *City and country in the ancient world*, ed. John Rich and Andrew Wallace-Hadrill, 211–39. London and New York: Routledge.

Cotter, Wendy J. 1996. The collegia and Roman law: State restrictions on voluntary associations 64 BCE–200 CE. In *Voluntary associations in the Graeco-Roman world*, ed. John S. Kloppenborg and Stephen G. Wilson, 74–89. London: Routledge.

Courcelle, Pierre. 1957. Les exégèses Chrétiennes de la quatrième eclogue. *Revue des études anciennes* 59:294–319.

Covino, Wm., and D. Jolliffe, eds. 1995. *Rhetoric: Concepts, definitions, boundaries*. Boston: Allyn and Bacon.

Cranfeld, C. E. B. 1966. Diakonia in the New Testament. In *Service in Christ: Essays presented to Karl Barth on his 80th birthday*, ed. James McCord and T. Parker, 37–48. Grand Rapids: Eerdmans.

Crawford, John S. 1990. *The Byzantine shops at Sardis*. Archaeological exploration of Sardis. Monograph 9. Cambridge, MA: Harvard University Press.

————. 1996. Multiculturalism at Sardis: Jews and Christians live, work and worship side by side. *BARev* 22/5:38–47, 70.

————. 1999. Jews, Christians, and polytheists in late-antique Sardis. In *Jews, Christians and polytheists in the ancient synagogue: Cultural interaction during the Greco-Roman period*, ed. Steven Fine, 190–200. BSHJ. London: Routledge.

Crawford, John S., George M. A. Hanfmann, and Fikret K. Yegül. 1983. The Roman and late antique period. In *Sardis from prehistoric to Roman times: Results of the archeological exploration of Sardis 1958–1975*, ed. George M. A. Hanfmann, 139–67. Cambridge, MA: Harvard University Press.

Crawford, Michael, ed. 1983. *Sources for ancient history*. Cambridge: Cambridge University Press.

Cumont, Franz. 1912. *Astrology and religion among the Greeks and Romans*. New York: G. P. Putnam's Sons. Repr. New York: Dover, 1960.

———. 1929. *Les religions orientales dans le paganisme Romain*. 4th ed. Paris: Guethner.

———. 1937. *L'Égypte des astrologues*. Repr. Brussels: Éditions Culture et civilisation, 1982.

———. 1958. Caelestis. *RE* 3/1: 1247–1250.

D'Angelo, Mary R. 2003. *Eusebeia*: Roman imperial family values and the sexual politics of 4 Maccabees and the Pastorals. *Biblical Interpretation* 11:139–65.

Davids, Peter H. 1990. *The First Epistle of Peter*. Grand Rapids, MI: Eerdmans.

Davies, J. G. 1962. *The origin and development of early Christian church architecture*. London: SCM.

Davies, Stevan L. 1980. *The revolt of the widows: The social world of the apocryphal Acts*. Carbondale, IL: Southern Illinois University Press.

De Boer, M. C. 1998. The Nazoreans: Living at the boundary of Judaism and Christianity. In *Tolerance and intolerance in early Judaism and Christianity*, ed. G. N. Stanton and G. Stroumsa, 239–62. Cambridge: Cambridge University Press.

Dehandschutter, B. 1979. *Martyrium Polycarpi: Een literair-kritische studie*. Louvain: Leuven University Press.

———. 1982. Le martyre de Polycarpe et le développement de la conception du martyre au deuxième siècle. *StPatr* 2:659–68.

de Jonge, Marinus. 1953. *The Testaments of the Twelve Patriarchs: A study of their text, composition and origin*. Assen: Van Gorcum.

———. 1960. Christian influence in *The Testaments of the Twelve Patriarchs*. *NovT* 4:182–235.

———. 1987. *The Testaments of the Twelve Patriarchs: Central problems and essential viewpoints*. *ANRW* II.20.1:359–420.

———. 1991. *Jewish eschatology, early Christian Christology, and The Testaments of the Twelve Patriarchs*. Leiden: Brill.

Delattre, A. 1895. *Gamart ou la nécropole juive de Carthage*. Lyons: Mougin-Rusand.

de Polignac, Francois. 1994. Meditation, competition, and sovereignty: The evolution of rural sanctuaries in Geometric Greece. In *Placing the gods: Sanctuaries and sacred space in Ancient Greece*, ed. Susan E. Alcock and Robin Osborne, 3–18. Oxford: Clarendon Press.

———. 1995. *Cults, territory, and the origins of the Greek city-state*. Chicago: University of Chicago Press.

deSilva, David A. 1997. Review of Malina 1995. *JBL* 116:763–65.

———. 2000. *Honour, patronage, kinship and purity*. Downers Grove, IL: InterVarsity Press.

Desjardins, Michel, and Stephen G. Wilson, eds. 2000. *Text and artifact in the religions of Mediterranean antiquity: Essays in honour of Peter Richardson*. ESCJ 9. Waterloo: Wilfrid Laurier University Press.

de Ste Croix, G. E. M. 1974a. Why were early Christians persecuted? In *Studies in ancient society*, ed. M. I. Finely, 210–49. London: Routledge and Kegan Paul.

———. 1974b. Why were early Christians persecuted? A Rejoinder. In *Studies in ancient society*, ed. M. I. Finely, 256–62. London: Routledge and Kegan Paul.

Dever, William G. 1993. *Preliminary excavation reports: Sardis, Bir Umm Fawakhir, Tell el-Umeiri, the combined Caesarea expeditions, and Tell Dothan.* AASOR 52. Ann Arbor: American School of Oriental Research.

———. 1996. *Preliminary excavation reports: Sardis, Idalion, and Tell el-Handaquq North.* AASOR 52. Ann Arbor: American School of Oriental Research.

DeVries, K., ed. 1980. *From Athens to Gordion: The papers of a memorial symposium for Rodney S. Young.* Philadelphia: University of Pennsylvania Museum.

Dibelius, Martin, and Hanz Conzelmann. 1972. *The Pastoral Epistles.* Philadelphia: Fortress.

Dickey, Samuel. 1928. Some economic and social conditions of Asia Minor affecting the expansion of Christianity. In *Studies in early Christianity*, ed. S. J. Case, 393–416. New York: Century.

Dodds, E. R. 1965. *Pagan and Christian in an age of anxiety.* Cambridge: Cambridge University Press.

Donaldson, Terence L. 1995. Proposal for the CSBS's seminar, Religious rivalries and the struggle for success: Jews, Christians and other religious groups in local settings in the first two centuries CE.

———. 1997. *Paul and the Gentiles: Remapping the apostle's convictional world.* Minneapolis: Fortress.

———. 2000. Introduction. In *Religious rivalries and the struggle for success in Caesarea Maritima*, ed. Terence L. Donaldson, 1–8. ESCJ 9. Waterloo: Wilfrid Laurier University Press.

———, ed. 2000. *Religious rivalries and the struggle for success in Caesarea Maritima.* ESCJ 9. Waterloo: Wilfrid Laurier University Press.

Donfried, Karl P., and Peter Richardson, eds. 1998. *Judaism and Christianity in first-century Rome.* Grand Rapids: Eerdmans.

Dörner, Frederick Carol. 1920. *Tituli Asiae Minoris collecti et editi auspiciis academiae litterarum austriacae.* Vindobonae: Academiam Scientiarum Austriacam.

Douglas, Mary. 1973. *Natural symbols: Explorations in Cosmology.* 2nd ed. London: Barrie and Jenkins.

———. 1975. *Implicit meanings.* Essays in anthropology. London: RKP.

Drijvers, H. J. W. 1976. *The religion of Palmyra.* Leiden: Brill.

Duff, P. W. 1926. The charitable foundations of Byzantium. In *Cambridge legal essays written in honour of and presented to Doctor Bond, Professor Buckland, and Professor Kenny*, ed. G. G. Alexander, 83–99. Cambridge: W. Heffer and Sons.

Duncan-Jones, Richard. 1982. *The economy of the Roman Empire: Quantitative studies.* 2nd ed. Cambridge: Cambridge University Press.

Dunn, J. D. G. 1991. *The parting of the ways.* London: SCM.

Edelstein, Emma J., and Ludwig Edelstein. 1945. *Asclepius: A collection and interpretation of the testimonies.* Vol. 1. Baltimore: Johns Hopkins University Press.

Eden, K. 1987. Hermeneutics and the ancient rhetorical tradition. *Rhetorica* 5:59–86.

———. 1997. *Hermeneutics and the rhetorical tradition: Chapters in the ancient legacy & its human reception.* New Haven: Yale University Press.

Edwards, Douglas R. 1996. *Religion and power: Pagans, Jews and Christians in the Greek east.* New York: Oxford University Press.

Edwards, Mark. 1995. Ignatius, Judaism, and Judaizing. *Eranos* 93:67–77.

Edwards, M., M. Goodman, and S. Price, eds. 1999. *Apologetics in the Roman Empire: Pagans, Jews, and Christians.* Oxford: Oxford University Press.

Elliott, John H. 1981. *A home for the homeless: A sociological exegesis of 1 Peter, its situation and strategy.* Philadelphia: Fortress.

———. 1986. Social-scientific criticism of the New Testament: More on methods and models. *Semeia* 35:1–33.

———. 1996. Phases in the social formation of early Christianity: From faction to sect; A social-scientific perspective. In *Recruitment, conquest, and conflict: Strategies in Judaism, Christianity, and the Greco-Roman world,* ed. P. Borgen, V. K. Robbins, and D. B. Gowler, 273–313. Atlanta: Scholars Press.

Engelmann, H., R. Merkelback, and H. Wankel. 1979–84. *Die Inschriften von Ephesos.* IGSK 11–17. Bonn: Rudolf Habelt.

Evans, Craig A., and Donald A. Hagner, eds. 1991. *Anti-Semitism and early Christianity: Issues of polemic and faith.* Minneapolis: Fortress.

Farrer, Austin. 1964. *The Revelation of St. John the Divine.* New York: Oxford University Press.

Feldman, L. H. 1992. Jewish proselytism. In *Eusebius, Christianity and Judaism,* ed. Harold W. Attridge and Gohei Hata, 372–408. Detroit: Wayne State University Press.

———. 1993a. *Jew and Gentile in the ancient world.* Princeton: Princeton University Press.

———. 1993b. Was Judaism a missionary religion in ancient times? In *Jewish assimilation, acculturation and accommodation: Past traditions, current issues and future prospects,* ed. Menahem Mor, 24–37. Lanham, MD: University Press of America.

Feldman, L. H., and Meyer Reinhold. 1996. *Jewish life and thought among Greeks and Romans.* Minneapolis: Fortress.

Ferguson, Everett. 1987. *Backgrounds of early Christianity.* Grand Rapids: Eerdmans.

———. 1993. *Backgrounds of early Christianity.* Updated ed. Grand Rapids: Eerdmans.

Ferguson, George. 1961. *Signs and symbols in Christian art.* New York: Oxford University Press.

Ferguson, John. 1970. *The religions of the Roman Empire.* Ithaca and London: Cornell University Press and Thames and Hudson.

Festugière, A. J. 1937. *L'idéal religieux des Grecs et l'évangile*. Paris: Lecoffre.

———. 1950. *La révélation d'Hermès Trismégiste 1: L'astrologie et les sciences occultés*. Paris: Gabalda.

Feuchtwang, David. 1915. Der Tierkreis im der Tradition und im Synagogenritus. *Monatschrift für Geschichte und Wissenschaft des Judentums* 59:241–267.

Feuillet, André. 1963. *L'Apocalypse: État de la question*. Studia Neotestamentica 3. Paris: Brouwer.

Fine, Steven, ed. 1999. *Jews, Christians and polytheists in the ancient synagogue: Cultural interaction during the Greco-Roman period*. BSHJ. London: Routledge.

Finely, M. I., ed. 1974. *Studies in ancient society*. London: Routledge and Kegan Paul.

Finney, Paul Corby. 1990. Early Christian architecture: The beginning. *HTR* 81:319–39.

Fiorenza, Elizabeth Schüssler. 1985. *The Book of Revelation: Justice and judgment*. Philadelphia: Fortress.

Flesher, Paul V. M., and Dan Urman. 1995. *Ancient synagogues: Historical analysis and archaeological discovery*. Leiden: Brill.

Foerster, Gideon. 1987. The zodiac in ancient synagogues and its place in Jewish thought and literature. *Erets-Yisrael* 19:380–91.

———. 1992. The ancient synagogues of the Galilee. In *The Galilee in late antiquity*, ed. Lee I. Levine, 289–319. New York: The Jewish Theological Seminary of America.

Foss, Clive. 1976. *Byzantine and Turkish Sardis*. Cambridge, MA: Harvard University Press.

Foss, Clive, and Jane Ayer Scott. 2002. Sardis. In *The economic history of Byzantium: From the seventh through the fifteenth century*, ed. Angeliki E. Laiou, 615–22. Dumbarton Oaks Studies 39. Washington, DC: Dumbarton Oaks Research Library and Collection.

Fox, R. Lane. 1986. *Pagans and Christians*. San Francisco: Harper and Row.

Francis, Fred O., and J. Paul Sampley. 1975. *Pauline parallels*. 2nd ed. Philadelphia: Fortress.

Fränkel, Max. 1890–95. *Die Inschriften von Pergamon*. Altertümer von Pergamon 8. Berlin: Spemann.

French, Valerie. 1986. Midwives and maternity care in the Roman world. *Helios* 13:69–84.

Frend, W. H. C. 1967. *Martyrdom and persecution in the early church*. Oxford: Blackwell.

———. 1980. *Town and country in the early Christian centuries*. London: Variorum Reprints.

———. 1984. *The rise of Christianity*. Philadelphia: Fortress.

———. 1996. *The archaeology of early Christianity: A history*. Minneapolis: Fortress.

Frerichs, E., and Jacob Neusner. 1985. *To see ourselves as others see us: Jews, Christians, "others" in late antiquity*. Scholars Press studies in the humanities. Chico, CA: Scholars Press.

Freyne, Sean. 1992. Urban–rural relations in first-century Galilee: Some suggestions from the literary sources. In *The Galilee in late antiquity*, ed. Lee I. Levine, 75–91. New York: The Jewish Theological Seminary of America.

Friesen, S. J. 1993. *Twice Neokoros: Ephesus, Asia and the cult of the Flavian imperial family*. Leiden: Brill.

Gager, John G. 1972. *Moses in Greco-Roman paganism*. Nashville: Abingdon.

———. 1983. *The origins of anti-Semitism: Attitudes towards Judaism in pagan and Christian antiquity*. Oxford: Oxford University Press.

———. 1994. Moses the magician: Hero of an ancient counter-culture? *Helios* 21:179–88.

Gallagher, Eugene V. 1991. Conversion and salvation in the apocryphal Acts of the Apostles. *SecondCent* 8:13–29.

Gardner, Richard B., Julian Victor Hills, and Robert Jewett, eds. 1998. *Common life in the early church: Essays honoring Graydon F. Snyder*. Harrisburg: Trinity Press International.

Garnsey, Peter. 1974. Aspects of the decline of the urban aristocracy in the empire. *ANRW* II.1:229–52.

———. 1988. *Famine and food supply in the Greco-Roman world*. Cambridge: Cambridge University Press.

Gaston, Lloyd. 1986a. Judaism of the uncircumcised in Ignatius and related writers. In *Anti-Judaism in early Christianity: Separation and polemic*, ed. Stephen G. Wilson, 33–44. ESCJ 2. Waterloo: Wilfrid Laurier University Press.

———. 1986b. Retrospect. In *Anti-Judaism in early Christianity: Separation and polemic*, ed. Stephen G. Wilson, 163–74. ESCJ 2. Waterloo: Wilfrid Laurier University Press.

Gauthier, Philippe. 1987. *Nouvelles inscriptions de Sardis II*. Centre de recherches d'histoire et de philologie. Geneva: Librarie Droz.

———. 1989. *Nouvelles inscriptions de Sardes II: Archeological exploration of Sardis*. Hautes études du monde gréco-romain 15. Geneva: Librairie Droz.

Geertz, Clifford. 1966. Religion as a cultural system. In *Anthropological approaches to the study of religion*, ed. M. Barton, 1–46. London: Tavistock.

———. 1973. *The interpretation of culture*. New York: Basic Books.

———. 1983. *Local knowledge: Further essays in interpretive anthropology*. New York: Basic Books.

Germanos, Bishop of Sardis. 1928. *Historike Melete peri tes Ekklesias ton Sardeon*. Constantinople.

Giangrande, I., ed. 1956. *Vitae sophistarum: Ioseph Giangrande recensuit; Eunapius, ca. 345–ca. 420*. Rome: Typis Publicae Officinae Polygraphicae.

Gibson, E. 1978. *The "Christians for Christians" inscriptions of Phrygia: Greek texts, translation and commentary*. HTS 32. Missoula: Scholars Press.

Gilliam, J. F. 1961. The plague under Marcus Aurelius. *AJP* 82:225–51.

Glueck, Nelson. 1965. *Deities and dolphins*. New York: Farrar, Straus and Giroux.

Godwin, Joscelyn. 1981. *Mystery religions in the ancient world*. London: Harper and Row.

González, Justo L. 1990. *Faith and wealth: A history of early Christian ideas on the origin, significance and use of money*. San Francisco: Harper and Row.

Goodblatt, David. 1994. *The monarchic principle: Studies in Jewish self-government in antiquity*. Tübingen: Mohr Siebeck.

Goodenough, Erwin R. 1935. *By light, light: The mystic gospel of Hellenistic Judaism*. New Haven: Yale University Press.

———. 1953–69. *Jewish symbols in the Greco-Roman period*. Bollingen Series 37. Princeton: Princeton University Press.

———1992. *Jewish symbols in the Greco-Roman Period*, ed. and abridged Jacob Neusner. Princeton: Princeton University Press.

Goodman, Martin. 1977. *The Roman world: 44 BC–AD 180*. London: Routledge.

———. 1992. The Roman state and the Jewish patriarch in the third century. In *The Galilee in late antiquity*, ed. Lee I. Levine, 127–39. New York: The Jewish Theological Seminary of America.

———. 1994. *Mission and conversion: Proselytizing in the religious history of the Roman Empire*. Oxford: Clarendon.

Goodman, Martin, ed. 1998. *Jews in a Graeco-Roman world*. Oxford: Clarendon.

Goold, G. P., trans. 1977. Marcus Manilius, *Astronomica*. LCL. Cambridge: Harvard University Press.

Grabar, Andre. 1988. *Early Christian art, A.D. 200–395: From the rise of Christianity to the death of Theodosius*. New York: Odyssey.

Granfield, P., and J. A. Jungmann, eds. 1970. *Kyriakon: Festschrift Johannes Quasten*. Vol. 1. Münster: Aschendorff.

Grant, Michael. 1973. *The Jews in the Roman world*. New York: Simon and Schuster.

———. 1992. *A social history of Greece and Rome*. New York: Scribners.

———. 1994. *The Antonines: The Roman Empire in transition*. London: Routledge.

Grant, Robert M. 1957. *Second-century Christianity: A collection of fragments*. London: SPCK.

———. 1977. *Early Christianity and society: Seven studies*. San Francisco: Harper and Row.

———. 1980. The social setting of second-century Christianity. In *Jewish and Christian self-definition*. Vol. 1, *The shaping of Christianity in the second and third centuries*, ed. E. P. Sanders, 16–29. London: SCM.

———. 1988. *Greek apologists of the second century*. London: SCM.

———. 1996. Review of *The rise of Christianity: A sociologist reconsiders history*. Princeton: Princeton University Press. Repr. as *The rise of Christianity: How the obscure, marginal Jesus movement became the dominant religious force in the Western world in a few centuries*, by Rodney Stark, *Christian Century* 113:1081–82.

Greenewalt, Crawford H., Jr., 1978. The Sardis campaign of 1976. *BASOR* 229:57–73.

———. 1982. The Sardis campaigns of 1979 and 1980. *BASOR* 249:1–44.

Greenewalt, Crawford H., Jr., C. Ratté, and M. L. Rautman. 1990. The Sardis campaigns of 1990 and 1991. *AASOR* 52:1–13.

Greenewalt, Crawford H., Jr., and Marcus L. Rautman. 1998. The Sardis campaigns of 1994 and 1995. *AJA* 102:469–505.

————. 2000. The Sardis campaigns of 1996, 1997, and 1998. *AJA* 104:643–81.

Greenewalt, Crawford H., Jr., Nicholas D. Cahill, Philip T. Stinson, and Fikret K. Yegül. 2003. *The city of Sardis: Approaches in graphic recording.* Cambridge, MA: Harvard University Museum Publications.

Greenewalt, Crawford H., Jr., and Sebastian Payne. 1978. *Ritual dinners in early historic Sardis.* Berkeley: University of California Press.

Griffiths, J. Gwyn. 1970. Plutarch. *De Iside et Osiride,* ed., trans., comm. J. Gwyn Griffiths. Cardiff: University of Wales.

————. 1975. *The Isis-Book* [Metamorphoses, Book XI]. Leiden: Brill.

Gruen, Erich. 1984. *The Hellenistic world and the coming of Rome.* Vol. 1. Berkeley: University of California Press.

Gschnitzer, Fritz. 1986. Eine persiche Kultstiftung in Sardeis und die "Sippengötter" Vorderasiens. In *Im Bannkreis des Alten Orients: Studien zur Sprach- und Kulturgeschichte des Alten Orients und seines Ausstrahlungsraumes,* ed. W. Meid and H. Trenkwalder, 45–54. Innsbrucker Beitrage zur Kulturwissenschaft 24. Innsbruck: Institut für Sprachwissenschaft der Universitat Innsbruck.

Gundel, Hans. 1972. Zodiakos. *RE* 2 (10A): 462–98, 543–709.

Gundel, W. 1950. Parthenos. *RE* 18 (4): 20–28.

————. 1958. Heimarmene. *RE* 1 (7): 2622–45.

————. 1966. Astrologie. *RAC* 1: cols. 817–31.

Gunkel, Hermann. 1895. *Schöpfung und Chaos in Urzeit und Endzeit, Eine religionsgeschichtliche Untersuchung über Gen. 1 und Ap. Joh. XII.* Göttingen: Vandenhoeck and Ruprecht.

Guralnick, Eleanor, ed. 1987. *Sardis: Twenty-seven years of discovery.* Chicago: Chicago Society of the Archaeological Institute of America.

Gutmann, Joseph, ed. 1975. *The synagogue: Studies in origins, archaeology and architecture.* New York: KTAV.

Hagedorn, Anselm C., and Jerome H. Neyrey. 1996. It was out of envy that they handed Jesus over (Mark 15:10): The anatomy of envy and the Gospel of Mark. Paper from the 1997 Context Group meeting, Portland, OR.

Halfmann, Helmut. 2001. *Städtebau und Bauherren im römischen Kleinasien: Ein Vergleich zwischen Pergamon und Ephesos.* Istanbuler Mitteilungen 43. Tübingen and Berlin: Wasmuth.

Hall, S. G. 1971. Melito in light of the Passover Haggadah. *JTS* 22:29–46.

————, ed. 1979. *Melito of Sardis: On Pascha and fragments, text and translation.* OECT. New York: Oxford University Press.

Halton, T. P. 1970. Stylistic device in Melito, PERI PASCA. In *Kyriakon: Festschrift Johannes Quasten.* Vol. 1, ed. P. Granfieldand and J. A. Jungmann, 249–55. Münster: Aschendorff.

————. 1999. *Saint Jerome: On illustrious men.* Washington, DC: The Catholic University of America Press.

Hamel, Gildas. 1990. *Poverty and charity in Roman Palestine.* Berkeley: University of California Press.

Hammond, Mason. 1972. *The city in the ancient world.* Cambridge, MA: Harvard University Press.

Hanfmann, George M. A. 1960a. Excavations at Sardis, 1959. *BASOR* 157:8–43.

———. 1960b. *Sardis und Lydien*. Mainz: Akademie der Wissenschaften und der Literatur.

———. 1962. The fourth campaign at Sardis (1961). *BASOR* 166:1–57.

———. 1972. *Letters from Sardis*. Cambridge, MA: Harvard University Press.

———. 1980. On Lydian Sardis. In *From Athens to Gordion: The papers of a memorial symposium for Rodney S. Young*, ed. K. DeVries, 99–131. Philadelphia: University of Pennsylvania Museum.

Hanfmann, George M. A., ed. 1983. *Sardis from prehistoric to Roman times: Results of the archeological exploration of Sardis 1958–1975*. Cambridge, MA, and London: Harvard University Press.

Hanfmann, George M. A., and Nancy H. Ramage. 1978. *Sculpture from Sardis: The finds through 1975*. Archaeological exploration of Sardis. Report 2. Cambridge, MA: Harvard University Press.

Hanfmann, George M. A. and Jane S. Waldbaum. 1975. *A survey of Sardis and the major monuments outside the city walls*. Archaeological exploration of Sardis. Report 1. Cambridge, MA: Harvard University Press.

Hanfmann, George M. A., Louis Robert, and William E. Mierse. 1983. The Hellenistic period. In *Sardis from Prehistoric to Roman Times: Results of the Archeological Exploration of Sardis 1958–1975*, ed. George M. A. Hanfmann, 100–108. Cambridge, MA: Harvard University Press.

Hansen, A. 1968. The *Sitz im Leben* of the Paschal Homily of Melito of Sardis with special reference to the Paschal Festival in early Christianity. Ph.D. diss., Northwestern University.

Harland, Philip A. 1996. Honours and worship: Emperors, imperial cults and associations at Ephesus (first to third centuries C.E.). *SR* 25:319–34.

———. 2000. Honouring the emperor or assailing the beast: Participation in civic life among associations (Jewish, Christian and other) in Asia Minor and the Apocalypse of John. *JSNT* 77:99–121.

———. 2002. Connections with the elites in the world of the early Christians. In *Handbook of early Christianity and the social sciences*, ed. Anthony J. Blasi, Jean Duhaime, and Paul-André Turcotte, 385–408. Walnut Creek: AltaMira Press.

———. 2003. *Associations, synagogues, and congregations: Claiming a place in ancient Mediterranean society*. Minneapolis: Fortress.

———. 2005. The declining polis? Religious rivalries in ancient civic context. In *Religious rivalries in the early Roman Empire and the rise of early Christianity*, ed. Leif E. Vaage. ESCJ. Waterloo: Wilfrid Laurier University Press.

Harmon, A. M. (trans.). 1925. *Lucian*. LCL. Cambridge, MA: Harvard University Press.

Hasan-Rokem, G. 1999. *The web of life: Folklore in rabbinic literature; The Palestinian Aggadic Midrash Eikha Rabba*. Stanford: Stanford University Press.

Hawkin, David J., and Tom Robinson, eds. 1987. *A study in changing horizons: Essays in appreciation of Ben F. Meyer from former students*. Lewiston: Mellen Press.

———. 1990. *Self-definition and self-discovery in early Christianity: A study in changing horizons*. Lewiston: Edwin Mellen Press.

Hazlett, Ian. 1991. *Early Christianity: Origins and evolution to A.D. 600.* London: SPCK.

Head, Barclay V. 1901. *Catalogue of Greek coins of Lydia in the British Museum.* London: British Museum Department of Coins and Medals.

———. 1911. *Historia numorum: A manual of Greek numismatics.* 2nd ed. Oxford: Clarendon.

Hegedus, Tim. 2003. The Magi and the star in the Gospel of Matthew and early Christian tradition, *LTP* 59:81–95.

———. 2004. *Attitudes to astrology in early Christianity: A study based on selected sources.* New York: Peter Lang.

Hemer, C. J. 1969. A study of the letters to the seven churches of Asia Minor with special reference to their background. Ph.D. diss., Manchester University.

———. 1972. The Sardis letter and the Croesus tradition. *NTS* 19:94–97.

———. 1986. *The letters to the seven churches of Asia in their local setting.* Sheffield: JSOT Press.

Herrmann, Peter. 1995. Sardeis zur Zeit der iulisch-claudischen Kaiser. In *Forschungen in Lydien*, ed. E. Schwertheim, 21–36. ISGK 18. Bonn: Rudolf Habelt.

———. 1996. Mystenvereine in Sardeis. *Chiron* 26:315–48.

———. 1998. Demeter Karpophoros in Sardeis. *REA* 100:495–508.

Hill, Charles E. 1999. The *Epistula Apostolorum*: An Asian tract from the time of Polycarp. *JECS* 7:1–53.

Hirschland, Nancy. 1967. The head capitals of Sardis. *BSR* 35:12–22.

Hoffmann, Adolf. 1998. The Roman remodeling of the Asklepieion. In *Pergamon: Citadel of the gods*, ed. Helmut Koester, 41–62. Harrisburg, PA: Trinity Press International.

Hohlfelder, Robert L., ed. 1982. *City, town and countryside in the early Byzantine era.* New York: East European Monographs and Columbia University Press.

Hollander, Harm W., and Marinus de Jonge. 1985. *The Testaments of the Twelve Patriarchs: A commentary.* Leiden: Brill.

Holman, Susan R. 1999. The hungry body: Famine, poverty, and identity in Basil's *Hom.* 8. *JECS* 7:337–63.

Hopkins, Keith. 1998. Christian number and its implications. *JECS* 6:185–226.

Horsley, G. H. R., ed. 1981. *New documents illustrating early Christianity.* Vol. 1, *A review of the Greek inscriptions and papyri published in 1976.* NewDocs 1. North Ryde, Australia: Ancient History Documentary Research Centre, Macquarie University.

Humann, Carl et al., eds. 1898, *Altertümer von Hierapolis.* Jahrbuch des kaiserlich deutschen Archäologischen Instituts, Ergänzungsheft 4. Berlin: Georg Reimer.

Humphrey, Edith M. 1995. Collision of modes? Vision and determining argument in Acts 10:1–11:18. *Semeia* 71:65–84.

Isaac, Benjamin. 1998. Jews, Christians and others in Palestine: The evidence from Eusebius. In *Jews in a Graeco-Roman world*, ed. Martin Goodman, 65–74. Oxford: Clarendon.

Jackson, John. 1931–37 Tacitus, *Annals.* 3 vols. LCL. Cambridge, MA: Harvard University Press.

Johnson, Sherman E. 1961. Christianity in Sardis. In *Early Christian origins: Studies in honor of H. R. Willoughby*, ed. A. Wikgren, 81–90. Chicago: Quadrangle Books.

———. 1968. Sabazios inscription from Sardis. In *Religions in antiquity: Essays in memory of E. R. Goodenough*, ed. Jacob Neusner, 542–50. SHR 14. Leiden: Brill.

———. 1975. Asia Minor and early Christianity. In *Christianity, Judaism, and other Greco-Roman cults: Studies for Morton Smith at sixty*, ed. Jacob Neusner, 1:77–145, 3 vols. Leiden: Brill.

Jones, A. H. M. 1931. Urbanization of Palestine. *JRS* 21:78–85.

———. 1937. *The cities of the eastern Roman provinces*. Oxford: Clarendon.

———. 1940. *The Greek city: From Alexander to Justinian*. Oxford: Clarendon. Repr. Oxford: Clarendon, 1966.

———. 1964. *The later Roman Empire, 284–602: A Social, economic and administrative survey*. Oxford: Clarendon.

———. 1966. *The decline of the ancient world*. New York: Holt, Rinehart and Winston.

———. 1970a. The caste system of the later Roman Empire. *Eirene* 8:79–82.

———. 1970b. *A history of Rome through the fifth century*. Vol. 2, *The Empire*. New York: Evanston and London: Harper and Row.

———. 1971. *The cities of the eastern Roman provinces*. 2nd ed. Oxford: Clarendon. Repr. Amsterdam: Hakkert, 1983.

———. 1974. *The Roman economy: Studies in ancient economic and administrative history*, ed. P. A. Brunt. Totowa, NJ: Rowman and Littlefield.

———. 1994. The place of astronomy in Roman Egypt. In *The sciences in Greco-Roman society*, ed. T. D. Barnes, 25–51. Edmonton: Academic Printing and Publishing.

Jones, C. P. 1990. Lucian and the Bacchants of Pontus. *EMC* 9:53–63.

———. 1998 Aelius Aristides and the Asklepieion. In *Pergamon: Citadel of the gods*, ed. Helmut Koester, 63–76. Harrisburg, PA: Trinity Press International.

Joseph, Howard et al., eds. 1983. *Truth and compassion: Essays on Judaism and religion in memory of Rabbi Dr. Solomon Frank*. Waterloo: Wilfrid Laurier University Press.

Joyce, Paul, David E. Orton, and Stanley E. Porter, eds. 1994. *Crossing the boundaries: Essays in biblical interpretation in honor of Michael D. Goulder*. Biblical Interpretation Series 8. Leiden: Brill.

Kearsley, R. A. 1992. Ephesus: Neokoros of Artemis. In *New documents illustrating early Christianity*. Vol. 6, *A review of the Greek inscriptions and papyri published in 1980–81*, ed. S. R. Llewelyn, 203–206. NewDocs 6. North Ryde, Australia: Ancient History Documentary Research Centre, Macquarie University.

Kee, Howard Clark et al., eds. *Christianity: A social and cultural history*. Upper Saddle River, NJ: Prentice Hall.

Keil, Josef. 1923. Die Kulte Lydiens. In *Anatolian studies, presented to Sir William Mitchell Ramsay*, ed. W. H. Buckler and W. M. Calder, 239–66. London: Manchester University Press.

————. 1928. *Monumenta asiae minoris antiqua*. Publications of the American Society for Archaeological Research in Asia Minor/JRSM. Manchester and London: Manchester University Press and the Society for the Promotion of Roman Studies.

Keil, Josef, and Anton von Premerstein. 1910. *Bericht über eine Reise in Lydien und der südlichen Aiolis*. Denkschriften der kaiserlichen Akademie der Wissenschaften in Wien, philosophisch-historische Klasse 53. Vienna: Alfred Hölder.

————. 1911. *Bericht über zweite Reise in Lydien*. Denkschriften der kaiserlichen Akademie der Wissenschaften in Wien, philosophisch-historische Klasse 54. Vienna: Alfred Hölder.

————. 1914. *Bericht über dritte Reise in Lydien*. Denkschriften der kaiserlichen Akademie der Wissenschaften in Wien, philosophisch-historische Klasse 57. Vienna: Alfred Hölder.

Kennedy, G. A. 1963. *The art of persuasion in Greece*. Princeton: Princeton University Press.

————. 1972. *The art of persuasion in the Roman world, 300 B.C.–300 A.D.* Princeton: Princeton University Press.

————. 1980. *Classical rhetoric under Christian emperors*. Chapel Hill: University of North Carolina Press.

————. 1983. *Greek rhetoric under Christian emperors*. Princeton: Princeton University Press.

————. 1984. *New Testament interpretation through rhetorical criticism*. Chapel Hill: University of North Carolina Press.

————. 1994. *A new history of classical rhetoric*. Princeton: Princeton University Press.

————. 1998. *Comparative rhetoric: An historical and cross-cultural introduction*. Oxford: Oxford University Press.

Klijn, A. F. J., and G. J. Reinink. 1973. *Patristic evidence for Jewish-Christian sects*. Leiden: Brill.

Kloppenborg, John S. 1993. Edwin Hatch, churches and *collegia*. In *Origins and method: Towards a new understanding of Judaism and Christianity*, ed. B. H. McLean, 212–38. *JSNT* Sup 86. Sheffield: JSOT Press.

————. 1996. Collegia and *Thiasoi*: Issues in function, taxonomy and membership. In *Voluntary associations in the Graeco-Roman world*, ed. John S. Kloppenborg and Stephen G. Wilson, 16–30. London: Routledge.

Kloppenborg, John S., and Stephen G. Wilson, eds. 1996. *Voluntary associations in the Graeco-Roman world*. London: Routledge.

Knapp, Henry M. 2000. Melito's use of scripture in Peri Pascha: Second-century typology. *VC* 54:343–74.

Koester, Helmut, ed. 1998. *Pergamon: Citadel of the gods*. Harrisburg, PA: Trinity Press International.

Kraabel, A. Thomas. 1968. Judaism in western Asia Minor under the Roman Empire: With a preliminary study of the Jewish community at Sardis, Lydia. Ph.D. diss., Harvard University.

————. 1969. *Hypsistos* and the synagogue at Sardis. *GRBS* 10:81–93.

———. 1971. Melito the bishop and the synagogue at Sardis: Text and context. In *Studies presented to George M. A. Hanfmann*, ed. D. G. Mitten, J. G. Pedley, and J. A. Scott, 77–85. Cambridge: Fogg Art Museum.

———. 1978a. The Diaspora synagogue: Archaeological and epigraphic evidence since Sukenik. *ANRW* II.19.1:477–510.

———. 1978b. Paganism and Judaism: The Sardis evidence. In *Paganisme, Judaïsme, Christianisme: Influences et affrontements dans le monde antique: Mélanges offerts à Marcel Simon*, ed. André Benoit et al., 13–34. Paris: de Boccard.

———. 1981. The disappearance of the "God-fearers." *Numen* 28:113–26.

———. 1982. The Roman Diaspora: Six questionable assumptions. *JJS* 33:445–64.

———. 1991. *Goodenough on the beginnings of Christianity*. Atlanta: Scholars Press.

———. 1992a. Afterword. In *Diaspora Jews and Judaism: Essays in honor of, and in dialogue with, A. Thomas Kraabel*, ed. J. Andrew Overman and Robert S. MacLennan, 347–57. SFSHJ 41. Atlanta: Scholars Press.

———. 1992b. Impact of the discovery of the Sardis synagogue. In *Diaspora Jews and Judaism: Essays in honor of, and in dialogue with, A. Thomas Kraabel*, ed. J. Andrew Overman and Robert S. MacLennan, 269–91. SFSHJ 41. Atlanta: Scholars Press.

———. 1992c. Melito the bishop and the synagogue at Sardis: Text and context. In *Diaspora Jews and Judaism: Essays in honor of, and in dialogue with, A. Thomas Kraabel*, ed. J. Andrew Overman and Robert S. MacLennan, 197–207. SFSHJ 41. Atlanta: Scholars Press.

———. 1992d. Paganism and Judaism: The Sardis evidence. In *Diaspora Jews and Judaism: Essays in honor of, and in dialogue with, A. Thomas Kraabel*, ed. J. Andrew Overman and Robert S. MacLennan, 237–55. SFSHJ 41. Atlanta: Scholars Press.

———. 1992e. Social system of six Diaspora synagogues. In *Diaspora Jews and Judaism: Essays in honor of, and in dialogue with, A. Thomas Kraabel*, ed. J. Andrew Overman and Robert S. MacLennan, 257–68. SFSHJ 41. Atlanta: Scholars Press.

———. 1992f. The synagogue at Sardis: Jews and Christians. In *Diaspora Jews and Judaism: Essays in honor of, and in dialogue with, A. Thomas Kraabel*, ed. J. Andrew Overman and Robert S. MacLennan, 225–36. SFSHJ 41. Atlanta: Scholars Press.

———. 1994. Immigrants, exiles, expatriates, and missionaries. In *Religious propaganda and missionary competition in the New Testament world: Essays honoring Dieter Georgi*, ed. Lukas Bormann, Kelly Del Tredici, and Angela Standhartinger, 71–88. NovTSup 74. Leiden: Brill.

———. 1995. The Diaspora synagogue: Archaeological and epigraphic evidence since Sukenik. In *Ancient synagogues: Historical analysis and archaeological discovery*, ed. Paul V. M. Flesher and Dan Urman, 95–126. Leiden: Brill.

Kraabel, A. Thomas, and Eric M. Meyers. 1986. Archaeology, iconography, and nonliterary remains. In *Early Judaism and its modern interpreters*, ed. R. A. Kraft and G. W. E. Nickelsburg, 175–210. Philadelphia: Scholars Press.

Kraabel, A. Thomas, and Birger A. Pearson, eds. 1991. *The future of early Christianity: Essays in honor of Helmut Koester*. Minneapolis: Fortress.

Kraeling, Carl H. 1956. *The excavations at Dura-Europos conducted by Yale University and the French Academy of Inscriptions and Letters: Final report VIII, Part I; The Synagogue*. New Haven: Yale University Press.

Kraemer, Ross S. 1989. On the meaning of the term *Jew* in Greco-Roman inscriptions. *HTR* 82:35–53.

———. 1992. On the meaning of the term *Jew* in Greco-Roman inscriptions. In *Diaspora Jews and Judaism: Essays in honor of, and in dialogue with, A. Thomas Kraabel*, ed. J. Andrew Overman and Robert S. MacLennan, 311–29. SFSHJ 41. Atlanta: Scholars Press.

Kraft, R. A., and G. W. E. Nickelsburg, eds. 1986. *Early Judaism and its modern interpreters*. Philadelphia: Scholars Press.

Krautheimer, Richard. 1939–45. *Corpus Basilicarum Christianarum Romae*. 5 vols. Monumenti de antichitta Christians II/2. Vatican City: Pontificio istituto di archeologia cristiana.

———. 1978. *Early Christian and Byzantine architecture*. 3rd ed. Pelican History of Art. New York: Penguin.

———. 1983. *Three Christian capitals: Topography and politics*. Berkeley: University of California Press.

Kraybill, Nelson J. 1996. *Imperial cult and commerce in John's Apocalypse*. *JSNT* 132. Sheffield: Sheffield Academic Press.

Krier, Jean. 1980. Zum Brief des Marcus Aurelius Caesar an den dionysischen Kultverein von Smyrna. *Chiron* 10:449–56.

Kroll, John H. 2001. The Greek inscriptions of the Sardis synagogue. *HTR* 94:5–55.

Lake, Krisopp. 1913. *The apostolic fathers*. Cambridge, MA: Harvard University Press.

———. 1926. *Eusebius: The ecclesiastical history*. Cambridge, MA: Harvard University Press.

Lake, Kirsopp, and Frederick John Foakes-Jackson. 1922–33. *The beginnings of Christianity*. 5 vols. London: Routledge and Kegan Paul.

Lambrecht, J., ed. 1980. *L'Apocalypse johannique et l'Apocalyptique dans le Nouveau Testament*. BETL 53. Louvain: Leuven University Press.

Lampe, G. W. H. 1966. Diakonia in the early church. In *Service in Christ: Essays presented to Karl Barth on his 80th birthday*, ed. James McCord and T. Parker, 49–64. Grand Rapids: Eerdmans.

Lane, E. N. 1989. *Corpus cultus Iovis Sabazii (CCIS): Conclusions*. EPRO 100. Leiden: Brill.

Laurence, R., and J. Berry, eds. 1998. *Cultural identity in the Roman Empire*. New York: Routledge.

Laurent, V. 1928. A propos de l'oriens Christianus. *Echo* 29:176–92.

Lebreton, Jules, and Jacques Zeiller. 1942. *The history of the primitive church.* New York: MacMillan.

Leon, Harry J. 1995. *The Jews of ancient Rome.* 2nd ed. Peabody: Hendrickson.

Lesko, Leonard H. 1991. Ancient Egyptian cosmogonies and cosmologies. In *Religion in ancient Egypt: Gods, myth, and personal practice,* ed. Byron E. Shafer, 88–122. Ithaca: Cornell University Press.

Levine, Lee I. 1979. The Jewish patriarch (Nasi) in third-century Palestine. *ANRW* II.19.2:649–88.

———. 1985. *Ma'amad HaHakhamin Be'Eretz Yisra'el BiTequfat HaTalmud.* Jerusalem: Yad Yitzhaq ben Tzvi.

———, ed. 1987. *The synagogue in late antiquity.* Philadelphia: The American School of Oriental Research.

———, ed. 1992a. *The Galilee in late antiquity.* New York: The Jewish Theological Seminary of America.

———. 1992b. The sages and the synagogue in late antiquity: The evidence of the Galilee. In *The Galilee in late antiquity,* ed. Lee I. Levine, 201–22. New York: The Jewish Theological Seminary of America.

———. 1996. The status of the patriarch in the third and fourth centuries. *JJS* 47:1–32.

———. 1998a. *Jerusalem and Hellenism in antiquity: Conflict or confluence?* Seattle: University of Washington Press.

———. 1998b. Synagogue leadership: The case of the Archisynagogue. In *Jews in a Graeco-Roman world,* ed. Martin Goodman, 195–213. Oxford: Clarendon.

———. 2000. *The ancient synagogue: The first thousand years.* New Haven: Yale University Press.

Lichtenberger, H. 1993. *Josephus und Paulus in Rom. Juden und Christen in Rom zur Zeit Neros: Begegnungen zwischen Christentum and Judentum. Festschrift für H. Schreckenberg.* Göttingen: Vandenhoek and Ruprecht.

Lieberman, S. 1944. Roman legal institutions in early Rabbinics and in the *Acta Martyrum. JQR* 35:1–57.

Lieu, Judith M. 1992. History and theology in Christian views of Judaism. In *The Jews among Pagans and Christians in the Roman empire,* ed. Judith M. Lieu, John North, and Tessa Rajak, 79–96. London: Routledge.

———. 1994a. Do God-fearers make good Christians? In *Crossing the boundaries: Essays in biblical interpretation in honour of Michael D. Goulder,* ed. Paul Joyce, David E. Orton, and Stanley E. Porter, 329–45. Biblical Interpretation Series 8. Leiden: Brill.

———. 1994b. "The parting of the ways": Theological construct or historical reality? *JSNT* 56:101–19.

———. 1996. *Image and reality: The Jews in the world of the Christians in the second century.* Edinburgh: T. & T. Clark.

———. 1998. Accusations of Jewish persecution in early Christian sources, with particular reference to Justin Martyr and the *Martyrdom of Polycarp.* In *Tolerance and intolerance in early Judaism and Christianity,* ed. G. N. Stanton and G. Stroumsa, 279–95. Cambridge: Cambridge University Press.

Lieu, Judith M., John North, and Tessa Rajak, eds. 1992. *The Jews among pagans and Christians in the Roman Empire*. London: Routledge.

Lighfoot, J. B. 1992. *The Apostolic Fathers: Greek texts and English translations*. 2nd edition. Grand Rapids: Baker.

Lightstone, Jack N. 1984. *The commerce of the sacred: Mediation of the Divine among the Jews of the Graeco-Roman Diaspora*. Chico, CA: Scholars Press.

———. 2001. Urbanization in late second- and early third-century Roman Palestine as reflected in the earliest rabbinic literature. Paper presented to the CSBS Religious Rivalries seminar, Quebec City, May 24.

———. 2003. City life in the southern Levant as the early rabbis imag(in)ed it: What the sources from Tosefta (Tractates Berakot through Eruvin) say. Paper presented to the CSBS Religious Rivalries seminar, Halifax, May 31.

Limor, Ora, and Guy G. Stroumsa, eds. 1996. *Contra Iudaeos: Ancient and medieval polemics between Christians and Jews*. Tübingen: Mohr Siebeck.

Littman, R. J., and M. L. Littman. 1973. Galen and the Antonine plague. *AJP* 94:243–55.

Llewelyn, S. R. 1992. *New documents illustrating early Christianity*. Vol. 6, *A review of the Greek inscriptions and papyri published in 1980–81*. NewDocs 6. North Ryde, Australia: Ancient History Documentary Research Center, Macquarie University.

Lloyd, Seton, and Hans Wolfgang Mueller. 1980. *Ancient architecture*. New York: Electra/Rizzoli.

Lohse, B. 1969. Meliton von Sardes un der Brief des Ptolemäus an Flora. In *Der Ruf Jesu und die Antwort der Gemeinde: Exegetische Untersuchungen Joachim Jeremias zum 70sten Geburtstag*, ed. Eduard Lohse, 179–88. Göttingen: Vandenhoeck and Ruprecht.

———, ed. 1970. *Der Ruf Jesu und die Antwort der Gemeinde: Exegetische Untersuchungen Joachim Jeremias zum 70sten Geburtstag*. Göttingen: Vandenhoeck and Ruprecht.

———. 1971. *Colossians and Ephesians: A commentary*. Philadelphia: Fortress.

Loisy, Alfred F. 1923. *L'Apocalypse de Jean*. Paris: Cerf.

Lüderitz, Gert. 1983. *Corpus jüdischer Zeugnisse aus der Cyrenaika*. Beihefte zum Tübinger Atlas des vorderen Orients. Wiesbaden: Ludwig Reichert.

———. 1994. What is the Politeuma? In *Studies in early Jewish epigraphy*, ed. J. W. van Henten and P. W. van der Horst, 183–225. AGJU 21. New York, Leiden, Köln: Brill.

MacCormack, Sabine. 1998. *Shadows of poetry: Vergil in the mind of Augustine*. The Transformation of the Classical Heritage 26. Berkeley: University of California Press.

MacDonald, Dennis R. 1983. *The legend and the apostle: The battle for Paul in story and canon*. Philadelphia: Westminster Press.

MacDonald, Margaret Y. 1988. *The Pauline churches: A socio-historical study of institutionalization in the Pauline and Deutero-Pauline writings*. Cambridge: Cambridge University Press.

Mack, Burton. 1987. *Anecdotes and arguments: The Chreia in antiquity and early Christianity*. Claremont, CA: Institute for Antiquity and Christianity.

————. 1990. *Rhetoric and the New Testament*. Philadelphia: Fortress.

MacLennan, Robert S. 1989. *Early Christian texts on Jews and Judaism*. BJS 194. Atlanta: Scholars Press.

————. 1990. *Early Christian texts on Jews and Judaism*. BJS 194. Atlanta: Scholars Press.

MacMullen, Ramsay. 1966. *Enemies of the Roman order*. Cambridge, MA: Harvard University Press.

————. 1974. *Roman social relations, 50 BC to AD 284*. New Haven: Yale University Press.

————. 1982. The epigraphic habit in the Roman Empire. *AJP* 103:233–46.

————. 1984a. *Power and persuasion in late antiquity: Towards a Christian empire*. Madison: University of Wisconsin Press.

————. 1984b. *Christianizing the Roman Empire, AD 100–400*. New Haven: Yale University Press.

————. 1986. Frequency of inscriptions in Roman Lydia. *ZPE* 65:237–38.

MacMullen, Ramsay, and Eugene N. Lane, eds. 1989. *Paganism and Christianity 100–425 CE: A sourcebook*. Minneapolis: Fortress.

MacRae, G. W., and G. W. E. Nickelsburg, eds. 1983. *Christians among Jews and Gentiles*. Philadelphia: Scholars Press.

Macro, A. D. 1980. The cities of Asia Minor under the Roman imperium. *ANRW* II.7.2:658–97.

Magie, David. 1950. *Roman rule in Asia Minor*. 2 vols. Princeton: Princeton University Press.

Maier, Harry O. 2002. *The social setting of the ministry as reflected in the writings of Hermas, Clement and Ignatius*. ESCJ 11. Waterloo: Wilfrid Laurier University Press.

————. 2002. *Apocalypse recalled: The book of Revelation after Christendom*. Minneapolis: Fortress.

Malay, Hasan. 1994. *Greek and Latin inscriptions in the Manisa Museum*. Ergänzungsbände zu den Tituli Asiae Minoris 19. Vienna: Verlag der österreichischen Akademie der Wissenschaften.

Malherbe, Abraham J. 1981. *Social aspects of early Christianity*. 2nd ed. Philadelphia: Fortress.

Malina, Bruce J. 1986. *Christian origins and cultural anthropology: Practical models for biblical interpretation*. Atlanta: John Knox.

————. 1993. *The New Testament world: Insights from cultural anthropology*. Westminster: John Knox.

————. 1995. *On the genre and message of Revelation: Star visions and sky journeys*. Peabody, MA: Hendrickson.

Manis, A. M. 1987. Melito of Sardis: Hermeneutic and context. *GOTR* 32:387–401.

Marshall, John W. 2001. *Parables of war: Reading John's Jewish Apocalypse*. ESCJ 10. Waterloo: Wilfrid Laurier University Press.

Martin, Luther H. 1991. The pagan religious background. In *Early Christianity: Origins and evolution to A.D. 600*, ed. Ian Hazlett, 52–64. London: SPCK.

Mattingly, Harold. 1954. *Christianity in the Roman Empire*. Dunedin, NZ: University of Otago Press. Repr. New York: Norton, 1967.

Mazzolani, Lidia Storoni. 1970. *The idea of the city in Roman thought: From walled city to spiritual commonwealth*. London: Hollis and Carter.

McCord, James, and T. Parker, eds. 1966. *Service in Christ: Essays presented to Karl Barth on his 80th birthday*. Grand Rapids: Eerdmans.

McCready, Wayne O. 1990. Johannine self-understanding and the synagogue episode of John 9. In *Self-definition and self-discovery in early Christianity: A study in changing horizons*, ed. David J. Hawkin and Tom Robinson, 147–66. Lewiston: Edwin Mellen Press.

McDonagh, Bernard. 1989. *Turkey: The Aegean and Mediterranean coasts*. Blue Guide. London: Black and Norton.

McKnight, Scott. 1991. *A light among the Gentiles: Jewish missionary activity in the second Temple period*. Minneapolis: Fortress.

McLean, B. H., ed. 1993. *Origins and method: Towards a new understanding of Judaism and Christianity*. *JSNT* Sup 86. Sheffield: JSOT Press.

McNeill, William H. 1976. *Plagues and peoples*. New York: Anchor Books.

Meeks, Wayne A. 1983. *The first urban Christians: The social world of the Apostle Paul*. New Haven: Yale University Press.

Meeks, Wayne A., and Robert L. Wilken. 1978. *Jews and Christians in Antioch in the first four centuries of the Common Era*. Missoula: Scholars Press.

Meid, W., and H. Trenkwalder, eds. 1986. *Im Bannkreis des Alten Orients: Studien zur Sprach- und Kulturgeschichte des Alten Orients und seines Ausstrahlungsraumes*. Innsbrucker Beitrage zur Kulturwissenschaft 24. Innsbruck: Institut für Sprachwissenschaft der Universitat Innsbruck.

Meiggs, Russell. 1960. *Roman Ostia*. Oxford: Clarendon Press.

Meinardus, O. F. A. 1974. The Christian remains of the seven churches of the Apocalypse. *BA* 37:69–82.

Mellor, Ronald. 1975. *THEA RŌMĒ: The worship of the goddess Roma in the Greek world*. Göttingen: Vandenhoeck and Ruprecht.

———. 1981. The goddess Roma. *ANRW* II.17.2:950–1030.

Mendelson, Alan. 1988. *Philo's Jewish identity*. Atlanta: Scholars Press.

Merkelbach, Reinhold. 1978. Die ephesischen Dionysosmysten vor der Stadt. *ZPE* 36:151–56.

———. 1988. Dionysische Vereine in der römischen Kaiserzeit. In *Die Hirten des Dionysos: Die Dionysos-Mysterien der römischen Kaiserzeit und der bukolische Roman des Longus*. Stuttgart: Teubner.

Métreaux, Guy P. R. 1971. A new head of Zeus from Sardis. *AJA* 75:151–59.

Meyer, B. F. 1986. *The early Christians: Their world mission and self-discovery*. Wilmington, DE: Michael Glazier.

Meyer, Elizabeth A. 1990. Explaining the epigraphic habit in the Roman Empire: The evidence of epitaphs. *JRS* 80:74–96.

Meyer, Marvin, and Richard Smith, eds. 1994. *Ancient Christian magic: Coptic texts of ritual power*. San Francisco: Harper.

Meyers, Eric M. 1982. Byzantine towns in the Galilee. In *City, town and countryside in the early Byzantine era*, ed. Robert L. Hohlfelder, 115–32. New York: East European Monographs and Columbia University Press.

———. 1988. Early Judaism and Christianity in the light of archaeology. *BA* 51:69–79.

———. 1992a. Roman Sepphoris in light of new archaeological evidence and recent research. In *The Galilee in late antiquity*, ed. Lee I. Levine, 321–38. New York: The Jewish Theological Seminary of America.

———. 1992b. Sardis. In *The Oxford Encyclopedia of Archeology in the Near East*. 3 vols. Oxford: Oxford University Press.

Meyers, Eric M., and J. F. Strange. 1982. *Archeology, the rabbis and early Christianity: The social and historical setting of Palestinian Judaism and Christianity*. Nashville: Abingdon.

Meyers, Eric M., and L. Michael White. 1986. Jews and Christians in a Roman world. *Arch* 42:26–33.

Mierse, William E. 1983. The Persian period. In *Sardis from prehistoric to Roman Times: Results of the archeological exploration of Sardis 1958–1975*, ed. George M. A. Hanfmann, 109–38. Cambridge, MA: Harvard University Press.

Mihailov, Georgius. 1958–1970. *Inscriptiones graecae in Bulgaria repertae*. Institutum Archaeologicum, Series Epigraphica 6. Sofia: Academia Litterarum Bulgarica.

Millar, Fergus. 1977. *The emperor in the Roman World (31 BC–AD 337)*. Ithaca: Cornell University Press.

———. 1983. Epigraphy. In *Sources for ancient history*, ed. Michael Crawford, 80–136. Cambridge: Cambridge University Press.

———. 1992. The Jews of the Graeco-Roman Diaspora between paganism and Christianity, AD 312–438. In *The Jews among pagans and Christians in the Roman Empire*, ed. Judith M. Lieu, John North, and Tessa Rajak, 97–123. London: Routledge.

Millett, Martin. 1991. Roman towns and their territories: An archaeological perspective. In *City and country in the ancient world*, ed. John Rich and Andrew Wallace-Hadrill, 169–89. London: Routledge.

Mimouni, S. C. 1992. Pour une définition nouvelle du Judéo-Christianisme ancien. *NTS* 38:161–86.

Mingana, Alphonse. 1917–18. Some early JudæoChristian documents in the John Rylands Library. *BJRL* 4:59–118.

Mitchell, Stephen. 1990. Festivals, games and civic life in Roman Asia Minor. *JRS* 80:183–93.

———. 1993. *Anatolia: Land, men, and gods in Asia Minor*. 2 vols. Oxford: Clarendon.

———. 1999. The cult of Theos Hypsistos between pagans, Jews, and Christians. In *Pagan monotheism in late antiquity*, ed. Polymnia Athanassiadi and Michael Frede, 81–148. Oxford: Clarendon Press.

Mitten, D. G. 1966. A new look at ancient Smyrna. *BA* 29:38–68.

Mitten, D. G., J. G. Pedley, and J. A. Scott, eds. 1971. *Studies presented to George M. A. Hanfmann*. Cambridge: Fogg Art Museum.

Mitten, D. G., and Andrew Ramage, eds. 1986. *Sardis: Twenty-seven years of discovery*. Chicago: Archaeological Institute of America.

Moehring, Horst R. 1975. The *Acta pro Judaeis* in the *Antiquities* of Flavius Josephus: A study in Hellenistic and modern apologetic historiography. In *Christianity, Judaism, and other Greco-Roman cults: Studies for Morton Smith at sixty*, ed. Jacob Neusner, 124–58. 3 vols. Leiden: Brill.

Mor, Menahem, ed. 1991. *Jewish assimilation, acculturation and accommodation: Past traditions, current issues and future prospects*. Lanham, MD: University Press of America.

Morris, A. E. J. 1979. *History of urban form*. 2nd ed. New York: Wiley.

Mounce, Robert H. 1977. *The book of Revelation*. Grand Rapids: Eerdmans.

Moxnes, H. 1991. Honor and shame. *BTB* 23:167–76.

Muir, Steven C. 1995. Touched by a god: Aelius Aristides, religious healing, and Asclepius cults. In *SBL 1995 Seminar Papers*, ed. Eugene H. Lovering, 362–79. SBLASP 34. Atlanta: Scholars Press.

———. 2005. Look how they love one another. Paper presented at the CSBS Religious Rivalries Seminar, Lennoxville, June 1. In *Religious rivalries in the early Roman Empire and the rise of early Christianity*, ed. Leif E. Vaage. ESCJ. Waterloo: Wilfrid Laurier University Press.

Muir, Steven C., ed. Forthcoming. *Religious rivalries and the struggle for success in North Africa*. ESCJ. Waterloo: Wilfrid Laurier University Press.

Mullin, Redmond. 1984. *The wealth of Christians*. Maryknoll: Orbis.

Murray, Michele. 2004. *Playing a Jewish game: Gentile Christian Judaizing in the first and second centuries CE*. ESCJ 13. Waterloo: Wilfrid Laurier University Press.

Musurillo, H., ed. and trans. 1972. *The Acts of the Christian martyrs*. Oxford: Clarendon Press.

Nau, F. 1910. La cosmographie au VIIᵉ siècle chez les Syriens. *Revue de l'orient chrétien*, 2ᵉ sèrie, 15:225–54.

Neusner, Jacob, ed. 1968. *Religions in antiquity: Essays in memory of E. R. Goodenough*. SHR 14. Leiden: Brill.

———. 1975. *Christianity, Judaism, and other Greco-Roman cults: Studies for Morton Smith at sixty*. 3 vols. Leiden: Brill.

Neyrey, Jerome H. 1998. *Honor and shame in the Gospel of Matthew*. Louisville: Westminster John Knox.

Nickelsburg, George W. E. 2001. *1 Enoch: A commentary on the book of 1 Enoch*. Hermeneia. Minneapolis: Fortress.

Nilsson, Martin P. 1925. *A history of Greek religion*. Oxford: Clarendon.

———. 1948. *Greek piety*. Oxford: Clarendon.

———. 1953. The bacchic mysteries of the Roman age. *HTR* 46:175–202.

———. 1955. New evidence for the dionysiac mysteries. *Eranos* 53:28–40.

———. 1957. *The Dionysiac mysteries of the Hellenist and Roman age*. Lund: Gleerup.

Noakes, K. W. 1973. Melito of Sardis and the Jews. *StPatr* 13:244–49.

Nock, Arthur Darby. 1925. Studies in the Graeco-Roman beliefs of the empire. *JHS* 45:84–101.

———. 1935. Religious developments from the close of the republic to the death of Nero. In *The Cambridge Ancient History*, 10:481–503. Cambridge: Cambridge University Press.

———. 1964. *Early Gentile Christianity and its Hellenistic background*. New York: Harper and Row.

Noll, Ray Robert. 1993. *Christian ministerial priesthood: A search for its beginnings in the primary documents of the apostolic fathers*. San Francisco: Catholic Scholars Press.

Norberg-Schulz, Charles. 1975. *Meaning in Western architecture*. New York: Praeger.

Norris, F. W. 1986. Melito's motivation. *ATR* 68:16–24.

Olster, David M. 1994. *Roman defeat, Christian response, and the literary construction of the Jew*. Philadelphia: University of Pennsylvania Press.

Oppenheimer, Aharon. 1992. Roman rule and the cities of Galilee in talmudic literature. In *The Galilee in late antiquity*, ed. Lee I. Levine, 115–25. New York: The Jewish Theological Seminary of America.

Osiek, Carolyn. 1981. The ransom of captives: Evolution of a tradition. *HTR* 74:365–86.

———. 1983. The widow as altar: The rise and fall of a symbol. *SecondCent* 3:156–69.

Overman, J. Andrew. 1992. The God-fearers: Some neglected features. In *Diaspora Jews and Judaism: Essays in honor of, and in dialogue with, A. Thomas Kraabel*, ed. J. Andrew Overman and Robert S. MacLennan, 145–52. SFSHJ 41. Atlanta: Scholars Press.

Overman, J. Andrew, and Robert S. MacLennan, eds. 1992. *Diaspora Jews and Judaism: Essays in honor of, and in dialogue with, A. Thomas Kraabel*. SFSHJ 41. Atlanta: Scholars Press.

Parkes, James. 1969. *The conflict of the church and the synagogue: A study in the origins of anti-Semitism*. New York: Atheneum. Repr. of 1934 edition.

Patterson, John R. 1991. Settlement, city and elite in Samnium and Lycia. In *City and country in the ancient world*, ed. John Rich and Andrew Wallace-Hadrill, 147–68. London: Routledge.

Patterson, Stephen J. 1985. A note on an Argive votive relief of Selene. *HTR* 78:439–43.

Pedley, John Griffiths. 1968. *Sardis in the age of Croesus*. Norman: University of Oklahoma Press.

———. 1972. *Ancient literary sources on Sardis*. Archaeological exploration of Sardis monograph 2. Cambridge, MA: Harvard University Press.

———. 1992. Sardis. *ABD* 5:982–84.

Perkins, J. 1985. The apocryphal Acts of the Apostles and the early Christian martyrdom. *Arethusa* 18:211–30.

———. 1995. *The suffering self*. London: Routledge.

Perler, O. 1970. Typologie der Leiden des Herrn in Melitons *Peri Pascha*. In *Kyriakon: Festschrift Johannes Quasten*. Vol. 1, ed. P. Granfield and J. A. Jungmann, 256–65. Münster: Aschendorff.

Perring, Dominic. 1991. Spatial organization and social change in Roman towns. In *City and country in the ancient world*, ed. John Rich and Andrew Wallace-Hadrill, 273–93. London: Routledge.

Petzl, Georg. 1974. Urkunden der Smyräischen Techniten. *ZPE* 14:77–87.

———. 1977. Aus alten Inschriftenkopien. *Talanta* 8–9:80–99.

———. 1978. Inschriften aus der Umgebung von Saittai (I). *ZPE* 30:249–73.

———. 1979. Inschriften aus der Umgebung von Saittai (II). *ZPE* 36:163–94.

———. 1982–90. *Die Inschriften von Smyrna*, IGSK 23. 2 vols. Bonn: Rudolf Habelt.

———. 1983. T. Statilius Maximus: Prokonsul von Asia. *Chiron* 13:33–36.

———. 1994. Die Beichtinschriften Westkleinasiens. *AE* 22:1–175.

Pharr, Clyde. 1952. *The Theodosian code and novels and the Sirmondian constitutions: A translation with commentary, glossary, and bibliography*. New York: Greenwood.

Phillips, C. S. 1930. *The new commandment: An inquiry into the social precept and practice of the ancient church*. London: SPCK.

Pippin, Tina. 1992. *Death and desire: The rhetoric of gender in the Apocalypse of John*. Louisville: Westminster John Knox.

Pleket, H. W. 1965. An aspect of the emperor cult: Imperial mysteries. *HTR* 58:331–41.

Porton, Gary G. 1994. *The stranger within your gates: Converts and conversion in rabbinic literature*. Chicago: University of Chicago Press.

Potter, D. S. 1991. Smyrna. *ABD* 6:73–75.

Potter, T. W. 1992. Towns and territories in southern Etruria. In *City and country in the ancient world*, ed. John Rich and Andrew Wallace-Hadrill, 191–209. London: Routledge.

Praet, Danny. 1992–93. Explaining the Christianization of the Roman Empire: Older theories and recent developments. *Sacris Erudiri* [Brugge] 33:5–119.

Preisendanz, Karl, ed. 1973. *Papyri Graecae magicae: Die griechichen Zauberpapyri*. 2 vols. Stuttgart: Teubner.

Prestige, G. L. 1952. *God in patristic thought*. 2nd ed. London: SPCK.

Price, S. R. F. 1984. *Rituals and power: The Roman imperial cult in Asia Minor*. Cambridge: Cambridge University Press.

Prigent, Pierre. 1959. *Apocalypse 12: Histoire de l'exégèse*. BGBE 2. Tübingen: Mohr Siebeck.

———. 2001. *Commentary on the Apocalypse of St. John*. Tübingen: Mohr Siebeck.

Radin, Max. 1910. *Legislation of the Greeks and Romans on corporations*. Columbia: Morehouse and Taylor.

Rajak, Tessa. 1985. Jewish rights in the Greek cities under Roman rule: A new approach. In *Approaches to Ancient Judaism 5: Studies in Judaism and Its Greco-Roman Context*, ed. William Scott Green, 19–36. BJS 32. Atlanta: Scholars Press.

———. 2001. *The Jewish dialogue with Greece and Rome: Studies in cultural and social interaction*. Leiden: Brill.

Ramage, Andrew, and Paul Craddock. 2000. *King Croesus' gold: Excavations at Sardis and the history of gold refining*. Archaeological exploration of Sardis monograph 11. Cambridge, MA: Harvard University Press, 2000.

Ramage, Andrew, Sidney M. Goldstein, and William E. Mierse. 1983. Lydian excavation sectors. In *Sardis from prehistoric to Roman times: Results of the archeological exploration of Sardis 1958–1975*, ed. George M. A. Hanfmann, 26–52. Cambridge, MA and London: Harvard University Press.

Ramage, Nancy H. 1987. The arts at Sardis. In *Sardis: Twenty-seven years of discovery*, ed. Eleanor Guralnick, 26–35. Chicago: Chicago Society of the Archaeological Institute of America.

Ramsay, William M. 1895–97. *The cities and bishoprics of Phrygia*. Oxford: Clarendon Press.

———. 1898–99. The Greek of the early church and pagan ritual. *ExpTim* 10:9–13.

———. 1904. *The letters to the seven churches of Asia and their place in the plan of the Apocalypse*. London: Hodder and Stoughton.

———, ed. 1906. *Studies in the history and art of the eastern provinces of the Roman Empire, written for the quartercentenary of the University of Aberdeen by seven of its graduates*. Aberdeen University Studies 20. Aberdeen: University of Aberdeen.

———. 1924. Studies in the Roman province Galatia. *JRS* 14:172–205.

———. 1941. *The social basis of Roman power in Asia Minor*. Aberdeen: Aberdeen University Press. Repr. Amsterdam: Hakkert, 1967.

———. 1994. *The letters to the seven churches: Updated edition*, ed. Mark W. Wilson. Peabody: Hendrickson.

Ratté, Christopher, Thomas N. Howe, and Clive Foss. 1986. An early imperial pseudodipteral temple at Sardis. *AJA* 90:45–68.

Rawlinson, A. E. J. 1928. *Essays on the Trinity and the Incarnation*. London: Longmans.

Rehm, Albert. 1958. *Didyma*. Zweiter Teil. *Die Inschriften*, ed. Richard Harder. Deutsches Archäologisches Institut. Berlin: Gebr. Mann.

Rein, Mary Jane. 1993. The cult and iconography of Lydian Kybele. Ph.D. diss., Harvard University.

Remus, Harold. 1996. Voluntary associations and networks: Aelius Aristides at the Asclepieion in Pergamum. In *Voluntary associations in the Graeco-Roman world*, ed. John S. Kloppenborg and Stephen G. Wilson, 146–75. London: Routledge.

Reynolds, J. M., and R. Tannenbaum. 1987. *Jews and God-fearers at Aphrodisias: Greek inscriptions with commentary*. Cambridge: Cambridge Philological Society.

Rich, John, and Andrew Wallace-Hadrill, eds. 1991. *City and country in the ancient world*. London: Routledge.

Richardson, Cyril C., ed. 1953. *Early Christian fathers*. Vol. 1. Philadelphia: Westminster.

Richardson, G. Peter, 1969. *Israel in the apostolic church*. Cambridge: Cambridge University Press.

———, ed. 1986. *Anti-Judaism in early Christianity: Paul and the Gospels*. ESCJ 2. Waterloo: Wilfrid Laurier University Press.

———. 1996a. Early synagogues as collegia in the Diaspora and Palestine. In *Voluntary associations in the Graeco-Roman world*, ed. John S. Kloppenborg and Stephen G. Wilson, 90–109. London: Routledge.

————. 1996b. *Herod: King of the Jews and friend of the Romans*. Columbia: University of South Carolina Press.

————. 1998a. Augustan-era synagogues in Rome. In *Judaism and Christianity in first-century Rome*, ed. Karl P. Donfried and Peter Richardson, 17–29. Grand Rapids: Eerdmans.

————. 1998b. Architectural transitions from synagogues and house churches to purpose-built churches. In *Common life in the early church: Essays honoring Graydon F. Snyder*, ed. Richard B. Gardner, Julian Victor Hills, and Robert Jewett, 373–89. Harrisburg: Trinity Press International.

————. 2002. Religion and architecture in Roman Africa. Paper presented to the CSBS Religious Rivalries seminar, Toronto, May 28.

————. 2003. City and sanctuary and religious rivalries. Paper presented to the CSBS Religious Rivalries seminar, Halifax, May 31.

Riddle, Donald Wayne. 1938. Early Christian hospitality: A factor in the Gospel transmission. *JBL* 57:141–54.

Ridgeway, Brunilde Sismondo. 1993. Response. In *Images and ideologies: Self-definition in the Hellenistic world*, ed. Anthony Bulloch, Erich S. Gruen, A. A. Long, and Andrew Stewart, 231–43. Hellenistic culture and society 12. Berkeley: University of California Press.

Riedinger, Utto. 1956. *Die Heilige Schrift im Kampf der griechischen Kirche gegen die Astrologie. Von Origenes bis Johannes von Damaskos*. Innsbruck: Universitätsverlag Wagner.

Robbins, Vernon K. 1996a. *Exploring the texture of texts: A guide to socio-rhetorical interpretation*. Valley Forge, PA: Trinity Press International.

————. 1996b. *The tapestry of early Christian discourse: Rhetoric, society, and ideology*. London: Routledge.

Robert, Jeanne, and Louis Robert. 1954. *La Carie: Histoire et géographie historique avec le recueil des inscriptions antiques. Tome II: le plateau de Tabai et ses environs*. Paris: Adrien-Maisonneuve.

————. 1983. *Fouilles d'Amyzon en Carie. Tome I: Exploration, histoire, monnaies et inscriptions*. Commission des fouilles et missions archéologiques au ministère des relations extérieures. Paris: de Boccard.

Robert, Louis. 1937. *Études anatoliennes: Recherches sur les inscriptions grecques de l'Asie Mineure*. Études orientales publiées par l'Institut Français d'Archéologie de Stamboul 5. Paris: de Boccard.

————. 1940–60 *Hellenica: Recueil d'épigraphie de numismatique et d'antiquités grecques*. Paris: Adrien-Maisonneuve.

————. 1946. Un corpus des inscriptions juives. *Hellenica* 1:90–108.

————. 1960. Épitaphes d'Eumeneia de Phrygie. *Hellenica* 11–12:414–39.

————. 1964. *Nouvelles inscriptions de Sardes*. Hautes études du monde gréco-romain 15. Paris: Librairie D'Amerique et d'Orient Adrien Maisonneuve.

————. 1969–90 *Opera minora selecta: Épigraphie et antiquités grecques*. Amsterdam: Hakkert.

————. 1971. *Les gladiateurs dans l'orient grec*. Bibliothéque de l'École des Hautes Études IV^c section, sciences historique et philologiques. Paris: Champion, 1940. Repr. Amsterdam: Hakkert, 1971.

————. 1975. Une nouvelle inscription greque de Sardes: Règlement de l'autorité perse relatif à un culte de Zeus. *CRAIBL*: 306–30.

————. 1986. *Documents d'Asie Mineure*. Athens: École Française d'Athènes.

Robertson, R., ed. 1969. *Sociology of religion*. Baltimore: Penguin.

Robinson, David M. 1912. Greek inscriptions of Sardes. *AJA* 16:11–82.

————. 1924. A new Latin economic edit from Pisidian Antioch. *TAPA* 55:5–20.

————. 1925. Notes on inscriptions from Antioch in Pisidia. *JRS* 15:253–62.

Robinson, Thomas L. 1991. Oracles and their society: Social realities as reflected in the oracles of Claros and Didyma. *Semeia* 56:58–77.

Rohrbaugh, Richard L. 1996. *The social sciences and New Testament interpretation*. Peabody: Hendrickson.

Rokeah, D. 1983. *Jews, pagans and Christians in conflict*. Jerusalem: Magnes.

Rostovtzeff, M. 1957. *The social and economic history of the Roman Empire*. 2nd ed., 2 vols. Oxford: Clarendon.

Roueché, Charlotte. 1993. *Performers and Partisans at Aphrodisias in the Roman and late Roman periods: A study based on inscriptions from the current excavations at Aphrodisias in Caria*. JRS monographs 6. London: Society for the Promotion of Roman Studies.

Roussel, Pierre, Antonin Salav, Marcus Tod, et al. 1923. *Supplementum epigraphicum graecum*. Lugduni Batavorum: A. W. Sijthoff.

Rutgers, Leonard V. 1992. Archaeological evidence for the interaction of Jews and non-Jews in late antiquity. *AJA* 96:101–18.

————. 1995. *The Jews in late ancient Rome: Evidence of cultural interaction in the Roman Diaspora*. Leiden: Brill.

Rykwert, Joseph. 1976. *The idea of a town: The anthropology of urban form in Rome, Italy and the ancient world*. Princeton: Princeton University Press.

Safrai, S., and M. Stern, eds. 1974. *Jewish people in the first century: Historical geography, political history, social, cultural and religious life and institutions*. Vol. 1. Assen: Van Gorcum.

Sanders, E. P., ed. 1980. *Jewish and Christian self-definition*. Vol. 1, *The shaping of Christianity in the second and third centuries*. London: SCM.

————. 1992. *Judaism: Practice and belief, 63 BCE–66 CE*. London: SCM.

Satran, David. 1996. Anti-Jewish polemic in the *Peri Pascha* of Melito of Sardis: The problem of social context. In *Contra Iudaeos: Ancient and medieval polemics between Christians and Jews*, ed. Ora Limor and Guy G. Stroumsa, 49–58. Tübingen: Mohr Siebeck.

Schaeffer, Judith Snyder, Nancy H. Ramage, and Crawford H. Greenewalt, Jr. 1997. *Corinthian, Attic, and Lakonian pottery from Sardis*. Archaeological exploration of Sardis monograph 10. Cambridge, MA: Harvard University Press.

Schede, Martin. 1964. *Die Ruinen von Priene*. 2nd ed. Berlin: Walter de Gruyter.

Schneemelcher, Wilhelm, ed. 1991. *New Testament Apocrypha*. Louisville: Westminster John Knox.

Schoedel, William R. 1980. Theological norms and social perspectives in Ignatius of Antioch. In *Jewish and Christian self-definition*. Vol. 1, *The shaping of Christianity in the second and third centuries*, ed. E. P. Sanders, 30–56. London: SCM.

————. 1985. *Ignatius of Antioch: A Commentary*. Hermeneia. Philadelphia: Fortress.

Schreckenberg, H. 1982. *Die christlichen Adversos-Judaeos-Texte und ihre literarisches und historishces Umfeld*. Frankfurt: Lang.

Schultze, Victor. 1926. *Altchristliche Städte und Landschaften*. Vol. 2, *Kleinasien*. Gütersloh: C. Bertelsmann.

Schürer, Emil. 1986. *The history of the Jewish people in the age of Jesus Christ*. 4 vols. Rev. and ed. Geza Vermes, Fergus Miller, and Martin Goodman. Edinburgh: T. and T. Clark.

Schüssler Fiorenza, Elisabeth, ed. 1976. *Aspects of religious propaganda in Judaism and early Christianity*. Notre Dame: Notre Dame University Press.

Schwartz, Seth. 2001. *Imperialism and Jewish society: 200 BCE to 640 CE*. Jews, Christians and Muslims from the ancient to the modern world. Princeton: Princeton University Press.

Schwertheim, E., ed. 1980. *Die Inschriften von Kyzikos und Umgebung*. ISGK 18. Bonn: Rudolf Habelt.

————. 1995. *Forschungen in Lydien: Herausgegeben von Elmar Schwertheim*. Bonn: Rudolf Habelt.

Scobie, Alex. 1986. Slums, sanitation, and mortality in the Roman world. *Klio* 68:399–433.

Scobie, Charles H. 1993. Local references in the letters to the seven churches. *NTS* 39:606–24.

Seager, Andrew R., and A. Thomas Kraabel. 1983. The synagogue and the Jewish community. In *Sardis from prehistoric to Roman times: Results of the archeological exploration of Sardis 1958–1975*, ed. George M. A. Hanfmann, 168–90. Cambridge, MA: Harvard University Press.

Segal, Alan. 1991. Studying Judaism with Christian sources. *USQR* 44:267–86.

Setzer, Claudia. 1994. *Jewish responses to early Christians: History and polemics, 30–150 B.C.* Minneapolis: Fortress.

Shafer, Byron E., ed. 1991. *Religion in ancient Egypt: Gods, myth, and personal practice*. Ithaca: Cornell University Press.

Shepherd, Massey Hamilton. 1940. Smyrna in the Ignatian letters: A study in church order. *JR* 20:141–59.

Sherwin-White, A. N. 1952. The early persecutions and Roman law again. *JTS* 3:199–213.

————. 1963. *Roman society and Roman law in the New Testament*. Oxford: Clarendon.

————. 1974. Why were early Christians persecuted? An amendment. In *Studies in ancient society*, ed. M. I. Finely, 250–55. London: Routledge and Kegan Paul.

Siegert, F. 1973. Gottesfurchtige und Sympathisanten. *JSJ* 4:109–64.

Simon, M. 1986. *Versus Israel: A study of relations between Christians and Jews in the Roman Empire*. Oxford: Oxford University Press.

Skarsaune, O. 1997. *Om påsken: den eldste kristne påskepreken*. Kristne klassikere 1. Oslo: Luther.

Smallwood, E. Mary. 1976. *The Jews under Roman rule from Pompey to Dioclet-ian: A study in political relations.* 2nd ed. published 1981. SJLA 20. Leiden: Brill.

Smith, Jonathan Z. 1990. *Drudgery divine: On the comparison of early Christian-ities and the religions of late antiquity.* Chicago: University of Chicago Press.

Smith, Morton. 1984. The eighth Book of Moses and how it grew (PLeid. J. 395). In *Atti del XVII Congresso internazionale di papirologia,* 683–93. Naples: Centro Internazionale per lo studio di papiri ercolanesi.

Smith, R. R. R. 1987. The imperial reliefs from the Sebasteion at Aphrodisias. *JRS* 77:88–138.

———. 1998. Cultural choice and political identity in honorific portrait statues in the Greek east in the second century A.D. *JRS* 88:56–93.

Smith, R. W. 1974. *Art of rhetoric in Alexandria: Its theory and practice in the ancient world.* The Hague: Martinus Nijhoff.

Snyder, Graydon F. 1983. *Ante Pacem: Archaeological evidence of church life before Constantine.* Macon, GA: Mercer University Press.

Sokolowski, Franciszek. 1955. *Lois sacrées de l'Asie Mineure.* École française d'Athènes. Travaux et mémoires des anciens membre étrangers de l'école et de divers savants 9. Paris: de Boccard.

———. 1962. *Lois sacrées de cités grecques.* École française d'Athènes. Travaux et mémoires des anciens membre étrangers de l'école et de divers savants 10. Paris: de Boccard.

———. 1969. *Lois sacrées de cités grecques supplément.* École française d'Athènes. Travaux et mémoires des anciens membre étrangers de l'école et de divers savants 11. Paris: de Boccard.

Sordi, M. 1962. Le polemiche intorno al cristianesimo nel II secolo, a la loro influenza ugli sviluppi della politica imperiale verso la Chiesa. *RSC* 16:1–28.

Sparks, H. F. D., ed. 1984. *The apocryphal Old Testament.* Oxford: Oxford University Press.

Stanton, G. N., and G. Stroumsa, eds. 1998. *Tolerance and intolerance in early Judaism and Christianity.* Cambridge: Cambridge University Press.

Stark, Rodney. 1996. *The rise of Christianity: A sociologist reconsiders history.* Princeton: Princeton University Press. Repr. as *The rise of Christianity: How the obscure, marginal Jesus movement became the dominant religious force in the Western world in a few centuries.* San Francisco: Harper Collins, 1996.

Stern, M. 1974–80. *Greek and Latin authors on Jews and Judaism.* 2 vols. Jerusalem: Israel Academy of Sciences and Humanities.

Stewart-Sykes, A. 1997. Melito's anti-Judaism. *JECS* 5:271–83.

———. 1998. *The Lamb's high feast: Melito,* Peri Pascha *and the Quartodeciman Paschal liturgy at Sardis.* VCSup 42. Leiden: Brill.

———. 2001. *From preaching to prophecy: A search for the origins of the Christian homily.* VCSup 59. Leiden: Brill.

Stillwell, R., ed. 1974. *The Princeton Encyclopedia of Classical Sites.* Princeton: Princeton University Press.

Stone, Michael E. 1975. *The Armenian version of the Testament of Joseph: Intro-duction, critical edition, and translation.* SBLTT 6. Missoula: Scholars.

Stoneman, Richard. 1997. *Alexander the Great*. London: Routledge.

Stoops, Robert F. 1992. Christ as patron in the *Acts of Peter*. *Semeia* 56:143–57.

Strobel, A. 1980. *Das Heilige Land der Montanisten: eine religionsgeographische Untersuchung*. Religionsgeschichtliche Versuche und Vorarbeidten 37. Berlin: Walter de Gruyter.

Sukenik, E. L. 1934. *Ancient synagogues in Palestine and Greece*. London and Oxford: Humphrey Milford and Oxford University Press.

Tabbernee, W. 1997. *Montanist inscriptions and testimonia: Epigraphic sources illustrating the history of Montanism*. Patristic monograph series 16. Macon: Mercer University Press.

Talbert, Richard J. A., ed. 1985. *Atlas of classical history*. London: Routledge.

Tassel, Janet. 1998. The search for Sardis. *Harvard Magazine* (March–April): 50–60, 95.

Taylor, J. E. 1990. The phenomenon of early Jewish-Christianity: Reality or scholarly invention? *VC* 44:313–34.

———. 1993. *Christians and the holy places: The myth of Jewish-Christian origins*. Oxford: Clarendon.

Taylor, Miriam S. 1995. *Anti-Judaism and early Christian identity: A critique of the scholarly consensus*. Leiden: Brill.

Tcherikover, Victor. 1964. *HaYehudim BeOlam HaYevani-Romi*. Tel Aviv: Neuman Press.

———. 1970. *Hellenistic civilization and the Jews*. New York: Atheneum.

Tcherikover, Victor, and Alexander Fuks, eds. 1957–64. *Corpus Papyrorum Judaicarum*. 3 vols. Cambridge, MA: Harvard University Press.

Telfer, W. 1936. The cultus of St. Gregory Thaumaturgus. *HTR* 29:225–344.

Theissen, Gerd. 1982. *The Social setting of Pauline Christianity in the first three centuries*. 2 vols. London: William and Norgate.

Thompson, Leonard. 1990. *The book of Revelation: Apocalypse and empire*. New York: Oxford University Press.

Thurston, Bonnie Bowman. 1989. *The widows: A woman's ministry in the early church*. Minneapolis: Fortress.

Tod, Marcus N. 1932. *Sidelights on Greek history*. Oxford: Blackwell.

Tomlinson, Richard. 1992. *From Mycenae to Constantinople: The evolution of the ancient city*. London: Routledge.

Torrey, C. C. 1917. The bilingual inscriptions from Sardis. *AJSL* 34:185–98.

Trebilco, Paul R. 1991. *Jewish communities in Asia Minor*. Cambridge: Cambridge University Press.

Trevett, Christine. 1992. *A study of Ignatius of Antioch in Syria and Asia*. Lewiston: Edwin Mellen Press.

———. 1996. *Montanism: Gender, authority and the new prophecy*. Cambridge: Cambridge University Press.

Turcan, Robert. 1996. *The cults of the Roman Empire*. Oxford: Blackwell.

Vaage, Leif E. 1995. Religious rivalries and the struggle for success: Jews, Christians, and other religious groups in local (urban) settings (63–330 CE). Paper presented to the CSBS Religious Rivalries seminar, Montreal, May 31.

————, ed. Forthcoming. *Religious rivalries in the early Roman Empire and the rise of early Christianity*. ESCJ. Waterloo: Wilfrid Laurier University Press.

Valée, Gérard. 1999. *The shaping of Christianity*. Mahwah, NJ: Paulist.

van der Horst, Pieter Willem. 1984. Chaeremon, Egyptian priest and stoic philosopher: The fragments collected and translated with explanatory notes. EPRO 101. Leiden: Brill.

van Henten, J. W. 1989. *Die Entstehung der jüdischen Martyrologie*. Leiden: Brill.

————. 1997. *The Maccabean martyrs as saviours of the Jewish people: A study of 2 & 4 Maccabees*. Leiden: Brill.

van Henten, J. W., and P. W. van der Horst, eds. 1994. *Studies in early Jewish epigraphy*. AGJU 21. New York, Leiden, Köln: Brill.

Vann, Robert Lindley. 1982. Byzantine street construction at Caesarea Maritima. In *City, town and countryside in the early Byzantine era*, ed. Robert L. Hohlfelder, 165–98. New York: East European Monographs and Columbia University Press.

————. 1995. *The unexcavated buildings of Sardis*. BAR International Series 538. Oxford: British Archaeological Review.

van Nijf, Onno M. 1997. *The civic world of professional associations in the Roman east*. Dutch Monographs on Ancient History and Archaeology 17. Amsterdam: J. C. Gieben.

Vanni, Ugo. 19808. L'Apocalypse johannique: État de la question. In *L'Apocalypse johannique et l'Apocalyptique dans le Nouveau Testament*, ed. J. Lambrecht, 21–46. BETL 53. Louvain: Leuven University Press.

Vermaseren, M. J. 1977. *Cybele and Attis: The myth and the cult*. London: Thames and Hudson.

————. 1987. *Corpus Cultus Cybelae Attidisque (CCCA)*. Vol. 1, *Asia Minor*. Leiden: Brill.

Vermeule, Cornelius. 1974. *The goddess Roma in the art of the Roman Empire*. 2nd ed. London: Spink and Son.

von Campenhausen, H. F. 1963. Bearbeitungen und Interpolationen des Polykarp-martyriums. In *Aus der Frühzeit des Christentums*, ed. H. F. von Campenhausen, 253–301. Tübingen: Mohr Siebeck.

————, ed. 1963. *Aus der Frühzeit des Christentums*. Tübingen: Mohr Siebeck.

von Gaertringen, F. Hiller et al. 1873. *Inscriptiones graecae, consilio et auctoritate Acadamiae Litterarum Borussicae editae*. Berlin: Walter de Gruyter.

von Harnack, Adolf. 1908. *The mission and expansion of Christianity in the first three centuries*. 2 vols. London: William and Norgate.

von Scherzer, Carl. 1873. *Smyrna. Mit besonderer Rücksicht auf die geographischen, wirtschaftlichen und Intellectuellen Verhältnisse von Vorder-Kleinasien*. Vienna: Holder.

Wagner, W. H. 1994. *After the apostles: Christianity in the second century*. Minneapolis: Fortress.

Waldbaum, Jane C. 1983. *Metal works from Sardis: The finds through to 1974*. Cambridge, MA: Harvard University Press.

Wallace-Hadrill, Andrew. 1991. Elites and trade in the Roman town. In *City and country in the ancient world*, ed. John Rich and Andrew Wallace-Hadrill, 241–72. London: Routledge.

Walmsley, Alan. 1996. Byzantine Palestine and Arabia: Urban prosperity in late antiquity. In *Towns in transition: Urban evolutions in late antiquity and the early Middle Ages*, ed. N. Christie and S. T. Loseby, 126–58. Aldershot: Scolar Press.

Walsh, Joseph. 1931. Refutation of the charges of cowardice made against Galen. *Annals of medical history* [N.S.] 3:195–208.

Walton, Alice. 1894. *Asklepios: The cult of the Greek god of medicine*. Ithaca: Cornell University Press. Repr. Chicago: Ares, 1979.

Walzer, Richard. 1949. *Galen on Jews and Christians*. Oxford: Oxford University Press.

Waltzing, Jean-Pierre. 1895–1900. Étude historique sur les corporations professionnelles chez les Romains depuis les origines jusqu'à la chute de l'empire d'Occident. 4 vols. Mémoires couronnés et autres mémoires publiée par l'Académie Royale des Sciences, des Lettres et des Beaux-Arts de Belgique 50. Bruxelles: F. Hayez.

Weiss, P. 1998. Götter, Städte und Gelehrte. Lydiaka und "Patria" um Sardes und den Tmolos. Forschungen in Lydien. Bonn: Rudolf Habelt.

Weiss, Ze'ev, and Ehud Netzer. 1996. *Promise and redemption: A synagogue mosaic from Sepphoris*. Jerusalem: Israel Museum.

Welburn, Andrew. 1991. *The beginnings of Christianity*. Edinburgh: Floris.

Werner, E. 1965. Melito of Sardes: The first poet of deicide. *HUCA* 37:191–210.

Wernicke, Konrad 1897. Pan im Tierkreis. In *Ausführliches Lexikon der Griechischen und Römischen Mythologie*, ed. W. H. Roscher, vol. 3 (1): 1347–1481. Leipzig: Teubner. Repr. Hildesheim: Olms, 1965.

White, L. Michael. 1990. *Building God's house in the Roman world*. Baltimore: Johns Hopkins University Press.

———. 1997. *The social origins of Christian architecture*. Vol. 2, *Texts and monuments for the Christian domus ecclesiae in its environment*. Valley Forge, PA: Trinity Press International.

———. 1998. *The social origins of Christian architecture*. Vol. 1, *Building God's house in the Roman world: Architectural adaptation among pagans, Jews and Christians*. Valley Forge, PA: Trinity Press International.

White, R. C. 1967. Melito of Sardis: Earliest Christian orator? *LTQ* 2:82–91.

Whittaker, John. 1979. Christianity and morality in the Roman Empire. *VC* 33:209–25.

Whittaker, M. 1988. *Jews and Christians: Greco-Roman views*. Cambridge: Cambridge University Press.

Wide, S. 1894. Inschrift der Iobakchen. *MDAI(A)* 19:248–82.

Wiegand, Theodor, and Hans Schrader. 1904. *Priene: Ergebnisse der Ausgrabungen und Untersuchungen in den Jahren 1895–1898*. Berlin: Georg Reimer.

Wifstrand, A. 1948. The homily of Melito on the Passion. *VC* 2:201–23.

Wikgren, A., ed. 1961. *Early Christian origins: Studies in honor of H. R. Willoughby*. Chicago: Quadrangle Books.

Wilde, R. 1949. *The treatment of the Jews in the Greek Christian writers.* Washington: Catholic University Press.

Wilder, A. N. 1964. *Early Christian rhetoric: The language of the gospel.* New York: Harper and Row.

Wilken, Robert L. 1976. Melito, the Jewish community at Sardis, and the sacrifice of Isaac. *Texts and studies* 37:53–69.

———. 1983. *John Chrysostom and the Jews.* Berkeley: University of California Press.

———. 1984. *The Christians as the Romans saw them.* New Haven: Yale University Press.

———. 1992. *The land called holy: Palestine in Christian history and thought.* New Haven: Yale University Press.

Will, E. 1969. Autour de culte des souverains (à propos de deux livres récents). *Revue de philology de littérature de l'historie ancienne* (3rd series) 34: 76–85.

Will, E., and C. Orrieux. 1992. *Proselytisme juif? Histoire d'une erreur.* Paris: Les Belles Lettres.

Williams, Margaret H. 1997. The meaning and function of *Ioudaios* in Graeco-Roman inscriptions. *ZPE* 116:249–62.

———. 1998. The structure of the Jewish community in Rome. In *Jews in a Graeco-Roman world*, ed. Martin Goodman, 215–28. Oxford: Clarendon.

Williamson, G. A., trans. 1965. *Eusebius. The history of the church from Christ to Constantine.* Minneapolis: Augsburg.

Wilson, Brian R. 1969. A typology of sects. In *Sociology of religion*, ed. R. Robertson, 361–83. Baltimore: Penguin.

———. 1973. *Magic and the millennium: A sociological study of religious movements of protest among tribal and third-world peoples.* New York: Harper and Row.

Wilson, Stephen G. 1985. Passover, Easter, and anti-Judaism: Melito of Sardis and others. In *To see ourselves as others see us: Jews, Christians, "others" in late antiquity*, eds. E. Frerichs and J. Neusner, 337–55. Chico, CA: Scholars Press Studies in the Humanities.

———, ed. 1986. *Anti-Judaism in early Christianity: Separation and polemic.* ESCJ 2. Waterloo: Wilfrid Laurier University Press.

———. 1986. Melito and Israel. In *Anti-Judaism in early Christianity: Separation and polemic*, ed. Stephen G. Wilson, 81–102. ESCJ 2. Waterloo: Wilfrid Laurier University Press.

———. 1995. *Related strangers: Jews and Christians 70–170 C.E.* Minneapolis: Fortress.

———. 1996. Voluntary associations: An overview. In *Voluntary associations in the Graeco-Roman world*, ed. John S. Kloppenborg and Stephen G. Wilson, 1–15. London: Routledge.

———. 2000. OI POTE IOUDAIOI: Epigraphic evidence for Jewish defectors. In *Text and artifact in the religions of Mediterranean antiquity: Essays in honour of Peter Richardson*, ed. Michel Desjardins and Stephen G. Wilson, 354–71. ESCJ 9. Waterloo: Wilfrid Laurier University Press.

Wineland, John D. 1992. Sepharad. *ABD* 5:1089–90.

Winter, Bruce W. 1988. Providentia for the widows of 1 Timothy 5:3–16. *TynBul* 39:83–99.

———. 1994. *Seek the welfare of the city: Christians as benefactors and citizens.* Grand Rapids: Eerdmans.

Witt, R. E. 1971. *Isis in the Graeco-Roman World.* London: Thames and Hudson.

Woolf, Greg. 1996. Monumental writing and the expansion of Roman society in the early empire. *JRS* 86:22–39.

Wright, James C. 1994. The spatial configuration of belief: The archaeology of Mycenaean religion. In *Placing the gods: Sanctuaries and sacred space in Ancient Greece*, ed. Susan E. Alcock and Robin Osborne, 37–78. Oxford: Clarendon Press.

Yamauchi, Edwin. 1980. *The archaeology of New Testament cities in western Asia Minor.* Grand Rapids: Baker.

Yates, Frances. 1975. *Astraea: The imperial theme in the sixteenth century.* London: Routledge and Kegan Paul.

Yegül, Fikret K. 1976. The marble court of Sardis and historical reconstruction. *JFA* 32:169–94.

———. 1982. A study in architectural iconography: *Kaisersaal* and the imperial cult. *ArtB* 64:7–31

———. 1986. *The bath-gymnasium complex at Sardis.* Archaeological exploration of Sardis. Report 3. Cambridge, MA: Harvard University Press.

———. 1987. Roman architecture at Sardis. In *Sardis: Twenty-seven years of discovery*, ed. Eleanor Guralnick, 46–61. Chicago: Chicago Society of the Archaeological Institute of America.

Young, F. 1999. Greek apologists of the second century. In *Apologetics in the Roman Empire: Pagans, Jews, and Christians*, ed. M. Edwards, M. Goodman, and S. Price, 81–104. Oxford: Oxford University Press.

Zanker, Paul. 1993. The Hellenistic grave stelai from Smyrna: Identity and self-image in the polis. In *Images and ideologies: Self-definition in the Hellenistic world*, ed. Anthony Bulloch, Erich S. Gruen, A. A. Long, and Andrew Stewart, 212–30. Hellenistic culture and society 12. Berkeley: University of California Press.

Zinn, Howard. 1995. *A people's history of the United States: 1492–Present.* Rev. and updated ed. New York: Harper Perennial.

MODERN AUTHORS INDEX

ANCIENT SOURCES INDEX

SUBJECT INDEX

Abraham 97
Aeolians 7, 47, 48, 141
Agdistis 42
Alexander the Great 6–9, 47, 197, 202, 205, 206, 209, 210, 214, 216, 220, 224, 232
Alexandria 24, 131, 237
Anatolian 6
angels 79
Antioch 8, 9, 136
Antiochus III 7, 17, 110, 142, 218
Antonius Pius 29, 41, 44, 58
Aphrodite 48, 81
Apollo 5, 48, 49, 54, 82, 125, 129
Apollonius of Tyana 8, 27, 32
Aquarius 73, 74, 75, 102
Aries/Mars 49, 67, 74, 80, 81, 100
Aristotle 32
Artemis 40, 41, 43, 44, 45, 76, 127, 131, 184, 248
artisans 54, 200
Asclepius 11, 44, 48, 126–29, 140, 248, 250, 251
associations, voluntary 18, 27, 42, 46, 47, 53, 54, 55, 56, 57, 59, 60, 61, 62, 63, 198, 200, 202, 226, 233, 248, 250, 251, 259, 294
Astarte 47
astrology 10, 67, 68, 69, 70, 71, 72, 75, 77, 85, 90, 91, 147
Athena 44, 81, 84, 128, 198, 201
Athens 71
athletes 49, 54, 62
Attis 44, 45, 54, 177, 184
Augustine 80
Augustus 29, 49, 52, 112, 162, 213, 217, 218, 229, 232
Aurelius (Marcus) 9, 29, 51, 58, 60, 128, 160, 161–63, 191, 246

banquets *see meals*
baptism 135, 161, 174
Basil of Cappadocia 139
benefaction *see patronage*
burial 141
Byzantine 11, 31, 174, 175, 176, 186, 207–8, 210, 216, 217, 219, 241, 246

Caesar 18, 32, 115, 149, 150, 152
Caesarea Maritima 3, 238, 245, 249, 252
cancer 74, 80, 102
Carthage 78
charity 11, 123–40
child 18, 79, 81, 82, 83, 84, 90, 94, 132
Christ *see Jesus*
citizen 221, 222, 224–26, 231, 237
Claudius 44, 112, 232
Clement 28, 31
Collegia see associations, voluntary
conflict, 12, 13, 24, 25, 35, 36, 37, 38, 142, 146
Constantine 33, 82, 123, 139, 140, 237
Constitutio Antoniniana 221, 224–26, 234
Cronus/Saturn 68
cross 175–89, 207, 248
crown 8, 33, 58, 76, 112, 117, 200
Cybele 8, 40, 41, 45, 47, 197, 199, 200–01, 206, 209, 273

David 167
Decius 36, 48
Demeter 54, 55, 63, 198, 250, 251
Diocletian 216–17, 220, 224
Dionysus 7, 43, 45, 48, 54, 57, 60, 62, 63, 76, 115, 250, 251
Domitian 112, 133, 161
donor *see patronage*
drinking 49, 62, 203

353

Series Published by Wilfrid Laurier University Press for the Canadian Corporation for Studies in Religion/Corporation Canadienne des Sciences Religieuses

Series numbers not mentioned are out of print.

Comparative Ethics Series /
Series no. Collection d'Éthique Comparée

Studies in Christianity and Judaism /
Series no. Études sur le christianisme et le judaïsme

Series no. The Study of Religion in Canada / Sciences Religieuses au Canada

Series no. Studies in Women and Religion / Études sur les femmes et la religion

* Only available from Les Presses de l'Université Laval

Series discontinued

Available from:

Wilfrid Laurier University Press
Waterloo, Ontario, Canada N2L 3C5
Telephone: (519) 884-0710, ext. 6124
Fax: (519) 725-1399
E-mail: press@wlu.ca
Website: http://www.wlupress.wlu.ca